Japanese Economics and Economists since 1945

In this book, leading Japanese scholars present an objective study of Japanese economics since 1945, based on statistical data and analysis.

In Part I, the impact and influence of Japanese economics within the international academy is assessed. The book demonstrates the increasingly important contribution of Japanese approaches to theoretical and mathematical economics, and includes a detailed case study of the relationship between Japanese and Marxist economic theory.

In the post-war era, Japanese economists have been increasingly woven into the fabric of Japanese administrative and political life. In this context, Part II investigates the impact of Japanese economics on policy-making. The book dissects the formulation of the famous 'industrial structure policy', and compares Japanese economics with American and Korean models.

Presenting a wealth of original empirical data, and a new perspective on international economic theory, this book will be of interest to historians, applied economists, political scientists and policy-makers alike.

Aiko Ikeo is professor of intellectual history at Waseda University, Japan. She is widely published in the history of twentieth-century economic thought, and is the editor of *Economic Development in Twentieth-Century East Asia* (Routledge, 1997).

Routledge Studies in the Growth Economies of Asia

Japanese Economics and Economists since 1945

Edited by Aiko Ikeo

London and New York

First published 2000
by Routledge
11 New Fetter Lane, London EC4P 4EE

Simultaneously published in the USA and Canada
by Routledge
29 West 35th Street, New York, NY 10001

Routledge is an imprint of the Taylor & Francis Group

Typeset in Baskerville by
MHL Typesetting Ltd, Coventry
Printed and bound in Great Britain by
TJ International Ltd, Padstow, Cornwall

British Library Cataloguing in Publication Data
A catalogue record for this book is available
from the British Library

Library of Congress Cataloging in Publication Data
Japanese economics and economists since 1945/edited by Aiko Ikeo.
      p.   cm.
      Includes bibliographical references and index.
      1. Economics–Japan.   2. Japan–Economic conditions–1945–.
      I. Ikeo, Aiko, 1956–

HB126.J2 J374 2000   99-056799
330'.0952'09045–dc21

ISBN 0-415-20804-1

To the late Martin Bronfenbrenner

Contents

Figures

Tables

Contributors

Michio Akama, Faculty of Law and Letters, Ehime University
Chapter 4

Aiko Ikeo, School of Commerce, Waseda University
Preface, Introduction, Chapters 1, 5 and Section 7.2, and Appendix to Chapter 2, (with T. Okuyama)

Masahiro Kawamata, Department of Sociology, Hosei University
Chapter 3

Takeo Minoguchi, Graduate School of Economics, Hitotsubashi University
Sections 7.1 and 7.4

Tamotsu Nishizawa, Institute of Economic Research, Hitotsubashi University
Section 7.3

Asahi Noguchi, Department of Economics, Senshu University
Chapter 8

Kiichiro Yagi, Graduate School of Economics, Kyoto University
Chapter 2 except Appendix and Chapter 6

Preface

Aiko Ikeo

This book is the result of the three-year project entitled 'A statistical study of Japanese economics since 1945', which was backed by Japan's Ministry of Education, Science, Sports and Culture from April 1995 till March 1998. This project was originally solicited by another project entitled 'Post-1945 internationalization of economics', which was organized by Bob Coats. At the initial stage, Coats aimed to examine the process and degree of the Americanization of economics in each country in the post-1945 period. However, we found this plan misleading, because what is regarded as American economics was found in Europe before 1945. Moreover, the internationalization of economics had started before the United States of America became an active participant in the formation of the international community for economists. The title was changed and the internationalization of economics was traced prior to 1945 as well. The final result of the HOPE-Duke project was published under the title of 'Post-1945 internationalization of economics' as the annual supplement to the *History of Political Economy* in December 1996.

In preparing for the HOPE-Duke conference, Coats suggested that the participants collect the relevant statistical data in making country-based studies such as Britain, Australia, India, Sweden, Italy, Brazil, Korea, and Japan. He wanted to avoid an 'impressionist' approach to this kind of comparative study. The economics of any country has those elements which are fully internationalized as well as those which are not. With regard to Japanese economics, the impressions held by foreign scholars differ from one group to another. There are diverse impressions held by many scholars without measuring a relevant weight. We aimed to make an objective study of comparative economics, that is to say, we clarified the characteristics of institutional arrangements for both economic research and economic policy making in Japan, collected as much data as we could, and tried statistical analysis of Japanese economics.

Honestly speaking, we started with the examination of those data which were available to us. In May 1996, we created the electronic mailing list exclusive for these project members. The list made it possible for us to exchange information and ideas every day. Thanks to the daily communication, we could save real meeting time and enhance research productivity enormously because we live in remote places from each other in Japan. We used not only EconLit (CD-ROM) but also the on-line database provided by the Academic Information Center (Ministry of Education) and other governmental agencies. We came into contact with some governmental agencies and interviewed officials and economists. We cannot attach too much importance to either electronic information or electronic network in proceeding with our research. Without them, our research would never have been completed.

In November 1997, we gave the papers which were to become chapters of this book at a forum of the annual meeting of the Japanese Society for the History of Economic Thought in Fukui and at the seminar on the comparison of Korean and Japanese economics in Kyoto. Professor Myoung-kyu Kang of Seoul National University (then) and Professor Young Back Choi of St. John's University, New York joined both the forum and the seminar, contributed to the sweeping away of parochialism from us, and made us take a big step forward to the completion of this book. It might be very natural *ex-post* that we characterize Korean and Japanese economics by paying attention to the differences between them. After the forum and the seminar, we decided to express our research results more cautiously in order for them to be better understood by foreigners than before.

The Japanese economy and its economic policies have been studied by Japanologists rather than by economists abroad. Japanese study is sufficiently established to support the academic journal entitled *Journal of Japanese Studies*. Japanologists have been picking up those themes and topics which are difficult to handle by economic analysis. In other words, there is a history that the peculiar aspects of the Japanese economy and economic policies are emphasized in this research tradition. We believe this book will be able to provide a firm foundation for promoting a more objective research of Japan by focusing upon Japanese economics and economists.

The economist Martin Bronfenbrenner was an exception among so many scholars who take non-economic approaches to Japan and the Japanese economy. We occasionally came across his writings in our research process and planned to interview him a couple of times. However, he passed away in June 1997 and we could get in touch with him only once. His comments were a little aggressive but constructive. We came to realize that we had missed the chances to hear about his intertwined relationships with so many Japanese historical personages. We pray for the repose of his soul and dedicate our five-year research results to him.

We received the Grant-in-Aid for Scientific Research for the academic years 1995–7 from the Ministry of Education, Science, Sports and Culture and conducted our project under the title of 'The Statistical Study of Japanese Economics since 1945'. The Japanese version of this book was published by Nihon Keizai Hyoron-sha in January 1999 with the Grant-in-Aid for Publication of Scientific Research Result for the academic year 1998. This English version is not a mere translation from the Japanese one, but a revised, second edition derived from further examination, consideration and discussion after we had completed the Japanese manuscript. This is fortunately published by Routledge.

We received various kinds of support from numerous scholars, economists, officials, librarians and research assistants. Each chapter includes special thanks to those who supported our painstaking research respectively.

Introduction

Aiko Ikeo

Prologue

This introduction summarizes the status of economics in Japan by focusing on the internationalization of economics, and discusses the impressions of Japanese economics in foreign countries. It also summarizes the changes in American economics after the mid-1940s relating to the experiences of Japanese economists. These changes in American economics are of vital importance for the study of economics in countries other than the United States.

Japanese economics and its internationalization

From 1930 on, the cooperation of leading economists of all cultural backgrounds was secured by the establishment of international journals of economics and prompt distribution of their issues, and the foundation of the Econometric Society (Ikeo 1993, 1994, 1996). More than half a century has passed since the end of World War II, which was *the* war for many Japanese. Increasing numbers of Japanese economists send their papers to scientific journals published in Europe and North America, participate in international conferences, and thus contribute to the international community of economists in various ways. Not only do Japanese economists travel abroad individually, but also they hold international conferences in Japan and invite economists from overseas to participate. Many economics associations and societies have made enormous efforts to promote communications with their counterparts abroad, and introduce new economic knowledge into the Japanese community. Although English has been a common language in many cases, other languages might be used in group research between two countries.

On the other hand, Japanese economists also use the Japanese language in writing scientific papers, in discussing economic policy matters, and in publishing textbooks. The works in Japanese are aimed at the Japanese audience, but they are sometimes read by Korean and Chinese economists while they are usually neglected by those economists who have other cultural backgrounds. Nonetheless, Japanese economists continue to produce many works in Japanese, set up a supporting system for economic studies, and create convenient classification codes for Japanese-speaking economists seeking the latest research. Part of the reason might exist in the fact that European languages are based on an alphabet, and in analyzing Japanese matters, a paper written in a European language without ideographs has less content than a paper of the same length written in Japanese.

It is relatively easy for Japanese economists to write papers in English for theoretical or econometric studies. Yet some economists write essays for a Japanese audience with a somewhat different tone and nuance from their scientific papers in English. For example, it seems that Tessa Moriss-Suzuki became interested in this fine distinction and in her *History of Japanese Economic Thought* (1989) picked up articles written by the Japanese economists who had been well known to Western economists thanks to their scientific publications in English. Therefore, it is not surprising her analysis of the post-WWII era did not reflect the whole of the research activities of Japanese economists very well. It is very difficult to make a full discussion of the Japanese system of scientific research and policy making in such a compact book. However, her book stimulated Japanese historians of economic thought and pushed them to publish a history of Japanese economics covering the Tokugawa period up to the present. This is the same period covered by Moriss-Suzuki (1989). For example, Shiro Sugihara and Toshihiro Tanaka edited *Economic Thought and Modernization in Japan* (1998) with support of the Society of the History of Economic Thought in Japan.

More than a few graduate schools of economics in Japan encourage students to write their theses in English, and also use English in presentations by Japanese scholars at seminars. On one hand, the research style and the education at graduate level will be more internationalized in Japan in the near future. On the other, Japan has many private universities and a decreasing number of people aged between 18 and 22. The situation of undergraduate and graduate courses in economics will be changed in the near future.

Beyond impressions

Foreign scholars may have many diverse impressions about Japanese economics in the post-WWII era. Such impressions tend to expand through the prism of a few Japanese economists who are well known abroad. There are some Japanese economists who perform research in the international environment, while others are engaged in research which is mainly for domestic consumption (Chapter 1). We can discuss some representative impressions that are held by foreign economists with reference to the research results in this book.

First, there has been the impression that Japan had a good number of excellent mathematical economists after 1945. It was true that young Japanese economists of the day published a series of papers on mathematical economics one after another a few years after Japan lost WWII. This impressed many international economists of the same generation. In the 1950s, the worldwide community of mathematical economists was expanding and becoming conspicuous in each country. Mathematical economists were a minority but, even so, influential beyond their numbers.

In the 1940s and 1950s, economics was mathematized in the United States more rapidly than ever before and in the 1950s several Japanese were staying there to make contributions. The changing economics was spread across the world through the prompt distribution of refereed scientific journals such as *Econometrica* (Chapter 3). This followed the model of knowledge dissemination in mathematics and physics. Therefore, the phenomenon of the internationalization of economics or the Americanization of economics was not the distribution of the economics made by Americans but the dissemination of new knowledge by way of the United States.

Second, many foreigners have the impression that there are many Marxian economists in Japan. Yet in the 1950s and 1960s, only a few Japanologists and the economists who had visited Japan knew this fact. The publication of *Marx's Economics* written by Michio Morishima, who was already well known outside Japan, provided many social scientists with the impression that Marxism was very widespread among Japanese economists (Ikeo 1999). As this book discussed Marx's economics mathematically with the use of the von Neumann model, only the title, rather than the discussion in the text, might bring the vivid impression to the international audience. A handful of Japanese Marxian economists began to publish books and articles in English on a regular basis. However, most of the works produced by Japanese Marxian economists were written in Japanese and not widely known to non-Japanese. Nonetheless, a few Japanese Marxian economists started to contribute to the production of electronic texts and information about Marx's works and related research with the use of the Internet (Chapter 4).

Third, it is doubtful how much standard economic knowledge contributed to the economic policies relating to the miraculous recovery of the Japanese economy just after the end of the war and the very high growth which followed. Martin Bronfenbrenner, an American economist, cynically said that a schizophrenic Japanese economist with an outside job arranging dumping or price fixing for a few industrial cartels would teach the economics of free competition and free trade in class (Bronfenbrenner 1956). Bronfenbrenner and Chalmers Johnson criticized Japan's policies of encouraging heavy and chemical industries as being Stalinist (Chapter 5). In the 1960s, some Japanese economists were critical of the control of 'excessive competition' and large-scale mergers propagated by the Ministry of International Trade and Industry (MITI) (Chapter 8).

It is noteworthy that the World Bank and the United Nations took part in the formation of development economics through the creation of economic plans for developing countries. Moreover, these international organizations and the IMF (International Monetary Fund) had contact with policy makers and disseminated standard economic ideas (De Vries 1996; Polak 1996). While taking it into consideration that Japanese policy makers had frequent interactions with these organizations, it can be said that there was a split between the development economics of the day and standard neoclassical economics including free competition and free trade. Therefore, many developing countries suffered as did Japan from 'schizophrenia'.

Fourth, MITI's policies became known outside Japan through the publication of Johnson's *MITI and the Japanese Miracle* (1982). Furthermore, this book stimulated more research on this topic made by other Japanologists (Calder 1993; Okimoto 1989). The collection of papers and chapters on the Japanese economy and economic policies written by Japanologists including these authors helped form a standard understanding of the Japanese economy (Ravenhill 1995). In Japan not only economic historians but also political scientists and administrative scientists focused on the relationship between Japan's economic development and government policies (Japanese Political Science Association 1992; Japanese Administrative Science Association 1972). Moreover, some Japanese economists analyzed Japan's industrial policies and rapid growth (Komiya, Okuno, and Suzumura 1984; Itoh, Kiyono, Okuno and Suzumura 1988; Aoki, Kim and Okuno-Fujiwara 1997). Collections of articles and chapters representative of this perspective are available in English (Yamamura and Yasuba 1987; Inoguchi and Okimoto 1988; Kumon and Rosovsky 1992).

There were some Japanese economists who supported artificial growth policies, namely the policies of promoting heavy and chemical industries that had high foreign currency earnings ratios, and the policy of restrictive competition such as the curtailment of output during recessions. In fact, we can probably quote passages supporting every MITI policy from Ichiro Nakayama's writings (Chapters 5 and 7). It is easier to cite the passages supporting the domestic policies of strengthening Japan's industries including the energy industry from Hiromi Arisawa's publications because he argued for such policies more often than did Nakayama. Some foreign scholars paid attention to Arisawa (Hein 1990; Gao 1997). On the other hand, Nakayama is less known to Japanologists, excepting for those who knew him personally. One scholar mistakenly regarded him as a Marxist economist (Sheridan 1993).

The changes in American economics

It is important to note that American economics began to change just after the end of WWII, when it was incorporating more mathematical and statistical elements than ever before (see Morgan and Rutherford 1998; Rutherford 1998). At the same time, Japanese economists began to publish mathematical papers one after another. There were only a few American economists who frequently used mathematical analysis. For instance, Allan Gruchy in his *Modern Economic Thought: The American Contribution* (1947) did not pay attention to mathematical economists like Irving Fisher. Most of the book addressed the contributions of institutional economists, who took a variety of approaches including quantitative and empirical analyses. Gruchy discussed Thorstein Veblen's institutional economics, John R. Commons's collective economics, Wesley C. Mitchell's quantitative economics, John M. Clark's social economics, Rexford G. Tugwell's experimental economics, and Gardiner C. Means's administrative economics. He spent one chapter discussing each economist.

In the 1940s, American economics was mathematized more rapidly than ever before partly because the US science policy was changed so that military-related research projects were promoted during WWII. Although the war ended in 1945, the Cold War between the United States and the Soviet Union started in 1947. Since then, scientific research has been generally promoted for defense purposes. It did not matter whether a project was directly related to defense or not (Ikeo 1996: 128). Interviews and memorial writings explored some projects. Harvey M. Sapolsky conducted interviews in his *Science and the Navy* (1990), and clarified the relations between the post-WWII science policies and the role of the Navy. His book was actually the history of the Office of Naval Research (ONR). He has found that ONR was essentially acting as the office of national research from 1945 until around 1957, the year in which the Soviet Union launched *Sputnik*, the first unmanned space satellite (Sapolsky 1990: 38). It managed to hobble the newly established National Science Foundation (NSF) by sending Navy-related people to the top of NSF (Sapolsky 1990: 54).

The ONR offered a great deal of money for research in mathematical science and mathematical economics. Only a few ONR contracts were classified, and foreigners including Japanese were allowed to join the projects supported by ONR. In the 1950s, Japanese mathematical economists such as Hukukane Nikaido, Hirofumi Uzawa, Kenichi Inada, Hajime Oniki and Takashi Negishi joined Kenneth J. Arrow's project at Stanford backed by ONR. They were encouraged to publish their research results and played active roles in the study of the existence and stability of a general equilibrium in a competitive economy, two sector growth models and welfare economics. Nonetheless they felt uneasy because they received money from the Navy and had to follow its way of using contracts for research instead of grants without knowing the reasons for the procedure. In the 1950s, the Cowles Foundation and Research and Development (RAND) Corporation were other important institutions for research in mathematical economics. A few Japanese economists visited the Cowles Foundation at the time.

In the 1950s, economics education at the American graduate level began to change. Statistics and mathematics were introduced into the curriculum while German and French were out at many graduate schools (Bowen 1953; Barber 1996). As several scholarship programs such as Fulbright became available, many Japanese economists came to study in the United States rather than in Europe. An increasing number of students were trained in economics at American graduate schools.

Outline of this book

Around 1994 the project 'Japanese economics and economists since 1945' was solicited by another project entitled 'Post-1945 internationalization of economics', which was organized by A. W. Coats and published as the annual supplement to the *History of Political Economy* from Duke University Press in December 1996. It is essential to avoid impressionist descriptions and to collect objective numbers with some quantitative analysis in order to provide information on Japanese economics that is useful for international comparison. Referring to Coats's project, our first step was to examine the materials available for quantitative analysis and how they were generated from original sources. We exchanged information and opinions all the time through an Internet mailing list. The required contents of our final results and lists of what to explore were kept updated on the Internet. The comparison between Japanese economics and Korean economics was conducted with the cooperation of Myoung-kyu Kang and Young Back Choi in the fall of 1997. Thanks to this comparative study, our research results are presented more objectively than before. The first Japanese version was published in January 1999.

Quantitative analysis needs stable institutions that generate numerical data. Therefore, we can analyze Japanese economics since 1955, when the immediate postwar recovery was complete, and most Japanese institutions had been stabilized. On the one hand, we have found the origins of the current academic institutions in the wartime period preceding it, namely the 1930s. We have found many elements that have continued from the time prior to and during WWII in the existing research environment and institutions, although there were major institutional changes resulting from 'democratization' just after the war. On the other hand, there was discontinuity in leadership. Old leaders were purged or forced to resign, while Marxian economists were rehabilitated and received university positions: in addition, younger economists gained a voice in academia. In the 1960s, the leadership shifted from Marxian economists and promoters of heavy and chemical industry to neoclassical economists, as the Japanese economy was de-controlled and grew rapidly. We place 'the internationalization of Japanese economics' at the center and pay attention to the institutional continuity and the personnel discontinuity.

This book has two parts relating to academic research and the making of economic policy. Part I 'Japanese economists and scientific research' explains how the Japanese institutions for economic research were renovated from around 1940. It summarizes the characteristics of Japanese economists' contributions centered around the internationalization of economics with accompanying quantitative analysis.

In Chapter 1 'Scientific research and internationalization', Aiko Ikeo surveys how Japanese economists have been seriously involved in societal activities by reviewing the activities of the Union of National Economic Associations in Japan (UNEAJ). UNEAJ is a non-governmental, nationwide federation of associations of scholars and experts on economics, commerce, and business administration organization. It was established on 22 January 1950 in order to complement the functions of the Third Division (economics and commerce at the time) of the Science Council of Japan (JSC). It had 50 member associations as of March 1999. There are a couple of reasons why we pay attention to UNEAJ. First, we can step forward to make an international comparison by comprehending how UNEAJ and its member associations have spent their energy in promoting international communications with their counterparts. What is internationalized is created from international communications, and it is differentiated from what is unique to the country. Second UNEAJ has much better historical materials for our research than JSC, the governmental organization.

Ikeo pays attention to UNEAJ's relations with the International Economic Association (IEA) and sheds light on global communication among economists in the world. UNEAJ has spent a considerable amount of money, which is mostly collected by donations, in communications with foreign economists and contributed to the enhancement of Japanese economics. During the two decades following 1945, Japanese economists could not communicate with Korean and Chinese economists due to the lack of diplomatic relations, but were able to communicate with American and European economists, who live far away from Japan. Therefore, the Japanese had difficulty communicating with the economists outside Japan without these organizational efforts.

In Chapter 2 'Economics in the academic institutions after 1945', Kiichiro Yagi sheds light on the post-1945 institutional framework for Japanese economics and the expansion of academic research in economics. Yagi has found some continuity in the establishment of economics associations and research institutes and the foundation of research grants from the period before and during the war. Yet there were major changes before and after the war such as the rehabilitation of Marxian economists, the purge of the economists who were believed to have incited the war and the democratization of academic associations and universities. Yagi processed the data on university education, research grants, the cohorts of economists, and economic literature.

In Chapter 3 'Scientific contributions to international journals', Masahiro Kawamata takes a quantitative approach to the scientific contributions made by Japanese economists. He used EconLit, the database of the American Economic Association, and examined the characteristics of economic research in general that appeared in prestigious journals written in English after 1945. He then extracted data on the contributions of Japanese economists to similar journals and has clarified the characteristics of Japanese contributions quantitatively. He has concluded that a large part of Japanese contributions were concentrated on mathematical theory or econometrics, while only a few contributions were made to the institutional or political aspects of economic activities. Then he looked at journals on applied economics as well. He has found that Japanese economists have kept pace with the development of economic theories and contributed a great deal to the advancement of pure and applied theories.

Chapter 4 'Marxian economics' is written by Michio Akama. Marxian economists have been powerful in various fields in Japan. Akama traces the study of Marxian economics in Japan by looking at symposium projects and major textbooks addressing consideration of orthodox Marxians, Uno School, the group of civil society, and mathematical Marxian economists. Japanese Marxian economists were vigorously rehabilitated soon after the end of the war, although they were repressed from the 1930s until 1945. They collaborated with non-Marxian economists on the reparation problem and the reconstruction of the

Japanese economy in the period immediately after the war. Yet they came to confront non-Marxian economists including neoclassical and Keynesian economists, and made a strong protest against the mainstream economics that was dispatched mainly from the United States. They were engaged in interpreting Marx's *Das Kapital* and analyzing modern capitalism. Some Japanese Marxian economists may disagree in several respects with Akama. Yet ten Japanese Marxian economists may write ten different stories of Japanese Marxian economics. Certainly Akama's story will help understanding of Japanese Marxian economics and the political influence of socialist countries including Japan's neighbors.

Part II 'Japanese economists and economic policies' examines how Japanese economists have contributed to the formation of economic policies and administrative reforms, and how economic knowledge has been used by national civil servants.

In Chapter 5 'Economists and economic policies', Ikeo describes how Japanese economists became involved in making economic policies after 1945, while paying attention to the historical background and the accompanying changes in the policy-making process. It examines Japan's 'economic plans' and shows that they were not economic plans in a strict sense. Then she considers the function of deliberation councils, and the members of those councils that have a relatively large number of economists. She also considers the shift in the members of these councils. Taking into consideration the European and American ideas of 'economic plans' since 1945, she clarifies the similarities with the Japanese case. She confirms that the concept of 'government failure' did not exist before 1970. Finally, she takes a brief look at the activities of economists in administrative reform during 1994–7.

In Chapter 6 'Bureaucrats and economics', Yagi examines the appointment system for Japanese bureaucrats including the Superior Appointment Examination, what they studied at universities, and which universities they graduated from. He has confirmed that graduates in law, not in economics, occupy the mainstream of the government offices in terms of power and prestige. Generalists who have knowledge of the law have held a dominant position over experts in Japanese administration since the pre-WWII period. Economists achieve superiority only in the Economic Planning Agency. Yagi conducted hearings about in-service training for officials from the National Personnel Authority. He has found first that economics is important in training courses. Second, some officials received jobs at universities and became economists. This was a marked difference from the cases of the United States and South Korea. Third, officials are sent to study in those countries that have graduate schools, especially in the United States. This suggests that graduate education in the United States is more efficient than in any other country. Chapters 7 and 8 pay attention to those economists who support or oppose the economic policies proposed by the government and administration.

Chapter 7 'From reconstruction to rapid growth' focuses on Ichiro Nakayama and Seiichi Tobata, who served on the Economic Council for the longest and second longest periods. First, Takeo Minoguchi examined how Nakayama acted as the chair or member for a variety of deliberation councils and committees, although he has found it hard to determine how Nakayama's mission contributed to the Japanese economy. It is noteworthy that each deliberation council or committee has a different degree of administrative power. Nakayama's proposal for 'wage doubling' became the source for the 'income doubling plan' announced by the Ikeda Cabinet in 1960, although Nakayama's proposal for the so-called income policy (anti-inflationary policy) did not come to pass. Nakayama's economics was based on Schumpeterian 'general equilibrium theory' and strongly influenced by Keynes's *General Theory* (1936). Next, Ikeo discusses the controversy between pro-trade and pro-domestic development forces from Nakayama's viewpoint, and points out how Nakayama gave full support for MITI's economic policies. Then, Nishizawa examines Nakayama's role as the chair for the Central Labor Committee and his contribution to union-capital cooperation by using the documents of Keizai Doyukai (Japan Association of Corporate Executives; formerly the Japan Committee for Economic Development). In the 1950s and 1960s, MITI took the initiative for the rationalization movement and made it easy to introduce labor-saving innovation in order to improve workers' lives through economic growth. It was a compromise between labor and capital from a longer perspective.

Minoguchi also discussed S. Tobata, the agricultural economist. Tobata decided to become a social scientist when he was shocked to see the rice riot of 1918. He searched for an environment of independence for farmers. Among the Japanese economists of the day Tobata was most strongly influenced by Schumpeter's *Theory of Economic Development* (1912). He played a role in establishing the Research Institute of Agriculture and advocated the importance of economic analysis in agriculture. He was also very much interested in the problems of developing countries and established the Institute for Developing Countries for the training of experts in 1959. Minoguchi traced Tobata's agricultural economics and pointed out that the self-sufficiency policy, which had been implemented in the early twentieth century, turned out to be an overly protectionist policy and therefore was a probable cause of the rice riot.

Asahi Noguchi in Chapter 8 'External liberalization and "industrial structure policy"' examines how Japanese economists discussed a series of economic policies proposed or executed by the government and administration faced with external liberalization in the 1960s. There were two groups of economists. One was a group which was positively cooperative with the formation of interventionist policies like MITI's 'industrial structure policy'. The other was critical of that kind of policy. The former had the protectionist, interventionist and developmental orientation which had been nurtured in the economic conditions from the Great Depression till the wartime-controlled economy. On the other hand, the opponents of MITI's policies had a neoclassical orientation, which in principle relied on the importance of competition in markets, admitting the role of the government as the maker of macroeconomic policies.

Moreover, Noguchi played the central role in collecting and processing the on-line data for our research, which we got from the National Center for Science Information Systems (Japan's Ministry of Education) and several libraries. Akama spent his effort in creating and maintaining the electronic mailing list for members of this project. Thanks to the mailing list through the Internet, we have been able to exchange information and ideas closely all the time. Although we had an original plan to spend a chapter on electronic information, we have dropped it because revolutionary changes have been occurring in information technology and this information is already widely spread.

Postscript

In order for non-Japanese scholars easily to understand Japanese economics since 1945, 'the internationalization of economics' was placed at the center although the theme of this book is Japanese economics. Moreover, this book did not handle economic education or its history in a systematic way. The rapid progress in electronic information technology has been changing the way historical studies are conducted. We cannot overemphasize how much our current research had relied on the spread of electronic information technology.

Acknowledgement

I thank Paul Pecorino for preparing the English version of this introduction.

References and further reading

Aoki, M., Hyung-Ki Kim and M. Okuno-Fujiwara (eds) (1997) *The Role of Government in East Asian Economic Development: Comparative Institutional Analysis*, Oxford: Clarendon Press.

Barber, W. J. (1996) 'Postwar changes in American graduate education in economics' in Coats (ed.) (1996), 12–30.

Bowen, H. R. (1953) 'Graduate education in economics', *American Economic Review* 43, suppl: Part 2 (September): xv, 223.

Bronfenbrenner, M. (1956) 'Economic thought and its application and methodology in the East: the state of Japanese economics', *American Economic Review* 46: 389–98. Also in Bronfenbrenner (1988).

Bronfenbrenner, M. (1961) *Academic Encounter: The American University in Japan and Korea*, New York: The Free Press of Glencoe.

Bronfenbrenner, M. (1988) *Keizaigaku Tokoro-Dokoro (Here and There in Economics)* Tokyo: Aoyama Gakuin University, School of International Politics, Economics and Business.

Calder, K. E. (1993) *Strategic Capitalism: Private Business and Public Purpose in Japanese Industrial Finance*, New Jersey: Princeton University Press.

Coats, A. W. (ed.) (1981) *Economists in Government: An International Comparative Study*, Durham, NC: Duke University Press.

Coats, A. W. (ed.) (1996) *The Post-1945 Internationalization of Economics*, annual supplement to volume 28 of *History of Economic Thought*, Durham, NC: Duke University Press.

De Vries, B. A. (1996) 'The World Bank as an international player in economic analysis' in Coats (ed.) (1996), 225–44.

Gao, B. (1997) *Economic Ideology and Japanese Industrial Policy: Developmentalism from 1931 to 1965*, New York: Cambridge University Press.

Gruchy A. G. (1947) *Modern Economic Thought: The American Contribution*, New York: Prentice-Hall, Inc. Reprint, Augustus M. Kelley Publishers, 1967.

Hein, L. E. (1990). *Fueling Growth*, Cambridge, MA: Harvard University, Council on East Asian Studies.

Ikeo, A. (1993) 'Japanese modern economics, 1930–1945' in vol. 9 of *Perspectives on the History of Economic Thought*, edited by R. F. Hebert, Cambridge: Edward Elgar.

Ikeo, A. (1994) *20 seiki no Keizaigakusha Network* (The Network of Economists in the Twentieth Century), Tokyo: Yuhikaku.

Ikeo, A. (1996) 'The internationalization of economics in Japan' in Coats (ed.) (1996), 123–41.

Ikeo, A. (1999) 'Japanese political economy' in *The Encyclopedia of Political Economy*, edited by Phillip O'Hara, London: Routledge.

Inoguchi, T. and D. I. Okimoto (1988) *The Political Economy of Japan*, Volume 2: The Changing International Context, Stanford, CA: Stanford University Press.

Ito, M., K. Kiyono, M. Okuno and K. Suzumura (1988) *Sangyo Seisaku no Kiso*, Tokyo: Tokyo Daigaku Shuppankai. *Economic Analysis of Industrial Policy*, tr. by Anil Khosla, San Diego CA: Academic Press. 1991.

Japanese Administrative Science Association (ed.) (1972) *Gyosei Keikaku no Riron to Jissai* (Theory and Practice of Administrative Planning). Tokyo: Keiso Shobo.

Japanese Political Science Association (ed.) (1992) *Sengo Kokka no Keisei to Keizai Hatten* (The post-WWII formation of the state and economic development). Tokyo: Iwanami Shoten.

Johnson, C. (1982) *MITI and the Japanese Miracle: The Growth of Industrial Policy, 1925–1975*. California: Stanford University Press.

Keynes, J. M. (1936) *The General Theory of Employment, Interest and Money*, London: Macmillan.

Komiya, R., M. Okuno and K. Suzumura (eds) (1984) *Nihon no Sangyo Seisaku*, Tokyo: Tokyo Daigaku Shuppankai. *Industrial Policy of Japan*, San Diego CA: Academic Press, 1987.

Kumon, S. and H. Rosovsky (eds) (1992). *The Political Economy of Japan*, Volume 3: Cultural and Social Dynamics, Stanford, CA: Stanford University Press.

Morgan, M. S. and M. Rutherford (eds) (1998) *From Interwar Pluralism to Postwar Neoclassicism*, annual supplement to volume 30 of *History of Political Economy*, Durham and London: Duke University Press.

Morishima, M. (1973) *Marx's Economics*, Cambridge: Cambridge University Press.

Moriss-Suzuki, T. (1989) *History of Japanese Economic Thought*, London: Routledge.

Okimoto, D. I. (1989) *Between MITI and the Market: Japanese Industrial Policy for High Technology*, Stanford: Stanford University Press.

Polak, J. J. (1996) 'The contribution of the International Monetary Fund' in Coats (ed.) (1996), 211–24.

Ravenhill, J. (ed.) (1995) *Japan*, 2 volumes, Aldershot: Edward Elgar. Title 1 of The Political Economy of East Asia.

Rutherford, M. (ed.) (1998) *The Economic Mind in America: Essays in the History of American Economics*, London: Routledge.

Sapolsky, H. M. (1990) *Science and the Navy: The History of the Office of Naval Research*, Princeton: Princeton University Press.

Schumpeter, J. A. (1912) *Theorie der wirtschaftlichen Entwicklung*, Leipzig: Dunker & Humblot, 2nd edn, 1926. *The Theory of Economic Development*, MA: Harvard University Press, 1934.

Sheridan, K. (1993) *Governing the Japanese Economy*, Cambridge: Polity Press.

Sugihara, S. and T. Tanaka (1998) *Economic Thought and Modernization in Japan*, Cheltenham: Edward Elgar.

Yamamura, K. and Y. Yasuba (eds) (1987). *The Political Economy of Japan:* Volume 1: The Domestic Transformation, Stanford, CA: Stanford University Press.

Part I

Japanese economists and scientific research

1 Scientific research and internationalization

Aiko Ikeo

Introduction

This chapter gives an overview of Japanese economists' societal activities in a wide range of specialized fields by examining the organization and contributions of the Union of National Economic Associations in Japan (UNEAJ) from a historical perspective. UNEAJ assists Japanese economists to communicate with economists abroad and keeps close contact with the International Economic Association (IEA). It contributes to the enhancement of the academic distinction of Japanese economists. The communication of UNEAJ and member societies with their counterparts abroad also reflects the enduring efforts of internationally oriented economists worldwide.

1.1 UNEAJ, Third Division of the Science Council of Japan (JSC) and the IEA

Japanese economists could not continue societal activities during the closing years of the Asian and Pacific War (1937–45) and the chaotic period right after Japan lost the war. After this period, Japanese scholars gradually built up the domestic system of scientific research accommodated to the new post-war environment, including the Science Council of Japan (JSC) and the Union of National Economic Associations in Japan (UNEAJ). On the other hand, they also came into contact with a new international organization that was coming to shape international communications in economics, namely the International Economic Association (IEA). UNEAJ especially aimed at systematic communication not only among themselves but also between non-Japanese and Japanese economists. Therefore, UNEAJ tried to keep these economists of the member associations as a whole involved in international communication through the formation of organizations, while each individual economist could join international or foreign academic societies. When we look at the history of Japanese economics since 1945, what was of importance were UNEAJ and the Third Division of the JSC, and IEA.

The Union of National Economic Associations in Japan (UNEAJ) is the nation-wide federation of associations of scholars and experts on economics, commerce, and business administration. It is a non-governmental and non-profit organization. The main aims and objectives of UNEAJ are to support the scholarly activities of its member associations and to promote academic exchanges not only among members themselves but also between Japan and academic societies overseas. The secondary aim is to help communications between the Third Division (economics, commerce and business administration) of the Science Council of Japan and the voluntary societies in the same fields.

The Science Council of Japan (JSC) mainly aims to encourage and develop scientific research, and to promote science in government administration, industry and national life. The Third Division of JSC has representatives from the fields of economics, commerce and business administration. The Science Council is a governmental organization. In order to secure its independence of government policies, it is not attached to the Ministry of Education, Science and Culture but to the Prime Minister's Office. UNEAJ was established by several members of the Third Division (economics and commerce at the time) of JSC on 22 January 1950, exactly a year after the foundation of JSC on 22 January 1949. Therefore, the relationship between the Third Division of JSC and UNEAJ is often expressed as two sides of a coin.

The International Economic Association (IEA) is an international federation of national academic associations or committees representing the economists of each country. It is a non-governmental and non-profit organization with purely scientific aims. It has been headquartered in Paris since it was founded in 1950, at the instigation of the Social Science Department of UNESCO and a group of French economists. 'The general purpose of the IEA is to initiate or coordinate measures of international collaboration designed to assist the advancement of economic knowledge' (Article 2 of the Statutes). Representing Japan, the Third Division of JSC is now a formal member association of IEA.

An economist has only an indirect relationship with UNEAJ or IEA through individual membership of societies or associations, because UNEAJ is a federation of societies or associations within Japan, and IEA is a federation of societies or associations representing each country. Therefore, economists are not very conscious of their relation to UNEAJ or IEA. Moreover, there is a big difference because JSC is a governmental organization whereas neither UNEAJ nor IEA is. Nonetheless their relations are hard to grasp because they have been evolving in order to fulfill their aims and objectives.

Section 1.2 discusses the aims and organization of UNEAJ based on its constitution. Section 1.3 traces the expansion of UNEAJ. Section 1.4 gives an overview of its activities and pays attention to the international collaboration with IEA from a perspective of international communication. Section 1.5 summarizes several observations and considerations.

1.2 Purpose and organization of UNEAJ

We will discuss the purposes and organizational characteristics of UNEAJ by taking a look at its current constitution and changes in past constitutions. The first constitution was promulgated on 22 January 1950. The constitution was revised in 1952, 1954, 1967, 1975, 1981, and 1983–84.

As we have seen in Section 1.1, the main aims and objectives of UNEAJ are to support the scholarly activities of its member associations and to promote academic exchanges not only among members themselves but also between Japan and academic societies overseas, and to contribute to the development of economics, commerce and business administration (Article 2). In 1950 economics and commerce were the only fields designated in the constitution but business administration was added when the constitution was revised in 1967.

Article 4 prescribes UNEAJ activities for the above purposes as follows:

1. It promotes mutual communication and exchanges not only among member associations but also between its member associations and their counterparts overseas.
2. It promotes communication between the Third Division of the Science Council of Japan (JSC) and the member associations (of the Third Division of JSC and UNEAJ) in the fields of economics, commerce and business administration.
3. It examines the systems supporting scientific research overseas and in Japan.
4. It organizes meetings for researchers and public lectures.
5. It publishes periodicals and books.
6. It will do other things that are necessary to fulfill its aims and objectives.

There have been no changes since 1950, except for the ordering of items 1 and 2. In other words, communication between the Third Division of JSC and member societies was given the first priority for UNEAJ.

Articles 5 to 11 provide the organizational structure of UNEAJ. UNEAJ has directors, councilors, the president and auditors (Article 5). The board of councilors consists of two persons selected from each member association for a three-year term (Article 6) and it makes final decisions (Article 7). A member association is allowed to re-elect the same person or change councilors (Article 6). The board of councilors is to meet twice a year (Article 7). The board of directors, which has 10 directors elected in the board of councilors, manages UNEAJ's activities (Article 8). Moreover, the board of directors may have a few more directors from the members of the Third Division of JSC if it is necessary for smooth administration with the approval of the board of councilors. These additional directors are allowed to attend the meetings of the board of councilors (Article 8). The president is elected in the board of directors and represents UNEAJ for a three-year term (Article 9). Two auditors are elected to the board of councilors and serve for three years (Article 10).

The constitution was revised in 1983. Prior to this change, the board of councilors consisted of two persons selected from each member association and the members of the Third Division of JSC. The ten councilors consisted of the chairperson, vice-chairperson and two secretaries of the Third Division of SCJ, and four persons elected from the board of councilors (Old Article 8). Thus the old constitution supposed that there were personnel overlapping between the UNEAJ board of directors and the members of the Third Division of JSC. The Old Article 8 also stated that the board of directors could add a few persons to the above ten directors in order to guarantee the continuity of UNEAJ activities if necessary.

The conditions for membership became an article (Article 3) in the 1967 revisions. As mentioned, UNEAJ is the nation-wide federation of associations of scholars and experts on economics, commerce, and business administration. An association is allowed to join UNEAJ if it satisfies the following conditions:

- it is a nation-wide association
- its main members are researchers
- it holds academic conferences regularly
- its executive members are reshuffled regularly and
- it issues periodicals.

In other words, an association that engages in these kinds of activities is regarded as an academic association or society in Japan. Moreover, the following documents are needed for an association to apply for membership:

1. application form
2. a constitution including the procedure of selecting directors
3. a list of directors
4. a list of members
5. a statement of account for the past five years
6. a prospectus
7. a record of activities including programs of meetings for research
8. a copy of the periodicals for the past five years.

Therefore, a newly established society is qualified to apply for membership only after at least five years of activities since its foundation.

An application is followed by a formal screening at the secretariat, the deliberation of the board of directors, the deliberation of the board of councilors, the deliberation of the board of directors with an interview of the representatives from the applicant association. If there is no objection from the board of directors, the board of councilors is supposed to approve the application at the next meeting. As the board of councilors meets twice a year, it takes at least six months for an applicant association to obtain membership.

Articles 12 to 14 describe the budgeting and accounting procedures. Member associations must contribute their quota of money according to the number of their members (Article 12). UNEAJ is allowed to receive donations for the fulfillment of its purposes (Article 13). Article 14 states the accounting period. Iwao (1988: 4) said, 'UNEAJ's budget is always under strict supervision of the Ministry of Finance. The secretariat always keeps accounts and materials in order, and is audited. In the first two years after its foundation (1950), UNEAJ was helped by the Third Division of JSC with its expenses of holding meetings, and received a Grant-in-Aid for Publication of Scientific Research from the Ministry of Education. In 1951, it was decided that UNEAJ should collect dues from member associations and organized a fund drive in fiscal year (FY) 1952 (*Bulletin*, J, 1951: (2) 100). In April 1952, not only did UNEAJ stand on its own two feet, but it also gave financial aid to the Third Division of JSC (*Bulletin*, J, 1952: (3/4) 179).

The secretary general is chosen from the directors by the President (Article 15). Article 1 states that the secretariat should be placed in Tokyo. The constitution of 1950 stated that the secretariat of UNEAJ should be placed in the secretariat of JSC, and in reality it was done by clerks of the JSC secretariat on the side (*Bulletin*, J, 1952: (3/4) 179). In April 1952, the secretariat of UNEAJ was moved from JSC to the Japan Society for the Promotion of Science (JSPS), causing the UNEAJ constitution to be revised a little further (*Bulletin*, J, 1954: (5) 258–9). Both JSC and JSPS were in Ueno Park at the time. From 1952 on, clerks in the general affairs section of JSPS assisted in the editorial work for the Japanese version of the periodical *Bulletin* for UNEAJ. In 1963, when Takeei Shintani (JSPS), who had assisted UNEAJ for many years died, the secretariat was moved from JSPS to a university.

Like many non-profit organizations, UNEAJ has both financial and managerial problems. In his 'UNEAJ director for a quarter century' (J, 1988) Iwao explained these problems as follows: 'The quotas from member associations could not cover the expenses for international exchanges, or the whole secretarial expenses'. Iwao (1993: 3) also said:

> We hope to handle all the secretarial jobs (including the whole domestic affairs) within the quota revenue. Yet in order to do this, we need either to raise the quota of money or to get more member associations. Both are not easy at all. Even if this was solved, we have to collect donations for international exchanges like attending or organizing international conferences. We need donations. Therefore, we always need a president and advisers who are good at raising money.

There are only a few universities that are allowed to house the secretariat for UNEAJ. 'The secretariat can be placed neither in universities in Kansai area (Kyoto, Osaka and Tokyo), nor in national universities (for the sake of donation). I really hope that the secretariat should be placed among so-called giant private universities in rotation.' (Iwao 1988: 3). Iwao, a professor of Chuo University, admitted that his university could not assist in the secretarial jobs, although he was a director for 25 years (Iwao 1988: 3).

The secretariat of UNEAJ moved out of JSPS in 1963, and moved into the Research Institute of Labor Science at Hosei University, for which Takeshi Fujimoto, the secretary general, worked. It settled there until 1969. Fujimoto served as a secretary for the Third Division of JSC during 1963–65 and was the Vice-Chairperson during 1966–68. In April 1969 the secretariat of UNEAJ formally moved into the graduate school of Meiji University, and Heihachiro Aso became the secretary general. Yet the temporary secretariat was placed at the residence of Tetsuo Okubo in Sumida-ku until June 1970, when the secretariat was moved to the graduate school of Meiji University. Beginning in April 1972, the secretariat was located in Keio University for sixteen and a half years. The secretary general was assumed first by Noboru Yamamoto, then by Takashi Shiraishi from April 1975, and finally by Norio Tamaki from June 1986. In October 1988, the secretariat moved to Waseda University. The secretary general was assumed first by Koichi Otani, and has been held by Kenichi Enatsu since November 1991.

Seiichiro Takahashi, who was the Chairperson of the Third Division of JSC, became the first President of UNEAJ, and Torajiro Takagaki became the second. Kaname Hayashi was both the President of UNEAJ and the Chairperson for the Third Division of JSC during 1960–69. So were Kohachiro Takahashi during 1969–75, Jokichi Uchida during 1975–81, and Yoshio Ando during 1981–83. Susumu Takamiya became the acting President during 1983–84 and became both the President of UNEAJ and the Chairperson of JSC during 1984–85. Takashi Shiraishi was the President of UNEAJ during 1985–89 and Masao Uno has been the President since 1989.

1.3 Member associations of UNEAJ

The Union of the National Economic Associations in Japan (Tables 1.1 and 1.2) was organized by 15 associations on 22 January 1950. Its initial name in English was Japan Union of Associations of Economic Sciences. Its initial member associations' most recent English names and their initial foundation year (in parentheses), in Japanese alphabetical order, are as follows (*Bulletin*, J, (1951: 1))

> Japan Society of Monetary Economics (1943)
> Society for the History of Economic Thought (1949–50)
> Japan Society of Public Utility Economics (1949)
> Socio-Economic History Society (1930)
> Division of Economics in the Humanities Committee (1946)
> Political Economy and Economic History Society (1942)
> Japan Accounting Association (1937)
> Japan Society of Business Administration (1926)
> Japan Economic Policy Association (1940)
> Japan Society of Transportation Economics (1941)
> Japanese Institute of Public Finance (1940)
> Japan Statistical Society (1931),
> Economic Division in Democratic Scientists' Association (1946),
> Agricultural Division in Democratic Scientists' Association (1946)
> Association of Theoretical Economics (1934).

As seen from the foundation years, there were several associations which had been established during the Asian-Pacific War (1937-45). Some broke up and others changed their names.

First, the predecessor of the Japan Society of Transportation Economics is the East Asian Society of Transportation Economics. Its first general assembly began at noon on 8 December 1941.

> Accidentally it was the very day on which the Pacific War started. The foundation meeting went on with the live report of the air raid on Hawaii coming from the radio. . . . At the time when the European war was becoming intensified and the East Asian front was growing tense, both the Railroad Minister and the Communication Minister were about to strengthen the war-time controls over transportation and were ready to support this new society. Therefore, both ministries became the co-founders, gave the society donations, and made the society a foundational juridical person. It was named the East Asian Society of Transportation Economics in order for the national companies and their members in Manchuria and China to become members easily (*Newsletter* 1974: 41).

In the spring of 1946, the society was divided into the Transportation Research Bureau as a foundational jurisprudential person and the Japan Society of Transportation Economics as a voluntary, academic society. The purposes of the society are 'to promote the study of history, economic analysis, business administration, and policy in transportation (railroad, roads, marine routes, airways and communication), the publication of research results, and the spread of the knowledge' (*Newsletter* 1980: 38).

Second, the Humanities Committee was established by the ordinance of the Ministry of Education of 3 September 1946. It had five divisions, namely literature, history, philosophy, law and economics; members were appointed by the Ministry of Education. Most of the members were active scholars in their research fields and academic associations. For the purpose of smooth communication in an early period, a few members joined the Humanities Committee from the Imperial Academy and the Liaison Committee. According to Kurosawa (1973: 14), the Humanities Committee played an important part in the deliberations on the allocation of grant-in-aid for scientific research for the Ministry of Education. Yet after the establishment of the Science Council of Japan, the job has been taken over by the Scientific Research Fund Committee, attached to the Ministry of Education, whose members are recommended by the Science Council of Japan. On 13 April 1950, it became a private organ named the Japan Humanities Society without the Division of Economics. It formally left UNEAJ on 25 April 1952, and broke up during 1953–4. It can be said that the Humanities Committee was *ad hoc* and had completed its function.

Third, the Democratic Scientists' Association, with the Economic and Agricultural Divisions, was established on 16 January 1946. The purposes of the Economic Division were 'to enhance the level of economics and spread economic

Table 1.1   The Union of National Economic Associations in Japan

Current Name	Enrolment year	Foundation year	Journals	Per year	March 1999 (N)
The Japan Society of Monetary Economics	1950	1943	Review of Monetary and Financial Studies	2	1,052
The Society for the History of Economic Thought	1950	1950	The Annual Bulletin of the Society for the History of Economic Thought	1	858
The Japan Society of Public Utility Economics	1950	1949	Journal of Public Utility Economics	1	425
Socio-Economic History Society	1950	1930	Socio-Economic History	6	1,272
The Political Economy and Economic History Society	1950	1948	The Journal of Political Economy and Economic History	4	914
The Japan Accounting Association	1950	1937	Accounting	12	1,654
The Japan Society of Business Administration	1950	1926	Journal of Business Management	3	2,077
Japan Economic Policy Association	1950	1940	The Annals of the Japan Economic Policy Association	1	1,273
Japan Society of Transportation Economics	1950	1941	Annual Report of Transportation Economics	1	402
The Institute of Public Finance	1950	1940	Annual Report of the Japan Institute of Public Finance	1	711
Japan Statistical Society	1950	1931	Journal of the Japan Statistical Society	2	1,436
Japanese Economic Association	1950	1934	Japanese Economic Review	4	2,538
			Trend in Contemporary Economics	1	
The Agricultural Economics Society of Japan	1950	1924	Journal of Rural Economics	4	1,420

Society	Founded	Journal	Founded	No.	Circulation
The Japan Society of International Economics	1950	International Economy	1950	2	1,272
Japan Society of Commodity Science	1950	Studies on Commodities	1935	4	282
The Society of the Study of Social Policy	1950	Annals of the Society of the Study of Social Policy	1950	1	930
The Japanese Society of Insurance Science	1951	Journal of Insurance Science	1940	4	1,319
Japan Society of Marketing and Distribution	1953	Journal of Marketing and Distribution	1951	2	880
The Japan Association of Economic Geographers	1959	Annals of the Japan Association of Economic Geographers	1954	4	757
The Japan Association for Asian Political and Economic Studies	1959	Asian Studies	1953	4	1,000
Japan Society of Political Economy	1960	The Annual Bulletin of the Society of Political Economy	1959	1	1,013
Japan Business English Association	1959	JBEA Annual Studies	1934	1	225
Japan Society of Business Mathematics	1960	Journal of Japan Society of Business Mathematics	1959	1	135
Business History Society of Japan	1964	Japan Business History Review	1964	4	860
		Japanese Yearbook on Business History		1	
Japan Academy for Foreign Trade	1964	The Annual Bulletin of the Japan Academy for Foreign Trade	1960	1	451
The Japan Section of the Regional Science Association International	1966	Studies in Regional Science	1962	2	665
The Society for the Economic Studies of Securities	1970	Annals of the Society for the Economic Studies of Securities	1966	1	535

Table 1.1 The Union of National Economic Associations in Japan (Continued)

Current Name	Enrolment year	Foundation year	Journals	Per year	March 1999 (N)
The Population Association of Japan	1971	1948	The Journal of Population Studies	1	358
The Association for Comparative Economic Studies	1973	1967	Bulletin of the Association for Comparative Economic Studies	1	246
The Academic Association for Organizational Science	1976	1959	Organizational Science	4	1,572
Japan Society for Personnel and Labor Research	1979	1970	Annual Report of Japan Society for Personnel and Labor Research	1	799
The Society of Economic Sociology	1985	1966	The Annual of the Society of Economic Sociology	1	351
Japan Finance Association	1984	1977	The Annual Report of the Japan Finance Association	1	479
Japan Association for Planning Administration	1985	1977	Planning Administration	4	1,312
Japan Auditing Association	1986	1978	Modern Auditing	2	429
Japan Academy for Consumption Economy	1990	1976	Annals of the Japan Academy for Consumption Economy	1	503
Japanese Association for International Accounting	1990	1984	Annual Report of Japanese Association for International Accounting Studies	1	493
Japan Society for Applied Management	1991	1967	The Practice of Management	1	543
Nippon Urban Management and Local Government Research Association	1991	1984	Journal of Urban Management and Local Government Research	1	350
Japan Port Economic Association	1991	1962	The Annual Report of the Japan Port Economics Association	1	350

Society		Journal		(N)	
Nippon Academy of Management Education	1991	Annals of the Nippon Academy of Management Education	1979	1	841
The Academy of Management Philosophy	1991	The Annual Report of the Academy of Management Philosophy	1984	1	342
Japan Risk Management Society	1991	JARMS Report (Report and Insurance Management)	1978	1	465
Japan Logistics Society	1992	Journal of Japan Logistics Society	1983	2	326
Japan Association for the Comparative Studies of Management	1993	Annual Report of Japan Association for the Comparative Studies of Management	1976	1	254
The Society for Industrial Studies	1994	Annals of the Society for Industrial Studies in Japan	1975	1	334
Japan Association for Management Systems	1994	Journal of Japan Association for Management Systems	1981	2	427
The Japan Association for Research on Business Administrative Behavior	1994	The Annals of the Japan Association for Research on Business Administrative Behavior	1991	1	360
CIRIEC Japanese Section (Japan Society of Research and Information on Public and Co-operative Economy)	1994	International Public Economy Study	1985	1	318
The Japan Society for Social Science of Accounting	1998	Annals of the Japan Society for Social Science of Accounting	1986	1	194

Source: From the *Bulletin* of 1998. The number of regular, individual members.

Note
(N) The number of regular, individual members.

Table 1.2　The Union of National Economic Associations in Japan: number of member associations and their individual members

	08/1969	10/1974	11/1980	02/1983	02/1984	02/1985	02/1986
Current Name ¦ The Number of Member Associations	26	29	31	32	32	33	34
The Japan Society of Monetary Economics	547	499	591	642	642	672	672
The Society for the History of Economic Thought	429	553	689	741	780	780	780
The Japan Society of Public Utility Economics	290	293	298	280	280	376	376
Socio-Economic History Society	660	832	989	1,018	1,039	1,047	1,039
The Political Economy and Economic History Society	642	700	900	923	923	923	978
The Japan Accounting Association	1,005	1,250	1,460	1,500	1,540	1,540	1,527
The Japan Society of Business Administration	1,340	1,533	1,745	1,788	1,804	1,804	1,804
Japan Economic Policy Association	880	835	898	982	982	1,086	1,036
Japan Society of Transportation Economics	358	356	350	352	352	388	353
The Institute of Public Finance	352	386	502	543	562	565	562
Japan Statistical Society	631	820	1,046	1,120	1,080	1,114	1,080
Japanese Economic Association	764	1,068	1,493	1,612	1,612	1,612	1,612
The Agricultural Economics Society of Japan	600	1,000	1,100	1,100	1,100	1,311	1,200
The Japan Society of International Economics	610	734	795	1,000	1,000	1,000	1,000
Japan Society of Commodity Science	410	384	310	295	306	299	306
The Society of the Study of Social Policy	554	640	730	757	757	792	787
The Japanese Society of Insurance Science	927	880	848	767	787	849	780
Japan Society of Marketing and Distribution	429	494	550	582	582	622	611
The Japan Association of Economic Geographers	537	638	603	630	650	641	646
The Japan Association for Asian Political and Economic Studies	380	500	600	600	600	600	600
Japan Society of Political Economy	1,000	947	947	1,000	1,000	1,000	1,000
Japan Business English Association	120	163	170	170	185	185	190
Japan Society of Business Mathematics	80	81	71	75	75	107	107
Business History Society of Japan	374	480	600	601	673	673	673
Japan Academy for Foreign Trade	254	246	257	245	245	302	310
The Japan Section of the Regional Science Association International	227	322	389	452	519	493	519
The Society for the Economic Studies of Securities		268	303	321	340	355	340
The Population Association of Japan		297	283	281	286	296	286
The Association for Comparative Economic Studies		134	198	209	217	218	218
The Academic Association for Organizational Science			834	953	953	1,052	1,021
Japan Society for Personnel and Labor Research			405	427	470	502	500
The Society of Economic Sociology				310	310	310	315
Japan Finance Association						360	360
Japan Association for Planning Administration							1,482
Japan Auditing Association							
Japan Academy for Consumption Economy							
Japanese Association for International Accounting							
Japan Society for Applied Management							
Nippon Urban Management and Local Government Research Association							
Japan Port Economic Association							
Nippon Academy of Management Education							
The Academy of Management Philosophy							
Japan Risk Management Society							
Japan Logistics Society							
Japan Association for the Comparative Studies of Management							
The Society for Industrial Studies							
Japan Association for Management Systems							
The Japan Association for Research on Business Administrative Behavior							
CIRIEC Japanese Section							
The Japan Society for Social Science of Accounting							

Note

The number of members reported from a member association sometimes includes non-individual members.

03/1987	03/1988	03/1989	03/1990	03/1991	03/1992	03/1993	03/1994	03/1995	03/1996	03/1997	03/1998	03/1999
35	35	35	35	37	43	44	45	49	49	49	49	50
718	718	827	827	870	920	931	961	981	981	1,044	1,052	1,052
793	795	802	802	808	808	808	819	817	824	824	826	858
313	313	406	332	344	439	462	462	461	478	485	500	425
1,086	1,086	1,104	1,126	1,140	1,147	1,161	1,182	1,188	1,196	1,208	1,239	1,272
1,005	1,005	1,005	1,005	1,005	1,005	1,005	1,005	929	929	929	914	914
1,552	1,552	1,631	1,631	1,621	1,636	1,654	1,671	1,671	1,630	1,634	1,654	1,654
1,852	1,852	1,852	1,880	1,930	1,974	1,974	1,996	2,029	2,049	2,049	2,075	2,077
1,036	1,111	1,111	1,134	1,191	1,226	1,226	1,251	1,241	1,265	1,291	1,285	1,273
353	365	395	354	359	417	417	417	409	409	409	459	402
600	600	600	613	620	620	643	640	640	651	665	710	711
1,161	1,161	1,175	1,196	1,215	1,308	1,321	1,321	1,322	1,358	1,358	1,367	1,436
1,800	1,800	1,903	1,943	1,938	2,018	2,070	2,140	2,241	2,253	2,333	2,428	2,538
1,186	1,186	1,233	1,087	1,051	1,223	1,229	1,271	1,289	1,315	1,354	1,411	1,420
1,000	1,000	1,000	1,100	1,118	1,171	1,162	1,160	1,193	1,229	1,171	1,266	1,272
297	297	309	290	273	297	283	277	268	268	266	290	282
812	812	825	825	829	824	860	860	870	870	882	894	930
696	696	755	688	723	814	814	1,119	1,119	1,297	1,410	1,500	1,319
611	660	676	700	716	759	759	761	810	810	846	873	880
646	650	689	680	680	690	730	730	742	756	764	764	757
620	620	620	700	700	700	740	830	850	900	988	1,000	1,000
1,000	1,026	1,010	1,002	1,017	1,017	1,032	1,047	1,044	1,044	1,044	1,031	1,013
182	182	205	197	209	219	221	236	236	236	236	239	225
109	109	120	120	120	122	124	134	134	135	135	135	135
672	672	757	710	710	757	797	817	818	828	840	868	860
310	310	293	293	308	308	354	370	370	370	386	423	451
543	543	587	587	563	563	563	582	582	582	598	599	665
390	390	426	441	448	461	480	480	495	526	534	524	535
295	295	354	347	340	347	367	378	388	388	403	416	358
210	219	220	220	222	224	223	224	217	217	217	240	246
1,028	1,028	1,115	1,108	1,147	1,188	1,251	1,260	1,296	1,412	1,489	1,527	1,572
500	500	565	619	632	663	698	708	708	729	752	752	799
334	334	372	300	310	310	310	310	342	384	378	331	351
365	365	400	400	421	449	449	455	451	451	451	465	479
1,254	1,254	1,254	1,307	1,141	1,136	1,288	1,297	1,300	1,322	1,308	1,304	1,312
345	345	380	380	372	409	415	423	421	419	421	429	429
					310	328	328	411	416	446	503	503
				334	482	433	439	449	471	471	493	493
					776	768	710	730	696	696	731	543
					255	270	270	267	267	267	306	350
					326	350	350	350	350	350	350	350
					746	783	801	801	847	860	854	841
					287	293	293	293	325	285	345	342
					417	488	488	488	488	609	609	465
						286	305	300	300	320	331	326
							258	248	240	243	256	254
								302	264	285	329	334
								369	314	312	410	427
								234	386	386	334	360
								313	329	334	334	318
												194

knowledge for the establishment of scientific spirit', and 'to reconstruct Japan democratically' (*Newsletter* 1980: 14). The Economic Division had 278 members in June 1950. It was included in the list of member associations for March 1961 but it broke up before 1970. The purposes of the Agricultural Division were 'to promote scientific research in agricultural economics, agricultural science, and agricultural technology, and to spread the research results'. According to its brief history, it aimed to attract many democratic agricultural scholars, to demand democratic operation of the post-WWII agrarian reform, and to make a scientific foundation for Japanese agriculture (*Bulletin*, J, 1951: (1) 52–4). The Agricultural Division was on the list of UNEAJ member associations for March 1956 but not on the list for 1960. It broke up before March 1961 (*Newsletter* 1980: 13).

Fourth, the Japan Society of Monetary Economics was founded in 1943. Its predecessor, the Study Group for the Monetary System, was started in November 1922 and held a regular meeting once a month until the 1927 financial crisis. In July 1932, the Study Group for the Currency System was started in order 'to study both the domestic and international economic conditions, and to find the best currency system for Japan to adopt in the future'. The research fund was donated by the Study Group on Finance at Mitsui Bank. Those who had participated in the Study Group for the Currency System kept in touch with each other through the magazine entitled *Toyo Keizai Shinpo*, and proposed the establishment of the Japan Society of Monetary Economics at the insistence of Torajiro Takagaki in 1943. Takagaki said that the final outcome of the Pacific War was not clear as yet but the discussions on the international monetary system for the post-war period had already begun in the UK and US, and therefore we had 'to initiate the discussion of the post-war matters promptly in Japan as well' (*Newsletter* 1974: 25; 1980: 20). In June 1943, the foundation assembly took place and Kakujiro Yamazaki became the first President. After October, several committees were started and made studies of the current problems such as 'the essence and the future of the managed currency system, the future of exchange and international finance centered on Japan', and 'the essence of savings and the plan of fund allocation'. The purpose of the society is 'to study the theory and policy of finance and its related matters, and to contribute to the progress of knowledge and economic development' (*Newsletter*, J, 1974: 25; 1980: 21).

Fifth, the Society for the History of Economic Thought is one of the founding member associations of UNEAJ, although its official foundation day is 23 April 1950, the date on which the inaugural meeting took place. *Bulletin* (J, 1951: (1) 35) said: 'The society was formed in December 1949, and was established at the first general assembly on 23 April 1950'. *A Ten-Year History of the Study of the History of Economic Thought* (J, 1961: 10) said: 'Thanks to the effort of Kubota, one of the founders of the society, UNEAJ allowed the society to become one of the original member associations'. Mitsuteru Kubota became the first President of the society. Kinnosuke Otsuka and Tsuneo Hori, founders of the society, attended the inaugural meeting of UNEAJ as councilors from member associations of UNEAJ based on its constitution. Its *Ten-Year History* said in the conclusion: 'Thus, the society could get a citizenship in the Japanese community of economists before its formal establishment. This fact shed bright light on the steps of the society.' This indicates that membership in UNEAJ was significant for this association. The purpose of the society is to study the history of economics and economic thought, and communications with other associations inside and outside Japan.

Sixth, the predecessor of the Association of Theoretical Economics is the Japanese Economic Association, which was established in 1934 but whose membership was restricted to theoretical economists teaching the principles of economics at universities and colleges (*Bulletin* J 1950: (1) 54). According to *Bulletin* (J, 1951: (1) 54–5), in 1949 its steering policy was changed, and the past directors were all released from their posts. New members were recruited from theoretical economists nation-wide. The name of the association was changed from the Japanese Economic Association to the Association of Theoretical Economics. In October 1950, the Japanese Econometric Society was established and joined UNEAJ in April 1952. This society and the association made it a rule to hold regular conferences together, and there was extensive overlapping in their membership (*Newsletter* 1980: 43). Therefore, the merger of the two became an issue but it was decided to go ahead at the general assembly of October 1967. At the next general assembly of October 1968 it was decided that the new name be the Japanese Association of Economics and Econometrics (*Newsletter* 1967: 48; 1980: 43). At the general assembly of September 1997, the name was changed to the Japanese Economic Association, which was the original name for the association.

As regards the activities of the Japanese Economic Association, there is something special to note on the internationalization of economics. In 1950, the leaders in the community of Japanese economists launched the scientific journal in Japanese entitled *Kikan Riron Keizaigaku*. This became the journal of both the Association of Theoretical Economics and the Japanese Econometric Society in 1959. A referee system was introduced in 1960. In order to promote the internationalization of the journal, its formal name was changed to an English one, *Economic Studies Quarterly*. A British publisher was found for the journal, and the name became the *Japanese Economic Review*. Moreover, the Econometric Society is an international organization, which individual economists can join from all over the world. This society and the Japanese Economic Association had jointly held a Far Eastern meeting every other year since the former Japanese Association of Economics and Econometrics decided to do so at its 1987 general assembly. The Japanese Association of Economics and Econometrics gave its full support to the 1995 world congress of the Econometric Society held in Tokyo, and did not hold a Far Eastern meeting.

Let us look now at the association that survives today with the initial names in order of establishment year. The Japan Society of Business Administration was founded in 1926 and is the oldest among the original member associations. The objective of the society at foundation was to set up a joint research organization in order to promote the study of commerce and business administration. It held its first nation-wide meeting in Tokyo in November 1926 and recommended that the government introduce an accounting system. It holds an annual meeting, which includes symposium sessions and individual papers on a common theme (*Bulletin*, E, 1981: 24).

The Socio-Economic History Society was established in December 1930. *Bulletin* (E, 1981: 112) said:

> As economic studies progressed in Japan in the 1920s, a variety of economic historical studies began to be conducted by an increasing number of experts. In 1929, a group of scholars (mainly from Kyoto University) began to study economic history. It should be noted that in the 1920s in Britain, the Economic History Society was inaugurated and *Economic History Review* started publication, while in France *Annales d'histoire economique et sociale* came into being. Reflecting such situations inside and outside of the country, there was a growing need among Japanese scholars of economic history to establish a nation-wide organization [Originally written in English but modified to fit in the context by the author.]

With regard to the two original purposes of the society, one was to break down academic sectarianism in order to promote the study of economic history through academic exchange among scholars in Japan. Another was to organize both economic historians and scholars of related fields such as political history, social history, legal history, history of ideas and history of economic thought (*Bulletin*, E, 1981: 112). This society has kept its liberal and interdisciplinary tradition until the current day.

The Japan Statistical Society was founded in 1931 by Hiromi Arisawa, Yuzo Morita, Ichiro Nakayama, Iwasaburo Takano, and other relatively young statisticians. It was because they recognized the need to organize a nation-wide academic society to help in the collection and manipulation of statistical data as well as to strengthen the theoretical and methodological background. The society has contributed to developing statistical theory, has helped improve the quality of official statistics, and has made it popular to think with the use of statistics among educated people. Recently, a number of researchers in biology, engineering, finance, medical science, technology, and other applied areas of statistics have joined the society, so that the annual meeting now offers a convenient place where statisticians from all fields can get together to exchange their ideas (*Bulletin*, E, 1994: 67).

The Japan Accounting Association was established in 1937, evolving from the Japan Society of Accounting, which had been established in 1917. This society was the only nation-wide organization for the study of accounting at the time, but the majority were accounting practitioners, whose numbers were increasing. Professors of accounting, who taught at universities and colleges, needed to create another organization to promote a purely academic study of accounting (*Newsletter* 1974, 35–6).

The Japan Economic Policy Association held its first meeting in May 1940. The association was organized on the initiative of scholars of economic policy who had something to do with the 23rd Study Committee (small and middle-sized manufacturing) of the Japan Society for the Promotion of Science. The founders aimed to meet the needs of the times for the promotion of scientific studies of economic policy in theoretical and practical terms. The association was open in principle to every scholar who was interested, whereas the Japanese Economic Association was not at the time (*Newsletter* 1974: 39). Although it promptly got started with 306 members at the beginning of the Sino-Japanese War (1937–45), its activities were suspended during and immediately after the Asian Pacific War (1941-5). Its annual nation-wide meeting was resumed in 1948. It sets a central theme for every annual meeting reflecting current economic policies, and examines the past economic policies every ten years (*Bulletin*, E, 1994: 21).

The Japan Institute of Public Finance was established in 1940, with 63 initial members. Its former English name was the Japanese Association of Fiscal Science. It seeks to encourage research on public finance, to foster the exchange of the results, and to facilitate friendly communication among its members. With the strong trend of internationalization, the institute is eager to promote international activities, such as sponsoring the annual conference of the International Institute of Public Finance that took place in Tokyo in 1981.

The Political Economy and Economic History Society was established in June 1948. Its former English name was the Agrarian History Society. It aimed to study the historical meaning of the agrarian reform during the post-WWII occupation by the Allies and its relationship with the reproduction structure. Its activities were suspended for a while after it published *The Upshot of the Agrarian Reform* in Japanese in 1951. It shifted the aims of research to the characteristics of landownership after the reform, agricultural productivity and the stratification of farmers, and its relationship with the reproduction structure. 'The objective of this society's foundation is to contribute to the progress of the Japanese people and the development of world history through a political-economic and historical study of current situations in the world' (*Bulletin*, E, 1998: 49). Now it has four divisions, namely economic history and current analysis, Japanese economic history, agrarian problems, and foreign economic history.

The Japan Society of Public Utility Economics was founded in 1949. It aims to foster the study and investigation of public utilities from political, economic and technical points of view, and to improve the general conception of public services, so as to induce their healthy development and thus to contribute to public welfare. *Bulletin* (J, 1950: (1) 36–7) said:

> Public utilities are a variety of natural monopoly enterprises which supply those services indispensable to our daily life, such as electric power, gas, water, railroads, urban transportation, bus, regular shipping, postal mail, telecommunication, and broadcasting. These differs in fare systems, services, government control, corporate form, and working conditions from general business enterprises in the respect that they are public goods and are usually monopolized by a company in a region. Therefore the policies for public utilities receive special treatment from legal, economic, and social principles different from those for general enterprises.

The first president was Masamichi Royama.

Let us look at the associations that joined UNEAJ after its founding in the order of their entry. The foundation of each association and the procedure for entry reflected contemporary practice. In 1950, the Agricultural Economics Society of Japan (1924), the Japan Society of International Economics (1950), the Japan Society of Commodity Science (1935), and the Society for the Study of Social Policy (1950) all joined UNEAJ. The number in parentheses after the name of an association denotes its foundation year.

The Agricultural Economics Society of Japan was established in November 1924, and joined UNEAJ on 24 January 1950. Its former name in English was the Agricultural Economic Society of Japan. After WWI, the issues of agriculture and rural community raised important problems in Japan (*Bulletin*, E, 1981: 19). It was gradually understood that agricultural problems were not confined to agriculture, rural villages or farmers, but could have a serious influence on Japanese society as a whole. However, the study of agriculture and rural problems had been largely ignored from the viewpoint of social science (*Bulletin*, J, 1974: 50; 1980: 47). The purpose of the society was stated in the prospectus as follows: 'The Agricultural Economics Society of Japan aspires to study all problems related to agriculture and rural societies. Regardless of how such problems are approached – from agricultural management, agricultural policy, agricultural statistics, agricultural history or other theories to accomplish its purposes.' (*Bulletin*, E, 1997: 1).

At the fourth meeting of directors, the qualifications for entry were decided. Based on this new rule, the third meeting of councilors approved the entry of the Japan Society of International Economics, while it turned down the application of the Economic Exchange Society by 8 to 16, because of the problems in the geographical distribution of the members and expertise.

The Japan Society of International Economics was established in 1950, stimulated by both the conclusion of the war and the foundation of UNEAJ. It aims to promote academic research of theoretical, empirical and policy-oriented international economics. In their view international economic organizations were being reconstructed based on the principles of freedom and peace to prevent another war from occurring. Therefore, international relations were becoming very important for Japan's economic recovery and rehabilitation in the international community. Taking this situation into consideration, academic study of the international economy was set in motion and the research environment was geared to this direction (*Bulletin*, J, 1951: (1) 38). *Bulletin* (E, 1981: 73) stated:

> Members pursue the theoretical and policy aspects of international economics as well as the historical and current analysis of international economic situations. Recently, with the rapid development and changes in the world economy, the contents of the subject of international economics and business have been much diversified into detailed division of trade, finance, investment and the problems of less developed countries including

oil producing countries. We also see the difficulties of exchange, trade and industrial adjustment even among the developed countries.

It is noteworthy that the society has both Marxian and non-Marxian economists, who were actively debating with each other on the issue of international trade and development in the 1950s (Ikeo 1999).

The Japan Society of Commodity Science was reorganized in 1950 and joined UNEAJ in October 1950. Its predecessor, the Commodity Science Council, was founded by experts on commodity science teaching at universities and colleges. The name was changed to the Japan Society of Commodity Science in 1937. Its activities were suspended during and immediately after the war. In 1949, a local meeting was held in Tokyo to form a closer academic relationship for the development of commodity science.

The Society for the Study of Social Policy was newly established in July 1950 and joined UNEAJ in November. It inherited its name and some of its members from a society of the same name, the Society of the Study of Social Policy, which was formed as the second academic society for social scientists in Japan in 1896. The old society attracted a very wide range of influential scholars, who had a reformist orientation. In the 1920s, its activities were suspended mainly due to internal conflict. After the end of WWII, the new society started over with the concentration of its focus on social problems and social policies including management and labor studies (*Newsletter* 1974: 57; 1980: 50).

The associations which joined UNEAJ during 1951–9 were the Japanese Society of Insurance Science (1940), the Japanese Econometric Society (1950), the Japan Society of Marketing and Distribution (formerly Japan Society of Commercial Sciences) (1951), the Japan Association of Economic Geographers (1954), the Japan Association for Asian Political and Economic Studies (1953), and the Japan Business English Association (1934). There were 23 associations in March 1960.

The Japanese Society of Insurance Science was established in November 1940. There was an older society named the Society of Insurance Science that had been established as the first society of social scientists in Japan in 1895. The old society made great contributions to the development of the insurance industry and academic circles for many years through the publication of insurance journals. However, it failed to give enough opportunities for young members directly to exchange their ideas at annual nation-wide conferences. Then young members inaugurated a separate organization, the Japanese Society of Insurance Science in 1940. The activities of both societies were suspended in 1944. After the war, in 1950, the two societies were merged into one, and joined UNEAJ in April 1951.

The Japanese Econometric Society was established in 1950 and joined UNEAJ in April 1952. As noted, it merged with the Association of Theoretical Economics in 1967, and the new name was settled as the Japanese Association of Economics and Econometrics in 1968. The name of the association changed to the Japanese Economic Association in 1997.

The Japan Society of Marketing and Distribution was established in April 1951 after holding a series of scholarly meetings from around November 1950. It was the time when commercial transactions were becoming normal after the end of WWII, and the theoretical and practical studies of commerce, trade, and securities were called for (*Newsletter* 1974: 62; 1980: 57). It has played a big role in both theoretical and empirical research on marketing and distribution in Japan. Its initial English name was the Japan Society of Commercial Sciences, although its Japanese name remains unchanged. It joined UNEAJ in April 1953.

The Japan Association of Economic Geographers was founded in April 1954 for scholars of economic geography as a social science. The study of economic geography was started in the 1930s and was producing some results. In the 1950s, economic geographers started to search for a new direction in dealing with humanities and social phenomena (*Newsletter* 1974: 65; 1980: 70–1). It joined UNEAJ in April 1959.

The Japan Association for Asian Political and Economic Studies was founded on 5 May 1953, aiming at doing purely academic but comprehensive studies on Asia. At the time the San Francisco Treaty had just been signed and the Korean War was coming to an end. *Bulletin* (E, 1994: 8) continues to say:

> The Association was not the only one which was involved in Asian studies at that time, but was unique in the sense that it was politically neutral while most other similar organizations were deeply influenced by Marxist ideology and leftist movements, against the background of the political atmosphere in Japan in the early 1950s. ... In 1957, it was authorized by the Ministry of Foreign Affairs as a public service corporation (*koeki hojin*). It is one of the few academic associations that are officially permitted as foundational juridical persons (*zaidan hojin*) in Japan. Although the Ministry of Foreign Affairs is its competent authority, ... the Association has never lost its academic freedom in its history of 41 years. [Originally written in English, but slightly modified to fit in the context.]

The association joined UNEAJ in April 1959.

The Japan Business English Association was established in July 1934 and joined UNEAJ in 1959.

> The objective of the association in its early years was to promote studies in Business English and foreign trade to meet the needs of the times for persons with a good command of English and expertise in the principles and practice of foreign trade. The scope has been gradually enlarged with the diversification and internationalization of business as well as progress in the means of communication. In spite of the modest name of the association, the present members' research efforts range over wide fields, from legal and technical aspects to linguistic and cultural aspects of international business, and tend toward an interdisciplinary science of international business communication (*Bulletin*, E, 1981: 29).

In the 1960s, the Japan Society of Political Economy (1959), the Japan Society of Business Mathematics (1959), the Business History Society of Japan (1964), the Japan Academy of Foreign Trade (1960), and the Japan Section of the Regional Science Association International (1962) joined UNEAJ.

The Japan Society of Political Economy was established in May 1959 and joined UNEAJ in April 1960. Scholars who were interested in Marx's economics decided to establish the society in April 1959 after holding a preparatory meeting in the summer of 1958. The prospectus stated:

> The objective of the Japan Society of Political Economy, the first independent organization of its kind, is to promote studies on basic economic theory through academic exchange among scholars not only of Marx's economics but also in other related fields. For instance, scholars of social policy, dealing with wages, or indeed profit theory might have academic relations with the society (*Bulletin*, E, 1981: 86).

Influenced by the collapse of actual socialism, member economists have recently discussed the viability of socialism, testify to the viability of Marxist economics by applying the theory to the reality of capitalism, and take up the contemporary world and the contemporary Japanese economy more often than before (*Bulletin*, E, 1994: 64–5).

The Japan Society of Business Mathematics was established in July 1959 and joined UNEAJ in April 1960.

> It aims to promote research and the application of quantitative approaches in business. Quantitative approach refer to methods which utilize mathematical models to solve problems encountered in the process of planning and control in management. These approaches encompass a variety of methods, such as investment theory and practice, production management, management science, operations research, and computer simulation (*Bulletin*, E, 1995: 39).

The Business History Society of Japan was established in 1964 and joined UNEAJ in the same year. It was born out of a study group for business history, which had started in 1960. It aims first to examine the entrepreneurial role in the light of the cultural environment by using sociological methods, second to clarify the relationship between entrepreneurship and economic performance, and third to study managerial history through examining the activities of business organizations (*Bulletin*, E, 1981: 32).

The Japan Academy of Foreign Trade was founded in September 1960 and joined UNEAJ in 1964. It hopes to attract a wide variety of researches such as the theory and policy of trade, trade management, trade history, transnational enterprise, North-South trade, and business practice. In the 1960s, its members' research was concentrated on the relationship between trade and economic growth. In the 1970s, it was broadened to cover the international movement of productive factors such as technology transfer, the activities of multinationals, exports of industrial plant and engineering services, and business practice of international consortia (*Bulletin*, E, 1981: 66). In the 1980s and 1990s, trade trends and environments are taken into consideration from a medium- to long-run (*Bulletin*, E, 1994: 26).

The Japan Section of the Regional Science Association International was established in 1962 and joined UNEAJ in 1964. The Regional Science Association is an international association for the advancement of regional and related special and area studies. The Japan Section operates as an objective, scientific organization without political, social, financial, or nationalistic bias. Its main purposes are to hold an annual domestic conference, to hold and to sponsor an international conference, and to publish and to distribute the papers and proceedings of the Japan Section (*Bulletin*, E, 1981: 97). The fifth World Congress of the Regional Science Association International was held in Tokyo in May 1996. Attending were 400 scientists and 100 spouses from 42 countries on six continents, and 100 Japanese Ph.D. students. It seemed very successful.

> Plenary sessions provided thoughtful overviews of emerging trends and issues, challenges and opportunities. Concurrent sessions allowed for testing of new approaches and perspectives before a thoughtful and critical audience. There were abundant opportunities to develop or expand scientific networks (*Bulletin*, E, 1998: 67).

Moreover, the report (on the same page) stated at the beginning: 'His Majesty the Emperor and Her Majesty the Empress of Japan opened the . . . Congress and then stayed on to have tea with visiting regional scientists. It is difficult to imagine a more dramatic start for a scientific congress.'

In the 1970s, the Society for Economic Studies of Securities (1966), the Population Association of Japan (1948), the Association for Comparative Economic Studies (1967), the Academic Association for Organizational Science (1959), and the Japan Society for Personnel and Labor Research (1970) joined UNEAJ. There were 31 member associations in March 1980.

The Society for Economic Studies of Securities was established in November 1966 with the purpose of promoting studies of securities and their markets, and joined UNEAJ in 1970. Most members are economists teaching at universities, but others are accountants, lawyers, securities analysts and practitioners working in financial markets. The survey conducted in its *Short History* (1996) classifies the past presentation at the official meetings into 15 areas such as the method for the research of securities, joint stock companies, primary (new issue) markets, secondary markets, securities markets within the financial system, derivatives, foreign securities markets, international capital markets, management of securities companies (brokers), corporate finance, securities (investments) analysis, investors, securities transaction law, regulation and administration for securities markets, and the history of securities markets.

The Population Association of Japan was established in November 1948 in order to facilitate the exchange of information and research results on population.

It was a time when rapid socio-economic changes were under way in Japan. It covers not only social sciences including, chiefly, economics but also natural sciences, because of the nature of population studies (*Bulletin*, E, 1981: 90). Its secretariat was in the National Academy of National Health from 1948 till March 1961. It was moved to the National Institute of Population Research at the Ministry of Health and Welfare in April 1961. It has been in the National Institute of Population and Social Security Research since 1997. The association joined UNEAJ in 1971.

The Society for the Study of Socialist Economies, currently the Association for Comparative Economic Studies, was founded in 1966, and joined UNEAJ in May 1973. It was organized by 57 young scholars who specialized in socialist economies and were not satisfied with the Japan Society of International Economics or the Japan Society of Political Economy, which had many socialist economists. The purpose of the society was to promote studies of socialist economies from both theoretical and empirical viewpoints. Its predecessor was the Study Group of Socialist Economies that was founded in 1963. The report in *Newsletter* (1974: 86; 1980: 72) said:

> Although the study of socialist economies was prohibited by the government until the end of the war [WWII], only a few front runners made a serious study of them. It is risky to make a special study of socialist economies because a limited number of university posts has been available for socialist economists. Overcoming a variety of obstacles, a young generation of scholars of socialist economies were nurtured and were getting ready for the establishment of the Society for the Study in Socialist Economies (Author's translation).

The society changed its name to the Association for Comparative Economic Studies because of the international environment during the mid-1980s and the mid-1990s. The report in *Bulletin* (E, 1998: 1) said:

> On the one hand, after Mikhail Gorbachev became the general secretary of the Communist Party of the Soviet Union, the Soviet Union and Eastern European countries tried to change their systems to compete with Western developed countries, and in the end abandoned their socialist political and economic systems, stepping up the transformation of their systems into democratic market economies. On the other hand, since Deng Xiaoping seized power, China has been liberalizing its economy step by step, saying that China has reached the stage of 'socialist market economy'.

The Academic Association for Organizational Science (1959) was founded under the initiative of Keiji Baba in September 1959 to counter criticism against the tendency of narrow specialization in science. Its activities were suspended by the unexpected death of Baba in 1961. The society restarted in 1963. Its first purpose is to make a comprehensive study of organizational problems from viewpoints of business management, economics, law, political science, administration, sociology, psychology, behavioral science, engineering, and business practice. Its second purpose is to contribute to the improvement of organizations (*Newsletter* 1980: 87). The association joined UNEAJ in 1976.

The Japan Society for Personnel and Labor Research was established in December 1970. It aims to promote an interdisciplinary research of personnel management and industrial relations mainly at management level with the cooperation of experts in various fields such as business management, economics, sociology, psychology, and law. It also aims to supply new information and research results (*Newsletter* 1979: (15) 8; 1980: 89–90). It joined UNEAJ in 1979.

In the 1980s, the Society of Economic Sociology (1966), the Japan Finance Association (1977), the Japan Association for Planning Administration (1977), and the Japan Auditing Association (1977) joined UNEAJ. The number of its member associations became 35 in 1986.

The Society of Economic Sociology was established in 1966 for the purpose of a comprehensive and integrative study in various forms of economic and social life based on the mutual correlation of economics and sociology. Its activities flourished in its early years under the strong influence of Yasuma Takata, who was a distinguished scholar in both economics and sociology (*Bulletin*, E, 1995: 44). The society joined UNEAJ in 1982.

The Japan Finance Association was founded in 1977 to promote academic research in the field of corporate finance and financial management. Since its foundation, the association has contributed to intellectual interactions between researchers in academic institutions and those in business and governmental institutions (*Bulletin*, E, 1996: 18). It joined UNEAJ in 1984. The Japan Association for Planning Administration was established in 1977 as a multidisciplinary forum consisting of academic researchers, government planning experts and administrators, and corporate planners. It aims first at the systematic development of knowledge of planning science based on interchange of both the practical observations from the processes of planning, implementation, and assessment and the analytical outcomes from planning theory and natural and social fundamentals. It joined UNEAJ in 1985. The Japan Auditing Association was established in 1978 and joined UNEAJ in 1986. It aims to promote research in auditing and to provide an intellectual link among researchers in auditing (*Bulletin*, E, 1995: 13).

In the 1990s up to March 1999, 15 associations joined UNEAJ and the number of member associations became 50. In 1990, two associations joined UNEAJ. The Japan Academy for Consumption Economy was founded in 1976 for the purpose of making a comprehensive study of consumption economy and consumer affairs. Next, the Japanese Association for International Accounting was established for the promotion of international accounting studies in 1984.

In 1991, six associations joined UNEAJ. The Japan Society for Applied Management was established in 1967 for the purpose of making a comprehensive study of strategic application of management, and the exchange of ideas and the promotion of joint studies. The Nippon Urban Management and Local

Government Research Association was established in 1984 for a comprehensive study of urban management. The Japan Port Economic Association was established in 1962 for a comprehensive and integrative study of port economics. The Nippon Academy of Management Education was established in 1979 for a comprehensive study of Japanese management practices, management education, management development, and international management. The Academy of Management Philosophy was established in 1984 for a comprehensive and integrative study of management philosophy. The Japan Risk Management Society was established in 1978 for a comprehensive study of risk management.

In 1992, the Japan Logistics Society, which was established in 1983 for a comprehensive study of logistics management, joined UNEAJ. In 1993, the Association for the Study of Socialist Enterprise, which was established in 1976 for a comprehensive study of socialist enterprise, joined UNEAJ. It changed its name to the Japan Association for the Comparative Studies of Management in March 1995.

In 1994, four associations joined UNEAJ. The Society for Industrial Studies was established in 1975 for a comprehensive study of industries. It published the post-WWII History of Japanese Industries (in Japanese, 1995), which was very useful for our current study in Part II. The Japan Association for Management Systems was established in 1981 for a comprehensive study of management systems. The Japan Association for Research on Business Administration was established in 1991 for a comprehensive study of business administrative behavior. CIRIEC Japanese Section (the Japan Society of Research and Information on Public and Co-operative Economy) was established in 1985 as the Japanese section of the International Center of Research and Information of Public and Cooperative Economy. It aims to promote the study of public economies and an international public economy.

In 1998, one association joined UNEAJ and the number of member associations became 50. The fiftieth association was the Japan Society for Social Science of Accounting, which was established in 1986 for a comprehensive study of accounting theory as social science.

It is interesting to list the member associations of UNEAJ that have the most individual members from the top. The number in parentheses after the name of an association indicates the number of individual members. According to *Newsletter* (1999), there are two associations that have more than 2,000 individual members, namely the Japanese Economic Association (2,538) and the Japan Society of Business Administration (2,077). There are eleven associations that have more than 1,000 but less than 2,000 members. From the third from the top, they are the Japan Accounting Association (1,654), the Academic Association for Organizational Science (1,594), the Japan Society of Insurance Science (1,416), the Agricultural Economics Society of Japan (1,471), the Japan Statistical Society (1,436), the Japan Association of Planning Administration (1,312), the Japan Economic Policy Association (1,279), the Socio-economic History Society (1,272), the Japan Society of International Economics (1,284), the Japan Society of Monetary Economics (1,052), the Japan Society of Political Economy (1,013), and the Japan Association for Asian Political and Economic Studies (1,000). The fifty member associations had 38,002 members in total. Usually many Japanese economists sign up for two or more academic associations, while some join no association. I guess that the number of Japanese economists might be a half or a third of the total number of members in UNEAJ.

1.4 UNEAJ and international communication

The general purpose of the UNEAJ is to contribute to the development of economics, commerce and business administration. As seen in Section 1.2, it is necessary to support the scholarly activities of its member associations and to promote academic exchange of ideas not only among members themselves but also between Japanese and academic societies overseas. UNEAJ has been organizing events needed to attain this purpose since its establishment.

In fact, UNEAJ has been spending considerable energy and funds in promoting international communication among economists. First, UNEAJ provides travel funds for the member economists who participate in academic gatherings overseas and for the member associations who invite foreign economists to Japan. Second, UNEAJ keeps close contact with the International Economic Association (IEA) through the Third Division of the Science Council of Japan (JSC), and plays the role of secretariat when IEA holds a round-table conference in Japan. In fact when the fifth world congress of IEA was held in Japan, the Third Division of JSC, UNEAJ, and the Japan Statistical Society co-sponsored it with the full support of related associations.

The larger a planned event or project becomes, the more flexibly the organizer has to adjust both the organizing association and the relationship among related organizations by making close contact with their counterparts abroad in order to put the plan into practice. Although the Third Division of JSC is the formal member association for IEA representatives from Japan, it has some limitations in taking such steps as promptly as the occasion demands, because it is a governmental organization. For example, it takes too much time to get permission from the government when it plans to raise money. Therefore UNEAJ, a non-governmental organization, needs to step in occasionally. As a result, the relationship among concerned organizations tends to become complicated although it is frequently clarified at formal meetings (*Newsletter* 1978: (13)).

UNEAJ reports its events and projects in its periodicals such as *Bulletin* and *Newsletter*. In the rest of this section, we first see the internal communication collaboration among member associations of UNEAJ and the international collaboration between UNEAJ and IEA.

1.4.1 Communications

The periodicals written in Japanese of UNEAJ are *Bulletin* (J, 1951–61) and *Newsletter* (1970–). The periodicals written in English are *Japan Science Review, Economic Sciences* (1953–64) and *The Information Bulletin for the Union of National*

Economic Associations in Japan (1981–). UNEAJ has published several books in order to survey the latest activities and research results of member associations. Since its foundation it has been organizing information gathering including invited lectures for those researchers working in economics, accounting and business administration.

The first *Bulletin* in Japanese was issued during 1951–61 with reports of activities of UNEAJ and its member associations, communications with both the Third Division of JSC and IEA, and scientific papers. Both the first and second issues appeared in 1951, the third and fourth joint issue in 1952, the fifth in 1954, the sixth in 1955, the seventh in 1956, the eighth in 1960, and the ninth in 1961. The interval between issues became longer because an increasing number of member associations did not keep the deadline. Some university libraries have a copy of *Bulletin* (J) and the UNEAJ secretariat has a set of photocopies.

The first article in the first issue of *Bulletin* (J) was Shigeto Tsuru's 'Reflections of an economist' (J). He pointed out that although Japanese economists tended to undervalue applied economics and to concentrate on theoretical studies, there were few original contributions to economic theory. He called such scholars *keizaigaku-gakusha*, which means something like scholars of economics as opposed to economists. Tsuru's cynical argument is still an occasional topic of conversation. The second article was Wasaburo Kimura's 'Changes in accounting theory under monopolistic financial capitalism'.

The second issue of *Bulletin* (J) carried Ichiro Nakayama's 'Economics and vision', Shinjiro Kitazawa's 'Human basis for public relations' and Tadao Yanaihara's 'Research system for social sciences in the United States'. The joint third and fourth issue carried Tsuneo Mori's 'D. Stueart's economic doctrine' and Tsukumo Shionoya's 'New advancement of economic development'. The fifth issue carried Tatsuo Takenaka's 'Research development of public-service companies in Japan'. But there were no articles in the sixth issue. The issues from two to six had summaries of research made by individual economists and the activities of member associations. The seventh and eighth issues carried only activities of member associations. The ninth issue carried the report of the third general assembly entitled 'On the thirteenth round table of the International Economic Association: Economic development with special reference to East Asia', written by Kenjiro Ara. It also included the new trend in economic theory, economic development and international trade, demographic statistics, economic history, economic geography, long-term plans for business administration, accounting, and the study of public service as well as activities of member associations.

The old *Bulletin* tells us of the energetic activities of Japanese economists and the formal procedures for entry in the 1950s. UNEAJ issued no periodicals from 1962 to 1969. Moreover, no records of formal meetings remained in the secretariat. We can conjecture part of its activities in the report of the Third Division of JSC in *A Twenty-Five Year History of the Scientific Council of Japan* (SCJ 1977).

Second, UNEAJ has been issuing *Newsletter* in Japanese since 1970. The board of directors discussed in 1969 that *Newsletter* should be issued for communication among member associations, with the Science Council of Japan (*Newsletter*, J, 1970: (1) 6). *Newsletter* usually carries the report from the board of councilors and the board of directors, and the report made by the participants in international gatherings who were supported by travel grants. On special occasions *Newsletter* takes a journal form. The joint eighth, ninth and tenth issue of 1974 was *the Special Issue for the 25th Anniversary*, and the 17th issue of 1980 was *the Special Issue of the Thirtieth Anniversary*. Both provide us with a good historical record of UNEAJ. The thirteenth issue of 1978 was the Special Issue for the Fifth World Congress of IEA, which was the official account of the congress that was held in Tokyo in 1977.

Third, *Japan Science Review: Economic Sciences* in English was issued ten times from 1953 till 1964. Few libraries had the whole series, and even the secretariat has none. The first issue appeared in 1953, the second to fifth issues from 1955 till 1958, the sixth to ninth issues from 1960 till 1963, and the tenth issue in 1965. Publication was stopped because the financial condition of UNEAJ was deteriorating.

The first and second issues were filled with surveys of the research done by individual economists in member associations in various fields. The first issue carried surveys in monetary economics, the history of economic thought, international economics, Western economic history, fiscal science, economic theory, commodity science, insurance, and accounting. The second issue included surveys in the study of public services, the study of economic policy, the post-WWII Marxian political economy, and the Marxian study of agrarian problems. The third issue also included lists of publications made by individual economists of member associations as well. Many member associations spent an enormous amount of energy in compiling bibliographies. The field of survey articles in the second issue was statistics and its related field, in the fifth monetary economics and the history of economic thought, in the sixth international economics, in the seventh economic geography, in the eighth monetary economics, the history of social and economic thought, (Marxian) political economy, Asian political and economic studies, in the ninth international economics, commercial English, in the tenth statistics, (non-Marxian) theoretical economics and econometrics. Instead of surveys, the fourth issue carried the report of the first world congress of IEA held in Rome (the theme was stability and progress in the world economy). Ichiro Nakayama gave the report to a symposium organized by UNEAJ after he came back to Japan.

Fourth, *The Bibliography of Japanese Publications on Economics, 1946–1975* was planned by Kohachiro Takahashi (*Newsletter* 1978 (13): 4) and given to the participants in the Tokyo Congress of IEA in 1977. It carried brief summaries of the member associations of UNEAJ and listed one or two titles, in English, German or French, of the main contributions made in Japanese by each of about 5,500 Japanese economists after the end of WWII. It allowed the international participants to understand that Japanese economists had been making energetic studies in various fields, and this satisfied the directors of UNEAJ. Jokichi Uchida, one of the directors of the day, said, 'European and American participants were surprised by the many contributions in all the fields made by Japanese. . . . UNEAJ spent a lot of money for this project. But it was worth doing even if our funds were exhausted' (*Newsletter* 1978 (13): 4).

Fifth, the largest project of UNEAJ was the publication of *Keizaigaku no Doko* (The Trend in Japanese Economics, 1975), a memorial project to celebrate the 25th anniversary of UNEAJ. It was a comprehensive report of the development of economics in post-WWII Japan. It covered non-Marxian economic theory, Marxian economic theory, statistics, the history of social and economic thought, economic history, socialist economics, economic policy, agricultural economics, social policy, public finance, monetary economics, international economics, population, geographic economics and regional science, business administration, accounting, commerce, commodity science, insurance, transportation economics, and the study of public service.

Kohachiro Takahashi, the president of the day, talked about the aim and the future plan of this project as follows (Takahashi 1975: i–ii):

> It is imperative to make an objective record of the latest research results in order effectively to accumulate the common property of the academic world and to maintain a high level of research activity and to make progress. . . . Therefore, this book includes a general survey and description of the research trend in each field and a bibliography of the basic literature. This book is a kind of national report on the economic studies that had been made in Japan for the past quarter century. It is desirable to publish a similar report every five years or every decade. This report will become a systematic historical record of the development of economics in Japan [Author's translation].

The second collection of *The Trend in Japanese Economics* was published in 1982 for the celebration of the thirtieth anniversary of UNEAJ. A third collection has never been published.

UNEAJ celebrated its thirtieth anniversary in 1980. According to Takashi Shiraishi (1980: 16), a series of memorial events were planned. Fortunately, the targeted total of donations, 50 million yen, for the plan was almost reached, and the plan could be gradually implemented. Shiraishi (1980: 16) noted that especially important were three projects promoting international communication among member associations, which are still effective today.

First, a grant supporting part of hotel expenses for foreign scholars studying in Japan was started in FY1980. Second, a travel grant for those who participate in international conferences held abroad was started in FY1981. A member association is supposed to apply for a grant for its individual scholars after formal approval from the association. The funded scholars are obliged to make a report of the conference abroad in which they participate and *Newsletter* (J) carries the report.

Third, *Information Bulletin for the Union of National Economic Association* written in English has been issued every year for the purpose of public relations with its counterparts abroad since 1981 (Shiraishi 1980: 18). It carried a special article at the opening of each issue and the report given from all the member associations including yearly activities and brief general information until the eleventh issue of

1991. *Bulletin* started to carry a brief history of some ten member associations and a more detailed report of their activities with the list of all the member associations, their contact addresses, the year of their establishment, and so on. Each member association is supposed to make a detailed report every five years or so. Copies are distributed to about 500 institutions and universities abroad every year.

1.4.2 *Collaboration with international organizations*

UNEAJ maintains contact with several international organizations. Focusing on international collaboration, its relationship with the International Economic Association (IEA) is the longest and most important.

As noted, IEA is a federation of national academic associations or committees representing the economists of each country. It is a non-governmental and non-profit organization with purely scientific aims (Article 1 of the Statutes). It has been headquartered in Paris since it was founded in 1950. Article 2 of the Statutes gives us the general purpose of the IEA as follows:

> The general purpose of the Association is to initiate or co-ordinate measures of international collaboration designed to assist the advancement of economic knowledge. And in particular: (a) to secure and develop personal contacts between economists of different countries, by organizing round table discussions and conferences; (b) to encourage the provision of international media for the dissemination of economic thought and knowledge (such as bibliographies, abstracts, dictionaries, translations, etc.).

The creation of IEA came out of the discussion between R. Mosse and the staffs of the Department of Social Science at UNESCO (United Nations Educational, Scientific, and Cultural Organization) during the fall of 1948. It moved with the invitation of a small number of scholars to an international conference in Monaco. Under the leadership of Julian Huxley, seven economists got together in the headquarters of UNESCO in Paris. They were R. Mosse (France), Jacques Rueff (France), Austin Robinson (United Kingdom), Gottfried Haberler (United States), E. Roland Walker (Australia), W. Keilhau (Norway), and G. de Leener (Belgium). Haberler was an official representative from the American Economic Association (AEA) because it was announced at the earliest stage that AEA would join IEA. The economists who joined the founding group were J. W. Bell, J. A. Schumpeter, John V. Van Sickle, J. A. Willits, and F. C. Mills. Although the IEA nominating committee named Schumpeter as president in 1949, he passed away in January 1950 prior to the real creation of IEA (Allen 1991: 226). IEA was brought formally into existence in September 1950 at the invitation of Rueff then minister of State of the Principality when its first provisional council met in Monaco to approve its statutes (Robinson 1963: 3). It was followed by the first formal international conference of IEA with the theme of the problem of long-term international balance.

The headquarters of IEA was located in Paris while the secretarial work was done in Cambridge University and A. Robinson (1897–1993) took care of most of it. A. Cairncross's biography entitled *Austin Robinson* (1993) told us of Robinson's activities for IEA. Robinson made programs for international conferences, raised funds for IEA activities, took care of residences for attendees to stay in and edited many proceedings, making them publishable English. At the 1995 World Congress in Tunis, there was a special session in which K. J. Arrow gave a memorial talk on Robinson's activities and efforts for IEA. Arrow and Atkinson (1994: 4) said: 'Throughout his long association with the IEA, Austin worked tirelessly to fulfil these objectives, bringing together economists from a wide range of countries, and ensuring that "lively minded theoretical economists mixed with specialists in applied economics".'

Because it was thought to be efficient and inexpensive, IEA has no individual members but is a federation of national economic associations. France, Italy, and Australia established associations representing their countries immediately because they had had no such associations. Representative associations from Europe and America proposed joining the new international organization and managed to found IEA. Soon the associations representing Italy, (West) Germany and Japan joined IEA.

Japan had no association representing Japanese economists. Therefore UNEAJ applied to IEA at its Cambridge-Oxford conference in July 1952. Shigeto Tsuru and Minoru Tōyosaki, the two scientists representing Japan, completed the necessary procedure and the application was approved. In 1965, the member association representing Japan was changed to the Third Division of JSC from UNEAJ. In short, UNEAJ formally left IEA. Yet the individual members of the Third Division of JSC paid the quota for 1965–68. From then on, the Third Division of JSC sent representatives to IEA while UNEAJ played the part of secretariat when a world congress or round-table conference was organized and held in Japan.

The main activities of IEA are to hold a world congress every three years, and to organize three or four round-table conferences every year (Hayami 1997). On one hand, a world congress is open to every individual economist in the world and its program is supposed to cover most fields in economics. On the other hand, the organizer of a round-table conference can set up a particular theme and invite 40–50 expert economists in order to make the discussion concentrate on the theme and contribute to scholarly knowledge.

In Japan, the fifth world congress of IEA was held in Tokyo in 1977. In addition, Japan hosted five round-table conferences. The proceedings entitled *Economic Growth and Resources* were published by Macmillan. The part relating to Japan's economic problems was edited by Shigeto Tsuru and published by the *Asahi Evening News* as well (Tsuru 1978). As noted, the thirteenth issue (1978) of *Newsletter* (J) was devoted to the fifth world congress of IEA.

The themes of the round-table conferences held in Japan were 'Economic development in relation to East Asia' (1960), 'Economics of health and medicine' (1973), 'Economics and choosing energy resources' (1982), 'Organizations in the new dynamic society' (1987), and 'East Asian institutional basis for East Asian economic development' (1996). Kenjiro Ara's report on the round-table conference of economic development appeared in number 9 of *Bulletin* (J).

5 Some observations and conclusions

It can be said that we have described Japanese economics since 1945 by tracing the activities and the history of the Union of National Economic Associations in Japan (UNEAJ). It is worth summarizing our observations in order to make it possible to compare our results with related studies.

First, the period of the 1940s witnessed the establishment of new economics associations one after another. UNEAJ started with 15 associations but its establishment itself triggered the foundation of a series of new economics associations, which subsequently joined UNEAJ and led to an increase in the number of member associations. The decade of the 1990s has seen another rapid increase in that number.

Second, UNEAJ spent an enormous amount of energy in creating bibliographies, including the basic literature in each field and the comprehensive list of achievements made by individual scholars of the member associations. On the other hand, Shigeto Tsuru's plan of establishing a Japanese *Economic Journal* did not come to pass (*Bulletin*, J, 1960: (8) 2, 11). It seems that Tsuru advocated the establishment of an economic journal written in English representing Japan although no evidence has remained of the detail.

Third, UNEAJ has been sending out *Bulletin* in English and *Newsletter* (J) to institutions inside and outside of Japan to inform them of the latest activities of member associations. However, it would be more convenient if a homepage were available.

Fourth, the importance of international communication and collaboration are weighted differently among member associations of UNEAJ. Some associations are so fully internationalized that they hold international conferences or keep a close contact with their counterparts abroad. Others cannot find any counterpart abroad to contact.

Fifth, IEA has been very much concerned about economic growth especially in underdeveloped countries (*Newsletter* 1970: (2) 14). It is an important fact to take into consideration when we think about the role of IEA in the post-WWII history of economic thought.

Acknowledgements

I would like to thank Masao Uno, Takashi Shiraishi, and Yoshiko Ishii for providing the information about the Union of National Economic Associations in Japan. Uno and Ishii have given us permission to include 'The Purport and Process of Formation of the Union of National Economic Associations in Japan', which appeared in *Bulletin* (J, 1951), in this book. I further thank Takashi Negishi, Hiroji Nakamura, Michio Akama, Kiichiro Yagi, Kinsaburo Sunaga, Yoshiro Himuro, Masahiro Okuno, and Atushi Komine for the related information. I also thank Paul Pecorino for editing the English version.

APPENDIX: PURPORT AND PROCESS OF FORMATION OF THE UNEAJ (JAPAN UNION OF ASSOCIATIONS OF ECONOMIC SCIENCES)

For the progress of modern science, regardless of their spheres of learning, it is desirable that research cooperation and interflow be kept up among scholars, associations of sciences, and scientific circles at home and abroad; for isolation and partiality will make it absolutely impossible for the progress of modern sciences to be realized. With regard to the organization of research on economic and commercial sciences in Japan, it is true that many associations of sciences in the various fields of learning on a national scale have already been, or are expected in future to be, established but there has been as yet no system to enable such scientific associations by mutual cooperation and interflow to contribute to the progress of economic and commercial sciences in Japan and in the world.

This fact has been a matter of regret for many of the men of economic sciences. Among others, the Third Division (Economic and Commercial Sciences) of the Science Council of Japan, finding it of especial importance to make up for the lack of such a system, decided at the division meeting on 28 April 1949, to establish a 'Committee for the Organization of Researches on Economic Sciences' to investigate the proposed formation of a national organization covering all the branches of study in economic sciences. Subsequently, several meetings of the committee were held but, in order that such a national organization might be formed, it was found necessary to seek not only the opinions of the members of the Third Division of the Council constituting the committee, but also those of scholars in all fields of research. Accordingly, with a view to forming a national organization of Japanese economists, two round-table conferences were held, one in Tokyo on 7 October of the same year, and the other in Kyoto on 7 November. At the conferences were present the members of the Third Division of the Science Council of Japan as well as the representatives of various associations of sciences, making a free and active exchange of their opinions as to the character, objects, activities, officers, branches, expenditure, etc., of the proposed organization. As a result of those round-table conferences, two committees were organized, one for drafting the regulation of such a national organization and the other to prepare for the foundation thereof, consisting of the representatives, one for each, of the thirteen associations of sciences, and four officers of the Third Division of the Science Council of Japan. Those two committees met twice in Tokyo on 3 and 17 December, 1949 and, in accordance with their respective functions, completed the drafting of the regulation, and the preparation for the foundation of a national organization which is provisionally called the 'Japan Union of Association of Economic Sciences'. Accordingly, the first general meeting of 'Japan Union of Association of Economic Sciences' was held in Tokyo on 22 January, 1950, attended by the representatives, two for each of fifteen associations and all the members of the Third Division of the Science Council of Japan. After careful discussion, they decided the regulation of the organization on the basis of the original draft previously prepared by the drafting committee, and appointed the officers of the organization in accordance with the regulation. In this way, 'Japan Union of Association of Economic Sciences' has been officially organized.

As specified in the regulation, the Union is composed of national scientific associations specialized in economic and commercial sciences and other corresponding organizations in Japan and it has for its objects research cooperation and interflow among all the specialized branches of economic sciences and, in addition thereto, the maintenance of intimate relationships between Japanese and foreign scientific circles, thus contributing to the progress of economic sciences in Japan and in the world. The Union is earnestly desirous that, as a result of its formation, not only the defect in the system of research on economic and commercial sciences in Japan may be remedied, but also its activities will lead to a vigorous interflow between Japanese scientific circles and those of foreign countries, thereby promoting the progress of economic sciences in the world.

Publications of the UNEAJ

(1951–60) *Bulletin* (J) (in Japanese) (1–9), Tokyo: Japan Society for The Promotion of Science. (1), 1951; (2), 1951; (3/4), 1952; (5), 1954; (6), 1955; (7), 1956; (8), 1960; (9) 1961.

(1953–65) *Japan Science Review: Economic Sciences*, Japan Union of Associations of Economic Sciences (in English). (1), 1953; (2), 1955; (3), 1956; (4), 1957; (5), 1958; (6), 1960; (7), 1961; (8), 1962; (9), 1963; (10), 1965.

(1970-99) *UNEAJ Newsletter* (J) (Nihon Keizai Gakkai Rengo Nyusu), (1–35), Tokyo: UNEAJ Secretariat.

(1974) *UNEAJ Newsletter* (J) (Nihon Keizai Gakkai Rengo Nyusu), (8, 9, and 10), Special Issue for the 25th Anniversary.

(1975) *Keizaigaku no Doko* (The Trend in Japanese Economics), 3 volumes, Tokyo: Toyo Keizai Shinpo-sha.

(1977) *Bibliography of Japanese Publications on Economics, 1946–1975*, Tokyo: University of Tokyo Press.

(1978) *UNEAJ Newsletter* (J) (Nihon Keizai Gakkai Rengo Nyusu), (13), Special Issue on the 5th World Congress of the International Economic Association.

(1980) *UNEAJ Newsletter* (J) (Nihon Keizai Gakkai Rengo Nyusu), (17), Special Issue for the 30th Anniversary.

(1982) *Keizaigaku no Doko* (The Trend in Japanese Economics), No. 2, Tokyo: Toyo Keizai Shinpo-sha.

(1981–98) *Information Bulletin for the Union of National Economic Associations in Japan* (1–18), Tokyo: UNEAJ Secretariat.

References and further reading

Allen, R. L. (1991) *Opening Doors: The Life and Work of Joseph Schumpeter*: Volume Two: America, New Brunswick: Transaction Publishers.

Anon. (1950) 'Plans for an International Economic Association', *American Economic Review*, 40(2): 173–6.

Anon. (1951) 'Nihonkeizaigakkairengo kessei no shushi to keika', *Bulletin* (J) (1): 24–5. English version as 'The purport and process of formation of the Japan Union

Associations of Economic Sciences', *Bulletin* (J) (1): 25–6.

Anon. (1951) 'Nihonkeizaigakkairengo gijikiroku gaiyo' (UNEAJ record: the foundation meeting), *Bulletin* (J) (1): 26–8.

Arrow, K. J. and A. B. Atkinson (1994) 'Sir Austin Robinson and the IEA', *International Economic Association Newsletter* 22 July.

Cairncross, A. (1993) *Austin Robinson: The Life of Economic Adviser*, London: St. Martin's Press.

Hayami, Y. (1997) 'IEA Tokyo entaku kaigi oyobi IEA rijikai houkoku' (Report on the Tokyo round-table and the official meeting of Directors of IEA), *UNEAJ Newsletter* (33): 21–25.

Hayami, Y. (1998) 'IEA 1997nend hokoku' (Report on IEA for 1997), *UNEAJ Newsletter* (34): 18–20.

Ikeo, A. (1994) *20seiki no Keizaigakusha Network* (The Network of Economists in the Twentieth Century), Tokyo: Yuhikaku.

Ikeo, A. (1996) 'Internationalization of economics in Japan' in A. W. Coats (ed.) *The Post-1945 Internationalization of Economics*, annual supplement to volume 28 of the *History of Political Economy*, 121–39.

Ikeo, A. (1999) 'Japanese political economy' in *The Encyclopedia of Political Economy*, edited by Phillip O'Hara, London: Routledge.

International Economic Association (IEA) (1979) *International Economic Association: Past and Future*, Paris: IEA.

Iwao, H. (1988) '4hanseiki no keizaigakkairengo riji' (Director of UNEAJ for a quarter century), *UNEAJ Newsletter* (J) (24): 2–4.

Kurosawa, K. (1973) 'Nihonkeizaigakkairengo no Kaiko' (UNEAJ in retrospect), *UNEAJ Newsletter* (J) (6): 13–16.

Robinson, A. (1963) *The International Economic Association, 1950–62*, Paris: IEA.

Science Council of Japan, Editorial Committee for a 25-Year History (1977) *Nihongakujutukaigi 25nenshi* (A Twenty-Year History of Science Council of Japan), Tokyo: Gakujutsu Shiryo Hanpukai.

Shiraishi, T. (1980) '30-shunen kinen jigyo no hossoku' (Starting the thirty-year memorial enterprise), *UNEAJ Newsletter* (17): 16–19.

Society for the History of Economic Thought, Japan, (ed.) (1961) *Nihon niokeru Keizaigakushi Kenkyu 10nen no Ayumi* (Ten Year Steps of the Society for the History of Economic Thought), Society for the History of Economic Thought, Japan.

Takahashi, K. (1975) 'Jo' (Introduction), UNEAJ (1975) pp. i–iv.

Tsuru, S. (1951) 'Ichi keizaigakuto no hansei' (Reflection of an economist), *Bulletin* (J), (1): 1–10. First published in *Chuo Koron* May 1950. Also included in his *Keizaigaku no Hansei* (Reflection of Economics), June 1950.

Tsuru, S. (ed.) (1978) 'Growth and Resources Related to Japan: Proceedings of Session VI of the Fifth World Congress of the International Economic Association held in Tokyo', Tokyo: *Asahi Evening News*.

2   Economics in the academic institutions after 1945

Kiichiro Yagi

Introduction

Many impressionistic remarks have been so far made on the economics and economics professions in Japan after 1945.[1] Although those by Japanese economists are founded on their real experience, they are often limited by their research fields or biased by the schools to which they belong.[2] To obtain an objective view of Japanese economics in this period, this chapter summarizes available quantitative data that are related to Japanese academic economics. However, it is also necessary to explain the academic system after 1945 on which the quantitative growth of Japanese economics professions has developed for nearly a half century since then.

As it can be maintained in several fields of post-war development in Japan, the heritage of the wartime years is important to the academic development of economics after 1945. These years are often considered as a dark age when the freedom of learning was totally denied. However, on the other hand, it was in these years that new imperial universities were founded in Osaka and Nagoya, the activities of the Japan Science Promotion Society was expanded, the Grant in Aid of the Scientific Research was established, and the public scholarship program appeared. The promotion of learning in these years was focused on natural science and technology; however, economics also benefited in a diminished degree from this wartime national policy. Those economists who were motivated by urgent national problems joined various policy research projects and organized several special academic societies. Although most of them were dissolved in 1945, at least for a while, their experience and network were succeeded by post-1945 Japanese economics.

Accordingly, this chapter begins with an overview of the academic institutions in wartime years, and proceeds to its change during occupied years. A non-Marxian academic orthodoxy was being formed in wartime years by the activity of the Japanese Economic Association (established 1934) and the Japan Economic Policy Association (established 1940). This orthodoxy, however, was dissolved in the turbulent years after 1945 by criticism of the collaboration to wartime policies.[3] A new generation of modern economists who had studied contemporary theoretical achievements in Western economics was not prepared well enough to take over from their seniors. It was Marxian economics that extended the influence in the academic world. Marxian economists not only enthusiastically advocated the democratization of society, but also launched lively disputes in various economic journals. However, due to the dissolution of the Democratic Scientists Association (called *Minka*), the umbrella organization of the progressive researchers in natural and social sciences, Marxian economists could not establish an academic society until 1959, when the Japan Society of Political Economy was established. On the contrary, in the camp of modern economics, steady efforts such as journal publication and international communication were made by those who were eager to catch up to the standard of economics in the English-speaking world.

From the last years of the Occupation to economic recovery under the conservative government, those who had been purged from public offices and teaching jobs were rehabilitated into Japanese society. The Science Council of Japan that was constituted on a democratic election system came in conflict with the government. Despite these so-called 'reverse course' trends, the elitist authoritarianism of the pre-1945 type was not revived. The new university system of 1949 supplied the institutional basis for the quantitative growth of economics education that proceeded hand in hand with economic development after the 1950s. The educational background of academic researchers shows a contrast between researchers in economics and those in management sciences. While graduates of national universities such as the University of Tokyo, Kyoto University, Kobe University, Hitotsubashi University, have dominance in economists, the graduates of private universities such as Waseda University, Keio University, and Meiji University keep the rivalry in management studies. Both in public universities and in private universities the late-comer graduate courses have begun to produce academicians. After the mid-1970s economists with an American PhD in economics joined the leading group of academic economists in Japan. But still now the share of graduates of overseas universities in the total economics professions in Japan is under 10 percent. The decreasing tendency of research interest in Marxian economics and classical studies is represented by stagnation in the membership of related academic societies as well as its age structure.

In the final part of this chapter, the items of economic literature after 1955 are provided under the classification of the research areas (Table 2.11).

2.1 Academic environment of economics in wartime years

Properly speaking, the wartime regime of Japan was established from 1938 to 1941, when the Sino-Japanese War lost any hope of cease-fire in its early stage. However, judging from the general social atmosphere and policy measures that were apparently prepared for the war, quasi-wartime had begun already in 1931 with the Manchurian Incident. If we consider economics in this period from the viewpoint of academic institutions, we find both severe political repression on

Table 2.1 Economists expelled from universities pre-1945

Tokyo Imp. Univ.	Tatsuo MORITO* (1920), Yoshitaro OMORI (1928), Moritaro YAMADA (1930), Tadao YANAIHARA (1937), Hyoue OUCHI(1938), Hiromi ARISAWA (1938), Yoshitaro WAKIMURA (1938), Eijiro KAWAI* (1939), Seibi HIJIKATA* (1939), Takao TSUCHIYA (1942), Yasuo KONDO (1943)
Kyoto Imp. Univ.	Hajime KAWAKAMI (1928), Koji ISHIKAWA* (1943)
Tohoku Imp. Univ.	Kozo UNO (1938), Eitaro HATTORI (1942)
Kyushu Imp. Univ.	Itsuro SAKISAKA (1928), Tomoyuki ISHIHAMA (1928), Yasoji KAZAHAYA (1928), Masao TAKAHASHI (1937)
Tokyo Univ. of Commerce	Kinnosuke OTSUKA (1933)
Osaka Univ. of Commerce	Yasuo TATSUNO (1942), Toichi NAWA (1943), Teijiro KAMIBAYASHI (1943), Kazusaburo KIMURA (1943), Shigeru IIDA (1943), Ryuichi ABE (1943), Jokichi UCHIDA (1943), Minoru TOYOSAKI (1943)
Hosei Univ.	Ryokichi MINOBE (1938), Isamu ABE (1938), Kinji MINAMI (1938), Kinsaku KASAGAWA (1938)
Senshu Univ.	Yoshimasa KOBAYASHI(1936)
Doshisha Univ.	Etsuji SUMIYA (1933),Fumio HASEBE (1933), Yoshisada FURUYA* (1935), Kaname HAYASHI (1936)
Waseda Univ.	Tsunao INOMATA (1923)
Keio Univ.	Shiro TOYODA (1943)
Sugamo College of Commerce	Hyoue SERIZAWA (1938)

Note
* Non-Marxian economist

one hand and beneficial progress in academic organizations and research funds on the other hand.[4]

Political intervention in learning was not solely directed to economics but repression in economics is particularly harsh, since Marxism had established its position sufficiently to put a number of young and spirited academics under its influence. This repression extended further to liberal scholars such as Eijiro Kawai. Even a national communitarian, Koji Ishikawa, was forced to stop teaching under suspicion of being a disguised communist. Young researchers that learned from Marx had to hide their original research interest in the textual interpretation of non-Marxian classics or in detailed empirical researches. Forty

Table 2.2 Subvention to economic research by JSPS (The Third Regular Committee)

| Year | Individual research | | | Joint research | | |
	Project	Amount	%	Project	Amount	%
1933	17	26,056	5.8	1	2,230	3.7
1934	20	25,120	5.5	1	6,559	4.1
1935	15	20,410	4.5	1	10,127	4.5
1936	16	21,230	5.3	3	12,804	4.3
1937	10	15,520	4.9	2	23,555	4.4
1938	6	10,600	3.4	3	23,728	2.9
1939	8	11,312	3.9	4	50,521	4.6

names of economists that were forced to leave lecture halls are in Table 2.1. This is not a small number when one thinks of the number of academic economists in pre-1945 years.

Turning our eyes to progress in the academic institutions, the establishment of the Japan Society for the Promotion of Science (JSPS) in 1932 is important. This was an extra-governmental organization that canalized the governmental subvention as well as donations from private sectors to ground-breaking scientific researches. Economics was registered as an independent research field for the distribution of the JSPS funds. The Science Promotion Aid of the Ministry of Education that was founded in 1918 was limited to the natural sciences. The JSPS organized twelve regular committees in each field including human and social sciences to distribute the research fund. It was the Third Regular Committee that dealt with economics and management studies. The JSPS subsidized not only individual researches but also 'synthetic studies' that were organized according to urgent topics. Synthetic studies on the 'Basic Policy of Rice', 'Landed Farmers', 'Retail Shop Problem', 'Small and Medium-sized Industry', and 'Consumer Prices Problem' were performed by *ad-hoc* subcommittees organized under the Third Regular Committee.[5] Further, the special committee of the JSPS (see Table 2.2) organized a larger-scale joint study on the 'Economy of Manchuria, Mongolia and China'. Further, in 1943 the Grant of Scientific Research of the Ministry of Education that was introduced in 1939 was widened so as to cover the human and social sciences. But the inflow from the fund was rather small compared with the research fund of the Army and the Navy in the extraordinary military budget from 1942. As there is much evidence that military officers requested research and advice to economists, considerably huge amounts of money are assumed to have flowed into economics from this source also.

On the side of universities, the initiative to add new chairs for the study area that fitted the current policy problem, or to establish special research institutes that served as recipients of various funds appeared in several universities. In the case of Kyoto University, the Faculty of Economics succeeded in realizing the chair of 'Economic Policy of East Asia' and that of 'Theory of Japanese Economics' in 1939, and established the Research Institute of the East Asian Economy the next year. In the case of the Hitotsubashi (then Tokyo University of

Commerce), she opened the Research Institute of the East Asian Economy in 1939 and succeeded in 1942 in establishing it as an official organ of the university. Various research projects that included overseas field researches were organized in these newly established institutions. However, mainly due to the incineration of materials just after the surrender, details of those researches are still unknown.

Wartime years are the period in which several academic associations in economics were founded. In 1934 the Japanese Economic Association was founded after a decade's hiatus since the dissolution of the Association for the Study of Social Policy.[6] The main reason for the dissolution of the latter was the growing cleavage among members due to the strengthening influence of Marxism after the First World War. It is not clear whether the exclusion of Marxian economists was aimed for by the foundation of the Japanese Economic Association. However, judging objectively, the situation of the mid-thirties that most Marxian economists were expelled from academic positions or were forced to keep silence was the basis of the general direction of this association that condemned the political bias of Marxian economics. Most members were academic economists that were on either the course of theoretical economics or the history of economic theory. Due to this restriction, its membership was not large. Of the 40 approved members at the first meeting, 29 were founding members. This level of membership increased and reached the eighties at its height.

As the activity of the Japanese Economic Association was confined to economic theory, another association, the Japan Economic Policy Association, was organized in May 1940. The applicants for this association amounted to over three hundred at the foundation and the founding meeting had over one hundred and fifty attendants. Further, the Japanese Association of Fiscal Science was formed in October of the same year, and it was followed in June 1943 by the Society of Monetary Economics. The dissolved Association for the Study of Social Policy was a comprehensive society that covered most fields of economics as well as theory, empirical investigation, and policy. In contrast, the specialization of academic societies began in this period. This reflects on the other hand the quantitative growth of academic economists and their specialization.

In the case of the Economic Policy Association, the joint research project that was supported by the special committee for the study of small and medium-sized industry stimulated her foundation. She stated its aim as 'promoting jointly the research of economic policy under the current national emergency-interest among economists supported the association'. She was still cautious about excess politicization and conformism as she stated 'she aims to develop the economic policy of the nation both in theory and practice while firmly retaining a purely academic stance'.[7]

Such themes as the development of productive powers and its measures, theory and practice of controlled economy, theory and policy of the bloc economy, became main topics of economists in this period. Further, various efforts were made to create 'political economy', 'Kodo (Royal road) economics', and 'Japanese economics' that were to be established on the ground of the national community as the alternative to Western economics based on economic liberalism. However, it seems that a subtle conflict between active collaborators to the controlled economy and expansive Asian policy and moderate economists of more academic traits appeared in most universities. In the case of the University of Tokyo, the elimination of the so-called 'Kakushin-ha' (Renovation-group) and the 'liberal group' was decided upon to calm the quarrel within the faculty. Also in Kyoto University, a similar cleavage existed during the war years.

If we look into the leadership of these academic societies, it seems that an orthodoxy whose core was composed of seniors that had the academic prestige since the 1920s was on the way to formation. Torajiro Takagaki (Tokyo University of Commerce), Yasuma Takata (Kyoto University), and Shinzo Koizumi (Keio University) were the main figures of this budding orthodoxy. On the other hand, a backbone group that supported seniors existed already. Takuma Yasui, Ichiro Nakayama, Kazuo Okochi, Eiichi Sugimoto, Hideo Aoyama, Takeyasu Kimura, Yasaburo Sakamoto, Yuzo Yamada, and so on belong to this group. For example, Yasaburo Sakamoto (Kobe University of Commerce) was in charge of the administration of the Japanese Economic Association; Eiichi Sugimoto (Tokyo University of Commerce) edited the annual bulletin of the Association. The following statement that introduced the first number of the annual bulletin of the Japanese Economic Association (1941) declared the stance of the academic group in this period.

> The aim of our association lies in raising the position of economic theory in Japan to attain the most advanced standard in the world. For this purpose we must first integrate all of the latest academic products of the world and then analyze and criticize them. Only by this effort can the original academic style of Japanese in economic theory be established and we become able to rank with the first-class nations in this science. For this reason, we do not adopt Marxism that intends to establish economics as a class theory and to make it serve the revolutionary practice. On the other side, we are not driven by the imaginary appeal that a Japanese economic theory could appear at once on the basis of the original thinking pattern while neglecting our science's two hundred year tradition and its remarkable developments in recent years. (Nihon Keizai Gakkai, 1941: 1)

Despite such an academic direction, however, the 'Kakushin-ha' and 'political economists' were allowed to join openly. The representative senior economist, Takata, himself had the traits that led him to a peculiar nationalism in his ethnic theory.[8] The eighth (1941) and the ninth (1942) meeting of the Japanese Economic Association chose 'Problems of Controlled Economy' as its common theme. A change seems to have been necessary for this pre-1945 association to be continued by post-1945 economists.

In the later stage of the war, economics and commercial studies together with other learning of humanities were regarded as the learning of peacetime. They became the target of mobilization for the war and munitions production. Academic societies in economics continued their activity until 1943. But the reduction of humanities and social sciences for the expansion of natural sciences and technology became the official policy of the government in the fall of 1943. Under this policy, the conversion of universities and colleges in humanities and social sciences into those of sciences and technology was declared together with the mobilization of students as workers in munition factories for one-third of the year. Under the prevalent view that denied the value of commercial education, most commercial colleges were reorganized into the technical colleges of industrial management. In September 1944 the Tokyo University of Commerce was renamed the Tokyo Industrial University and its junior course the Course for Industrial Management.[9] Students and teachers worked together at the factories located some distance from the *alma mater*. Not only students but teachers also were mercilessly drafted. In the later phase of wartime, economic rationality that was beyond mere administration of forcefully mobilized resources was neglected at the level of educational policy.

2.2 Changes in academic institutions post-1945

2.2.1 Early responses of economists

We have to begin with the dissolution of wartime mobilization and the movement to question the collaboration of the war policies. When Japan surrendered on 15 August 1945, the campuses of Japanese universities were empty due to mobilization and evacuation. Following the cabinet decision of February 1945, all lectures at the universities were suspended. It was a month after the surrender that lectures began one by one and students and teachers gradually returned to the campus. In most universities, the recovery of the campus itself was the first serious problem because many campuses or buildings had been offered to the military or the government in the end of the war and after the surrender were requisitioned by the occupation army. After the settlement of this problem, the question of supporting the war intensified its power.

The first directive of the Supreme Commander of the Allied Powers (SCAP) on educational reform was issued on 22 October 1945. This directive declared that the removal of militaristic and ultra-nationalistic ideologies from education and the purge of teachers and officials that advocated such ideologies as well as the return of the distanced liberal or anti-military teachers and officials as its basic direction. The second directive of the education reform (30 October 1945) showed the concrete procedure of the examination of the teachers. After a six-month interval the Japanese government brought it into the Imperial Ordinance No. 263 on the 'Investigation, Removal, and the Permission of the Teachers and Related Officials'.

In most universities and their faculties, presidents and deans resigned. Chairs and institutions that had names of militaristic or expansionist flavor were renamed or reorganized under more neutral or pacifist names. Marxian economists and liberal economists that were expelled in wartime returned to the lecture room with applause and scholars that were blamed for their support of the war left the chairs. In as much as the prestige of the senior professors who were responsible for academic administration in wartime was eclipsed, so the voices of the middle class and youth, including the associate professors and lecturers increased its influence.

It was Iwasaburo Takano's article on the *Teikoku Daigaku Shimbun* (Campus Paper for the Imperial University) of 1 November 1945, 'Definite measures to clean the campus: clearance and reconstruction of the Imperial University of Tokyo' that guided the general opinion of academics to democratization. In this article Takano demanded the following:

1. Abolition of the name 'Imperial University' and renaming it 'the University of Tokyo';
2. Deletion of the nationalistic clauses in the University Decree and the cut of the powers of the minister of education;
3. Reshuffling of the faculty members (rehabilitation of the expelled professors and associate professors, and removal of militarists and war-collaborators through the examination of a special committee);
4. Promoting the democratic spirit of students and participation in labor movements, social services, elementary and adult education;
5. Introduction of lectures on the history of social thought as a general course for all students;
6. Systematization of lectures on economics and promotion of competitive lectures;
7. Opening of lectures to the public;
8. Admission of female students;
9. Development of the international activity of the university.[10]

On the same day, with the issuing date of that number of the *Teikoku Daigaku Shimbun*, Chogoro Maiide assumed the office of dean of the Faculty of Economics of the University of Tokyo. He declared that he would 'observe and perform the directives of Commander MacArthur loyally' and make contact with the Hyoue Ouchi/Hiromi Arisawa group immediately. Maiide rehabilitated Tadao Yanaihara, Hyoue Ouchi, Hiromi Arisawa, Yoshitaro Wakimura, Takao Tsuchiya, and Moritaro Yamada, and then asked Takeyasu Kimura, who had resigned with his liberal mentor Kawai, to return. Their chairs were offered following the resignation of the ex-dean Akio Hashizume and Haruo Naniwada before the start of the questioning of the militarists and further by voluntary retreat of Kotaro Araki, Toyokichi Yumoto, Tomonaga Nakagawa, and others. Takano's proposal had massive resonance in the reconstruction period of the academies with the support of journalists who demanded also the democratic reform of the universities.

Takano's proposal of the academic reform reflected his unique position in economics that combined Marxism and liberalism with a broad perspective for social problems. In contrast, Takuma Yasui offered another proposal to the academic economists on the same media in the number dated ten days after. His article, 'Fill the gap in the scientific level on the new trends in Economics', began with a harsh criticism of the economics in wartime. He also anticipated the recovery of Marxian economics but regarded catching up to the level of modern economics in the English-speaking world as the urgent task of Japanese economists.[11]

In Yasui's view, economic theory made remarkable progress in the 1930s and the early 1940s in the United States and Britain. However, a misconception of the essence of modern economics prevailed among Japanese economists even after the retreat of Marxists. 'It is all but a pity that economic theory could not proceed along its due course, but continued the distorted rotation and stagnation as its reaction instead'.

Yasui's proposal was not confined to the serious study of the 'mainstream of modern economics whose core is the equilibrium theory'. He also evaluated American institutionalists and their works with three aspects of research – sociological, statistical and inductive – that would suggest how to establish economic sociology. He also recommended the scientific level of discussions with Marxian economics be raised by studying the reappraisal of Marxian economic theory from the viewpoint of modern economics in such a way as done by Oskar Lange, Wasily Leontiev and Joan Robinson. However, to the economists on both sides, this advice seemed to be too roundabout, for modern economists became so busy in absorbing the latest theories in mainstream economics while Marxian economics were engaged in the democratic revolution with the vocabulary of Marx-Leninism.

2.2.2 *Purge of economists*

How large was the impact of post-war adjustment to the world of economists? As we saw in the case of the University of Tokyo, resignation or early retirement to evade the accusation of wartime collaboration began in 1945. It took six months for the directive of the SCAP to be brought into legislation by the Japanese government and the procedure of examination to be put into practice. In the meantime universities rather preferred mild measures such as voluntary resignation or transfer to other institutions that would not totally ruin the honor and the living of the retired. The total number of teachers (not confined to the higher educational institutions), ca. 560,000 persons, that were in teaching positions as of 7 May 1946 when the Ordinance No. 263 was issued were investigated and ca. 5,000 persons were eliminated. However, over 110,000 persons retired voluntarily before the start of the investigation.[12]

In each university or in each faculty, a 'screening committee' was organized, following the directive of the Ministry of Education that had been issued simultaneously with the Imperial Ordinance No. 263. Members that were elected by the mutual votes of professors and associate professors investigated the public activities of colleagues during wartime. The 'Central Screening Committee' was constituted as the second instance for the dissatisfied. But the Civil Information and Education Section of the SCAP strictly monitored its activity.

Table 2.3 Unacceptable screenees of university staff

Ryukoku Univ. 10	Tohoku Univ. 3	Rikkyo Univ. 1
Kyoto Univ. 9	Toyo Univ. 3	Hosei Univ. 1
Waseda Univ. 6	Hiroshima Univ. 3	Tokyo Jikei Univ. 1
Ritsumeikan Univ. 6	Kobe Univ. 2	Naniwa Univ. 1
Univ. of Tokyo 5	Kyushu Univ. 2	Tokyo Agricult. Univ. 1
Nihon Univ. 5	Niigata Univ. 2	Tokyo Pedagogic Univ. 1
Otani Univ. 5	Koyasan Univ. 2	Kansai Univ. 1
Tokyo Inst. of Technology 4	Komazawa Univ. 1	Osaka Economic Univ. 1
Hitotsuibashi Univ. 3	Meiji Univ. 1	Kwansei Gakuin Univ. 1
Keio Univ. 3	Hokkaido Univ. 1	Kurume Univ. 1

Source: Isao Nagahama (1984)

Note
Acceptable 24,886. Unacceptable 86. Total 24,582 screenees.

The total number of those purged by examination within universities was 86, as shown in Table 2.3. Though the number does not seem to be large, there were several universities that had over five purged from their staff. In addition, 326 persons were automatically dismissed because of their careers in the military or military police according to the 'Special Table 2.' As well as the graduates of the overseas universities based on the idea of the East Asian Community, the Kenkoku University in Manchuria and the Toa Dobun Shoin in Shanghai, those of the department of colonization were also regarded automatically as unqualified. This is also a related branch of economics.

In the University of Tokyo, Kyoto University, and Osaka University of Commerce, a large-scale replacement occurred due to the questioning and examination as stated above. In the Economics Faculty of the University of Tokyo, Susumu Takamiya was judged as unqualified by the screening committee within the faculty on 16 October 1946. Though Takao Tsuchiya and Tokusaburo Kitayama were judged as qualified at this level, Kitayama resigned in January 1947 and Tsuchiya was judged as unqualified by the Central Screening Committee in April 1947. Tsuchiya was dismissed in September 1947 and returned to the chair after five years. Further, two professors and an associate professor retired voluntarily from the end of 1946 to the next year. So, altogether the Economics Faculty lost 10 staff out of 20 full and associate professors as of 15 August 1945.[13]

In case of the Osaka University of Commerce (after 1949 Osaka City University), the repression of the resistance of 1943 by which over twenty students and staff had been arrested, became the background of the growing movement of questioning of the collaborators. On 26 February 1946 all professors submitted their resignation to give the new president, Kyo Tsuneto, the opportunity to reappoint those who should remain. As a result, 'the faculty that had been so proud of its staff of more than 30 was more than halved'.[14]

Professors of the Economics Faculty in Kyoto preceded by a week their colleagues in Osaka in the unanimous submission of their resignation. Hajime

Kawakami's death on 30 January 1946 revived the criticism of the attitude of the Faculty that could be regressed up to the approval of the government's intervention in Kawakami's forced resignation (1928). Held on 19 February 1946 was an 'unusual meeting where all staff from full professors to lecturers gathered and were guaranteed to be able to speak equally'. At this meeting the following three statements were confirmed:

1. We regret the long-continued direction of the Faculty up to the end of the war and criticize ourselves that our efforts to maintain the freedom of learning was not sufficient.
2. We approve the resignation of the dean Ninagawa and elect a new dean. All the staff submit their resignations to the new dean with the spirit of unanimous penitence.
3. The new dean deals with the delivery of the resignations with a cautious consideration of the reconstruction of the faculty.

The newly elected dean, Hitoshi Shizuta, conveyed resignations of six professors, Shotaro Kojima, Saburo Shiomi, Kichihiko Taniguchi, Torazo Ninagawa, Kei Shibata, and Yonosuke Nakagawa, and approved their retirement. On this occasion, one associate professor, one lecturer and two assistants left the faculty in spite of the persuasion of the dean.[15]

SCAP also kept a keen interest in the development of the Economics Faculty of Kyoto. The Chief of the Civil Information and Education Section, D. R. Nugent, ordered confidentially the investigation of nine professors of Kyoto University on 4 March 1996. This list included six economics professors, Koji Ishikawa, Koji Matsuoka, Yonosuke Nakagawa, Torazo Ninagawa, Kei Shibata, and Kichihiko Taniguchi, and three philosophers of the so-called 'Kyoto School', Iwao Koyama, Masaaki Kosaka, and Shigetaka Suzuki, who were regarded to have legitimized the war by the 'philosophy of world history'. By the memorandum of the SCAP to the government, dated 2 May, Ishikawa was dismissed; by that of 15 May, Shibata and Taniguchi followed Ishikawa as 'active exponents of militarism and ultra-nationalism'. Later, Nakagawa was purged by a similar charge, Matsuoka was dismissed due to his concurrent service as a military officer. Further, Kiyoyuki Tokunaga was dismissed due to his voluntary service in the Military Police.

Twenty staff that remained or were newly invited underwent the examination procedure. Out of them Ichiro Otsuka and Yasuma Takata (then honorary professor) were judged unqualified. Takata demanded the re-examination of the Central Screening Committee, but the Central Committee, too, judged him unqualified on 18 June 1947. Takata repeated his claim to special examination by Ministers of Education successfully and at last on 19 June 1951 he obtained a certificate of qualification from the then Minister Teiyu Amano.

The surviving full professors were only three, Hitoshi Shizuta, Yasuzo Horie, and Fumio Hozumi. The Economics Faculty promoted three associate professors, Hideo Aoyama, Minoru Nakatani, and Senpei Sawa, to full professor in July 1946 and invited Seijiro Kishimoto and Minoru Toyosaki to form the team of the professors.

In the Tokyo University of Commerce (Hitotsubashi University after 1949), Keio University, and Waseda University, the loss of staff was quite small. However, the first three professors, Takanosuke Kaneko, Ryuzo Maitani, and Toshita Tokiwa, were judged unqualified by the examination in the university and one professor of the preparatory course, Joji Ezawa, was judged unqualified by the examination committee of the Ministry of Education. In Keio, Tadao Takemura was judged unqualified.[16] In Waseda, three professors of the Faculty of Politics and Economics, Susumu Mizugaki, Masamichi Royama, and Shigetaka Uchida, were judged unqualified. Further, the ex-president in the war years, Tomio Nakano, was judged unqualified by the examination outside.[17] In Kansai University, in addition to one professor who was judged within the university, the newly elected president, Keiji Masai, was purged by special examination of the Ministry of Education.[18] The investigations of the author do not cover all universities but according to information given by published university histories, two staff of the Faculty of Law and Letters of Kyushu University, and one of the Faculty of Law and Letters of Tohoku University were declared unqualified.

2.2.3 *Democratization of academic organizations*

Of the official academic institutions that worked beyond the individual universities and disciplines, three existed in pre-1945 years. The first was the Imperial Academy that had the tradition since the Meiji Era. The second was the Council for Science Research that was constituted in 1920 for the purpose of international exchange in sciences. The third was the Japan Society for the Promotion of Science that was established in 1932 with the aim of channeling donated funds from the private sector to promising researches in sciences. In wartime, under the title of the 'New Regime in Science and Technology', a special committee named 'Mobilization Committee of Science and Technology' was constituted in the Council for Science Research. This committee selected 'urgent tasks' and discussed the selection and mobilization of researchers, research funds, research equipment and materials and the use of research results related to those tasks.

After the defeat a severe conflict arose between the former leaders of the academic circle and the science policy and the growing wave to question the wartime collaboration of scientists. However, both establishment and the anti-establishment shared a naive admiration of science. While established scientists regarded the gap in science and technology as the reason of defeat, young scientists thought the lack of scientific rationality led Japan into the desperate war. Scientists of the anti-establishment persuasion gathered in the Democratic Scientists' Association (*Minka*) that was constituted at the beginning of 1946. Though this Society dissolved due to political manipulation of the Communist Party, in its early stage the initiative of scientists with progressive beliefs was manifest. On the other hand, the group that was in charge of the area of science and technology within SCAP thought that democratization would not be realized by giving a free hand to the Japanese government and established scientists. They tried to establish various routes to intervene in the inner structure of the scientists' community and would use the movement of progressive scientists also for their purpose.

The complicated interaction among the three, the group of established conservative scientists, the group of progressive anti-establishment scientists, and American advisers around Dr Kelly, was seen in the discussion of the Renovation Committee of the Academic System that was constituted in August 1947. Three groups came in accord to create a new organ 'Science Council of Japan' as a 'parliament of scientists' based on the direct election of scientists. In July 1948 the Law of the Science Council passed the Diet. After the registration of the scientists in October and the first election in December, the Science Council started its activity in January 1948. However, its history since then has been that the idealistic consensus of the scientists at the starting point was paralyzed step by step by the real politics and the interest conflicts between scientists. While the Council was to have an important role in the distribution of research funds according to its original concept, the Ministry of Education resisted it and endeavored constantly to make the Council a mere honorary organization. Among scientists, researchers in the engineering sciences were generally favorable to cooperation with the government. They often did not support criticism of the government's policy raised by the Council. Conservative governments neglected most of the advice of the Council and established the Agency of Science and Technology in 1956 to implement a government-led science and technology policy. Further, the significance of the Council was reduced by the Council for Science and Technology and the Council for Learning. After 1965 the Science Council received no consultation from the government and the budget has been fixed since then.

The Science Council is composed of 210 members that belong to seven departments with 30 members each. The third department (Economics and Management Sciences) was to be composed of 23 members elected from national districts (5 from Economics, 5 from Commercial and Management Studies, 13 with no special research fields) and 7 members from regional districts. The tenure of members is three years. Since the first election of 1948, eleven elections have been held up to the abolition of direct election by the revision of the Law of Japan Science Council in 1983. After this revision members have been recommended by registered academic societies. Table 2.4 shows the overview of the elections of the members of the third department. As can be seen in every department of the Council, candidacy as well as all voting rates have declined since the 1960s.

In the reorganization of the academic system of the post-1945 years, economists (including researchers in commercial and management studies) do not seem to have contributed much. The main reasons would be the relatively small share of economists in the total number of scientists and their remoteness from the world of researchers in natural sciences and engineering. The interest of economists was directed more to the real problems of democratization of the economy and inflation or to the more local problems of personnel policy in the replacement of professorial chairs at each university. In the so-called 'Reverse Course' years, the third department that had many Marxist members was a source of trouble not

Table 2.4 Elections of Members of Science Council, Third Division

	Electorate	National candidates	Regional candidates	Votes	Rate of voting (%)
1948	1,024	108	41	926	76.9
1950	1,139	63	17	1,002	88.0
1953	1,573	49	12	1,426	90.8
1956	1,737	33	11	1,538	88.5
1959	2,151	31	8	1,797	83.5
1962	2,391	32	9	1,981	82.9
1965	2,678	29	9	2,174	81.2
1968	3,061	22	8	2,016	65.9
1971	3,324	24	10	2,261	68.0
1974	3,499	24	6	2,266	64.6
1977	3,736	27	7	2,594	69.4
1980	4,150	25	7	2,900	69.9

Source: Nihon Gakujutsu Kaigi (1977) (1985)

because of its opinions in science policy but through direct conflict with the government. The government rejected the appointment of its member, Katsujiro Yamada, to the Science and Technology Administration Council (1949), despite the recommendation of the Science Council. The membership of Fumio Moriya was refused because of allegations of his participation in editing the banned organ of the Japan Communist Party in 1950. The third department joined actively in academic exchange with Soviet Union and China in years when Japan had no diplomatic relations with them. In the period of the revision of the Security Treaty of Japan and United States, the third department was one of the cores that opposed the participation of the president of the Council, Seiichi Kaya, in the Japan–USA Committee for Cooperation. Looking into the list of members, Marxian economists did not always form the majority of the department. In my estimation, a third would be more correct. However, Marxian economists assumed a chief position several times. This might have contributed to the creation of an exaggerated impression on outsiders or foreigners of the dominance of Marxian economics in Japan.[19]

The third department organized the Union of National Economic Associations in Japan in 1950. The historical development of this federation and its member societies are described in Chapter 1, I confine myself here to only two points related to modern economics and Marxian economics.

The first is that a democratic organizational reform was introduced in the reorganization process of the Japanese Economic Association. In this reorganization, all of the officials of the pre-1945 Association were dismissed and mitigation of the membership criterion (at least two years experience in the theoretical research of economics) was introduced. None of the pre-1945 officials were elected as the officials of the new Association. Since the pre-1945 Association was known by its closure and strong authority of its officials, democratization and a change of generation were intended in the renewed start.

The second was the failure of Marxian economists to form the open academic society, though the Economic Department of the Society of Democratic Scientists joined the Federation of Economics Societies together with its Agriculture Department. However, as loyalty to the policy of the Japan Communist Party prevailed in this Association, it turned out to be no longer an academic society in the eyes of non-communist members or more academic members. In reality, it was said that the most powerful organization of Marxian economists then was the Research Department of the Communist Party that had ca. 300 staff in its prospering period.[20] This is surely not a small number when one considers that registered scientists (economists) at the election of the third department of the Japan Science Council amounted to just over 1000. However, mainly due to the split of the Communist Party in 1950, many economists left its research department and also the Association of Democratic Scientists.

2.3 Quantitative growth of the academic economics

2.3.1 *Economics and the new university system*

At present, most of the economists in Japan are academics who teach economics courses at universities and colleges. However, several alternatives for exerting their influence in the real world seem to have existed in the short period just after 1945. The governments invited many economists to various committees that were newly created for the sake of recovery and reform of the economy. In particular, the Economic Stabilization Board became a center for the devoted economists headed by Shigeto Tsuru. On the other hand, many young economists volunteered to work as researchers or instructors in political or social movements. Even if not involved directly in politics, the flourishing of journalism in this period might have provided an opportunity to young journalists to absorb economic knowledge through their daily work. However, once ministerial bureaucracy succeeded in reconstructing its career system, the possibility for outsiders to assume significant positions was ruled out. Also in politics and social movements, the rigid ideological control over intellectuals under the intensifying political confrontation estranged most of the once devoted economists. Further, due to the so-called 'red purge' the environment in politics as well as journalism was changed drastically. It was thus the only remaining way for economists to live as academics in the universities and colleges that were enlarged by the educational reform.

If we take the fiscal year 1935, universities where economics was taught systematically numbered 21: four imperial universities had economics faculties (Tokyo and Kyoto) or faculties of law and letters (Tohoku and Kyushu); three commercial universities in Tokyo, Osaka, and Kobe; 14 private universities were equipped with economics faculties or departments (Keio, Waseda, Meiji, Hosei, Chuo, Nihon, Doshisha, Senshu, Rikkyo, Ritsumeikan, Takushoku, Kwansei-Gakuin, Kansai, and Sophia). The number of the total registered students for the economics courses of the above universities amounted to 14,720. Further, elementary or practical economics was taught also at 11 public commercial colleges, two public professional commercial schools, and 11 private professional commercial schools. In today's school system, these correspond to technical colleges and junior colleges. If we add students of the preparatory course of the above universities to the students of these commercial schools, we obtain 14,102 students who studied elementary or practical economics in this year.[21] Since the expansion of economics education was halted in wartime, the extent of economics education in 1945 was nearly the same.

Now we compare the figure above with present statistics. In the fiscal year 1997, Japanese universities had 303 faculties that had a name related to economics. The total admission complement of students amounts to 126,756. This is about ten times the number of economics students in 1935. In addition to the teaching staff of these faculties, there is also the need for economics lecturers that teach basic economics courses as a part of general education. Also teacher colleges and junior colleges in economics or commercial studies need teaching staff in economics. So, we can safely conclude that the market for academic economists has expanded around forty times from the pre-1945 years. On the supply side, we can now count 60 graduate courses that end with master degrees and 115 graduate courses that lead to a doctorate in economics and economics related studies.[22]

The institutional basis for this expansion was the new university system that was introduced with the comprehensive education reform in 1947. The United States Education Mission that visited Japan in 1946 advocated that promotion of 'free thought, brave quest, and action for the people' was necessary in the reform of higher education. It recommended the Japanese government to found universities in the regions, guarantee equality of the sexes, provide financial support to students, and extend general study. Four-year universities were to occupy the top of the new school system that was composed of six-year elementary schools, three-year middle schools, and three-year high schools. The plural school system that separated education of elite and supporting experts was discarded and most professional schools were elevated to universities, though a part of them remained two-year junior colleges. By integration and reorganization of various colleges and schools, every prefecture could have at least one national university. Further, the criteria for the founding of universities became easier than before.[23]

In 1945 the number of universities in Japan was 48. In the fiscal year 1949 when the new university system was introduced, Japan had 70 national, 17 public and 81 private universities (in total 168). In three years following this year, 46 (mostly public and private) universities followed. However, the largest rush to establish universities came when the first baby boomers were grown up to the age of higher education. Three national, five public, and 103 private universities were founded from 1964 to 1968 fiscal years. Further, there was the second wave that corresponded to the children of the first baby boomers in the mid-1990s. The rush of new universities was not so great due to anticipation of the fall of the need after this second peak. Still, since this was the last chance for the new foundation of universities or promotion to the university rank, 63 universities were founded from FY1993 to FY1997.

2.3.2 *Research fund*

How is the research fund distributed in the universities after 1949? Since the situation of private universities differs largely in each case, I use here the data of a national university that I am working for. Table 2.5 shows the budgetary situation of the Economics Faculty of the Kyoto University from FY1983 to FY1993.

The basis of the budget was compiled by the accounting unit of school cost per staff under the so-called Koza-sei (chair hierarchy). In the 1992 fiscal year, for the experiment chair 3,774,000 Yen was budgeted for a full professor, 2,255,000 Yen for an associate professor, 1,363,000 Yen for a full-time lecturer, and 613,000 Yen for an assistant. For the non-experiment chair, 983,000 Yen was budgeted for a full professor, 548,000 Yen for an associate professor, 329,000 Yen for a full-time lecturer, and 283,000 Yen for an assistant. The difference between the two was very large. In that year, three out of seven chair-groups were approved as experiment chairs. In addition, 109,250 Yen for a full professor, 92,340 Yen for an associate professor or a full-time lecturer, 61,370 Yen for an assistant were distributed as travel costs. In this year the faculty has 23 full professors, 15 associate professors, 3 lecturers and 1 assistant, in total 42 teaching staff. Furthermore, the faculty received additional monies during the fiscal year so the total budget amounted to 145,987,000 Yen.

From this budget, an overhead administrative cost was extracted and other necessary expenditure followed. As a result, the budget that reaches the hands of staff as their disposable research fund turns out to be very small. In traditional universities like the Kyoto University, each faculty or department has its own library and books are mainly purchased by the common fund for that library. Accordingly, the allowance for individual use of the staff was only 150,000 Yen at that year. In comparison, the budgets of most regional national universities were compiled by the course system (Gakkamoku-sei) under which the standard of compiling unit is lower than that of the chair system. But the budgetary situation of the local national universities has been improved at least partially by their efforts at reorganization into the chair-group system or transfer of non-experiment chair to experiment chair. In some cases, as regional universities have no departmental library and small graduate courses, the remaining disposable amount for individual research is larger than that of the staff in traditional universities. Even in cases of ex-imperial universities under the privileged chair system, regular budget was totally deficient when staff performed concentrated research.

Another way of acquiring public resources for research is based on the individual application. The Grants-in-Aid for Scientific Research of the Ministry of Education is distributed through the examination of the research fund department of the Gakujutsu-Shingikai. Table 2.6 shows the distribution of this grant to the area of economics in the 1996 fiscal year. In case of the Economics Faculty of Kyoto, the adopted researches of the staff were only from 1 to 4 years in 1975–85, but increased after 1987 to the level of 5 to 8. As an additional distribution system, Kyoto University has a special budget for educational

Table 2.5 Composition of research and administrative budget (Faculty of Economics, Kyoto University, 1983–92)

Fiscal year	Total budget	Dept. library	Research archive	Publication	Copy expenditure	Student expenditure	Working environment	Information system	Common administration	Special purpose
1983	68,178,000	(5,776,411) 24,142,504	(31,488) 4,554,239	885,800	1,889,946	1,973,490	1,509,870	(51,714) 159,768	(10,047,986) 18,080,850	(1,734,155) 14,981,533
1984	82,020,000	(6,067,301) 28,983,963	5,166,541	1,685,200	2,137,909	2,074,040	2,301,840	(59,990) 3,128,603	(10,517,369) 17,185,908	(1,932,250) 19,355,996
1985	92,329,000	(8,636,451) 28,520,527	5,244,446	2,826,400	2,193,311	2,125,507	1,795,450	(109,596) 3,134,272	(11,008,888) 16,979,589	(2,166,178) 29,631,599
1986	105,576,000	(7,003,644) 28,220,762	(887,783) 5,131,710	1,893,800	2,418,968	2,057,987	2,989,000	(100,944) 3,134,272	(11,468,420) 20,701,225	(5,204,067) 39,028,276
1987	115,743,000	(7,096,433) 33,537,183	(826,705) 5,925,099	1,986,400	2,572,546	2,775,067	5,122,490 (1,446,774)	4,103,690	(11,986,359) 19,284,036	(3,395,958) 40,436,489
1988	108,722,000	(7,348,796) 33,290,527	(1,519,272) 5,938,902	2,037,080	2,584,681	3,129,757	8,129,122	3,874,071	(12,572,203) 23,192,807	(3,740,772) 26,545,053
1989	143,385,000	(7,231,774) 34,461,942	(1,846,674) 6,093,692	1,626,370	3,385,560	3,307,042	7,193,864	4,361,816	(15,650,025) 26,370,073	(3,837,663) 56,584,641
1990	124,732,000	(8,317,169) 38,419,263	6,753,006	787,641	3,830,659	3,017,338	5,683,786	7,839,319	(16,809,115) 26,302,674	(3,409,957) 32,098,314
1991	122,115,000	(9,183,993) 43,218,559	(1,847,094) 7,352,821	1,712,327	3,963,930	2,448,485	5,484,420	3,404,446	(17,145,895) 27,560,357	(2,559,117) 26,969,655
1992	145,987,000	(9,651,627) 43,767,174	(1,933,222) 7,547,272	2,870,198	4,251,368	2,539,567	3,202,099	6,810,061	(17,517,723) 28,650,140	(4,547,835) 46,349,121

(Japanese Yen)

Source: Faculty of Economics, Kyoto University (1994)

Note
( ) signifies wages paid from the amount below.

Table 2.6 Economics in the distribution of Grant-in-Aid for Scientific Research

Division	Application in Dept. of Economics	Adopted projects in economics	Distributed amount (1,000 Yen)	Involved researchers (persons)	Adopted projects in total	Distributed amount in total (1,000 Yen)
Scientific research (A)	76	26 (continued 18)	89,700	258	3,177	17,829,000
Scientific research (B)	130	61 (continued 34)	39,900	157	4,857	12,953,400
Scientific research (C)	595	275 (continued 40)	206,800	369	11,961	13,481,800
Exploratory research	43	15	14,500	20	977	1,423,100
Encouragement of young scientists	260	92	88,500	92	5,490	5,403,400

Source: Monbusho (1996)

research and a special research budget to which teams of staff apply for their joint research projects. Further, after 1992 the Economics Faculty received a special budget for improving research and education (15,000,000 Yen) along with the extension policy of graduate courses.

Private funding is publicly introduced as the research donation or trusted research fund. In the case of the Economics Faculty of Kyoto the former is preferred to the latter. Donations vary from small (under 500,000 Yen) to large ones (ca. 10,000,000 Yen). Further, research funds obtained from private foundations can be trusted to the accountant of the faculty, though the accounting is done sometimes by applicants themselves.

Many universities or faculties, organized supporting funds or societies to facilitate the research of staff. Semi-official research institutes sometimes serve a similar purpose. It is usual that house journals or research monographs are published by affiliated societies or institutes that can receive the membership fee or donations easily.

2.3.3 *Composition of academic economists and graduate schools*

Comprehensive research of the recruitment of Japanese academic economists was performed once by Shozaburo Fujino and Koichi Hatanaka. Based on the individual data collected from the personnel catalogues of universities from 1958 to 1983, they provide us with rich quantitative data and interesting findings. The fifth and sixth chapters of Fujino's *University Education and Market Mechanism* (in Japanese, 1986) are the summaries of their research. Next, Toshihiro Iwata analyzed the properties of teaching staff in economics at Japanese Universities in his *Introduction to the Study of Economics Education* (in Japanese, 1992) based on the data up to 1989. In our investigation, we have to admit that far from surpassing the predecessors, we confined ourselves in a very easy analysis based on the existing online data base, 'Researchers Directory'[24] of the National Center for Science Information Systems (NACSIS) and its book-styled abridged version, *Catalogue of Researchers and Research Topics*.

Fujino and Hatanaka discovered that after 1970 there were two peaks of academic economists, one composed of economists born in 1931–2 and another of those born in 1942–7. The present shape of these two peaks is shown by Figure 2.1. Although we can recognize the first peak, its height is considerably lower due to death and retirement. Now it is like a small hill covering those born from 1929 to 1935. In contrast, the second has grown to a massif of a decade's generation that has a first peak in those born in 1943 and a main peak in those born in 1947. Behind this massif a plateau covering those born from 1952 to 1962 follows. This plateau has nearly the same height as that of the decaying first peak. In the near future, the recruitment need for economists to replace those leaving in their late sixties is anticipated to form a new peak or at least extend this plateau for several years.

Fujino explained the reason for the emergence of the first peak and the decline after it as follows.[25] First, the expansion of job opportunities for academic economists caused by the introduction of the new university system stimulated

Source: Online database 'Researchers' of NACSIS, August 1998.

Figure 2.1 Birth year of researchers in economics and management studies.

private universities and late-starting national or public universities to extend or begin to supply young economists to the job market. The result was an excess supply situation of academic economists after 1958. The favorable conditions for economics graduates in getting jobs in private firms in the prosperous years (1958–63) diminished the attraction of further study in graduate courses. The combined effects of this relatively diminished attraction on students' side and the restricted admission policy of universities to cope with the excess supply job market is shown by the valley that started with those born in 1933. The graph bottoms for economists born in 1938 and then enters a steep rise. This is because the job market turned out to have excess demand due to the rushed openings of universities/faculties/departments that aimed to supply economics graduates to the rapidly growing economy.

Thus, the difference in expected remuneration between academic and non-academic job markets, as well as universities' policy on their graduate courses are the two key factors in Fujino's explanation. However, the former seems not to be the case with the generation of the second peak that graduated in the still prosperous years before the first oil crisis. The significance of the supply factor in

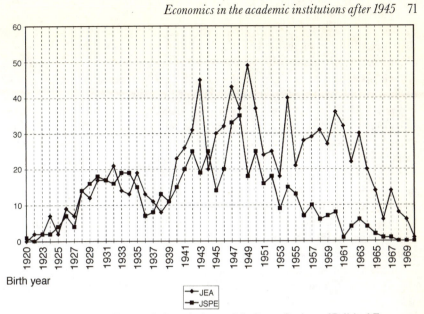

Figure 2.2 The Japanese Economic Association and the Japan Society of Political Economy: birth year of members.

the academic job market may be explained by the relatively long period of job searching by young economists. In Japan it begins usually in the higher part of the doctor course and continues several years including a few years after five years normal enrollment on the graduate course. However, in Iwata's view, the job

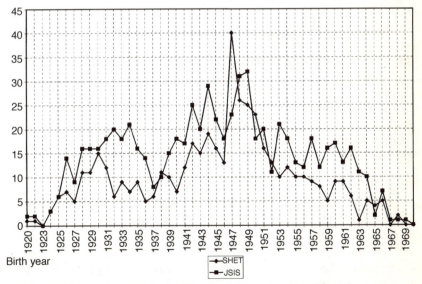

Figure 2.3 The Society for the History of Economic Thought and the Japan Society of International Economics: birth year of members

market for academic economists is basically a customer's market and sensitivity to the supply-demand gap is weak.[26]

Our interesting finding is the difference in the ageing patterns of academic economists in their research fields as well as in their directions. This is revealed by making the graph of birth-year composition of members of academic associations. Figure 2.2 shows the contrast between the Japanese Economic Association and the Japan Society of Political Economy that compete with each other in the field of theoretical economics. As explained before, the former is the gathering of so-called 'modernists' and the latter, that of Marxian economists. The members of both societies on the online database were nearly a half of their total registered members in both cases. The rivalry that is manifest in the first peak is not sustained in the second peak and after the generation born in 1955, members of the JSPE turned out to be a genuine minority. While the members of JEA in this generation make successive peaks, those of JSPE were less than their seniors leaving in the first peak. The often remarked loss of the vigor of Marxian economists is a reflection on this diminished number of its younger generation that are capable of absorbing new approaches and challenging the task of the creation of new theory. A similar difference is shown in Figure 2.3 between the Japan Society of International Economics and the Society for the History of Economic Thought. While membership of the former draws a plateau after the second peak, that of the latter shows a clear decline after the salient height of those born in 1947.

The preference of graduate students seems to be not enough to explain the difference shown above. It is assumed that the demand factor of the universities intended a selective expansion. While international economics is one of the favorite branches in economics when higher education in economics was expanded in the 1980s and 1990s, history of economics has been downgraded in these years. Since being in the curriculum of Japanese universities, the history of economics is placed generally in the course group of economic theory, the recruitment of its lecturer is sometimes neglected because of the need for new theoretical courses. In the case of modern economics and Marxian economics, the competitive or substitutive factor in course groups of theoretical economics is stronger than in the case of the history of economics. The author of this chapter belongs to the generation of the second peak and recollects that the graduate students in the fields of Marxian economics and history of economics were never minorities. However, many friends shifted their interest into a more specialized field or were obliged to leave research life due to difficulties in getting jobs.

Table 2.7 shows the fluctuations in the applicants and those admitted to the graduate course of economics of Kyoto University together with those who continued study in the advanced graduate course. Although the official capacity of students was 35 in each year grade, application was lower than the capacity in the years from 1957 to 1963. In these years, the number of those admitted did not often reach double figures. This period of unpopularity of graduate studies in economics corresponds correctly to the valley in the age structure of academic economists. It is after 1963 that the number entered in this graduate course

Table 2.7 Applicants and admissions to a graduate course in economics (Kyoto University, 1953–93)

Year	Applicants	Admitted	Enrolled in the third grade
1953	38	17	
1954	42	10	
1955	53	12	11
1956	44	7	7
1957	33	10	8
1958	29	6	6
1959	22	4	9
1960	12	5	7
1961	17	10	2
1962	14	3	6
1963	26	13	12
1964	37	10	2
1965	38	11	12
1966	54	11	8
1967	64	10	9
1968	74	10	11
1969	71	18	10
1970	96	13	8
1971	109	13	17
1972	173	16	14
1973	146	17	12
1974	130	17	17
1975	127	8	18
1976	114	10	18
1977	128	15	11
1978	106	13	13
1979	101	15	17
1980	95	16	15
1981	96	14	17
1982	79	14	19
1983	67	16	19
1984	68	12	15
1985	65	16	18
1986	72	19	14
1987	105	35	16
1988	70	22	18
1989	85	20	35
1990	95	22	13
1991	111	18	16
1992	104	26	27
1993	120	29	21

Source: Faculty of Economics, Kyoto University (1994)

Table 2.8 Visited graduate courses of academic economists in Japan

Graduate Course University	Research area								Total	Under-graduate study	Don't move	Moving out	Moving in
	Economic theory	Statistics	Economic policy	Economics history	Public finance/Monetary economics	Commercial studies	Management	Accounting					
Univ. of Tokyo (n)	159	41	277	207	82	15	99	20	574	736	369	367	205
Waseda Univ. (pr)	93	25	125	48	48	94	188	119	500	522	317	205	183
Kyoto Univ. (n)	152	33	246	116	64	30	98	16	486	486	294	197	192
Kobe Univ. (n)	139	30	147	38	61	58	165	86	463	245	176	69	187
Hitotsubashi Univ. (n)	118	32	119	73	63	22	95	49	380	251	148	103	232
Keio Gijuku Univ. (pr)	84	28	131	51	46	53	128	52	366	399	243	156	123
Meiji Univ. (pr)	42	11	70	32	33	48	138	77	284	207	159	48	125
Kyushu Univ. (n)	85	30	97	45	56	16	47	17	263	194	143	51	120
Osaka City Univ. (pu)	67	13	127	37	48	19	47	19	236	141	93	48	143
Tohoku Univ. (n)	56	7	85	52	28	8	24	12	185	157	104	53	81
Chuo Univ. (pr)	42	10	43	21	26	22	48	50	170	209	105	104	65
Osaka Univ. (n)	48	24	54	31	40	5	35	14	170	126	62	64	108
Hokkaido Univ. (n)	46	30	76	33	22	13	31	2	167	140	90	50	77
Nagoya Univ. (n)	66	9	58	27	26	7	38	17	163	123	85	38	78
Nihon Univ. (pr)	32	3	51	14	26	26	48	18	148	144	105	39	43
Doshisha Univ. (pr)	33	3	53	28	30	22	37	15	146	187	108	79	38

University													
Kwansei Gakuin Univ. (pr)	26	6	35	14	26	19	28	24	119	154	99	55	20
Tsukuba Univ. (n)	39	15	35	16	9	6	37	8	115	37	29	8	86
Kobe Commercial Univ. (pu)	27	5	22	8	14	21	29	21	95	63	26	37	69
Rikkyo Univ. (pr)	24	2	33	24	19	6	28	11	91	60	30	30	61
Kansai Univ. (pr)	18	7	21	9	16	14	21	13	80	84	47	37	33
Ritsumeikan Univ. (pr)	17	3	34	6	15	7	30	8	79	93	38	55	41
Aoyama Gakuin Univ. (pr)	22	12	20	5	9	5	31	13	74	70	33	37	41
Hosei Univ. (pr)	18	4	33	11	15	3	14	6	69	87	32	55	47
Hiroshima Univ. (n)	13	5	24	18	9	2	14	1	61	73	37	36	24
Fukuoka Univ. (pr)	21	7	20	7	4	13	11	7	60	50	34	16	26
Tokyo Institute of Technology (n)	16	6	10	3	5	4	25	1	58	51	34	17	24
Tokyo Metropolitan Univ. (pu)	22	2	25	18	9	0	5	1	49	44	14	30	35
Senshu Univ. (pr)	8	2	12	5	4	8	17	19	48	47	24	23	24
9 American Univ.*	67	30	71	7	41	3	28	2	146				
Researchers total	2,091	635	3,093	1,311	1,236	885	2,505	991	8,443				

* Stanford (22), Harvard (19), Rochester (18), Hawaii (17), Yale, Minnesota (15), Pennsylvania (14), Columbia, MIT (13)
(n): national university; (pu): public university; (pr): private university

Source: Online database 'Researchers' of NACSIS, July 1998.

constantly reached double figures. The outstanding number of applicants in 1972 and 1973 may be explained by the peculiar situation that many students who had experienced student revolt looked for shelter in the graduate course. Against this rush of applicants, the university seemed to respond rather coolly, i.e. the university did not increase admission considerably. The restraint of traditional universities such as Kyoto University contributed much to the dispersion of applicants to the late-starting graduate courses of other universities.

The policy of restraining admissions to under a half of the official capacity seems to have been continued up to the late 1980s. On the other hand, Kyoto did not reduce admissions in the period of a relative unpopularity of graduate studies (1982–8). After several years relaxation of the restraint, the reappraisal of graduate studies that included the creation of master courses for working students increased both applicants and the admitted. Since 1992 a full admission up to capacity was proposed with the idea of reorganizing the faculty to the graduate school.

Table 2.8 is the result of the search of the universities that academic economists in Japan visited in their undergraduate and graduate studies. The search was made in July 1998 using the same online directory 'RES' of the NACSIS. In the areas of economics, the University of Tokyo and Kyoto University occupy the first and the second place in Economic Theory, Statistics, Economic Policy, Economic History, and Public Finance and Financial Economics'. Of these research areas, two ex-imperial universities keep an outstanding share in Economic Policy and Economic History. The difference between the second and the third universities is not large in Economic Theory, Statistics, and Public Finance and Financial Economics. In Management Study, Commercial Study and Accounting, private

Table 2.9 Overseas graduate courses in the background of academic economists in Japan

	American universities			Other overseas universities			Overseas researchers	
	Japanese	*Foreigner*	*Sum*	*Japanese*	*Foreigner*	*Sum*	*Total overseas graduates*	*Total researchers*
Economic theory	108	6	114	30	2	32	146	1,316
Statistics/ Econometrics	30	1	31	3	2	5	36	243
Economic policy	61	4	65	13	7	20	85	1,452
Economic history	1	2	3	11	2	13	16	603
Public finance/ Monetary economics	25	2	27	3	0	3	30	670
Commercial studies	10	1	11	3	2	5	16	563
Management	60	8	68	12	6	18	86	1,544
Accounting	2	0	2	1	0	1	3	947
Total	297	24	321	76	21	97	418	7,338

Table 2.10 Classification of the *Keizaigaku Bunken Kiho*

Original Class. (1956)	Revision of No. 44/45 (1967)	Revision of No. 111 (1983)
	0. General	
1. General	1. Social Science and Social Thought	01. Humanities and Social Sciences
2. Economic Theory	2. Economic Theory (subsections introduced)	02. Economics and Economic Theory
3. History of Economic Thought	3. History of Economic Thought	03. History of Economic Thought
4. Economic History	4. Economic History	04. Economic History
5. Economic Geography	5. Economic Geography and Regional Economy (subsection introduced)	05. Economic Geography/ Regional Economics
6. Present Economic Conditions	6. International Economics	06. International Economics and World Economy
7. Economic Policy	7. Economic Policies and Present Economic Conditions	07. Economic Policies and Economic Conditions/ Country Studies
8. Agriculture and Industrial Economics	8. Industry	08. Industry
9. Commerce	9. Business	09. Business Economics
10. Accounting	10. Management	10. Management
11. Management and Enterprise	11. Accounting	11. Accounting/ Bookkeeping
12. Money and Finance	12. Money and Banking	12. Money and Banking
13. Public Finance	13. Public Finance	13. Public Finance
14. Labor and Social Problems	14. Population	14. Population
15. Sociology	15. Labor and Social Problems	15. Labor and Social Problem
16. Politics	16. Statistics	16. Statistics
17. Law	---------------	----------------
18. Statistics	---------------	----------------

Note:
From No. 44/45 all major divisions have subdivisions.
4 digits subdivision is introduced from No. 111.

universities such as Waseda, Keio, and Meiji are dominant, although among national universities Kobe University (national university) shows a relatively good score in these areas.

The lack of mobility of Japanese economists is often complained of but so far as the choice of graduate course is concerned, the rate of mobility is not small. Those who moved out and those who moved in rival those who entered the graduate course of the same university that finished the undergraduate study.

Lastly, a glance should be given to the share of academic economists who studied at overseas universities, in particular those who were trained on the graduate courses of American universities. The search result of the registered economists in the *Catalogue of Researchers and Research Topics* (1996) is shown in Table 2.9.[27] The share of those who mentioned American graduate courses in their academic background is highest in Statistics (this covers econometrics) with 12.8 percent. It is 8.7 percent in Economic Theory. In Economic Policy 4.5 percent, in Management Study 4.4 percent, in Public Finance and Financial Economics 4.0 percent, in Commercial Study 2.0 percent. In Economic History and Accounting it is under 1 percent. Since studying at American graduate courses for researchers in Marxian economics and history of economics is very rare, if the share is counted after excluding them, we can roughly estimate that almost 20 percent of Japanese 'modern' theoretical economists have a background of American graduate course training. It is rather surprising that the American share is relatively low in management studies and in the areas of applied economics. However, we can appreciate its that the motivation for studying abroad may be weaker in those areas where nation-wide particularity is stronger than those where pure theory matters.

2.4 Classified works of economists in Japan

The classification scheme of the *Journal of Economic Literature* is often used in international comparisons of economic literature. However, applying this to Japanese economic literature is very difficult. The representative of the bibliographical journal in economics is the *Keizaigaku Bunken Kiho* (Quarterly Bibliography of Economics) that has been published since 1956 (Table 2.10). It is a group of librarians with the name of the Association for Documentation in Economics that has maintained this journal. Since 1983 the bibliographical information compiled by this group has been made public by the online database 'KEIZAI' of NACSIS. However, the classification system was devised originally with reference to the curriculum in economic education in traditional universities. A comparison of the two classification systems is shown in the appendix to this chapter.

The classification system of QBE underwent considerable changes in 1967 and in 1983 and so we show the numbers of classified items of Japanese economic literature in three periods, 1956–66, 1967–83, and 1983–1996 separately (Table 2.11). The counting for the first and second periods was performed on the basis of issues of QBE, but as for the third, the counting was done by searching the online database. Probably because of the extension of coverage in the transition to the online database, numbers of the total items nearly doubled in the third period.[28]

If we pay attention to the composition, the share of 'Economic Theory' increased from 6.40 percent in the first period to 9.17 percent and 11.82 percent in the second and third periods respectively. But since the item of 'Economic Theory' within each period shows no trend of increase, it is too soon to say that the theoretical interest of Japanese economists has been intensified. On the other hand, Labor and Social Problems, that occupied 12.27 percent in the first period,

Table 2.11 Classified items of economics literature: (a) 1956–66; (b) 1967–83; (c) 1983–96
(a)

							Classification									
Year	1 General	2 Economic theory	3 History of economic theory and ideas	4 Economic history	5 Economic geography	6 Nation-wide situation	7 Economic policy	8 Agriculture/ Industry	9 Commerce	10 Accounting	11 Management/ Business	12 Money/ Finance	13 Public finance	14 Labor/ Social problems	18 Statistics	Total*
1956	209	530	274	691	100	474	323	1,298	782	762	894	860	377	1,465	105	10,717
1957	197	716	264	640	98	438	264	1,250	727	599	968	776	292	1,339	121	10,376
1958	204	679	205	686	96	483	202	1,232	641	594	911	714	248	1,092	74	9,161
1959	147	702	230	737	88	434	305	1,182	684	687	1,052	736	195	982	97	9,181
1960	236	497	231	568	102	428	288	1,210	683	711	946	751	261	1,017	75	8,935
1961	89	491	124	515	99	397	524	1,043	264	704	584	571	200	930	71	7,003
1962	105	509	166	617	162	627	617	1,283	386	669	902	616	287	1,113	87	8,574
1963	76	461	85	531	98	515	567	1,066	379	578	793	644	200	1,011	75	7,591
1964	118	505	120	450	182	512	645	970	460	719	1,130	636	199	946	85	8,135
1965	147	496	123	447	153	456	626	1,074	366	610	949	655	246	1,053	87	8,165
1966	88	537	154	449	184	423	559	1,052	419	742	957	623	261	792	70	7,850
56–66 sum	1,616	6,123	1,976	6,331	1,362	5,187	4,920	12,660	5,791	7,375	10,086	7,582	2,766	11,740	947	95,688
Share (%)	1.69	6.40	2.07	6.62	1.42	5.42	5.14	13.23	6.05	7.71%	10.54	7.92	2.89	12.27	0.99	86,462

Source: Keizaigaku Bunken Kiho, Nos.1–43.

Note
* Items of 15 Sociology, 16 Politics, and 17 Law are additionally included.

Table 2.11 Continued
(b)

Year	0+1 Social science and thought	2 Economic theory	3 History of economic theory and ideas	4 Economic history	5 Geography/Regional economy	6 International economy	7 Econ. policy/Nation-wide study	8 Industry	9 Business economy	10 Management	11 Accounting	12 Money and finance	13 Public finance	14 Population	15 Labor and social problems	16 Statistics	Total
								Classification									
1967	238	627	163	381	326	460	461	1,612	623	646	678	550	248	72	716	88	7,889
1968	187	612	154	382	319	512	540	1,220	415	694	685	571	188	49	551	82	7,161
1969	164	403	123	294	291	479	414	1,294	426	693	742	435	182	42	525	79	6,586
1970	254	513	112	215	303	398	393	1,092	306	612	643	507	200	38	596	75	6,257
1971	255	608	165	262	367	550	376	1,217	352	655	733	539	203	58	676	77	7,093
1972	266	622	131	267	404	592	365	1,138	341	497	690	417	172	53	652	87	6,694
1973	349	663	145	348	416	555	358	1,302	362	681	695	580	208	61	729	86	7,538
1974	247	764	151	311	414	419	412	1,427	489	587	700	553	243	54	816	82	7,669
1975	250	747	158	320	345	393	332	1,161	511	694	834	524	276	46	674	75	7,340
1976	269	716	162	341	414	369	305	1,295	460	718	776	495	247	39	689	63	7,358
1977	234	815	183	302	327	444	354	1,416	585	702	727	530	234	49	681	81	7,664
1978	248	695	149	316	409	435	314	1,317	421	636	699	498	233	41	667	99	7,177
1979	256	793	281	348	446	428	355	1,492	464	711	691	548	330	40	709	82	7,974
1980	309	773	207	350	429	435	416	1,654	463	716	801	503	298	96	779	98	8,327
1981	210	902	158	333	426	443	442	1,557	489	750	796	602	325	82	669	106	8,290
1982	245	716	180	276	448	477	420	1,481	518	778	758	540	282	86	748	109	8,062
1983	217	528	191	299	341	394	274	1,151	371	600	626	447	209	40	554	52	6,294
1967–83 sum	4,198	11,497	2,813	5,345	6,425	7,783	6,531	22,826	7,596	11,370	12,274	8,839	4,078	946	11,431	1,421	125,373
Share (%)	3.35	9.17	2.24	4.26	5.12	6.21	5.21	18.21	6.06	9.07	9.79	7.05	3.25	0.75	9.12	1.13	

(c)

Year	1 Humanities	2 Economic theory	3 History of economic thought	4 Economic history	5 Economic geography/ Regional economy	6 International economy /World economy	7 Country studies	8 Industry	9 Business economics	10 Management	11 Accounting	12 Money and banking	13 Public finance	14 Population	15 Labor and social problems	16 Statistics	Total
										Division							
1983	233	1,913	241	410	493	882	739	1,841	654	1,117	594	829	434	154	1,070	150	11,754
1984	378	2,477	304	528	788	1,124	765	2,284	787	1,701	1,058	995	586	187	1,472	194	15,628
1885	320	2,626	324	565	780	1,198	976	2,279	833	1,611	1,150	1,054	631	191	1,525	173	16,236
1986	290	2,268	294	539	759	1,105	1,116	2,174	780	1,641	1,052	1,087	577	172	1,431	178	15,463
1987	237	1,639	222	535	623	986	928	1,819	703	1,259	934	809	481	130	1,034	144	12,483
1988	299	1,298	232	441	819	1,143	1,277	2,202	860	1,182	813	872	508	101	1,120	139	13,306
1989	320	1,480	210	407	812	1,140	1,339	2,085	790	1,184	861	971	494	94	1,182	148	13,517
1990	414	1,493	220	396	936	1,238	1,430	2,084	836	1,364	818	916	468	126	1,210	111	14,060
1991	369	1,335	202	423	947	1,132	1,460	2,039	812	1,315	852	969	433	127	1,182	121	13,718
1992	269	1,312	212	413	917	1,126	1,423	2,154	965	1,342	901	976	404	133	1,188	122	13,857
1993	240	1,376	226	423	956	1,075	1,529	2,264	977	1,429	906	1,016	382	124	1,220	128	14,271
1994	238	1,382	216	380	966	1,094	1,662	2,123	1,063	1,455	904	1,077	479	109	1,304	131	14,583
1995	268	1,388	198	365	945	955	1,634	2,150	980	1,596	986	1,191	443	97	1,155	131	14,482
1996	168	1,322	161	357	905	908	1,474	2,079	998	1,659	1,007	1,139	415	94	1,065	115	13,866
83–96 sum	4,043	23,309	3,262	6,182	11,646	15,106	17,752	29,577	12,038	19,855	12,836	13,901	6,735	1,839	17,158	1,985	197,224
Share (%)	2.05	11.82	1.65	3.13	5.90	7.66	9.00	15.00	6.10	10.07%	6.51	7.05	3.41	0.93	8.70	1.01	100.00

Source: Online database 'Researcher' of NACSIS. Searched in August 1998.

decreased to 9.12 percent and 8.70 percent in the second and third periods respectively. In Industry, the share of Agriculture decreased. Behind such changes we can assume the influence of the structural change in Japanese economy on the research interest of economists. The introduction of International Economics, Business Economics, and Management as main divisions in the classification system is also a reflection of such structural change. However, it is regrettable that the alterations made the comparison numbers before and after 1967 impossible. For example, when the large division, International Economics was introduced in 1967, International Currency and Finance was transferred from Money and Finance to International Economics. Further, the new large division absorbed several sub- or sub-sub divisions from Present Economic Conditions, Economic Policy, and Commerce. Also, in the case of the separation of Business Economics and Management, making a correspondence before and after 1967 is too difficult.

In the second and third period, the share of History of Economic Thought as well as Economic History shows a considerable decrease. But absolute numbers did not change to a great extent. This decrease comes partly from the inclusion of non-academic journals to the bibliography. On the other hand the 9 percent share of Economic Policies and Economic Conditions/Country Studies in the third period compared with the lower percentage of Present Economic Conditions would be a reflection of the deepening of interest of foreign countries as well as the growth of expert researchers.

Acknowledgements

The author thanks NACSIS (National Center for Science Information Systems) and the librarians of the Keizai Shiryo Kyogikai (The Association for Documentation in Economics) for the use of the database and bibliographical publications mentioned in this chapter. He also acknowledges with thanks his friends and acquaintances for the information they kindly gave him about the history and current situation of the academic institutions with whom they are affiliated with.

Notes

1   See Bronfenbrenner (1956) (1988) and Ikeo (1990).
2   As examples see Ikeo (1996a) and Yamada (1998).
3   The viewpoint in this chapter is exclusively that of a sociologist of knowledge. For those who are interested in theoretical or intellectual problems of economists in this period, the author would like to suggest Yagi (1997) and Negishi (1998) as relevant literature.
4   It was Toru Hiroshige (Hiroshige 1965) that recognized first the significance of the wartime science promotion policy as the basis of the postwar development of academic science. His view was succeeded by Shigeru Nakayama who organized the project of general history of science and technology of postwar Japan (Nakayama 1996).

5   In these studies econometrics was first applied to the real problems of Japan. See Ikeo (1994) Chapter 4.

6   For the history of this association, see Fujii (1998). The influence of Marxism on Japanese economists is explained in Inoue and Yagi (1998).

7   See Nihon Keizai Seisaku Gakkai (1988).

8   I discussed Takata's ethnic theory and sociological foundation of power theory in economics in Chapter 6 of Yagi (1999).

9   As for the hardship that commercial universities faced in this period, see Hitotsubashi Daigaku Gakuenshi Kanko Iinkai (1995) pp. 152, 160f. Shirai (1996) contains important reports of the situation of such various private universities as Keio, Rikkyo, Sophia, Kwansei-Gakuen, Doshisha, Taisho, and Toa-Dobun-Shoin in this period.

10   This article was included in Takano's posthumous publication (Takano 1961).

11   This is reprinted in Yasui (1979).

12   Yamamoto (1994), pp. 337–9. Although several studies of the occupation purge exist, Yamamoto (1994) is the only one that dealt with the screening of teachers.

13   Tokyo Daigaku (1988), p. 1008f.

14   Osaka Shiritsu Daigaku (1987), vol. 1, p. 232.

15   Kyoto Daigaku (1997), p. 400.

16   Keio Gijuku (1956–68), Chu (Go), p. 1030. See also Shirai (1996).

17   Waseda Daigaku (1992), vol. 4, p. 306.

18   Kansai Daigaku (1986).

19   Nihon Gakujutsu Kaigi (1977), pp. 307–12. (Report of the Third Department).

20   Keizai Riron Gakkai (1980), p. 253.

21   Dainippon Teikoku Monbusho (1936).

22   Monbusho Gakujutsu-kyoku Daigaku-ka (1997).

23   Kaigo and Terasaki (1969) is a comprehensive study of the formation process of a new university.

24   This once-a-year online directory is based on the questionnaire that the Ministry of Education distributes to all researchers working for institutions of higher education and research. Since answering the questionnaire is not compulsory, the data of many researchers are missing, however eminent they may be. The *Catalogue* is based on the same data.

25   Fujino (1986), p. 110f.

26   Iwata (1992) p. 255, (1998) p. 104.

27   Denki-Denshi Johou Grakujutsu Shinko Zaiden (1997). The reason that the author used the *Catalogue* was to avoid the difficulty caused by various renderings of the names of American universities when one searches the online database. I still found several researchers that preferred to list their enrolled Japanese graduate course to the American one where they obtained their PhD when giving details of educational background.

28   The name of the online database of NACSIS is 'KEIZAI'. In case of this database, multiple classification seems to be allowed more often.

APPENDIX: COMPARISON OF TWO CLASSIFICATION SCHEMES

Keizaigaku Bunken Kiho (Quarterly Bibliography of Economics)	*Journal of Economic Literature*
01 Humanities and Social Sciences	
00 General	
10 Humanities and Social Sciences	A1 General Economics
20 Social Thought	A1 General Economics
	D6 Economic Welfare
	Z1 Cultural Economics
02 Economics and Economic Theory	
00 General	
10 General Economics: Methodology. Education. Relation to Other Disciplines	A1 General Economics
	A2 Teaching of Economics
	B4 Economic Methodology
20 Economic Theory in General	C6 Mathematical Methods and Programming
	D5 General Equilibrium and Disequilibrium
30 Microeconomics in General	C7 Game Theory and Bargaining Theory
	D Microeconomics (D1–D9)
31 Theory of Capital	E2 Consumption, Saving, Production, Environment, and Investment (E22 Capital: Investment (including Inventories))
32 Production. Value. Price. Resource Allocation. Theory of Firm	D2 Production and Organization
	D4 Market Structure and Pricing
	L1 Market Structure, Firm Strategy, and Market Performance
33 Distribution. Consumption. Saving	D1 Household Behavior and Family Economics
	D3 Distribution
40 Macroeconomics in General	E Macroeconomics and Monetary Economics (E1–E6)
41 National Income. Reproduction	E1 General Aggregate Models
	E2 Consumption, Saving, Production, Employment, and Investment
42 Economic Growth. Development. Plannning	O1 Economic Development
	O2 Development Planning and Policy

43 Economic Fluctuations. Business Cycle
50 Economics of Socialist Planning
60 Economic Systems

O4 Economic Growth and Aggregate Productivity
E3 Prices, Business Fluctuations, and Cycles
P2 Socialist Systems
F Economic Systems (F1–F5)

03 History of Economic Thought
00 General
10 History of Economic Thought in General
20 Japan
30 Asia & Islam
40 Europe & North America
50 Other Countries

B1 History of Economic Thought through 1925
B2 History of Economic Thought since 1925
B3 History of Thought: Individuals

04 Economic History
00 General
10 Economic History in General. World Economic History
20 Japan
30 Asia
40 Europe
50 Southwestern Asia & Africa
60 North America & Canada
70 Latin America
80 Oceania

N Economic History (N1–N7)

N1 Macroeconomics: Growth and Fluctuations
N2 Financial Markets and Institutions
N3 Labor, Demography, Education, Income, and Wealth
N4 Government, Law, and regulations
N5 Agriculture, Natural resources, and Extractive Industries
N6 Manufacturing and Construction
N7 Transport, Trade, Energy, and Other Services

05 Economic Geography. Regional Economics
00 General
10 Economic Geography
20 Regional Economics

30 Urban Economics	R Urban, Rural, and Regional Economics (R1–R5) R1 General Spatial Economics R2 Household Analysis R3 Production Analysis and Firm Location R4 Transportation System R5 Regional Government Analysis
40 Pollution. Environmental Problems	K3 Other Subjective Area of Law (K32) Q2 Renewable Resources and Conservation: Environment Management Q3 Nonrenewable Resources and Conservation

06 International Economics and World Economy   F International Economics (F1-F4)
00 General
10 International Economics. World   F2 International Factor Movement
Economy   F4 Macroeconomic Aspects of
                                     International Trade and Finance
20 International Trade: Theory.   F1 Trade
History. Policy
30 International Finance: Currency.   F3 International Finance
Exchange Rate. Balance of Payments

07 Economic Policies and Economic Conditions. Country Studies
00 General
10 Japan
20 Asia
30 Europe
40 Southwestern Asia & Africa
50 North America & Canada
60 Latin America
70 Oceania   E6 Macroeconomic Aspects of Public
                                     Finance, Macroeconomic Policy, and
                                     General Outlook
                                     H Public Economics (H1–H8)

08 Industry
00 General
10 Industry: Organization. Policy.   K1 Basic Area of Law
Resources. Technology   K2 Regulation and Business Law

	L1 Market Structure, Firms Strategy, and Market Performance
	L2 Firm Objectives, Organizations, and Behavior
	L4 Antitrust Policy
	L5 Regulation and Industrial Policy
	O3 Technical Change
	Q3 Nonrenewable Resources and Conservation
20 Agriculture. Forestry. Fishery	Q1 Agriculture
	Q2 Renewable Resources and Conservation: Environmental Management (Q22)
21 Agricultural Economics	Q1 Agriculture
22 Agricultural History	N5 Agriculture, Natural Resources, and Extractive Industries
23 Agricultural Policy and Conditions	Q1 Agriculture
24 Agricultural Market. Agricultural Cooperatives	Q1 Agriculture (Q13)
25 Agricultural Business and Finance	Q1 Agriculture (Q13, Q14)
26 Agricultural Labour. Agricultural Population	J4 Particular Labor Market (J43)
27 Stock-Breeding. Dairy-Farming	Q1 Agriculture
28 Forestry. Hunting	Q2 Renewable Resources and Conservation: Environmental Management (Q23)
29 Fishery. Water Culture	Q2 Renewable Resources and Conservation: Environmental Management (Q22)
30 Mining. Energy Industry	L7 Industry Studies: Primary Products and Construction
40 Manufacturing Industry	L6 Industry Studies: Manufacturing
41 Industrial Economics	L6 Industry Studies: Manufacturing
42 Industrial History	N6 Manufacturing and Construction
43 Industrial Policy and Conditions	L6 Industry Studies: Manufacturing
44 Textile	L6 Industry Studies: Manufacturing (L67)
45 Machinery. Arms	L6 Industry Studies: Manufacturing (L64)
46 Iron and Steel. Fabricated Metal Non-Ferrous Metals	L6 Industry Studies: Manufacturing (L61)
47 Chemicals. Drugs and Medicines	L6 Industry Studies: Manufacturing (L65)
48 Other Manufacturing Industries	L6 Industry Studies: Manufacturing (L62, L63, L66–L69)
50 Commerce. Service Industry	L8 Industry Studies: Services

60 Transportation. Communication Industry

L9 Industry Studies: Utilities and Transportation (L91–L93, L96)

70 Construction Industry. Other Housing Industries

R3 Production Analysis and Firm Location (R31)

L7 Industry Studies: Primary Products and Construction (L74)

80 Other Industries

09 Business Economics

00 General

10 Business Economics in General

L2 Firm Objectives, Organization, and Behavior

M2 Business Economics

20 Business and Entrepreneurial History

N6 Manufacturing and Construction

30 Big Business. Business Combination

L1 Market Structure, Firm Strategy, and Market Structure

40 International Business

50 Small Business. Cooperatives

L1 Market Structure, Firm Strategy, and Market Structure

60 Public Enterprise. Public Utilities

L3 Nonprofit Organization and Public Enterprise

L9 Industry Studies: Utilities and transportation

70 Enterprises in Socialist Countries

P3 Socialist Institutions (P31)

10 Management

00 General

10 Business Administration in General	M1 Business Administration
20 Management Science in General	M1 Business Administration
30 Management and Management Organization in General	M1 Business Administration
40 Production Management	M1 Business Administration
50 Marketing	M3 Marketing and Advertising
60 Financial Management	G3 Corporate Finance and Governance
70 Labour Management	J3 Wages, Compensation, and Labor Cost
80 Management Information System	M1 Business Administration
90 Management by Industry: Case Studies	M1 Business Administration

11 Accounting. Bookkeeping

00 General

10 Accounting in General	M4 Accounting
20 Bookkeeping	M4 Accounting
30 Financial Accounting	M4 Accounting

40 Cost Accounting	M4 Accounting
50 Management Accounting	M4 Accounting
60 Auditing	M4 Accounting
70 Tax Accounting	M4 Accounting
80 Other Types of Accounting	M4 Accounting
90 Accosting by Industry: Case Studies	M4 Accounting

12 Money and Banking
00 General

10 Money and Prices General	E3 Prices, Business Fluctuations, and Cycles (E31)
	E4 Money and Interest Rates
	E5 Monetary Policy, Central Banking, and the Supply of Money and Credit
20 Banking and Finance	G1 General Financial Market
	G2 Financial Institutions and Services (G21, G24)
30 Securities	G1 General Financial Market
40 Insurance	G2 Financial Institutions and Services (G22)

13 Public Finance
00 General

10 Public Finance in General. National Government Finance	E6 Macroeconomic Aspects of Public Finance, Macroeconomic Policy, and General Outlook
	H Public Economics (H1-H8)
20 Local Government Finance	H7 State and Local Government: Intergovernmental Relations
	R5 Regional Government Analysis

14 Population
00 General

10 Population in General	J1 Demographic Economics
20 State of Population. Movement of Population	J1 Demographic Economics
30 Migration	J1 Demographic Economics

15 Labour and Social Problems
00 General

10 Labour Problems in General	J1 Demographic Economics
20 Labour Conditions	J3 Wages, Compensation, and Labor Costs
30 Labour Markets	J2 Time Allocation, Work Behavior, and Employment Determination
	J4 Particular Labor Markets
	J6 Mobility, Unemployment, and Vacancies
40 Wages. Hours. Fringe Benefits	J3 Wages, Compensation, and Labor Costs

50 Trade Union. Labor Movement	J5 Labor-Management Relations, Trade Unions, and Collective Bargaining
60 Public Policies. Social Securities & Welfare	H5 National Government Expenditure and Welfare Grant K3 Other Subjective Areas of Law
70 Living Conditions	I1 Health I3 Welfare and Poverty
80 Social Problems and Movements	J1 Demographic Economics

16 Statistics
00 General

10 Theory & History of Statistics	C1 Econometric and Statistical Methods: General C2 Econometric Methods: Single Equation Models C3 Econometric Methods: Multiple/ Simultaneous Equation Models C4 Econometric and Statistical Methods: Special Topics C5 Econometric Modeling
20 Statistical Survey	C8 Data Collection and Data Estimation Methodology; Computer Programs
30 Overall Statistical Data	C8 Data Collection and Data Estimation Methodology; Computer Programs

Note
Compiled by Aiko Ikeo with the cooperation of Tomoki Okuyama.
Sources: Keizai Shiryo Kyogikai (1956–)

References and further reading

Bronfenbrenner, M. (1956) 'The state of Japanese economics', *American Economic Review* 46: 389–98.
Bronfenbrenner, M. (1988) *Keizaigaku Tokoro-Dokoro* (Here and There in Economics), Tokyo: Aoyama Gakuin University.
Dainippon Teikoku Monbusho (Ministry of Education, The Empire of Japan) (1936) *Dainippon Teikoku Monbusho Dai 63 Nenpo* (The 63rd Annual Report of the Ministry of Education, The Empire of Japan).
Denki-Denshi Johou Gakujutsu Shinko Zaidan (ed.) (Promotion Fund for Academic Use of Electronic Information) (1997) *Kenkyusha Kenkyu-kadai Soran, 1996* (Catalogue of Researchers and Research Topics, 1996), Tokyo: Kinokuniya.
Faculty of Economics, Kyoto University (1994) *Arata na Hisho wo motomete: Kyoto Daigaku Keizai-gakubu Jikotenken-hyoka Hokokusho* (In Quest of a new Flight: State of the Faculty of Economics, Kyoto University with Auto-evaluations), private publication.

Fujii, T. (1998) 'The Japanese social policy school: its formation and breakup' in Sugihara and Tanaka (eds) (1998), pp. 44–59.

Fujino, S. (1986) *Daigaku Kyoiku to Shijo Kiko* (University Education and Market Mechanism). Tokyo: Iwanami Shoten.

Hiroshige, T. (1965) *Kagaku to Rekishi* (Sciences and History). Tokyo: Misuzu Shobo.

Hitotsubashi Daigaku Gakuenshi Kanko Iinkai (1995) *Hitotsubashi Daigaku 120 nenshi* (120 Years of the Hitotsubashi University), private publication.

Ikeo, A. (1990). 'Japanese economics from another sociological perspective', *Kokugakuin Keizaigaku* (Kokugakuin University) 39 (1): 112–28.

Ikeo, A. (1994) *20 Seiki no Keizaigakusha Netto-waaku* (Networks of Economists in the 20th Century), Tokyo: Yuhikaku.

Ikeo, A. (1996a) 'Marxist economics in Japan', *Kokugakuin Keizaigaku* 44 (3/4), pp. 425–51.

Ikeo, A. (1996b) 'The advent of marginalism in Japan', *Research in the History of Economic Thought and Methodology* 14: 217–45.

Ikeo, A. (1998) 'Economic thought and economic development after World War II: non-Marxian economists on development, trade, and industry' in Sugihara and Tanaka (eds) (1998), pp. 131–51.

Inoue, T. and K. Yagi (1998) 'Two inquirers on the divide: Tokuzo Fukuda and Hajime Kawakami' in Sugihara and Tanaka (eds). (1998), pp. 60–77.

Iwata, T. (1992) *Keizaigaku Kyouiku-ron Josetsu* (Introduction to Research in Economics Education), Tokyo: Aoki Shoten.

Iwata, T. (1998) *Keizaigaku Kyouiku-ron no Kenkyu* (Study of Economics Education), Osaka: Kansai-Daigaku Shuppanbu.

Kaigo, T. and M. Terasaki (1969) *Daigaku Kyoiku: Sengo Nihon no Kyoiku Kaikaku 9* (University Education: Post-War Educational Reform in Japan, vol. 9), Tokyo: Tokyo Daigaku Shuppankai.

Kansai Daigaku Hyakunen-shi Hensan Iinkai (1986) *Kansai Daigaku Hyakunen-shi, Tsushi-hen 1* (Centennial History of the Kansai University, Part 1), private publication.

Keio Gijuku (1956–68). *Keio Gijuku Hyakunenshi* (A Centennial History of the Keio Gijuku), 3 books in 4 vols, private publication.

Keizai Shiryo Kyogikai (Association for Documentation in Economics) (1956–) *Keizaigaku Bunken Kiho* (Quarterly Bibliography of Economics). At present by Kinokuniya, Tokyo.

Keizai Riron Gakkai (Japan Society of Political Economy) (1980) 'Zadankai: Keizai Riron Gakkai no 20-nen' (Discussion: 20 years of the Japan Society of Political Economy), *Annual Bulletin of the Society of Political Economy* 17: 253–66.

Kyoto Daigaku Hyakunen-shi Henshu Iinkai (1997) *Kyoto Daigaku Hyakunenshi, Bukyoku-shi Hen 1* (A Centennial History of Kyoto University, History of Departments, Part.1). Kyoto: Kyoto Daigaku Koenkai.

Monbusho Gakujutsu-kyoku Daigaku-ka (University Section of the Ministry of Education: supervisor) (1997) *Zenkoku Daigaku Ichiran, Heisei 9 nendo* (National List of Universities, FY1997).

Monbusho (1996) *Monbusho Kagaku Kenkyu-hi Hojokin Saitaku Kadai, Kobo Shinsa Yoran* (Grant in Aid of the Research Fund of the Ministry of Education: Adopted Projects and Outlines of Examination), Heisei 8 (FY1996).

Morris-Suzuki, T. (1989) *History of Japanese Economic Thought*. London: Routledge.

Nagahama, I. (ed.) (1984) *Fukkoku Shiryo Koshoku Tsuiho II* (Reprinted Materials, Occupation Purge, II), Tokyo: Shiraishi Shoten.

Nakayama, S. (ed.) (1996) Tsushi: Sengo no Kagaku Gijutsu (General History: Science and Technology in the Post-War Period), 5 volumes. Tokyo: Gakuyo Shobo.

Negishi, T. (1998) 'General equilibrium theory and beyond: Yasuma Takata and Kei Shibata'. In Sugihara and Tanaka (eds) (1998) pp. 97–116.

Nihon Gakujutsu Kaigi (Science Council of Japan) (1977) *Nihon Gakujutsu Kaigi 25-nenshi* (25 Years of the Science Council of Japan) private publication.

Nihon Gakujutsu Kaigi (1987) *Nihon Gakujutsu Kaigi Zoku Jyunenshi* (The next 10 Years of the Science Council of Japan) private publication.

Nihon Keizai Gakkai (Japanese Economic Association) (1941) *Nihon Keizai-Gakkai Nenpo* (Annual Bulletin of Japanese Economic Association), no. 1.

Nihon Keizai Seisaku Gakkai (ed.) (1988) *Keizai Seisaku-gaku no Tanjo* (Birth of the Science of Economic Policy), Tokyo: Keiso Shobo.

Osaka Shiritsu Daigaku (1987) *Osaka Shiritsu Daigaku Hyakunen-shi, Zengakuhen* (A Centennial History of Osaka City University, General Part), 2 vols, private publication.

Shirai, A. (ed.) (1996) *Daigaku to Ajia-Taiheiyou Sensou* (Universities and the Asia-Pacific War), Tokyo: Nihon Keizai Hyoron-sha.

Sugihara, S. and T. Tanaka (eds) (1998) *Economic Thought and Modernization in Japan*. Cheltenham: Edward Elgar.

Sugiyama, C. and H. Mizuta (eds) (1988) *Enlightenment and Beyond: Political Economy Comes to Japan*. Tokyo: University of Tokyo Press.

Takano, I. (1961) *Kappa no He: Iko-shu* (Fart of a Kappa: posthumous publication), Tokyo: Hosei Daigaku Shuppankyoku.

Tokyo Daigaku Hyakunen-shi Henshu Iinkai (1988) *Tokyo Daigaku Hyakunen-shi, Bukyokushi 1* (A Centennial History of the University of Tokyo, History of Departments, Part 1), private publication.

Tsuru, S. (1964). 'Survey of economic research in post-war Japan', *American Economic Review* 54(4), part 2, supplement. pp. 79–101.

Union of the National Economic Associations in Japan (ed) (1977) *Biography of Japanese Publications on Economics, 1946–1975*, Tokyo: University of Tokyo Press.

Waseda Daigaku (1992). *Waseda Daigaku Hyakunenshi* (Centennial History of the Waseda University), private publication.

Yagi, K. (1997) 'Economic reform plans in the Japanese wartime economy: the case of Shintaro Ryu and Kei Shibata' in A. Ikeo (ed.) *Economic Development in Twentieth Century East Asia*, London: Routledge, pp. 100–15.

Yagi, K. (1999) *Kindai Nihon no Shakai-Keizaigaku* (Social Economics of Modern Japan), Tokyo: Chikuma Shobou.

Yamamoto, R. (1994). *Senryo-ka ni okeru Kyoshoku Tsuiho: GHQ/SCAP bunsho ni yoru Kenkyu* (Screening of Teachers under Occupation. Research based on GHQ/SCAP papers), Meisei-Daigaku Shuppanbu.

Yamada, T. (1998) 'After World War II: economic development and Marxian political economy' in Sugihara and Tanaka (eds) (1998), pp. 152–70.

Yasui T. (1979) *Keizaigaku to sono Shuhen* (Economics and Its Margins), Tokyo: Bokutaku-sha.

3 Scientific contributions to international journals

Masahiro Kawamata

Introduction

Recently, in each area and country, historians of economics have been interested in characterizing the post-1945 development of economics, based on the concepts of internationalization or Americanization of economics (Kyklos 1995; Coats 1996). Their research features positive analysis based on statistical data and it has been possible because of the post-1945 development of economics.

The first characteristic of the post-1945 development of economics is its formalization. In the development of mathematical economics since the marginal revolution, the problems of existence, stability, and uniqueness of competitive equilibrium had been increasingly important and therefore the economic theory had come to be expressed as a formal system in the 1950s. If an economic theory is expressed as a formal system, then expressions are universal and any economic theory can be understandable beyond the social background of language, culture, institution, and so on.

The second is the institutionalization of economics. Because of this institutionalization, academic contribution is assessed by the number of papers published in economics journals as opposed to the number of books published. Furthermore institutions, including universities, evaluate economists by using this criteria together with which economics journals economists appear in, and the number of times their papers are cited in other economists' papers (Sawa 1979, 1982; Sato 1989).

The third is the development of an information system. The data accumulated in economics journals are saved as a database. This makes it possible for every individual researcher to analyze the database quantitatively alone. Hong (1996) presents an example of Korean internationalization of economics where he analyzes a database quantitatively.

In the Korean case, Hong (1996) confirms the internationalization of Korean economics by showing the number of Korean Ph.D. in the USA, the utilization of mathematics and statistics, the contributions to international journals, the English papers of Korean authors published in domestic journals and the foreign contributors to domestic journals to be increasing. However, it is very difficult to construct an index to indicate the internationalization of economics itself.

In Japan there are the other difficulties proper to the Japanese academic environment, in analyzing the internationalization of Japanese economics based on the database available in Japan. First, Japanese economics is not sufficiently institutionalized in the sense that there are a few Japanese economics journals that have the refereeing process. Then, Japanese economists have published their papers in the faculty journal without any refereeing process. The faculty journal is generally called *Kiyo*, which is published by the faculty's association of the university where they are employed. Needless to say, the quality of papers published in the faculty journal could not be guaranteed and the data processed from it loses reliability as a database.

Second, as the result of the post-1945 development of economics, it is sure that the number of Marxian economists decreases and that of non-Marxian economists increases. But we cannot confirm this fact by the quantitative analysis of the database produced from the faculty journal because Marxian economists still publish their papers in their faculty journal while non-Marxian economists have been publishing their papers in the international journals of economics as far as they can. This is the reason why we analyze not the Japanese domestic database but the database of the USA.[1]

While Japanese economists have been publishing their papers in the international journals, it does not mean that Japanese economics is internationalized. We suppose that the internationalization and Americanization of Japanese economics is a local phenomenon within the fields of economics formally described. Japanese economists' contributions are confined to theoretical, econometric, mathematical, and statistical researches. However, these researches are one of the cores of economics, but a minor part of the whole system of economics, while applied economics, economic policy, institutional researches are a major part of economics.

Thus we investigate the following two problems: first, which type of analysis do Japanese economists make; theoretical, practical, mathematical, statistical, policy making, or institutional? Secondly, which fields of the JEL Alphanumeric Classification System do Japanese economists contribute to? We investigate the first problem in Sections 3.1 through 3.3 and the second in Section 3.4. The results of this investigation suggest that our supposition should be valid. In Section 3.5, we interpret the results of the quantitative analysis.

3.1 Selection of data

Economists contribute to economics by publishing papers in economic journals. We can observe, from certain databases, how many papers and in which journals each Japanese economist has published. However, all of the data is not necessarily effective in characterizing their contribution. Of course, the larger the amount of information, the more reliable is the result of the analysis. However, since it costs a great deal of time for an individual researcher to process much data, we have to confine the database to meaningful information by excluding the irrelevant in evaluating the contribution of Japanese economists.

What is the contribution in economics? We can consider that the academic contribution to economics is made by publishing papers in the economics journals that accept anonymous referee(s) examinations.[2] But we cannot consider all the papers published in the economics journals to be contributions, because about 70 percent of those papers are not read and cited by any other papers (Sato 1989: 174–7). Then, a contribution to economics is indicated by a subset of papers published in the economics journals. However, the index of the contribution will vary according to the criterion on which the selection of papers is based.

The first and immediate index is the citation by other papers, but this index is not appropriate to our purpose, because citations are made independently of the characteristics of the paper that the author intends and supposes to be a contribution. We use the second index and this is the amount of papers published in the core journals that always maintain high quality and influence other journals.

3.1.1 Classification of economics journals

We have two problems and we have to process respective data to solve them. The first problem is solved based on the data of general interest and comprehensive journals, because this is independent of the field of economics. The second is on the data of applied economics journals because of its very purpose. Fortunately, core journals are of general interest and comprehensive, and the applied economics journals are second to them except for some up-to-date fields such as finance and monetary problems.

Hawkins, Ritter and Walter (1973) suggest that the comprehensive journals of general interest and high prestige are as follows: *American Economic Review, Econometrica, Economic Journal, Economica, Journal of Political Economy, Oxford Economic Papers, Quarterly Journal of Economics, Review of Economic Studies, Review of Economics and Statistics*. These journals are of general interest and comprehensive so that the characteristic of every journal does not depend on the research fields.

3.1.2 Ranking of economics journals

We use the results of journal rankings by Liebowitz and Palmer (1984) and Laband and Piette (1994). Their results are based on the Social Science Citation Index (SSCI) that provides information on the total number of citations from journals covering all the social sciences. First, they rank journals by the total number of citations received from other journals for 1970, 1980, and 1990. They use the citations to articles published in the last five-year period because journals of recent birth have a much smaller inventory of articles to be cited and will certainly be at a disadvantage relative to older journals. Second, they adjust a journal's impact on other journals by the process of the following iteration. A journal's impact on highly influential journals is probably of greater value than its impact on less influential journals. They weight each citation according to the total number of citations received by the citing journal if it is on the list, otherwise

Table 3.1 Ranking of economics journals

	1970 Citations to articles published 1965–69		1980 Citations to articles published 1975–79		1990 Citations to articles published 1985–89	
1	Journal of Political Economy	100.0	Journal of Political Economy	100.0	American Economic Review	100.0
2	Review of Economic Studies	43.2	Journal of Financial Economics	99.0	Journal of Financial Economics	90.7
3	American Economic Review	41.4	American Economic Review	76.6	Econometrica	89.0
4	Quarterly Journal of Economics	34.4	Journal of Monetary Economics	61.1	Journal of Political Economy	79.1
5	Review of Economics and Statistics	30.2	Journal of Finance	60.1	Quarterly Journal of Economics	64.5
6	Journal of Finance	22.6	Journal of Economic Literature	55.0	Journal of Monetary Economics	59.3
7	Economic Journal	20.9	Econometrica	47.6	Journal of Economic Theory	51.1
8	Economica	20.7	Bell Journal of Economics (Rand J. of Econ.)	46.4	Journal of Finance	51.0
9	Econometrica	20.0	Brookings Papers on Economic Activity	37.0	Review of Economic Studies	47.6
10	Journal of Business	17.0	Review of Economic Studies	36.5	Bell Journal of Economics (Rand J. of Econ.)	46.5
11	American Economic Review Papers & Proceedings	16.3	Economica	36.2	Journal of Economic Perspectives	37.0
12	International Economic Review	15.0	Journal of Mathematical Economics	35.6	Journal of Mathematical Economics	32.4
13	Economic Planning	10.7	Quarterly Journal of Economics	35.2	Journal of Accounting and Economics	28.7
14	Oxford Economic Papers	8.6	Journal of Economic Theory	32.1	Journal of Business	27.1
15	Economic Records	6.6	American Economic Review Papers & Proceedings	31.4	Journal of Econometrics	26.8
16	Journal of the American Statistical Association	6.0	Review of Economics and Statistics	30.0	American Economic Review Papers & Proceedings	26.7
17	Southern Economic Journal	5.1	Journal of Econometrics	29.6	Journal of Financial and Quantitative Analysis	21.3
18	Journal of Law and Economics	4.1	Journal of International Economics	29.6	Journal of Economic Literature	18.6

19	Journal of Money, Credit, and Banking	17.9	International Economic Review	29.3	Journal of the Royal Statistical Society Ser. A-Gen.	4.0
20	Journal of Labor Economics	17.1	Journal of Human Resources	28.1	Journal of Economic History	3.7
21	International Economic Review	16.7	Journal of Money, Credit, and Banking	24.2	Yale Essays Economics	3.4
22	Brookings Papers on Economic Activity	14.7	Journal of Public Economics	23.6	Economic Inquiry (Western Economic Journal)	3.2
23	Review of Economics and Statistics	14.0	Economic Journal	22.5	Journal of Development Studies	2.7
24	Journal of Law and Economics	12.8	Economic Inquiry (Western Economic Journal)	22.4	Kyklos	2.7
25	Economic Journal	12.8	Scandinavian Journal of Economics	22.3	Economic Devel. Cult. Change	2.5
26	Journal of Business and Economic Statistics	12.4	Journal of Law and Economics	21.7	Lloyd's Bank Review	2.4
27	Journal of Economic Education	12.2	Journal of Business	21.1	National Tax Journal	2.3
28	Industrial and Labor Relations Review	11.7	Industrial and Labor Relations Review	18.5	Public Finance	2.2
29	Journal of Public Economics	10.8	Canadian Journal of Economics	18.0	Review of Social Economy	2.1
30	Journal of International Economics	10.8	Journal of Financial and Quantitative Analysis	13.2	Quarterly Review of Economic Business	2.0
31	Economic Letters	9.6	Journal of Industrial Economics	12.6	Journal of Regional Sciences	1.7
32	Journal of Industrial Economics	9.5	Southern Economic Journal	12.4	Weltwirtschaftliches Archiv	1.6
33	International Journal of Industrial Organization	8.5	Journal of Urban Economics	12.2	American Journal of Agricultural Economics	1.5
34	Journal of Economic Dynamics and Control	8.1	National Tax Journal	11.8	Journal of Industrial Economics	1.4
35	Social Choice and Welfare	7.3	Journal of Accounting Research	10.6	Manchester School of Economics and Soc. Studies	1.4
36	Journal of Human Resources	7.3	Kyklos	10.0	Land Economics	1.3
37	Journal of Banking and Finance	6.7	Manchester School of Economics and Soc. Studies	9.5	Economica Internazionale	1.2

Table 3.1 Continued

	1970 Citations to articles published 1965–69		1980 Citations to articles published 1975–79		1990 Citations to articles published 1985–89	
38	Explorations in Economic History	1.0	Journal of the American Statistical Association	7.5	Economic Inquiry (Western Economic Journal)	5.9
39	Scandinavian Journal of Economics	0.8	Journal of Legal Studies	7.3	Journal of the American Statistical Association	5.5
40	International Monetary Fund Staff Papers	0.8	Public Finance	7.2	Journal of Urban Economics	5.3
41	Industrial Relations	0.6	European Economic Review	6.5	Demography	5.1
42	Problems of Economics	0.5	Oxford Economic Papers	6.2	Journal of the Royal Statistical Society Ser. B. Meth	4.8
43	Economic History Review	0.2	Public Choice	5.3	Journal of Economic History	4.8
44	Business History Review	0.1	Public Finance Quarterly	4.7	Oxford Bulletin of Economics and Statistics	4.4
45	Industrial and Labor Relations Review	0.1	Journal of Regional Sciences	4.6	Journal of Financial Research	4.2
46	Indian Economic Journal	0.0	Applied Economics	4.1	Economica	4.1
47	Scottish Journal of Political Economy	0.0	Journal of Development Economics	3.7	Public Choice	3.9
48	S. African Journal of Economics	0.0	Industrial Relations	3.5	Journal of Risk and Insurance	3.8
49	Social and Economic Studies	0.0	Journal of the Royal Statistical Society Ser. A-Gen.	3.5	Journal of Accounting Research	3.7
50	Ger. Economic Review	0.0	Journal of Economic Education	3.2	European Economic Review	3.6
51			Journal of Environmental Economics and Management	3.2	Scandinavian Journal of Economics	3.6
52			British Journal of Industrial Relations	3.1	Econometric Theory	3.3
53			Weltwirtschaftliches Archiv	3.0	Journal of Comparative Economics	3.1
54			American Journal of Agricultural			

		Score			Score
	Economics	2.7		*Journal of Economic Behavior and Organization*	2.7
55	*Lloyd's Bank Review*	2.6		*Journal of Labor Research*	2.5
56	*Economic Letters*	2.5		*Explorations in Economic History*	2.4
57	*Journal of Consumer Research*	2.4		*Public Finance*	2.2
58	*Regional Science and Urban Economics*	2.2		*Cato Journal*	1.8
59	*Scottish Journal of Political Economy*	2.1		*Journal of Devel. Economics*	1.8
60	*Land Economics*	2.0		*American Journal of Agricultural Economics*	1.8
61	*Urban Studies*	1.9		*Southern Economic Journal*	1.7
62	*Journal of Economics and Business*	1.8		*Journal of Legal Studies*	1.6
63	*Oxford Bulletin of Economics and Statistics*	1.7		*Journal of Macroeconomics*	1.4
64	*Journal of Economic Issues*	1.5		*Industrial Relations*	1.1
65	*Inquiry*	1.5		*Kyklos*	1.1
66	*Quarterly Review of Economics and Business*	1.3		*Journal of Health Economics*	1.1
67	*Economic Records*	1.3		*Canadian Journal of Economics*	1.1
68	*Explorations in Economic History*	1.1		*Oxford Economic Papers*	1.0
69	*Journal of Economic History*	1.1		*Public Finance Quarterly*	1.0
70	*Economic Development and Cultural. Change*	1.1		*British Journal of Industrial Relations*	0.8

Source: Liebowitz and Palmer (1984), Laband and Piette (1994)

the citation receives a weight of zero. Then they have a new journal ranking. They iterate this procedure until the results converge. Third, they adjust the ranking by dividing the results by the total number of characters published by a journal in the last five-year period. This procedure makes the results independent of the journal style. The final results are shown in Table 3.1.[3]

We confine the journals to those maintaining a ranking above 25th on all of three occasions. The rankings of *Economica* and *Oxford Economic Papers* in 1970, 1980 and 1990 are as follows:

Economica	8	11	46
Oxford Economic Papers	14	42	68.

According to this criterion, we have to exclude *Economica* and *Oxford Economic Papers*.

3.1.3 *Quantitative analysis and reliability of the result*

In order for the quantitative analysis of the data to be meaningful, the amount of the data have to be enough for the result of analysis to be reliable.

When the journals are published

The oldest generation of Japanese economists who constantly contribute to the international economics journals consists of the economists Michio Hatanaka, Ken-ichi Inada, Takashi Negishi, Hukukane Nikaido, Miyohei Shinohara, and Hirofumi Uzawa, who are members of the honorary board of *Japanese Economic Review*, and several other economists including Shigeto Tsuru, Michio Morishima, Shin-ichi Ichimura. They have published papers since the 1950s. Therefore, the core journals that we take up already have to be publishing in 1950. *American Economic Review* was first published in 1911, *Econometrica* in 1933, *Economic Journal* in 1891, *Journal of Political Economy* in 1892, *Quarterly Journal of Economics* in 1891, *Review of Economic Studies* in 1933, *Review of Economics and Statistics* in 1920. Therefore, all of these journals satisfy the conditions.

Reliability

The amount of data has to be enough for the results of the quantitative analysis of the data to be reliable. In other words, Japanese economists have to contribute to the journal enough material for the quantitative analysis to be effective. However, the data of *Economic Journal* is too little for the results of the analysis to be reliable. It is because *Economic Journal* has confined its contributors to members of the Royal Economic Society that we have to exclude it from our analysis.

Thus, we analyze the data of the following journals, the abbreviations for which are indicated in parentheses: *American Economic Review* (AER), *Econometrica* (Em), *Journal of Political Economy* (JPE), *Quarterly Journal of Economics* (QJE), *Review* of *Economic Studies* (RES), *Review of Economics and Statistics* (RE&S). In these core journals, fortunately, Japanese economists have enough contributions to analyze their characteristics quantitatively.

3.2 Characteristics of economics journals

Each of the core journals has its own characteristics. AER is a journal published by the American Economic Association and Em by the Econometric Society. JPE is a journal published by the University of Chicago, QJE and RE&S by Harvard University. RES was originally published by a young group of British and American economists. Each of them is edited based on a proper editorial policy. For example, the style guides of AER indicate that 'it is the policy of the AER to publish papers only if the data used in the analyses are clearly and precisely documented and are readily available to any researcher for the purpose of replication. Details of the computations sufficient to permit replication must be provided'.

The scope of the Econometric Society confirms that:

> The Econometric Society is an international society for the advancement of economic theory in its relation to statistics and mathematics. The Society shall operate as a completely disinterested, scientific organization, without political, social, financial or nationalistic bias. Its main object shall be to promote studies that aim at the unification of the theoretical-quantitative and the empirical-quantitative approach to economic problems and that are penetrated by constructive and rigorous thinking similar to that which has come to dominate in the natural sciences.

In the first volume of JPE, Laurence Laughlin (1892: 19) states in his paper entitled 'The study of political economy in the United States', that:

> it has seemed that a distinct place exists for a journal of political economy which, while welcoming the discussion of theory, may be devoted largely to a study of practical problems of economics, finance and statistics. Inasmuch as existing scientific journals have a tendency largely towards discussions of theory, and as popular journals do not usually treat practical economic problems scientifically, the *Journal of Political Economy* may, therefore, find for itself in the scientific study of this latter class a free field.

RES states that: 'It is published by the Review of Economic Studies Ltd., whose object is to encourage research in theoretical and applied economics, especially by young economists, and publish the results in the Review of Economic Studies.'

The Prefatory Statement of RE&S states that 'The purpose of the Review is to promote the collection, criticism, and interpretation of economic statistics, with a view to making them more accurate and valuable than they are at present for business and scientific purposes'. These statements suggest that AER is a positive journal, Em features the mathematical and statistical research, JPE the theoretical and quantitative analysis of practical economic problems, QJE the research of actual phenomena, RES the theoretical and applied economics, RE&S promotes the collection, criticism, and interpretation of economic statistics. In this section, we confirm these features of the core economics journals by analyzing the distribution of key words in the economic fields quantitatively.

3.2.1 Database

We utilized the EconLit of AEA, where every paper published in the economics journals is characterized by a few key words according to the JEL Classification System. This system has two types of Numeric Classification System (NCS), which indicates every field by four digits and is used from 1969, and the Alphanumeric Classification System (ACS), which indicates every field by one letter and three digits and has been used since 1990. We use the data of key words according to NCS, because the data according to NCS is richer than the data according to ACS.

For every core journal that we selected, we make a distribution of key words of papers published in the journal. The number of key words for each journal is as follows: AER (5909), Em (3546), JPE (3914), QJE (2692), RES (2433), RE&S (4512).

JEL NCS is classified in detail; there are 150 items expressed by large letters and indicated by the three numbers of thousand digits, hundred digits, ten digits. Each of the 150 items is classified into more detail items expressed by the small letters and indicated by the number of unit digits. The number 0 of thousand digits indicates the field of economics in general, the number of hundred digits the fields of economic theory, history of economics, methodology of economics, economic history, economic system etc. Economic theory is classified into microeconomics and macroeconomics, which are indicated by the number of ten digits. Microeconomics is classified into consumer theory, producer theory etc., which are indicated by the number of unit digits. We have only to classify the fields into the fields indicated by the two numbers of thousand digits and hundred digits, because we characterize each journal by the characteristics of theoretical, statistical, practical, policy, institutional. As to the fields indicated by the numbers of the 200s, we classify them into the fields indicated by the number of ten digits, because the key words indicated by the numbers of the 200s are used frequently. In every journal, we count the key words of all the fields from the database EconLit, and make a distribution of the key words.

The more papers that are published in a journal, and the more key words that are indicated in a paper, the larger is the number of key words. We have only to know the percentage of the key words relative to the total number of words in order to characterize the economics journal by the distribution of key words over the NCS classification of fields. Therefore we have the distributions of individual key words per the total number of key words over the NCS classification of fields. The JEL NCS is indicated by Table 3.2. The distribution of the key words for every journal is shown by Table 3.3. The graph of Table 3.3 is given by Figure 3.1.

Table 3.2 JEL numeric classification system

Numeric	Classification
100	General economics
200	General economic theory
210	General equilibrium theory
220	Microeconomic theory
230	Macroeconomic theory
240	Welfare theory
250	Social choice and bureaucratic performance
260	Economics of uncertainty and information, game theory and bargaining theory (1975)
270	Economics of centrally planned economies (1978)
300	History of economic thought & economic methodology
400	Economic history
500	Economic systems
1100	Economic growth and development
1200	Economic studies of countries
1300	Economic fluctuations
2100	Econometric and statistical methods and models
2200	Economic and social statistical data and analysis
3100	Domestic monetary and fiscal theory and institutions .
3200	Fiscal theory and policy: public finance
4000	International economics
4100	International trade theory
4200	Trade relations; commercial policy; international economic integration
4300	International finance
4410	International investment and long-term capital movements
5100	Administration
5200	Business finance and investment
5300	Marketing and advertising
5400	Accounting
6100	Industrial organization and public policy
6200	Technological change; innovation; research and development
6300	Industry studies
6400	Economic capacity
7100	Agriculture
7200	Natural resources
7300	Economic geography
8100	Manpower training and allocation; labor force and supply
8200	Labor markets; public policy
8300	Trade unions; collective bargaining; labor-management relations
8400	Demographic economics
8500	Human capital
9100	Welfare, health, and education
9200	Consumer economics; levels and standards of living
9300	Urban economics
9400	Regional economics

Table 3.3 Distribution of key words (%)

NCS	AER	Em	JPE	QJE	RES	RE&S	Jpns
100	0.931	0.028	1.099	0.297	0.041	0.355	0.154
200	23.879	41.568	20.567	28.120	45.458	6.782	30.615
200	0.474	0.338	0.204	0.074	0.000	0.022	0.154
210	0.575	7.417	0.460	0.929	5.425	0.199	4.462
220	10.509	13.790	8.406	11.850	16.728	2.903	13.846
230	3.571	1.974	4.037	4.569	4.316	2.105	2.154
240	4.282	4.738	3.526	4.903	6.371	0.598	4.923
250	1.591	4.117	1.916	2.043	3.535	0.554	1.538
260	2.759	9.109	1.942	3.380	8.919	0.377	3.538
270	0.118	0.085	0.077	0.371	0.164	0.022	0.000
300	0.778	0.254	2.095	1.672	0.164	0.133	0.615
400	1.252	0.000	2.018	1.263	0.041	0.887	0.769
500	0.558	0.113	0.562	0.892	0.247	0.199	0.462
1100	2.318	2.707	2.453	4.235	6.042	0.997	6.615
1200	1.303	0.226	0.818	1.152	0.206	2.061	2.154
1300	5.720	2.030	4.829	4.421	3.411	4.167	3.538
2100	1.574	28.624	1.048	0.817	7.111	7.447	10.154
2200	2.217	2.115	1.712	2.340	1.028	4.344	1.385
3100	8.648	3.976	9.607	6.798	6.494	7.624	3.692
3200	7.125	2.171	7.077	6.092	4.069	4.167	4.462
4000	0.034	0.000	0.026	0.000	0.000	0.000	0.000
4100	3.266	0.705	2.734	3.380	2.178	1.130	5.385
4200	1.929	0.310	1.482	1.597	0.822	4.078	2.000
4300	2.149	0.367	2.529	2.563	1.521	2.371	2.923
4400	0.694	0.028	0.460	0.929	0.288	0.975	1.077
5000	0.000	0.000	0.000	0.000	0.000	0.000	0.000
5100	1.100	1.184	1.124	1.337	1.110	0.709	1.077
5200	1.794	1.043	1.252	2.415	1.850	2.593	1.538
5300	0.406	0.056	0.409	0.111	0.164	0.554	0.154
5400	0.237	0.056	0.102	0.000	0.000	0.089	0.000
6000	0.000	0.000	0.000	0.000	0.000	0.000	0.000
6100	4.992	1.100	3.960	4.086	1.767	6.161	2.769
6200	1.218	0.564	1.201	1.932	1.274	1.285	2.154
6300	2.335	1.128	2.913	2.563	1.315	7.624	2.923
6400	0.152	0.028	0.102	0.149	0.123	0.244	0.000
7100	1.202	0.254	1.763	0.892	0.452	1.795	1.231
7200	1.675	0.818	1.354	1.746	1.767	2.194	0.308
7300	0.034	0.028	0.051	0.260	0.164	0.111	0.154
8000	0.000	0.000	0.000	0.000	0.000	0.000	0.000
8100	0.914	0.310	1.099	0.594	0.822	1.662	0.462
8200	8.496	3.412	9.172	8.432	5.960	11.059	4.308
8300	0.795	0.254	0.818	1.597	0.452	0.997	0.462
8400	1.049	0.536	2.402	1.040	0.617	1.308	0.462
8500	1.286	0.254	2.708	0.632	0.288	1.463	0.923
9100	4.248	0.818	4.088	2.229	0.699	4.920	0.615
9200	1.963	1.748	2.529	1.412	1.397	4.233	2.308
9300	1.066	0.705	1.329	0.892	0.288	1.928	0.769
9400	0.660	0.479	0.511	1.114	0.370	1.352	1.385
Amount	100.000	100.000	100.000	100.000	100.000	100.000	100.000

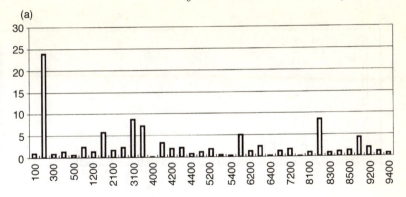

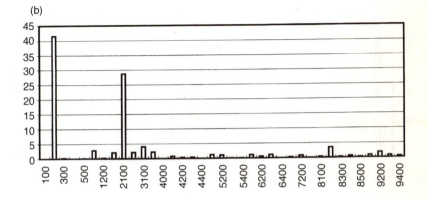

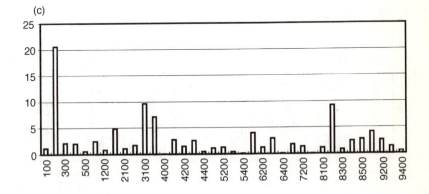

Figure 3.1 Distribution of key words: (a) AER; (b) Em; (c) JPE; (d) QJE; (e) RES; (f) RE & S; (g) Japanese.

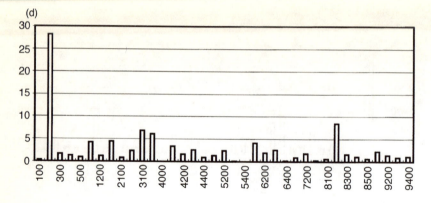

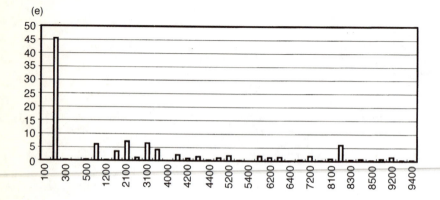

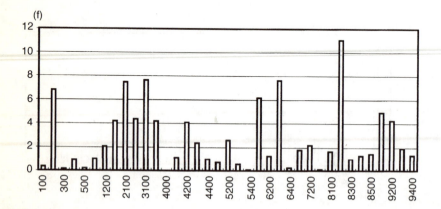

Figure 3.1 Continued.

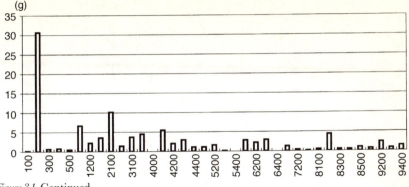

Figure 3.1 Continued.

3.2.2 *Characterizing economics journals*

Every field classified according to JEL NCS has respective characteristics. For example, the fields of the 200s are economic theory, namely theoretical research, the fields of the 2000s are econometrics, namely statistical research. The characteristics of some classifications are clearly policy, institutional, and practical. The classifications into the number of ten digits and one digit are too detailed to characterize the journals. We classify them based on the classification by the numbers of hundred digits. We have compiled Table 3.4 by observing the distribution of key words over the classification of the economics fields.

Pure theory is indicated by the key words of the 200s, the distribution of the core journals other than RE&S is from 20 percent through 45 percent, this respects the academic level of the core journals and has characteristics common to high-level journals. Looking at them in detail, Em and RES have a high percentage distribution on General Equilibrium Theory, Economics of Information, Game Theory, etc. and Mathematical Analysis in Econometrics has a large percentage. In particular, Em has more than 70 percent distribution in mathematically and statistically rigorous research, which exactly reflects Em's own editorial policy.

Table 3.4 Characteristics of economics journals

	AER	Em	JPE	QJE	RES	RE&S
Mathematical analysis		●		▲	●	
Pure theory	●	●	●	●	●	
Econometric & statistical theory		●			▲	▲
Positive analysis	●		●	●		●
Applied theory & policy	●		●	●	▲	●
Policy & institution	▲		▲	▲		▲

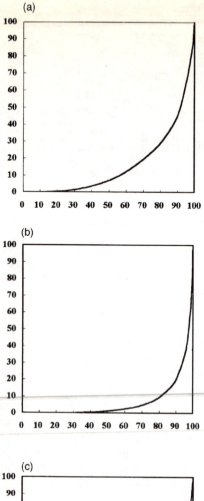

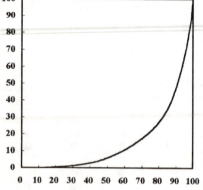

Figure 3.2 Lorenz curves: (a) AER; (b) Em; (c) JPE; (d) QJE; (e) RES; (f) RE & S.

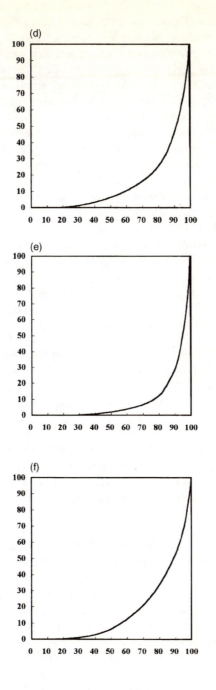

Economic Fluctuation in the 1300s, Economic and Social Statistical Data and Analysis in the 2200s, Technological Changes in the 6200s, Industrial Studies in the 6300s, Agriculture and Natural Resources in the 7000s, Labor Policy in the 8200s, Welfare, Education, Social Security in 9000s, are practical researches, which are not theoretical but statistical. In AER, JPE, QJE, and RE&S, there are many papers in these fields, which is quite different from Em.

The fields where pure theories are applied to make economic policies, are those of Fiscal and Monetary Theory in the 3000s, International Economics in the 4000s, Industrial Organization in the 6100s, Labor Markets and Public Policy in the 8200s and Public Economics in 9000s. In AER, JPE, QJE, and RE&S, there are many papers in these fields, which reflect the editorial policy of these journals that treat practical problems scientifically.

Institutional researches of economic policy consist of Economic History in the 400s, Economic System in 500s, Economic Development in the 1200s, Industrial Studies in the 6300s, Problems on Labor in the 8000s. In AER, JPE, QJE, and RE&S, there is a relatively large percentage in these fields of institutional approach to economic policy. This suggests that these journals are open to the institutional analysis of economic policies.

The six core journals are considered to be essentially general and comprehensive, but Em and RES has a clear bias with respect to mathematical, theoretical and statistical researches. By lining up fields in increasing order and accumulating the distribution, the graph is presented by Figure 3.2. It is called a Lorenz curve and the straight line means no bias and the sharply curved line means a strong bias in the distribution of key words in the field of economics. Em and RES curves sharply, and therefore they have a strong bias to theoretical, mathematical and statistical researches. Gini coefficients of core journals are as follows:[4] AER (0.5960), Em (0.5614), JPE (0.5904), QJE (0.5899), RES (0.5656), RE&S (0.5918).

These data suggest that AER, JPE, QJE, and RE&S are more general and comprehensive journals than Em and RES. Those journals are also open to the fields around economics such as History of Economic Thought, Methodology of Economics, Economic History, and Economic System respectively in the 300s, 400s, and 500s.

We can conclude that the characteristics of the core economics journals are subject to the editorial administration of their own. Em features the rigorous analysis on the mathematical and statistical method. RES features the theoretical research including the pure theory, the theory of econometrics, and the applied theory. RE&S promotes the researches based on the statistical method, and prefers the practical analysis to the theoretical analysis. AER is the most comprehensive journal in the core journals, and very positive. JPE and QJE reflect the academic characteristics of the Universities that publish those journals. JPE treats the practical problem scientifically, and QJE promotes the theoretical research.

3.3 Contributions to the core economics journals

The contributions made by different economists, belong to different institutions, different generations, different specialties. Therefore, we cannot know *a priori* if a certain set of characteristics is found in the data. We assume a representative Japanese economist who has a certain set of characteristics, and the data reflects the set of characteristics. In this section, we confirm the validity of our hypothesis such that the Japanese economist contributes to the theoretical, mathematical, statistical researches, but not to the practical, policymaking, institutional researches in the core economics journals. In order to confirm our hypothesis, we need information on how many pages the Japanese economist has published in every core journal and for every year. The results are summarized in Table 3.5.

3.3.1 Data

We used Heck's Economic Literature Database from 1951 through 1968 and EconLit from 1969 through 1995. Based on these databases, we proceed to process the database.

First, we import the data of author(s), title, institution of author, journal name, year, volume, number, page, key words, abstract from the above databases and saved them.[5]

Second, we chose the data of Japanese authors, and process the data to have the data of the number of pages of the papers that Japanese economists write, for every year. When the authors are plural and include those who are not Japanese, we divide the number of pages of the paper by the number of authors per Japanese author. This indicates the number of pages for which Japanese economists are responsible. The data may vary depending on the total number of pages and the style of the journal. The larger the number of pages of the journal, the larger may be the number of pages of Japanese economists' papers. The number of pages of the journal is gradually increasing every year because of publishing pressure.

Third, when the style of the journal changes, the number of pages of a paper may change. Then we identify Japanese economists' contributions with the number of the pages of Japanese economists' papers divided by the number of journals for every year.

Thus, we have data on the number of pages of Japanese economists' papers divided by the number of pages of the journal, for every journal, for every year from 1951 to 1995. This data is shown by Table 3.5 and Figure 3.3. The Japanese economist contribution is concentrated on Em and RES. Since the common characteristics of those journals are mathematical and theoretical research, we may expect that the Japanese economist contributes to the mathematical and theoretical research.

3.3.2 Principal component analysis of the data

We examine if the Japanese economists' contributions to international economics journals are theoretical, practical, mathematical, statistical, policy

Table 3.5 Contribution of Japanese economists

Year	AER	Em	JPE	QJE	RES	RE&S
1951	0	10	0	0	5	0
1952	0	27	0	0	0	0
1953	0	0	0	0	0	0
1954	0	4	0	0	4	0
1955	0	4	0	22	0	3.333
1956	0	11	0	0	7	0
1957	17	14	0	0	9	0
1958	0	43	0	0	0	0
1959	0	57	15	0	0	0
1960	0	22	0	12	30	17
1961	12	41	0	0	33	1
1962	4	85	0	5	20	13
1963	24.5	16	0	14	41	6
1964	28.9	79	0	9	100	15
1965	0	25	2	0	56	18.5
1966	19	46	0	38	24	0
1967	10	14.5	0	25	50	6
1968	11	45	5	40.667	24.5	18.5
1969	25	40.5	56.5	16.5	79.5	0
1970	21	15	16.5	27	52	8
1971	0	130	33.5	6	8	15
1972	20	45	33.5	0	18	13
1973	22	71	18	0	23	13
1974	47.5	146	32.5	80	66	13
1975	14	11.667	54	10	18	1.5
1976	19	48.5	44	1	51	36
1977	16	96	8.5	14	56	32
1978	21	48	19	46	22	28.167
1979	27.833	64	19	6	8	10
1980	29.333	124	0	15	64.5	19
1981	8	47.5	0	25	42.5	9
1982	41.333	68.667	22	11	12	7
1983	10.333	77	0	27	16	15
1984	21.833	25	23	15	17	0
1985	10.5	24	0	60.667	20	14
1986	14	33	43	0	21.5	13.5
1987	13	20	39	0	11	3
1988	2	17	0	19	25	20
1989	2	20	14	0	0	10
1990	42	30	11	11	15.333	10
1991	5	82	0	43.333	10	15
1992	46	10	20	0	77.833	0
1993	7.5	22.833	27	4	25	15
1994	2	0	0	0	0	27
1995	20	25.5	14	0	0	0
Amount	634.567	1885.667	570	603.167	1162.667	445.5

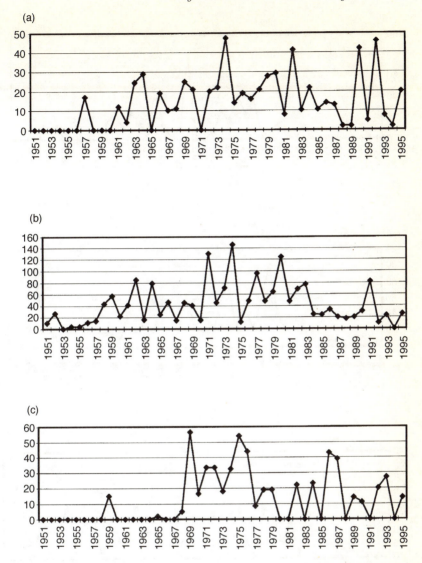

Figure 3.3 Contribution of Japanese economists: (a) AER; (b) Em; (c) JPE; (d) QJE; (e) RES; (f) RE & S.

making, or institutional by analyzing the data by principal component analysis.[6] It is one of the multivariate analyses and is useful, for example, in assessing a student's ability and inclination (based on the results of examinations in literature, history, mathematics, science and so on). Every economics journal has respective characteristics of theoretical, practical, mathematical, statistical, policy making, institutional, and so on, as we have shown in Section 3.2. The quantity of the Japanese economists' contribution

(d)

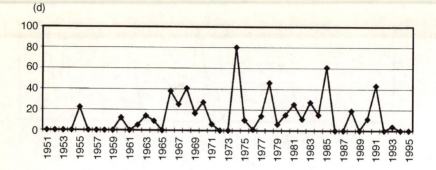

(e)

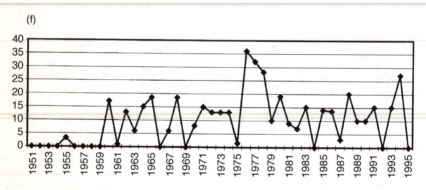

(f)

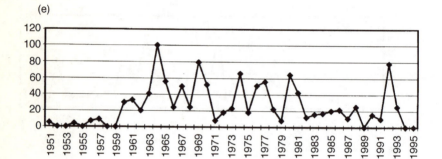

Figure 3.3 Continued.

should be larger in the journals whose characteristics are closer to those of the Japanese economist.

Table 3.5 shows the number of pages of Japanese economists' papers published in each journal every year, but this data may not be appropriate to be analyzed by principal component analysis because an ordinal researcher needs at least two or three years to complete a paper which will be published in the core economics journals. Therefore, it is better to aggregate the number of pages for every two years, for every three years, and so on. Of course, it makes no sense to aggregate the number of pages for too many years.

We have analyzed the data for every year, for every 2 years (omitting the data of 1995), for every 3 years, for every 4 years (omitting the data of 1995), and for every 5 years. The results of the first three analyses are quite different, but the results of the last two are similar to each other. We show the results of principal component analysis of the data for every 4 years in Table 3.6 and that of the data for every 5 years in Table 3.7. The tables consist of the correlation matrices, the eigenvalues of the correlation matrices, and the eigenvalue vectors.

3.3.3 *Interpretation of results*

We have to decide which principal components we should accept. We based our decision on criteria such that the cumulative proportion is close to one, and the

Table 3.6 Results of principal component analysis (every four years)
(a) correlation matrix

	AER	Em	JPE	QJE	RES	RE&S
AER	1	0.4025	0.5935	0.7335	0.273	0.6589
Em	0.4025	1	0.2164	0.4398	0.5154	0.3293
JPE	0.5935	0.2164	1	0.682	−0.0407	0.7653
QJE	0.7335	0.4398	0.682	1	0.4411	0.5449
RES	0.273	0.5154	−0.0407	0.4411	1	0.346
RE&S	0.6589	0.3293	0.7653	0.5449	0.346	1

(b) eigenvalue of correlation matrix

	Eigenvalue	Distribution	Proportion	Cumulative
PRIN1	3.38761	2.11932	0.564601	0.5646
PRIN2	1.26829	0.75164	0.211382	0.77598
PRIN3	0.51665	0.05419	0.086109	0.86209
PRIN4	0.46246	0.12828	0.077076	0.93917
PRIN5	0.33418	0.30336	0.055696	0.99486
PRIN6	0.03082		0.005136	1

(c) eigenvector

	PRIN1	PRIN2	PRIN3	PRIN4	PRIN5	PRIN6
AER	0.461448	−0.11235	−0.09155	−0.3885	−0.74764	0.236989
Em	0.324273	0.501927	−0.71995	0.348932	0.015419	−0.05093
JPE	0.420884	−0.49062	−0.08875	0.199013	0.428714	0.592342
QJE	0.475162	−0.00178	−0.02868	−0.58726	0.452169	−0.47335
RES	0.269232	0.677454	0.561705	−0.01693	0.122081	0.371305
RE&S	0.454428	−0.18918	0.386105	0.585274	−0.19401	−0.47796

Table 3.7 Results of principal component analysis (every five years)
(a) correlation matric

	AER	Em	JPE	QJE	RES	RE&S
AER	1	0.4718	0.6855	0.6433	0.2789	0.8158
Em	0.4718	1	0.3051	0.3358	0.6703	0.4435
JPE	0.6855	0.3051	1	0.5024	−0.2025	0.4047
QJE	0.6433	0.3358	0.5024	1	0.1558	0.2361
RES	0.2789	0.6703	−0.2025	0.1558	1	0.3386
RE&S	0.8158	0.4435	0.4047	0.2361	0.3386	1

(b) eigenvalue of correlation matrix

	Eigenvalue	Distribution	Proportion	Cumulative
PRIN1	3.1301	1.68604	0.521684	0.52168
PRIN2	1.44406	0.69173	0.240677	0.76236
PRIN3	0.75233	0.26897	0.125389	0.88775
PRIN4	0.48336	0.33313	0.08056	0.96831
PRIN5	0.15023	0.11033	0.025039	0.99335
PRIN6	0.03991		0.006651	1

(c) eigenvector

	PRIN1	PRIN2	PRIN3	PRIN4	PRIN5	PRIN6
AER	0.53094	−0.16297	−0.16738	−0.25326	0.172411	−0.75476
Em	0.406054	0.406369	0.19937	0.609408	−0.48262	−0.16105
JPE	0.378642	−0.51057	0.012156	0.534587	0.46812	0.301464
QJE	0.381817	−0.23408	0.688951	−0.44568	−0.24105	0.260831
RES	0.259699	0.700199	0.132332	−0.15473	0.603328	0.191886
RE&S	0.443424	0.050472	−0.66327	−0.23692	−0.31001	0.456802

eigenvalue of the principal component is more than one. The former requires that the accepted principal components have to explain what the original variables explain. The latter requires that every principal component accepted has to have more information than that of each original variable. Then, we accept the first principal component (PC1) and the second (PC2) based on the criteria.[7]

The results of Table 3.6 and Table 3.7 show that the correlation of AER, JEP, QJE and RE&S is high in PC1, and the correlation of Em and RES is high in PC2. We can interpret these facts as follows. PC1 reflects the fact that these four journals have the same characteristic of general interest and is comprehensive, and indicates the general ability of the Japanese economist to research. PC2 is more important in characterizing the Japanese economists' ability and means that the Japanese economists are able to do the theoretical research based on the mathematical and statistical analysis.

We can consider the results of principal component analysis to suggest that Japanese economists contribute to the research in a normal science, for example, puzzle solving in the field where the problem is already formulated. Table 3.3 and

Figure 3.1 show the distribution of key words in the papers of Japanese economists published in the core journals. The characteristics that we can read from the distribution are consistent with our results.

3.3.4 *Problems of the analysis*

The results of this section may not be clear, but we consider them to be enough to confirm the ability of the Japanese economist to research. Of course, the results have some problems because of our supposition and the limitation of the data. First, we suppose a representative Japanese economist, but the characteristics of Japanese economists' contributions may be a matter of individual ability to research, of generation, or of institution. If the characteristics of Japanese economists vary according to their individual ability, generation, institution, then it is impossible to find any stable characteristics.

Second, our analysis is confined to the core journals. As we can see from Figure 3.3, the number of pages of papers published in the core journals from 1970, especially from 1980, is decreasing. This reflects the fact that the journals in the applied fields and the contributions to them are sharply increased. Those journals include *Journal of Financial Economics, Journal of Industrial Economics, Journal of International Economics, Journal of Mathematical Economics, Journal of Monetary Economics, Journal of Money, Credit, and Banking, Journal of Public Economics, Journal of Urban Economics*, and are highly evaluated as is clear by Table 3.1.

3.4 Contributions to the applied fields

In order to investigate to which research field and how much Japanese economists contribute, we must classify all of the economics journals into a certain classification, for example, JEL alphanumeric classification (ANC) system and how many Japanese economists write papers to journals classified into the JEL ANC. Of course, it is impossible to take up all of the economics journals. We have to take up the entire field A to R of JEL alphabetical classification because of the purpose of our research. There are several journals which have a relatively long history, like the *Journal of Business* and *Journal of Finance*, but the journals in applied economics have been published since the 1970s. All journals in the field of applied economics are published after 1970s. Then, we will select journals within ranking of 1970, 1980 and 1990. However, we cannot take up journals where the history of the journals is too short to provide enough data for us to analyze or the prestige of the journals is too low to be considered valuable.

We research journals based on the following criteria.

1.   The journal has been published since 1975, and therefore it has had two opportunities to be ranked in the economics journal ranking of Laband and Piette (1994).
2.   At each opportunity, the journal is ranked according to the 'top-50' economics journal ranking of Laband and Piette (1994). We have to take up

relatively low-ranking journals to complete the list of JEL ANC in the fields of applied economics.

The economics journals that we research are as follows (for letters see Table 3.9): C: *Journal of Econometrics, Journal of Mathematical Economics, Journal of the American Statistical Association*, E: *Journal of Monetary Economics, Journal of Money, Credit, and Banking*, F: *Journal of International Economics*, G: *Journal of Finance, Journal of Financial and Quantitative Analysis, Journal of Financial Economics*, H: *Journal of Public Economics, Public Choice, Public Finance*, I: *Journal of Economic Education*, J: *Industrial and Labor Relations Review, Industrial Relations, Journal of Human Resources*, K: *Journal of Law and Economics*, L: *Journal of Industrial Economics*, M: *Journal of Accounting Research, Journal of Business*, N: *Explorations in Economic History, Journal of Economic History*, O: *Journal of Development Economics*, Q: *American Journal of Agricultural Economics, Journal of Environmental Economics and Management*, R: *Journal of Regional Sciences, Journal of Urban Economics*.

We used the database of EconLit from 1969 through 1992. Based on the database, we chose the data of Japanese authors, and sum up the pages of the papers for every year, for every field of economics. This data is shown in Table 3.9. It is too little for us to analyze quantitatively, but it suggests that the fields of economics where Japanese economists contribute are those where theoretical, mathematical, and statistical analysis are directly applied. Japanese economists contribute, for example, to mathematical economics, econometrics, theory of industrial organization, international economics, public economics, urban economics. Thus, Japanese economists' contribution has a strong relationship with the development of modern economic theory as a normal science.

Table 3.8 JEL alphanumeric classification system

A	General Economics and Teaching
B	Methodology and History of Economic Thought
C	Mathematical and Quantitative Methods
D	Microeconomics
E	Macroeconomics and Monetary Economics
F	International Economics
G	Financial Economics
H	Public Economics
I	Health Education and Welfare
J	Labor and Demographic Economics
K	Law and Economics
L	Industrial Organization
M	Business Administration and Business Economics; Marketing; Accounting
N	Economic History
O	Economic Development, Technological Change and Growth
P	Economic Systems
Q	Agricultural and Natural Resource Economics
R	Urban Rural and Regional Economics
Z	Other Special Topics

Table 3.9 Contributions to applied economics

JEL	C	E	F	G	H	I	J	K	L	M	N	O	Q	R
1969	23	19	0	0	0	0	0	0	12	0	22	0	23	0
1970	0	0	0	0	0	0	0	0	0	0	0	0	6	50
1971	26.33	0	33	1	0	0	3.5	0	0	29.5	118	0	0	32
1972	5	0	60	15.5	19	0	0	0	0	5	0	0	34	0
1973	25	0	28	4	10	0	8.5	0	0	0	49	0	8	23
1974	55.5	0	20	0	14	0	0	0	10	0	23	12	8	18
1975	17	5	24	39	9	0	0	0	0	24	0	14.5	17	0
1976	54	13.5	39	0	6	0	0	0	0	0	0	9	0	0
1977	23.5	23.5	33.5	0	17	0	0	0	0	0	47	0	7.67	42
1978	109	3.5	45	0	7.5	0	0	0	0	0	111	0	8	10.5
1979	20.5	0	58.5	0	19	0	0	0	13	0	9.5	0	7.5	7
1980	79	5	36	0	0	0	0	0	8	9	0	0	3	72.67
1981	74	0	55	0	33	0	0	0	8	0	20	31	3	18.33
1982	83	9	13.67	0	20.5	0	0	0	0	9	0	12	20	49.67
1983	68	0	53	0	30.67	0	0	0	21	0	0	0	0	72.5
1984	178	0	68	0	18	0	0	0	0	0	16	15	3	62.5
1985	84.5	12	15	57	33	4	0	0	5	0	0	13.33	16	97
1986	36.67	17	65	0	71	0	0	0	0	13.5	0	7	0	72.5
1987	54.5	50.5	31	0	84	0	20.67	22	15	0	8	12	10	32
1988	74.5	14	22	0	18	0	0	0	11	0	0	1.33	11	17
1989	26.5	15	18	19	33	0	8	0	21	0	34	28	34.17	110
1990	141	8	28	15	95	0	0	0	0	31	0	1.33	7.5	150.5
1991	51	0	6	17.67	39	0	62	0	6	16	23	29.5	8.17	70.5
1992	88.5	0	51.67	13.5	58	0	4.5	0	0	8	0	0	12.5	0
Amount	1398	195	803.33	181.67	634.67	4	100.67	22	122	145	480.5	186	239.5	1007.67

In the theoretical fields, the contributions to the applied topics of game theory are increasing, as game theory develops. It is sure that contributions to mathematical and statistical fields are many more than those to practical and institutional fields.

3.5 Concluding remarks

The results of the quantitative analysis are summarized as follows. Japanese economists contribute to international journals in the fields of theoretical, mathematical, and statistical analysis, but not in the fields of practical, institutional, and policy-making analysis. The former fields are abstract and formalized, and the latter concrete and difficult to be formalized. It should be natural that the abstract and formalized fields are easier to be internationalized than the practical fields. In this sense, Japanese economics is supposed to be internationalized.

Coats (1996) characterizes internationalization and Americanization of economics by the formalization and institutionalization of economics, both of which promote mutual understanding among people based on different backgrounds. The formalization is necessary for economics to be internationalized, because we cannot understand different economics without any formal consistency. However, even if every economic theory is completely formalized, there might remain respective parts for every theory not to be acceptable by one another. Both Euclidean geometry and non-Euclidean geometry are consistent in themselves but they are incompatible with each other. Since every local economy has its own social background rooted in its climate, culture, history, nation, religion, and so on, there have to remain some differences based on the practical and institutional background between economic theories, if they reflect their social background exactly. Such a theory is not useful for the other local economies, and therefore any practical and institutional economic theory is supposed not to be internationalized.

Institutionalization is necessary for economics to be standardized and constantly reproduced in respective local economies. As we have pointed out in the introduction, we cannot consider Japanese economics to be institutionalized in fields other than economic theory and econometrics. Institutionalization in the fields of economic theory and econometrics has been imported from the USA and advanced by the economists who have taken their Ph.D. at universities in the USA, and therefore it is Americanized (Sawa 1979, 1982). In the majority of other fields, even the refereeing process has not been established. In this sense, we consider Japanese economics to be far from being internationalized (Ikeo 1996).

In our research, quantitative analysis may not be enough to persuade readers, but we have to underline that quantitative analysis of the well-organized database should be more fruitful. Until the beginning of the twentieth century, economics was developed by several groups of economists, some of which were called schools, and they communicated with one another by correspondence. Therefore, in order to develop the history of economics until the beginning of the twentieth century, it is very successful to investigate their correspondence, as is shown by research into the formative process of the theories of Walras and Keynes.

The economics of the twentieth century feature the academic journals. As economics is institutionally organized, economics has come to be developed in the journals involving worldwide economists, and communication is open to all. In such an environment, we should accumulate data to make a database and utilize that to verify the fact. If we could organize the accumulation of database appropriately and develop the procedure to analyze the data quantitatively, we would have fruitful results.

Notes

1   In Korea since the Korean war, Marxian economists have gone to North Korea, and there remain only non-Marxian economists in South Korea. This is supposed to assist the Korean Economic Association to be Americanized. See Choi (1996).
2   Gans and Shepherd (1994) point out that classical papers were often rejected by the refereeing process. However, as Sato (1989: 174–7) states, the quality papers would eventually come to be accepted by some other core journal. In this sense, the refereeing process is significant if a journal does not restrict or discriminate applicants.
3   Liebowitz and Palmer (1984) state that this is probably the ranking closest to 'journal quality', and it might be instructive to compare the ranking with the survey of Hawkins, Ritter and Walter (1973). As Hodgeson and Rothman (1995) suggest, the procedure has a bias to ranking American journals in the higher orders. See Diamond (1989) and Burton and Phimister (1995) about the alternative procedures of journal ranking.
4   The closer to 1 is the Gini coefficient, the smaller is the bias of the distribution of key words.
5   We imported the data by Silver Platter SPIRS accompanied with EconLit and saved it. Then we imported, edited and saved it as a text file by EndNote. Moreover, we imported the data by excel and processed it. We are thankful to Asahi Noguchi for his instruction in processing the data.
6   We do not have any concrete model of how the Japanese economist contributes to international economics journals. We are going to support our expectation such that the Japanese economists' contributions are concentrated into the theoretical, mathematical and statistical researches. This is the reason why we analyze the data not by the factor analysis but by the principal component analysis. We referred to Okuno (1981) for the method of multivariate analysis including the principal component analysis. We used SAS to process the data (Takeuchi 1987).
7   There are more rigorous theories that explain how to select principal components, but we do not need rigorous argument here. We are thankful to Katsuya Yamamoto for his comment on the statistical analysis.

References

Burton M. P. and E. Phimister (1995) 'The core journals: a reappraisal of the Diamond List', *Economic Journal*, 105, March: 361–73.

Choi, Y. B. (1996) 'The Americanization of Economics in Korea', in Coats (1996: 97–122).

Coats, A. W. (ed.) (1996) *The Post-1945 Internationalization of Economics*, Annual Supplement to Volume 28, *History of Political Economy*, Duke University Press.

Diamond, A. M. (1989) 'The core journals of economics', *Current Contents* 21, January: 3–11.

Gans, J. S. and G. B. Shepherd (1994) 'How are the mighty fallen: rejected classic articles by leading economists', *Journal of Economic Perspectives* 8, 1: 165–79.

Hawkins, R. G., L. S. Ritter, and I. Walter (1973) 'What economists think of their journals', *Journal of Political Economy* 81, July/August: 1017–32.

Hodgeson G. and H. Rothman (1995) 'Institutions and power in economics: a preliminary paper', Paper read at the 1995 Conference of European Association for Evolutionary Political Economy, Cracow: Poland.

Hong, K. (1996) 'The growth and change of economic research in South Korea', *Research in the History of Economic Thought and Methodology* 14: 193–215.

Ikeo, A. (1996) 'The internationalization of economics in Japan'. In Coats (1996: 123–41).

Kyklos (ed.) (1995) 'Special Issue: Is There a European Economics?', *Kyklos*. 48, Fasc.2: 185–311.

Laband, D. N. and M. J. Piette (1994) 'The relative impacts of economics journals: 1970–1990', *Journal of Economic Literature* 32, June: 640–66.

Laughlin, J. Laurence (1892) 'The study of political economy in the United States', *Journal of Political Economy* 1, December: 1–19.

Liebowitz, S. J., and J. P. Palmer (1984) 'Assessing the relative impacts of economics journals', *Journal of Economic Literature* 22, March: 77–88.

Okuno, T., T. Haga, H. Kume, and T. Yoshizawa (1981) *Tahenryo Kaiseki-ho* (Methodology of Multivariate Analysis), revised version, Nikkagiren Shuppansha.

Sato, K. (1989) *Amerika no Shakai to Daigaku* (Society and Universities in the U.S.A.), Nihon Hyoron-sha.

Sawa, T. (1979) *Keizaigaku no Sekai: Amerika to Nihon* (The World of Economics: U.S.A. and Japan), Tokyo: Toyo Keizai Shinpo-sha.

Sawa, T. (1982) *Keizaigaku toha Nandarouka* (What is Economics?), Tokyo: Iwanami Shoten.

Takeuchi, K. (ed.) (1987) *SAS niyoru Deta-kaiseki Nyumon* (Introduction to the Data Analysis by SAS), Tokyo: Tokyo Daigaku Shuppankai.

4   Marxian economics

Michio Akama

Introduction

Japan is said to be a unique case in capitalist countries where Marxian economics was acknowledged as an important edifice of economic thought in the academy and as a basis for practical studies and political analysis. Marxian scholars were engaged in the studies of various fields in social sciences and used to receive much more attention than the present. Marxian economists gave impetus to the formation of economic policies in the period just after *the* war (WWII), when democratic reforms of Japan's economic system were desperately needed. They also exerted some influence on the actualization of these policies. In the latter half of the 1950s, they pointed out the pending problem of so-called double structure in Japan's economy. These are the reasons why a whole chapter is given to Marxian economics in a book on Japanese economics since 1945.

Borrowing the words from geneticist Hitoshi Kihara,[1] it can be said that 'the history of Marxian economics in Japan exists in its interpretation'. Yet many Japanese Marxian economists are always keen on political and economic problems of their time, and pay attention to the international tension between existing economic-social systems. They try to analyze contemporary problems basically and theoretically, and to interpret these problems in various ways by relating them to current economic-social systems in order to get a deep understanding of the problems and their causes.

As there are enormous numbers of research results produced by Japanese Marxian economists, an entire analysis of them is not easy for a single scholar. Moreover, ten Japanese Marxian scholars could write ten stories of Japanese Marxian economics. It might be interesting to summarize the analysis of the history of Marxian arguments by surveying the passionate controversies from time to time. However, this chapter focuses mainly on the 'series of publications', namely academic achievements, and aims to sketch the past, the present and the future of Japanese Marxian economics (in a capitalist country).

4.1 Academic freedom and Marxian economics: 'The season of politics' and 'confronting economics'

4.1.1 Tradition, regeneration and innovation

Considering the developments of Marxian economics after the war, the introduction and the publication of past achievements has an important meaning. Kawakami's *Shihonron Nyumon* (Introduction to *Das Kapital*, 1951–52) was a comprehensive survey of *Das Kapital* studies. Kushida's *Kushida Tamizo Zenshu* (Collected Works of Tamizo Kushida, 1947) and *Marx Kyokoron Kenkyu* (Study of Marxian Economic Crisis, 1949), and Uno's *Shihonron no Kenkyu* (Study of *Das Kapital*, 1949) were revisions of the monographs published before the war. Yamada's *Saiseisan Katei Hyoshiki Bunseki Joron* (Introductory Analysis of Process of Reproduction, 1948) and Uno's *Keizai Seisakuron* (Theory of Economic Policy, 1951) tried to develop new approaches to economics. Their achievements should be appreciated as monumental works. The flourishing study of Marxian economics after 1945 was not just a temporary phenomenon. The basis for these studies had been cultivated prior to and during the war, when Marxians, socialists and even liberals had a hard time retaining their ideology.

We must not forget other studies that tried to light up the realities of Japan by way of deepening the classic literature of economics, though standing somewhat apart from the study of Marxian economics. Takashima's *Adam Smith no Shimin Shakai Taikei* (Adam Smith's Civil Society, 1946) applied Smith's concept of civil society to a society in the Far East, far away from Europe. He recognized the question of whether the formation of a civil society could be analyzed scientifically or not. This is a type of academic study before the war. Sugimoto's *Kindai Keizaigaku no Kihon Seikaku* (Fundamental Character of Modern Economics, 1949) created his system of economics, including methodology and historical analysis of economic thought, by following the Marxian method of critical study, and emphasized the importance of 'hard work' on so-called modern economics (non-Marxian, neoclassical, or Keynesian economics). When we think of the fact that not only Marxian economics established its own place in the academy but also modern economics has come to exercise some influence, Sugimoto's struggle gave an important hint to Japanese Marxian economists.

Most Japanese remember 15 August 1945, when the Japanese Emperor announced the loss of the war on the radio, as the day when the old regime began to shake. Before the war, Japanese society had a hierarchical order with the Emperor at the apex. The Allied Forces, whose power formally became effective on 2 September 1945, later changed the old Japanese economic and political system drastically. In Japan, the development of Marxian economics had started in the 1920s, but Marxian economics was formally forbidden and illegal from around 1930 till 1945. It is true that the day of 15 August 1945 may symbolize liberation from the oppression of Marxians. Yet it was not a complete break. 'Japanese Marxian economics did not start completely new from the ruins in the defeated country', but 'could make advances based on the traditions and heritages shaped before and during the war' (Miyazaki 1984: 214, 215).

Of course there are new elements that came after the war. After 15 August 1945 the radical controversy which had been interrupted during the 1930s was reopened and the system of theories such as *Keizaigaku Kyokasho* (Textbook of Economics), formed under the authority of Stalin in the former Soviet Union, began to flow in. The theory of 'general crisis of capitalism' was revived by the Communist International, Lenin's 'theory of two ways' swept across the academy, and his 'state-monopolistic capitalism' also began to receive attention. After China was newly born under the leadership of Mao Tse-tung and the Chinese Communist Party in 1949, the Party intended to start a revolution against American capitalism. Marxian economists of the postwar era, who had grown up under rapid political changes, began their research facing not only the accumulated achievements of the old generation from the prewar era but also the fresh theories of the new generation.

4.1.2 The start of efflorescence

On the basis of achievements before the war, Japanese Marxian economists began to publish their studies and organize academic societies. One was to assemble many Marxian economists under the Economic Section of Democratic Scientists Associations (ESDSA) soon after the war. ESDSA was regarded as a leading member association of the Union of National Economic Associations in Japan. After the foundation of the Science Council of Japan in 1941, it led the third division of economics and commercial science.

As academic freedom was secured both in name and reality, the complete works of Karl Marx were published. *Choryu Koza Keizaigaku Zenshu* (Choryu Symposium on Economics, 1949) was a distinctive work done by many Marxian economists. ESDSA published *Koza Shihonron no Kaimei* (Symposium on the Elucidation of *Das Kapital*, 1951–53), and publisher Iwanami Shoten *Nihon Shihonshugi Koza* (Symposium on Learning the Textbook of Economics, 1953–54). It was an application of some incorrect propositions of Stalin's 'Some economic problems in the Soviet Union' (1952, translated into Japanese in the same year) and an observance of 'Thesis of 1951', which was the platform of the Japan Communist Party. ESDSA published *Keizaigaku Kyokasho Gakushu Koza* (Symposium on Learning the Textbook of Economics, 1955–56) as well. This also provided the dogmatic interpretation of Marx in the Soviet Union and had the intention of spreading it in Japan.

Many academic societies were founded to organize Marxian economists along with these attempts. For example, the (Japanese) Society for the History of Economic Thought (JSHET) was established as an academic society by Marxian economists in 1950. The Agrarian History Society, now the Political Economy and Economic History Society, was founded in 1950 with the aim of making clear the standards of reform in the postwar period. The Credit Theory Society was founded in 1954 with the purpose of researching Marx's credit theory. After ESDSA broke up, the Japanese Society of Political Economy (JSPE) was established in 1959 as a genuine academic society with the purpose of 'studying the basic theories of economics, mainly the Marxian'. JSPE started with 247 members but the number was doubled a few years later. The translation of Marx's *Das Kapital* was published by several publishers (Nihon Hyoronsha, Iwanami Shoten, Aoki Shoten, Kawade Shobo, etc).

Japanese Marxians have gone through many controversies. 'Japanese Capitalism Controversy' ('Nihon Shihonshugi Ronso' or 'Hoken Ronso') continued from the prewar period between 'Koza School' (Koza-ha) and 'Rono School' (Rono-ha). The main topic of the controversy was the characteristics of Japanese capitalism and the agrarian problem of the rents paid by tenant farmers. The controversy was not just a topic of the academies but also that of journalism. It helped spread Marxism and enhanced the level of academic research. After the war this controversy was connected with new problems, such as Japan's dependence on the United States, the revival of Japanese capitalism, structural reformation, and state-monopoly capitalism. Japanese Marxians did not live only in the field of interpretation but also in the analysis of modern capitalism.

From an international point of view we cannot disregard Marxian studies in other countries, other than the influences of the former Soviet Union and Stalin. With regard to capitalism after the war, there was a dispute on Valga's *Changes of capitalism as the result of World War II* (1947; original edition 1945). He was editing *World Economy and World Politics* from the prewar period, predicted the financial panic in 1929, and was known as a disputant of the former Soviet Union and the author of *History of World Economic Crisis* (translated by Nagasumi, Keio Shobo; original edition 1937). He argued that American capitalism should lead the economic revival of the world after World War II and was accused of being 'a right-wing opportunist' in his theory of nation and crisis. The controversy triggered by Valga evolved into a controversy on national monopolistic capitalism by K. Zieschang, a German theorist, in the late 1950s. The introduction of such controversies was a big help to Japanese Marxian economists in understanding modern capitalism.

The theory of capitalist development by P. Sweezy,[2] M. Dobb,[3] and European Marxian economists indicated different ways in the analysis of capitalism (financial capital and interests groups etc.). L. Meek's studies of the history of economic thought and value theory were translated into Japanese.[4] Dobb played the part of critical introducer of growth theory, development economics and welfare economics for Japanese Marxian economists. P. Sweezy and P. Baran's *Monopoly Capitalism* (1966) was widely read in Japan but their analysis of the idea of 'financial surplus' did not fit in with Japanese Marxian economics, which started with the labor theory of value. M. Kalecki and J. Robinson's criticism of neoclassical economics à la Marx was well read in Japan as well. Yet they did not have much influence on Japanese Marxian economists, who were taught a different system of economic principles. However, thanks to their criticism, a number of post-Keynesian economists appeared in Japan. They regarded the conflicts of interest between classes as of importance and shared the critical viewpoint of capitalism with Marxian economists. O. Lange, who assumed an important position in the Polish government and studied the theory of a planned economy with the use of cybernetics, had a big influence in Japan. The Japanese version of P. Sraffa's *Production of Commodities by Means of Commodities* (Cambridge, 1960) gave a chance to the revival of 'transformation problem' among Marxian economists. However, when it became clear that 'labor value' was regarded as 'an unnecessary detour' by Sraffa, Sraffians, and post-Keynesians, Marxian economists found themselves belonging to another group. The works of these foreign economists served as the basis for communication between Marxian economists and modern economists.

4.1.3 Academic independence of Marxian economics

From the prewar period, Japanese Marxian economists made great contributions to the historical study of economic thought. The foundation of the Japan Society for Political Economy (JSPE) expanded the fields for Marxian studies including basic theory and actual analysis. Marxian economists had posts at major universities, and established an education system for young scholars. Marxian economics was taught in the courses such as 'political economy', 'Marxian economics' and 'economic principles' (there are many other courses incorporating the methods of Marxian economics).

The science of business administration introduced from the United States was opposed to the critical science of business administration developed by Marxians. In most universities modern economists rivaled Marxian economists. Moreover, it became even harder for the students who had studied Marxian economics in school, to maintain their critical and theoretical opinions after getting jobs at commercial companies. A kind of 'conversion in getting a job' was already observed in the 1950s. Japanese Marxian economists critically learned econometric methods, neoclassical analysis of economic policies, the analysis of industrial relations, the concept of oligopoly, and national income analysis. However, even a part of modern economics was contradicted by the theoretical system constructed upon the economic principles of *Das Kapital*. The students, who had learned Marx in universities, could get jobs at government offices and commercial companies. Yet they were compelled to learn the basics of modern economics in the intensive training courses. Then the number of Marxian scholars began to decrease (see Chapter 2). The influence of Marxian economics on politics, ideologies and journalism dwindled from its peak of the 1950s.

4.2 Maturity and development: the centennial anniversary of volume one of *Das Kapital* (1967) and Marx's death (1983): 'series of publication' and forming of schools

4.2.1 Comprehensive survey of postwar Marxian economics

The years 1967 and 1983 were symbolic for Marxian economists. Celebrated in 1967 was the centennial anniversary of the first publication of *Das Kapital*, and in

1983 the centennial anniversary of Marx's death. After the mid-1960s, Japanese Marxian economists were split into schools and involved in joint academic projects with their colleagues. The period between 1967 and 1983 was the golden age of Marxian economics in Japanese academe. A great number of books were published by each group.

In the early 1950s, the Credit Theory Society edited *Koza Shinyoriron Taikei* (Symposium on Credit Theory, 1956), which was their first attempt to develop credit theory based on Marx's analysis since its foundation of 1954. Asobe edited *Shihonron Kenkyushi* (A History of Studying *Das Kapital*, 1958) and classified the disputed issues on *Das Kapital* from the prewar period on. Marxian economists were not only engaged in detailed studies of Marxian economics but also tried to learn from modern economics, namely the achievements of their rivals. Kishimoto and Tsuru edited *Koza Kindai Kezaigaku Hihan* (Symposium on the Critical Assessment of Modern Economics, 1956–57), and clarified the foundation, ideology and edifice of modern economics, and proposed a debate on actual economic issues with modern economists. It included the achievements of modern economics such as the theory of monopoly price, industrial relations, business cycle, and optimum distribution. Ikumi edited *Koza Kyokoron* (Symposium on the Theory of Crisis, 1958–59), which was a highly motivated study on industrial cycle or crisis both from a perspective of economic history and realistic analysis.

D. Rosenberg's *Shihonron Chukai* (Annotations to *Das Kapital*, 1962–64) represented the orthodox viewpoint of the former Soviet Union, and became the standard interpretation of *Das Kapital* in Japan in the 1960s. A series of symposium books followed. Watanabe edited *Ronso Gendai no Keizairiron* (Controversy: Modern Economic Theory, 1962), which attempted to summarize the theoretical questions that are related to contemporary problems. Uno edited *Gendai Teikokushugi Koza* (Modern Imperialism, 1963) with a big plan of analyzing the characteristics of modern capitalism as a whole by describing the characteristics of imperialism. Uno edited *Keizaigaku Taikei* (Economics, 1962–63) and presented theories on methodology, principles, imperialism, the world and Japanese economies. Asobe edited *Shihonron Koza* (Symposium on *Das Kapital*, 1963–64), Usami edited *Marx Keizaigaku Taikei* (Marxian Economics, 1966), and Uno edited *Shihonron Kenkyu* (A Study of *Das Kapital*, 1967–68) with the intention of looking at Japanese Marxian economics through *Das Kapital*. Asobe's book covers Japanese Marxian economics, Usami's Marxian 'orthodox' economics, and Uno's the Uno school. The first generation of Marxian economists surviving from the prewar period had established a system of reproducing successors. Hidaka edited *Nihon no Marx Keizaigaku* (Marxian Economics in Japan, 1967) and described each Marxian economist including himself. It included the lineage of Japanese Marxian economists from Toshihiko Sakai to Kozo Uno. It was a unique work on Marxian scholars with its method of describing how Uno succeeded in establishing the autonomy of Marxian economics. JSHET edited *Shihonron no Seiritsu* (The Formation of *Das Kapital*, 1967) in memory of the centenary of the first volume of *Das Kapital*. It described the birth of *Das Kapital* in comparison with the contemporary economists through the process of writing *Das Kapital* and its influence on other countries. Kuruma edited *Marx-Lexikon zur politischen Ökonomie* (1968–95) as his life work. It was a work on Marx, written in Marx's words and discussed from Kuruma's viewpoints of competition, method, materialistic view of history, crisis and money.

Studies on Marxian economics in Japan have produced important works on study about the formation of Marxian economics. *Grundrisse der Kritik der politischen Ökonomie (Rohentwurf) 1857–1858*, produced by the Marx-Engels-Lenin Institute Moscow, and published in 1953 by Dietz Verlag, Berlin, which is one of the manuscripts written in the latter half of the 1850s when Marx started his study on economics. It provided the information about the middle period of Marx's life and created a sensation at the time of publication. R. Rosdolsky's *Zur Entstehungsgeschichte des Marxschen 'Kapital', Der Rohentwurf des 'Kapital' 1857–1858*, 2 vols, 1969 (Japanese translation; 1973–74) discussed the making of Marx's economic theory on the basis of *Grundrisse*, published in Russian before the war. It pointed out a strong relationship between Hegel's *Logic* and Marx's *Grundrisse*. *Commentary Grundrisse*, a part of *Koza Marx Keizaigaku* (Symposium on Marxian Economics, 1974–76), made great progress for the study of *Grundrisse* in Japan. Clear motivation to promote the popularity of Marxian economics could be seen in the 1970s. Usami *et al.* edited *Marx Shugi Keizaigaku Koza* (Symposium on Marxian Economics, 1971), Shima *et al.* edited *Shin Marx Keizaigaku Koza* (New Symposium on Marxian Economics, 1972–76) Sugihara and Furusawa edited *Marx Keizaigaku Zensho* (Complete Works on Marxian Economics, 1973–incomplete), Ouchi *et al.* edited *Shihonron Kenkyu Nyumon* (Introduction to the Study of *Das Kapital*, 1976) and Sato *et al.* edited *Shihonron wo Manabu* (Learning *Das Kapital*, 1977). Uno edited *Teikokushugi no Kenkyu* (A Study of Imperialism) (1973–76), which was a comprehensive work of the Uno school on imperialism. Takasuka edited *Dokusen Shihonshugi no Tenbo* (Perspective on Monopoly Capitalism, 1978) and summarizes surveys of contemporary capitalism looking through monopolistic theory.

In 1983, one hundred years after Marx's death, there appeared many featured journal articles and events. Mita edited *Marx Shihonron no Kenkyu* (A Study of Marx's *Das Kapital*, 1980) and Kobayashi edited *Koza Shihonron no Kenkyu* (Symposium on the Study of *Das Kapital*, 1980–82). Tomizuka *et al.* edited *Shihonron Taikei* (Study Series on *Das Kapital*) (1983–incomplete). Hirata's *Commentary Das Kapital* (1980–83) was a monumental work of the 1980s and an antithesis to the trend of the age. But still Marxian economics finds its way out in the analysis of capitalism on the ground of analysis about real economy. Okishio *et al.* edited *Gendai Shihonshugi Bunseki* (Analysis on Contemporary Capitalism, 1980–incomplete), and *Koza Kon-nichi no Nihon Shihonshugi* (Symposium on Japanese Capitalism Today, 1981–82) went beyond the interpretation of *Das Kapital* and tried to apply Marxian methods to the analysis of contemporary capitalism.

The continuous flow in the tradition of Marxian economics can be seen in the effort of explaining Marxian ideas and trying to make them the intellectual property of all mankind. Kuruma *et al.* edited *Shihonron Jiten* (A Dictionary of *Das Kapital*, 1961), Osaka City University edited *Keizaigaku Jiten* (A Dictionary of

Economics, 1965) and *Keizaigaku Jiten* (A Dictionary of Economics, 1979) mostly based on the concept of Marxian economics. (The 2nd and 3rd edition of the second dictionary put back the color of Marxian economics and set forth the color of modern economics.) *Gendai Marxism-Leninism Jiten* (Contemporary Dictionary of Marxism-Leninism, 1981–1982) was contributed by more than 170 scholars and attempted to explain the history, idea and concept of Marx. *The Cyclopedia of Categories in Marx* (1998) was a new dictionary and a collaboration on Marxian fundamental concepts (collected works of categories), the new image of Marx, retrial of Marx and diversity of his ideas and theories.

4.2.2 Formation of the 'big four' schools and absence of 'Marx Renaissance'

The academic world of economics in Japan is characterized by the existence of the two separate powers of modern economics and Marxian economics. There are several groups inside Marxian economics.

> There exists no such thing as a school in physics or chemistry. The characteristic of physics or chemistry as science is that it has one objective system and in order to create the system, many scientists contribute to it and if the work is worth the name of scientific contribution it will be accepted as everybody's common knowledge. On the contrary, in the field of economics, the age of feudalism with conflict between schools continued too long. (Tsuru 1993: 194–5)

The above is a quotation from a context that argues that the 'Schumpeter school' did not exist. Marxian economics in Japan was affected by the 'conflicts among schools' on theory and their problems. There are four major groups; 'the orthodox school', 'Uno school', 'civil society school' and 'mathematical Marxian school'.

The 'orthodox school' thinks the following pairs are equal; Marxian economics and 'Marxist' economics, theory and practice, science and ideology, logic and history. It covers most of Japanese Marxian economists. Scholars other than 'Uno' and 'civil society' are sometimes included in this school. We may as well call it 'the school loyal to Marx'. The groups which study the formation of Marxian theory are included in this school.

> The Uno school basically differentiated theoretical study, historical study, and the study of actual capitalism from each other although the last two were often mixed in the research of the Uno school. Uno's heretical ideas stimulated controversy among Japanese Marxian economists, although he tried to purify Marx's *Das Kapital* and transcend Marx. It is noteworthy that he tried to distinguish science from ideology unlike the 'orthodox school'. His ideas were inspired by the controversy of the changes in capitalism after World War I in Europe (Bernstein, Kautsky, Hilferding and Lenin) and the controversy on Japanese capitalism between Koza school vs. Rono school

around 1930. He apparently resisted the Stalinist trend after World War II (Miyazaki 1984: 232).

The Uno school continued to have great influence on the following generation and is relatively well known to foreign Marxian economists (Uno 1980). The 'civil society school' continued research on classical economics and restored the long-neglected theory of civil society. This school, like the 'Uno school', excludes the dogmatic interpretation of Marx infringed by Stalinism.

Nobuo Okishio (Krueer and Flaschel 1984) is famous for his Marx-Okishio theorem (or Marx's fundamental theorem) and Okishio theorem. Okishio, along with Tsuneyoshi Seki, represents the mathematical development of Marxian economics in Japan. The Marx-Okishio theorem is a formularization of Marx's theory of income redistribution. The Okishio theorem states that when the actual wage rate is fixed, the lower the new technology cost is and the higher the profit rate becomes. There existed strong objections toward introducing a mathematical method into Marxian economics at first but it proved to be an important achievement to promote detailed studies of Marxian economics (Okishio 1965; 1977; 1987) and collaborative research with modern economists,[5] The fact that Okishio's theory was a bridge between Marxian economics and modern economics should not be forgotten. Also a dialogue between schools was made possible by the presence of Okishio. For example, Okishio published *Keizairiron to Gendai Shihonshugi* (Economic Theory and Contemporary Capitalism) with Makoto Itoh in 1987, *Keizaigaku* (Economics) with Mitsuhiko Tsuruta and Yasuhiko Yoneda, in 1988, *Marx, Keynes and Schumpeter* with Yoshitsugu Kotani and Jun Ikegami in 1991, *Nihon Keizai no Suryobunseki* (Econometric Analysis to Japan Economy) with Masanori Nozawa in 1983.

A 'Marx Renaissance' did not happen in Japan unlike Europe or North America. One of the reasons was the difference in attitude toward dogmatism. European and North American economists were absolutely against Stalinism and even against Leninism. Another reason was the existence of the tense relationship with neoclassical economics there. The economics taught in schools is neoclassical economics and there are many Marxian scholars who have knowledge of neoclassical theory. Marxian economics was supposed to stand against the neoclassical school. Marxian economics was already recognized as a 'system of economic knowledge' in Japanese academia and so it need not fight against modern economics for its acceptance. A third reason was the variety of Marxian interpretations. Japanese Marxian economists are traditionally engaged in reading Marx. 'Marx Renaissance' gave a chance to unique and distinctive works such as a constructive interpretation of *Das Kapital* (L. Althusser), the refusal of Marx's original concepts, the reformulation of value theory based on mathematical method (C. F. Clause), the re-evaluation of the controversy of the falling rates of profit and long wave movement (J. Grin, B. Satcriff and E. Mandel), subordinate theory of accumulation (S. Amin and A. G. Frank), and theory of exploitation and quantitative decision (J. E. Roemer). In the economically advanced countries other than Japan, Marxian economics was utterly excluded from academia until 'Marx Renaissance'. The foundations of the Congress of Socialist Economics (CSE) in the UK and the Union for Radical Political Economics (URPE) in the United States marked the peak of 'Marx Renaissance'. Marx used to be 'an insignificant Ricardian' in Samuelson's words but it is now 'a scandal' to ignore Marx. He is now recognized as 'a mathematical economist', like Walras in neoclassical economics.

The theories of Otsuka, Okochi and Sugimoto should not be forgotten. The historical theories of Otsuka were a great influence not just on economics but on social sciences in general. His interest was mainly in the economic history of modern Europe but he also extracted the consistency of history from modernization to civil society, and became deeply involved in the guidepost of 'undeveloped' Japan and the prospects of future society. Otsuka's theory and method had a immeasurable impact on Japanese Marxian economics. For example, the theory of pre-capitalist capital, the formation of capitalist society, formation of 'local market area', cooperative society, modern human type with economic and ethical conception and ethos, the method of social science known as the 'Weber-Marx problem'. Okochi's theory was so unusual that he tried to explain the necessity of social policy from the point of internal inevitability in capitalism, and stressed the hierarchical character of social policy. He maintained that the target of social policy was not laborers but labor itself. He believed that the essence of the Labor Protection Act existed in labor preservation. Okochi's theory derives from Weber as well as many other Japanese theories in social sciences. Sugimoto's argument that Marxian economics and modern economics should be unified stands out prominently in Japan. The essential part of Sugimoto's theory entrusts the analysis of the imbalance of market and price, which eventually ends up in world market crisis, the unsolved problem of the systematic criticism of Marxian economics, to dynamic economic analysis. He found a hope in the mathematical analysis of *Das Kapital*. His argument is still a serious theme left for Japanese Marxian economists to pursue.

4.2.3 The developments of Marxian economics

Marxian economics influenced the making of actual policy when Japan started over again after the war. Marxian economists joined the process of legislation and the practice of postwar democratization policy together with government officials. Many Marxian economists have worked in various committees both national and provincial. Shigeto Tsuru with his unique political economy (he was the writer of the first Economic White Paper in Japan after the war) put the basis of his work on the criticism of market economics which derives from his sympathy toward the institutional school, and American democracy and his affinity with Marxian economics.

Marxian economics proved its worth in the fields of business cycle theory, industrial structure, technical innovation, public finance, finance-credit-securities theory, agricultural theory, labor economics, etc. Marxian economists were the first to take up urban and environmental problems in Japan after 1960.

They have been working hard on the problem because the problem needed economic analysis. Collaboration with modern economists and scholars in other academic fields should be mentioned also. The first economic analysis of the urban problem is said to be *Sumiyoi Nihon* (Inhabitable Japan, Ito *et al.* 1964). The bases of the analysis here are the economic categories of social consumption and social cost, and the prescription for solution is sought in the principle 'means public, efficiency planned, subject democracy, outcome equal'. Miyamoto's *Shakai Shihonron* (A Theory of Social Capital, 1967) developed this argument.

> Concentration of capital and spatial accumulation of labor population happen in a city in capitalist society. Laborers needed a means of common consumption as a general condition of labor reproduction. The means of common consumption should be offered and supplied by social capital or public power. But a capitalist society has the tendency to cut down the means of social and common consumption in order to increase the profit rate of capital. The more the working population concentrates and the higher the labor value rises, so the necessity of the means of social and common consumption increases. Yet capital accumulation requires to cut it down. (Miyamoto 1967: 161)

He defined 'the urban problem' as 'the difficulties caused by the unfulfilled necessity of social and common consumption of the working class' in his *Nihon no Toshi Mondai* (Urban Problems in Japan, 1969).

The method of Marx was effective for the problem of pollution in a quickly growing economy. Shoji and Miyamoto's *Osoroshii Kogai* (Terrible Pollution, 1964) is an analysis of environmental pollution by both the methods of economics and natural science. Tsuru's *Gendai Shihonshugi to Kogai* (Contemporary Capitalism and Pollution, 1968) is a comprehensive study of pollution including the definition of pollution, the forms of pollution (industrial, urban, political) and the social expenses caused by pollution.

Ikegami's theory on human development is an attempt to consider public policy through information, education, and culture. Ikegami published many books including his *Zaiseigaku* (Public Finance, 1990) from 1965 to the present (see references). According to Ikegami it is a suggestion on the lineage from Hajime Kawakami, Ruskin to Marx.

4.3 Skeptism and new struggle: East European revolution 1989; Soviet Union dissolution 1991; relativity of Marx and Marx as a subject of economic history; *Das Kapital* (from a holy book to a classic)

4.3.1 Relativity of Marxian economics

First, with the end of political confrontation through revolutions in East Europe and the dissolution of the Soviet Union, the study of Marx is no longer absolute.

The paradigm of Marxian economics as the one and only truth was overthrown by the reality, and the study of Marx became only a field of economic history. This may seem a retreat for some Marxian scholars but it is not so. Marx exists right there liberated from the spell of ideology. Marx no longer belongs to a specific political regime or an ideology, but has become the common property of mankind.

Second, it is recognized that the superiority of Marxian economics cannot be proved in any other way than by the validity of analyzing reality. The key does not lie in interpretation of *Das Kapital* but in the analysis of reality. Bob Rowthorn pointed out precisely the weak point of Japanese Marxian economists in his preface to the Japanese edition of his *Logic of Contemporary Capitalism*. 'Marxian economists in Japan do not seem to have received much orthodox training in economics'.

The third is the awareness of crisis that various schools of Marxian economics, which were formed inevitably during the golden age of Marxism, must stop confronting each other with. Kitahara, Itoh and Yamada *Gendai Shihonshugi wo Domiruka* (How We See Contemporary Capitalism, 1997) suggest the importance of collaboration to overcome the crisis and the differences among schools.

Through 'Marx Renaissance' the co-existence of Marxian economics and modern economics has become a phenomenon not only in Japan but common through all developed capitalist countries. The co-existence of Marxian economics and modern economics which were separated by Marx's *Das Kapital* and marginalist revolution has become a common phenomenon throughout the world. The two economics have derived from two different ways of thinking. Marxian economics is now at its turning point.

There are new studies on Marx in Europe and America such as the new stream of study after 'Marx Renaissance', the structural macroeconomics and regulation school. Complexity economics is trying to create a new theory of economics using computer science and game theory. Its influence on Marxian economics cannot be avoided. Evolutionary economics, with many Marxian economists working on it, is another way for Marx to regenerate.

4.3.2 *The study of the manuscripts of Marx and Engels: the publication of MEGA and new possibilities*

Marxian economics must change now that we are breaking into a new age. Before concluding this chapter, the direction of the historical study of Marxian economics needs to be checked. It must start with recognition of the fact that the literatures of Marx and Engels were not completely made open for some political reasons. At last, at the end of the twentieth century, the publication of *MEGA* (since 1975) made it possible to reveal the total figures of Marx and Engels.

In November 1997, the foundation of Japanese MEGA-Arbeitsstelle was approved by the Internationale Marx-Engels-Stiftung (IMES, Amsterdam) committee. It was decided that Otani will edit *MEGA*, book II, vol. 11, no. 2 (Marx's Manuscripts no. III to no. VIII for *Das Kapital*, book II) and Omura's group Vol.12 and Vol.13 (Engels' editorial manuscripts of *Das Kapital*, book II and 1st and 2nd editions). The published part of *MEGA* has proved several hundred differences between Marx's original manuscript and Engels' published edition based on the outcome of research at the Internationaal Instituuto voor Sociale Geschiedenis (IISG, Amsterdam). Shibuya edited *Perfect Restoration Edition Deutsche Ideologie* (1998) based on IISG's original manuscript and bears the role of deciphering some editions of manuscript and of filling up the defects of the texts. The manuscript of *Das Kapital* was the first to be translated into Japanese as *Karl Marx: Ökonomische Manuskripte* (1978–94) among MEGA publications, which supported the study of Marx in Japan. In the study of the literature of Marx and Engels which supports the study of Marx and Engels, the deciphering of the original manuscript which was exclusively done in East Germany and the Soviet Union is now being undertaken by Japanese scholars. The publication of and study on basic texts made this possible.

Before MEGA *Marx-Engels-Werke* (MEW) was translated and published, the Japanese translation appeared as *Marx-Engels Zenshu* (1959–91). There were some other selected works published before this and they contributed to the study and popularization of Marxian economics (*Marx-Engels Selected Works*, 23 vols, 1946–52, *Marx-Engels Selected Works*, 8 vols, *Marx-Engels Selected Works*, 16 vols, 1956–57, etc.). These *Works* and *Selected Works* were not published by an institute belonging to some political party, as was so in East Germany or the Soviet Union, but by commercial publishers such as Otsuki Shoten and Shincho-sha, with editorship of Marxian economists. We should appreciate the fact that the texts of Marx and Engels have become the common property of all Marxian scholars in Japan. It is remarkable that this comprehensive work, which had been out of print due to stock problems, was revived as *CD-ROM Edition Marx-Engels-Werke* (1996) by using the technology of pictogram and picture processing. The original photocopy of Marx and Engels in Moscow and Amsterdam was also published (*Facsimile Edition Grundrisse der politischen Ökonomie (Rohentwurf)*, 1997). The fact that this semi-primary material has come out into the open at last means the study of Marx has become in name and reality an open subject to be pursued in academia. Now with the literature of Marx and Engels opened on the Internet the range of Marx study is certainly widening.

4.3.3 The historical study of Marxian economics and the application of its analysis

The literature of Marx and Engels is now changing from 'the holy book' to 'the classic'. To revive the study of Marx the complete study of the history of Marxian economics is essential. Even if Marxian economics in general is inactive, if only one field of study could attract scholars, then Marxian study will continue to live as a part of the historical study of economics.

In order for Marxian economics to continue having credence as the economics of the twenty-first century, it must stop 'conflict among schools', and make practical studies of contemporary capitalism. The co-existence of Marxian economics and modern economics has some significance only through hard work on both sides and mutual criticism. Marxian economics will shine more as a powerful tool to analyze and explain the realities of our world.

Notes

1   Hitoshi Kihara (1893–1986) said,'The history of the earth is recorded in the layers of its crust; the history of all organizations is inscribed in the chromosomes.'
2   *The Theory of Capitalist Development; Principles of Marxian Political Economy,* New York, 1942. *Karl Marx and the Close of His System* by E. von Böhm-Bawerk and *Böhm-Bawerk's Criticism of Marx* by R. Hilferding, New York, 1949. *Socialism,* New York, 1949. *The Present as History; Essays and Reviews on Capitalism and Socialism,* New York, 1953. *Cuba; Anatomy of a Revolution,* New York, 1960. (With Baran) *Monopoly Capital; An Essay on the American Economic and Social Order,* New York, 1966. (With H. Magdoff) *The Dynamics of U.S. Capitalism; Corporate Structure, Inflation, Credit, Gold, and the Dollar,* New York, 1972. *Modern Capitalism and Other Essays,* New York, 1972. (With H. Magdoff) *The End of Prosperity,* New York, 1978. *Post-Revolutionary Society,* New York, 1980.
3   There are many Japanese translations after World War II; *Political Economy and Capitalism; Some Essays in Economic Tradition,* London, 1937. *Studies in the Development of Capitalism,* London, 1946. *Soviet Economic Development since 1917,* London, 1948. *Some Aspects of Economic Development; Three Lectures,* Delhi, 1951. *On Economic Theory and Socialism; Collected Papers,* London, 1955. *Capitalism, Yesterday and Today,* London, 1958. *An Essay on Economic Growth and Planning,* London, 1960. *Papers on Capitalism; Development and Planning,* London, 1967. *Theories of Value and Distribution since Adam Smith,* Cambridge, 1973.
4   *Studies in the Labor Theory of Value,* London, 1956. 2nd edition, 1973. Some of his works were translated into Japanese; *Economics and Ideology, and Other Essays,* London, 1967; *Smith and After,* London, 1977.
5   Okishio was the president of the Japan Association of Economics and Econometrics (now, the Japanese Economic Association) in 1979–80.

References and further reading

Asobe, K. (ed.) (1958) *Shihonron Kenkyushi* (A History of Studying *Das Kapital*), Kyoto: Minerva Shobo.
Asobe, K. *et al.* (ed.) (1963–64) *Shihonron Koza* (Symposium on *Das Kapital*), Tokyo: Aoki Shoten.
Choryu Koza Keizaigaku Zenshu (Choryu Symposium on Economics) (1949), Tokyo: Choryu-sha.
Credit Theory Society (ed.) (1956) *Koza Shinyo Riron Taikei* (Symposium on Credit Theory), Tokyo: Nihon Hyoron Shin-sha.
Economic Section of Democratic Scientists Associations (ESDSA) (ed.) (1951–53) *Koza Shihonron no Kaimei* (Symposium on the Elucidation of *Das Kapital*), Tokyo: Rironsha.
Economic Section of Democratic Scientists Associations (ed.) (1955–56) *Keizaigaku Kyokasho Gakushu Koza* (Symposium on Learning the Textbook of Economics).
Hidaka, S. *et al.* (ed.) (1967) *Nihon no Marx Keizaigaku* (Marxian Economics in Japan), Tokyo: Aoki Shoten.

Hirata, K. (1980–83) *Commentary Das Kapital*, Nihon Hyoronsha.

Ikegami, J. (1965) *Kokka Dokusen Shihonshugiron* (Theory of State-monopolistic Capitalism), Tokyo: Yuhikaku.

Ikegami, J. (1977) *Kokka Dokusen Shihonshugi Ronso* (Controversy of State-monopolistic Capitalism), Tokyo: Aoki Shoten.

Ikegami, J. (1978) *Amerika Shihonshugi no Keizai to Zaisei* (The Economy and Public Finance in the US), Tokyo: Otsuki Shoten.

Ikegami, J. (1979) *Chiho Zaiseiron* (Theory of Regional Finance), Tokyo: Dobunkan.

Ikegami, J. (1980) *Gendai Kokkaron* (Theory of Contemporary State), Tokyo: Aoki Shoten.

Ikegami, J. (1981) *Nihon Keizairon* (Theory of the Japanese Economy), Tokyo: Dobunkan.

Ikegami, J. (1984) *Kanri Keizairon* (Theory of Administrative Economics), Tokyo: Yuhikaku.

Ikegami, J. (1984) *Johoka Shakai no Seijikeizaigaku* (Political Economy of Information Society), Kyoto: Showado.

Ikegami, J. (1990) *Zaiseigaku* (Public Finance), Tokyo: Iwanami Shoten.

Ikegami, J. (1991) *Keizaigaku* (Economics), Tokyo: Aoki Shoten.

Ikegami, J. (1994) *Gendai Keizaigaku to Kokyo Seisaku* (Contemporary Economics and Public Policy), Tokyo: Aoki Shoten.

Ikegami, J. (1996) *Multi Media Shakai no Seiji to Keizai* (Politics and Economy in Multimedia Society), Kyoto: Nakanishiya Shuppan, 1996.

Ikeo, A. (1996) 'Marxist economics in Japan', *Kokugakuin Keizaigaku* 44 (3/4): 425–51.

Ikumi, T. *et al.* (ed.) (1958-59) *Koza Kyokoron* (Symposium on the Theory of Economic Crisis), Tokyo: Toyo Keizai Shinpo-sha.

Ikumi, T. *et al.* (ed.) (1963) *Gendai Teikokushugi Koza* (Symposium on Contemporary Imperialism), Tokyo: Nihon Hyoron Shinsha.

Ishii, N. *et al.* (eds) (1998) *The Cyclopedia of Categories in Marx*, Tokyo: Aoki Shoten.

Ito, M. *et al.* (ed.) (1964) *Sumiyoi Nihon* (Inhabitable Japan), Tokyo: Yuhikaku.

JSHET (ed.) (1967) *Shihonron no Seiritsu* (The Formation of *Das Kapital*), Tokyo: Iwanami Shoten.

JSHET (ed.) (1984) *Nihon no Keizaigaku* (Economics in Japan), Toyo Keizai Shinposha.

Kawakami, H. (1951-52) *Shihonron Nyumon* (Introduction to *Das Kapital*), Tokyo: Aoki Shoten (1st edn., 1932).

Kishimoto. S. and S. Tsuru (eds) (1956–57) *Koza Kindai Keizaigaku Hihan* (Study Series: Criticism to Modern Economics), Toyo Keizai Shinposha.

Kitahara, I., M. Itoh and T. Yamada (1997) *Gendai Shihonshugi wo Domiruka* (How We See Contemporary Capitalism) Tokyo: Aoki Shoten.

Kobayashi, N. *et al.* (eds) (1980–82) *Koza Shihonron no Kenkyu* (Symposium on the Study of *Das Kapital*), Tokyo: Aoki Shoten.

Krüeer, M. and P. Flaschel (eds) (1984) *Nobuo Okishio: Essays on Political Economy*, Frankfurt am Main: Verlag Peter Lang GmbH.

Koza Gendai Keizaigaku Hihan (Study Series: Criticism to Contemporary Economics) (1974–75), Tokyo: Nihon Hyoron-sha.

Koza Kon-nichi no Nihon Shihonshugi (Symposium on Japanese Capitalism Today) (1981–82), Tokyo: Otsuki Shoten.

Koza Marx Keizaigaku (Symposium on Marxian Economics) (1974–76), Tokyo: Nihon Hyoron-sha.

Kozo, U. (1980) *Principles of Political Economy. Theory of Purely Capitalist Society*, Brighton: Harvester Press.

Kuruma, S. (1949) *Marx Kyokoron Kenkyu* (A Study of Marxian Economic Crisis), Hokuryukan, Revised edition, Tokyo: Otsuki Shoten.

Kuruma, S. (ed.) (1968–95) *Marx-Lexikon zur politischen Ökonomie*, Tokyo: Otsuki Shoten.

Kuruma, S. *et al.* (eds) (1961) *Shihonron Jiten* (A Dictionary of *Das Kapital*), Tokyo: Aoki Shoten.

Kushida, T. (1947) *Kushida Tamizo Zenshu* (Complete Works of Tamizo Kushida), Tokyo: Kaizosha.

Mita, S. *et al.* (eds) (1980) *Marx Shihonron no Kenkyu* (A Study of Marx's *Das Kapital*), Tokyo: Shinnihon Shuppansha.

Miyamoto, K. (1967) *Shakai Shihonron* (A Theory of Social Capital), Tokyo: Yuhikaku.

Miyamoto, K. (1969), *Nihon no Toshi Mondai* (Urban Problems in Japan), Tokyo: Chikuma Shobo.

Miyazaki, S. (1984) 'Sengo no Marx keizaigaku' (Marxian Economics after WWII), In JSHET (ed.) (1984).

Nihon Shihonshugi Koza (Symposium on Japan Capitalism) (1953–54), Tokyo: Iwanami Shoten.

Okazaki, N. (ed.) (1981–82) *Gendai Marx-Lenin Shugi Jiten* (Contemporary Dictionary of Marxism-Leninism), Tokyo: Shakai Shisosha.

Okishio, N. (1965) *Shihonsei Keizai no Kisoriron* (Basic Theory of Capitalistic Economy), Tokyo: Sobunsha. Revised edition, 1975.

Okishio, N. (1977) *Marx Keizaigaku* (Marxian Economics), Tokyo: Chikuma Shobo.

Okishio, N. (1987) *Marx Keizaigaku II* (Marxian Economics II), Tokyo: Chikuma Shobo.

Okishio, N. and M. Itoh (1987) *Keizairiron to Gendai Shihonshugi* (Economic Theory and Contemporary Capitalism) Tokyo, Iwanami Shoten.

Okishio, N., Y. Kotani and J. Ikegami (1991) *Marx, Keynes and Schumpeter*, Tokyo: Otsuki Shoten.

Okishio, N. and M. Nozawa (1983) *Nihon Keizai no Suryobunseki* (Econometric Analysis of Japan Economy), Tokyo: Otsuki Shoten.

Okishio, N., M. Tsuruta, Y. Yoneda (1988) *Keizaigaku* (Economics), Tokyo: Otsuki Shoten.

Okishio, N. *et al.* (eds) (1980–incomplete) *Gendai Shihonshugi Bunseki* (An Analysis of Contemporary Capitalism), Tokyo: Iwanami Shoten.

Ouchi, H. *et al.* (eds) (1976) *Shihonron Kenkyu Nyumon* (Introduction to the Study of *Das Kapital*), Tokyo: Tokyo Daigaku Shuppankai.

Osaka City University (ed.) (1965) *Keizaigaku Jiten* (A Dictionary of Economics), Tokyo: Iwanami Shoten.

Osaka City University (ed.) (1979) *Keizaigaku Jiten* (A Dictionary of Economics), Tokyo: Iwanami Shoten.

Rosenberg, D. (1962–64) *Shihonron Chukai* (Annotations to *Das Kapital*), Tokyo: Aoki Shoten.

Rosdolsky, R. (1969) *Zur Entstehungsgeschichte des Marxschen 'Kapital', der Rohentwurf des 'Kapital' 1857–1858*, 2 vols (Japanese translation; 1973–74).

Sato, K. *et al.* (eds) (1977) *Shihonron wo Manabu* (Learning *Das Kapital*), Tokyo: Yuhikaku.

Shibuya, T. (1998) *Perfect Restoration Edition Deutsche Ideologie*, Tokyo: ShinNihon Shuppansha.

Shima, Y. *et al.* (eds) (1972–76) *Shin Marx Keizaigaku Koza* (New Symposium on Marxian Economics), Tokyo: Yuhikaku.

Shoji, H. and K. Miyamoto (1964) *Osoroshii Kogai* (Terrible Pollution), Tokyo: Iwanami Shoten.

Sraffa, P. (1960) *Production of Commodities by Means of Commodities*, Cambridge: Cambridge University Press.

Sugihara, S. and T. Furusawa (ed.) (1973–incomplete) *Marx Keizaigaku Zensho* (Complete Works on Marxian Economics), Tokyo: Dobunkan.

Sugimoto, E. (1949) *Kindai Keizaigaku no Kihon Seikaku* (Fundamental Characters of Modern Economics), Tokyo: Nihon Hyoron-sha.

Sweezy, P. and P. Baran (1996) *Monopoly Capitalism: An Essay on the American Economic and Social Order*, New York: Monthly Review Press.

Takashima. Z. (1946) *Adam Smith no Shimin Shakai Taikei* (Adam Smith's Civil Society), Tokyo: Kawade Shobo.

Takasuka, Y. (ed.) (1978) *Dokusen Shihonshugiron no Tenbo* (Perspective on Monopoly Capitalism), Tokyo: Toyo Keizai Shinpo-sha.

Tomizuka, R. *et al.* (eds.) (1983–incomplete) *Shihonron Taikei* (Study Series on *Das Kapital*), Tokyo: Yuhikaku.

Tsuru, S. (ed.) (1968) *Gendai Shihonshugi to Kogai* (Contemporary Capitalism and Pollution) Tokyo: Iwanami Shoten.

Tsuru, S. (1993) [1964] *Kindai Keizaigaku no Gunzo* (Group of Modern Economics), Nihon Keizai Shimbun-sha, 1964; Shakai Shisosha, 1993.

The Union of National Economics Associations in Japan (ed.) (1974–75) *Keizaigaku no Doko* (Economics Trends), Tokyo: Toyo Keizai Shinpo-sha (2nd series, 1982).

Uno, K. (1949) *Shihonron no Kenkyu* (A Study of *Das Kapital*), Tokyo: Iwanami Shoten.

Uno, K. (1951) *Keizai Seisakuron* (Theory of Economic Policy), Tokyo: Kobundo.

Uno, K. (ed.) (1962–63) *Keizaigaku Taikei* (Economics), Tokyo: Tokyo Daigaku Shuppankai.

Uno, K. (ed.) (1967–68) *Shihonron Kenkyu* (A Study of *Das Kapital*), Tokyo: Chikuma Shobo.

Uno, K. (ed.) (1973) *Teikokushugi no Kenkyu* (A Study of Imperialism), Tokyo: Aoki Shoten.

Usami. S. *et al.* (eds) (1966) *Marx Keizaigaku Taikei* (Marxian Economics), Yuhikaku.

Usami. S. *et al.* (eds) (1971) *Marx Keizaigaku Taikei* (Marxian Economics), Tokyo: Shinnihon Shuppan-sha.

Valga, E.S. (1945) *Changes of Capitalism as a result of World War II, 1945*, Moscow: Progress Publishers (translated in Japanese 1947).

Watanabe, S. (ed.) (1962) *Ronso Gendai no Keizai Riron* (Controversy: Contemporary Economic Theory), Tokyo: Nihon Keizai Hyoron-sha.

Yamada, M. (1948) *Saiseisan Katei Hyoshiki Bunseki Joron* (Introductory Analysis of Process of Reproduction), Tokyo: Kaizo-sha.

Yamada, T. (1998) 'Economic development and economic thought after World War II: economic development and Marxian political economy', in Sugihara, S. and Tanaka, T. (eds.) (1998) *Economic Thought and Modernization in Japan*, Cheltenham: Edward Elgar.

Part II

Japanese economists and economic policies

5 Economists and economic policies

Aiko Ikeo

Introduction

This chapter mainly aims to describe how Japanese economists became involved in making economic policies after 1945, while paying attention to the historical background and the accompanying changes in the policy making process. It examines Japan's 'economic plans' and shows that they were not economic plans in a strict sense. Then we consider the function of deliberation councils, and the members of those councils that have a relatively large number of economists. We also consider the shift in the members of these councils. Taking into consideration European and American ideas of 'economic plans' since 1945, we clarify similarities with Japanese cases. We confirm that the concept of 'government failure' did not exist before 1970. Finally, we take a brief look at the activities of economists in administrative reform during 1994–7.

5.1 Historical overview

As regards the evolution of the system for policy making, the time from 1945 to 1955 should be regarded as the period of cleaning up the post-war mess, which witnessed major institutional changes even after the end of the occupation by the Allies. A variety of governmental committees appeared and disappeared one after another. During this period, Japanese economists joined several organizations such as the Special Committee at the Ministry of Foreign Affairs, the Board of Economic Stabilization, the Committee on Coal Mining, and the Committee for Economic Reconstruction. These economists prepared for talk on reparations with the Allied Occupation Force, estimated the optimal level for the single exchange rate, and discussed reconstruction plans for the Japanese economy. In this time the government and administration had a great advantage over the private sector in obtaining economic information.

Since 1955, Japanese economists have had formal or informal influences on the process of policy making and on policy makers themselves. For example, they became members of official and unofficial advisory bodies, have taught economics to civil servants in intensive special training courses, visited the research organs attached to ministries and agencies, advised senior officials and ministers directly, contributed timely essays to economics magazines and published books on economic problems and future prospects. Lectures given by economists in the courses for civil servants will be examined in Chapter 6, because they are considered to have had significant effects on creating the roots of economic knowledge and analysis throughout the administrative offices although the process took a long time. Moreover, the way Japanese economists talk about economic problems has changed since around 1990. This has resulted from the revolutionary changes in electronic communication, the rapid extension of informational networks, and the introduction of the European monetary unit, developments that have accelerated economic globalization.

In the period of economic recovery and economic growth, the Japanese government negotiated with the Occupation Forces and the international economic organizations for the importation of technology and capital, while it protected Japanese domestic industries. The monetary authority undertook its policy measures in order to keep a certain amount of foreign exchange reserves in its vault. Nonetheless the Japanese government gradually opened its markets in response to the demands from outside after it began to go into the trade surplus. Toyoo Gyoten gives an example of how Japanese officials utilized external demands to open its markets in the case of negotiations with the World Bank (which was also learning how to deal with Japanese), as follows:

> [The] Bank officials learned a mixed approach to dealing with the Japanese: sometimes they used coercive methods; in other cases they nurtured. When Japanese officials faced coercive demands, they, though superficially annoyed, sometimes exploited the demands as external leverage (*gaiatsu*) to launch difficult policy alterations. (Gyoten 1997: 291)

The government conducted massive public investment in infrastructure to set its economy on a smooth growth path, and set up a financial network reaching every corner of the country to collect savings for industrial investment. On the other hand, it suggested that fast-growing companies cooperate with other companies to avoid major changes and to maintain harmony in the industry. In economic depressions, cartels were regarded as necessary evils and the working of the market mechanism was blunted. After the end of the rapid growth era, the Japanese system did not change immediately, while mainly land and other asset prices kept rising. Finally after 1990, the system that had supported economic growth became fatigued, while the internationalization of economic activities demanded a global standard instead of a Japanese standard. The price of land has been declining in the subsequent period.

Section 5.2 focuses on the reconstruction period of 1945–55 and summarizes the activities of economists and the formation of economic administration. Section 5.3 examines Japan's 'economic plans' and shows that econometricians have been regarded as experts in making 'economic plans' since the Midterm Economic Plan (1965). Section 5.4 discusses the functions of official councils and analyses the members of the Economic Council from a historical perspective. We will pay attention to the development of economic ideas in Europe and America, and especially Jan Tinbergen's contributions to development plans for the United Nations and the enterprises of the World Bank.

5.2 Economic reconstruction, 1945–55

The Allies from September 1945 until April 1952 indirectly ruled Japan. The military officers and politicians who were supposed to have responsibility for waging the Asian and Pacific War (1937–45) were brought to trial or purged. The professorship of the economists who cooperated in the war effort was questioned (see Chapter 2). In the middle of the chaos just after the war, Japanese economists worked with government officials, and actively participated in a number of committees on reparations and economic reconstruction by supplying professional knowledge and an assessment of the situation based on their expertise.

5.2.1 Reparations

First, informal and formal talks on the post-war Japanese economy started around June 1945, two months before the conclusion of the war, in order to prepare for the expected reparation problem (Okita 1981). A meeting, which had been called by a couple of officials including Saburo Okita, happened to be held on 16 August 1945, the day after the Japanese emperor declared surrender. At the meeting, the attendees decided to form the Study Group on Post-War Problems. The study group became the official Special Committee at the Ministry of Foreign Affairs (MFA) in November with the aim of 'learning the exact conditions of the Japanese economy from the diplomatic point of view relating to the new post-war situation'. If this official expression of the aim might sound unclear, the real aim was to prepare for reparations. The economists who joined the main committee were Hyoe Ouchi, Seiichi Tobata, Ichiro Nakayama, Kozo Sugimura, Seijiro Kishimoto, Tokutaro Yamanaka, Kiyoshi Tsuchiya, Kozo Uno, Moritaro Yamada, Yasuo Kondo, Hiromi Arisawa, and Okita (Ministry of Foreign Affairs). They studied the post-war Japanese economy to get precise recognition of current conditions from an international point of view. The research committee was formed to obtain a theoretical comprehension of the Japanese economy and to study basic economic policies for the future. Its members were Teizo Taira, Harumaru Inoue, Susumu Takamiya, Kiyoshi Tsuchiya, Kozo Uno, Moritaro Yamada, Yasuo Kondo, Hiromi Arisawa, and the officials sent from the Ministry of Foreign Affairs and the Cabinet Investigative Bureau.

In November 1945, Edwin W. Pauley, Personal Representative of the President on Reparations, arrived in Japan and commenced investigation of the reparations program. The US reparation policy was that Japan was not to be pauperized, but neither was Japan to be allowed to rehabilitate her economic life in a form which would allow her to gain control, or to secure an advantage, over her neighbors. Put another way, while Japan should have the last priority in getting back on the road to prosperity, Japan was not to be barred from getting back on it (US Reparations Policy for Japan, 31 October, 1945; p. 435). Pauley promptly released the Interim Reparation Policy, the so-called Pauley Report, on 7 December, the fourth anniversary of the Pacific War in the American standard time. (The attack was on 8 December, Japanese time.) Then on 18 December, he submitted to President Truman a more detailed report entitled 'Reparations from Japan: Immediate Program', the so-called Pauley Interim Report. It was a harsh program based on the idea of reparations through movement of industrial plant and equipment. For example, the following categories (with some exceptions) were considered to be made available for Australia and South East Asian countries as soon as possible for reparations (MOF 1982: 20, 443–9):

1. Half of the capacity for the manufacture of machine tools;
2. All tools and equipment located in Army and Navy arsenals except for equipment useful solely for making arms, ammunition and implements of war, which will be destroyed;
3. The aircraft industry of Japan, all plants manufacturing ball and roller bearings, and all plants manufacturing aircraft engines;
4. All equipment and accessories in twenty shipyards;
5. All steel-making capacity in excess of 2,500,000 tons per year. (This was based on a comparison with 1930, when Japan produced 2,300,000 tons of ingots and consumed 1,700,000 tons of finished steel);
6. Half of the thermal (coal) electricity generating plants, all contact process sulfuric acid plants, the largest Solvay process soda-ash plant, and twenty of the most modern large plants for the manufacture of caustic soda and chlorine.

The Japanese had to prepare statistical material in order to rebut this harsh reparations program. Okita (1981: 66–7) characterized Pauley's idea of reparations of industrial plant and equipment, as follows: 'It was such a severe program that Japan would be pulled back to a primitive agricultural country.' Young officials from the Ministry of Foreign Affairs, the Ministry of Commerce and Industry, the Ministry of Agriculture and Forestry, and the Ministry of Finance began to make a rational and concrete examination of the scope of industries which could maintain a peacetime economy for Japan (Nakayama *et al.* 1993: 79). The Japanese had to show statistical estimates of aggregate demand for goods based on calorie calculations and population to clarify Japan's capacity for reparations. Later, the material became the report 'The Japanese economy and standard of living' (September 1946) by adding the national income account.

The conditions for the reparation question were changed in 1947. First, the industrial plant and equipment that had been brought from Japan based on the interim reparations program never worked well in developing countries. Second, the countries that were to receive the reparations preferred cash to industrial plant and equipment. Third, the confrontation between the United States and the Soviet Union initiated the Cold War between the Western and Eastern blocs. The

United States held power in the occupation policy in Japan and changed the target to the reconstruction of the Japanese economy as a free nation. The Allies could not reach any consensus on Japan's compensation and had no systematic reparation policy as the Cold War proceeded. Japan negotiated with each individual country that was to receive an indemnity. It gave its goods and services to Burma, the Philippines, Indonesia, and Vietnam, while it offered economic grants to Laos, Kampuchea, Burma, South Korea, Malaysia, Singapore, and Thailand (Kashima Peace Research Institute and Hagiwara 1972: 133–55).

5.2.2 *Control of economic reconstruction*

On the other hand, the main goal of economic policy was recovery in production, the establishment of order in the distribution of products, and restoration of stability in economic life. After the loss of the Asian-Pacific War, not only did military production stop, but other production also fell drastically. Food shortages and extensive inflation attacked the Japanese economy. The Supreme Commander of Allied Occupation (SCAP) ordered the Japanese government to devise a plan for controlling prices strictly and rationing necessities. However, the Japanese government conceived a plan of reduced controls in order to achieve a smoother distribution of rationed goods. SCAP denied permission for this plan and emphasized that there was a greater need to control the Japanese economy for its recovery than during the war itself (Nakayama 1993: 9–10).

On 12 August 1946, the Economic Stabilization Board and the Agency of Prices (a price control agency) were established in order to overcome the crisis of the Japanese economy. Article 1 of the Ordinance of the Economic Stabilization Board states:

> The Economic Stabilization Board is under the control of the Prime Minister and is to do office work in making emergent policies for economic stability relating to the production, distribution and consumption of goods, services, prices, finance, transportation and others, and to do office work for the coordination, inspection, and promotion of stability.

The Economic Stabilization Board had very strong power to execute the above missions 'through the Prime Minister by ordering concerned ministries and agencies to cooperate with it if necessary'. At first this ordinance was to be inactive for a year but later several detailed editions came into force (EPA 1997).

In May 1946, three months before the establishment of the Economic Stabilization Board, Shigeru Yoshida became Prime Minister as well as the minister of foreign affairs, and held lunchtime meetings unofficially in the ministry room once a week. The meetings were organized by Hiroo Wada, the minister of agriculture and forestry, attended by Arisawa, Ichiro Nakayama, Seiichi Tobata, Seiji Kaya, Shunichi Uchida, Yoshimichi Hori, Jiro Shirasu, and Tomohiko Ushiba, and recorded in notes taken by Okita. Their theme was the reconstruction of the Japanese economy. It was at one of the meetings that Arisawa for the first time spoke of a recovery plan named 'priority production system', that is, putting a priority on resources allocated for the two key industries of coal mining, and iron and steel production. His plan originated from the mixture of ideas such as W. Leontief's inter-industry analysis, K. Marx's reproduction scheme, and the Austrian conception of the superiority of roundabout methods of production. The last of these was the basis for the Austrian theory of capital and states that more time-consuming methods of production which are 'wisely chosen' are more productive. It is hypothesized that capitalist production – namely producing capital goods first and then using them to produce consumables – is an efficient detour, that is to say, more productive than direct production of consumables with primitive methods. Arisawa (1989a) stated: 'Roundabout methods of production took place almost nowhere at the time. To resume roundabout production meant to resume production. We could not expect the increase in industrial production without getting the physical structure for reproduction ready'.[1]

Thanks to the intensive discussions at the informal lunch time meetings, the formal Committee on Coal Mining was established and the priority production plan which targeted '30 million tons of coal per year' was created under the leadership of Arisawa, and joined by Hidezo Inaba, Toshihiko Yoshino, Okita and Goto from the Ministry of Foreign Affairs, and other officials. After a few months delay due to Yoshida's inappropriate statement on workers' behavior, the plan was finally set in motion.[2] Wada became the chief of the Economic Stabilization Board, Shigeto Tsuru the sub-chair for comprehensive adjustment and Okita the chief secretary for the Prime Minister. Thus the priority production system was carried out under the Katayama cabinet. Coal miners were given twice as much as the normal food ration and better living conditions in order to execute the plan because they were supposed to work 45 minutes longer in collieries. In the fiscal year 1947, coal production was 2,932 tons and industrial production was increased by 22 percent compared with the previous year, and by 46 percent in the fiscal year 1948 (Okita 1981: 75–6).

5.2.3 *The emergence of white papers and 'government economists'*

In July 1947 the Economic Stabilization Board produced the first white paper on the Japanese economy. Its formal name was *Keizai Jisso Hokokusho* (The Report on the Real State of Economic Affairs), and the catchphrase was 'Fiscal deficit, corporate deficit, and household deficit'. Shigeto Tsuru drafted the general situation of the Japanese economy while Saburo Okita and Hitoshi Matsuo wrote on particular aspects. Coming across the British economic paper, *Economic Perspectives*, released by the Attlee Cabinet in February 1945, Hiroo Wada, Tsuru, and Okita agreed that Japan should make a similar detailed report on the analysis of general economic conditions and an outline of required economic policies and the basic attitude in budgeting (Okita 1981: 98).

Tsuru studied at Harvard from 1933 and received his PhD in 1940. He returned to Japan by exchange ship in 1942 with those Japanese diplomats, businessmen, scholars, and students who had been in the United States when Japan opened the war against the United States. Tsuru's orientation was close to classical economists, or institutional economists who were the majority in the United States until around 1940. Nonetheless, he brought back not only a cosmopolitan attitude but also imported American economic language into the community of Japanese economists and economic officials. His non-Marxian, non-historical style of analysis of the current Japanese economy was impressive because many Japanese economists of the day focused on Japanese capitalism from a historical perspective and included the end of the Tokugawa era and the Meiji restoration of 1868, even in the analysis of the current conditions. A white paper has been published every year and the authors have followed Tsuru's analytical style of writing since then.

The *White Paper on the Japanese Economy* has been widely known since the period of Yonosuke Goto's authorship. He wrote six white papers from 1952 till 1958, not including 1955, more than any other author. In 1956 he said, 'It was not postwar anymore' because the production level went over the highest level of the prewar period. This phrase convinced the Japanese people that postwar was really over. In 1957, Goto used and spread the phrase 'dual structure', which economists began to use in describing differentials in working hours and wages between large and small companies in Japan. Goto's exquisite use of phrases in expressing some characteristics of current conditions made *Economic White Paper* popular. It also became known that there were some economic experts in the government who could write a report on economic affairs. Yet Goto's economic forecast did not come to pass in 1958. He expected a prolonged economic setback, which he named the recession of 'the flat bottom of a pan', to come because business people were pessimistic after the Jinmu boom, which was named after the first Japanese Emperor, from December 1954 till July 1957. However, the Japanese economy enjoyed a boom of a record length, from July 1958 till December 1961, which was to be called the Iwato boom meaning the best boom since the era of Japanese myths.[3]

5.2.4 Establishment of the Ministry of International Trade and Industry and economic decontrol

In May 1948, the Committee for Economic Reconstruction Planning was established under the Ashida Cabinet. The chairperson was the Prime Minister, who also held the post of the governor of the Economic Stabilization Board at the establishment. The vice-chairperson of the committee was the secretary general of the Economic Stabilization Board. Several officials from relevant ministries and agencies, leaders of the business world, and people of experience or academic standing, including economists Seiichi Tobata, Shigeto Tsuru, Ichiro Nakayama, and Hiromi Arisawa, joined the committee. In May 1949 they made the final report of the five-year Economic Reconstruction Plan, which basically targeted rational economic circulation from production through distribution to consumption to support the economy in the fiscal year 1953. It was the first plan that gave priority to an increase in capital accumulation rather than the enhancement of living standards, and especially emphasized for the first time the encouragement of heavy and chemical industries. The ratio of foreign currency earnings per industry, which was obtained by dividing domestic value-added by the export price, was high in these industries. It was believed in the Economic Stabilization Board that the higher the ratio, the larger the increase in domestic income gained from the same amount of exports (Fujii 1988: 211).[4] Yet when the plan was reported, it was rejected by Shigeru Yoshida, who was the prime minister, probably because the plan supposed that Japan required considerable amounts of foreign aid in the process of recovery (Arisawa and Nakamura 1990: 248). Moreover, commodity prices began to decline in the black markets, the price level was finally stabilized, and the value of currency became stable by the implementation of the so-called Dodge Line or Nine-Part Directive on Stabilization (the strong anti-inflationary policy recommended by the American delegate Joseph M. Dodge). The Dodge Line also aimed to maximize production for export (Ikeo 1998: 138).

In August 1947, commercial trade abroad was resumed. In April 1949, the single exchange rate was fixed at \$1=¥360 by SCAP and the Japanese yen became convertible into foreign currencies. Restrictions on trade were gradually relaxed and a move toward the liberalization of trade (and later capital import) began. On 25 May 1949, the Ministry of International Trade and Industry (MITI) was established by reshuffling the Ministry of Trade and Industry. This ministry was first established in 1925, absorbed into the Ministry of Munitions during the war and reestablished after WWII. MITI took the prime principle of international trade to be the promotion of exports in order to secure the import of necessities. It inherited the traditional bottom-up production policy of encouraging the production of key industries at maximum level without considering profitability. Around this time, economic controls were losing their significance because there were partial gluts of several basic materials under the Dodge Line. MITI also cut administrative work for economic controls.

Several councils including the Advisory Council (Komon Kaigi), the Councilor Council (Sanyo Kaigi), the Imports Council (Yunyu Kyogikai), the Exports Council (Yushutsu Kyogikai), the Export Inspections Council (Yushutsu Kensa Shingikai), the Export Credit and Insurance Council (Yushutsu Shinyo Hoken Shingikai), the Nationwide Coal Mining Council (Zenkoku Tanko Kanri Shingikai), the Industrial Technology Council (Kogyo Gijutsu Unei Shingikai), the Council on the Encouragement of Invention (Hatsumei Shorei Shingikai), and others were established for economic democratization at the same time MITI was established. The power of the Economic Stabilization Board was gradually weakened, and the Council of Economic Reconstruction Planning, the Natural Resources Investigation Committee, the Economic Reconstruction Service Council, the Food and Nutrition Council, and the Currency Issue Council were established as accessories. In July 1949, a Cabinet meeting discussed industrial rationalization, and decided to make basic industries submit rationalization plans and to give official guidance to them. For the promotion of rationalization, it also decided to relax control over materials to a great extent, to decontrol commodity prices, to reevaluate assets, to ease corporate tax, and to improve communications and transportation. In December 1949, MITI established the major Industrial Rationalization Council, which discussed measures for rationalization in the steel and coal-mining industries. The government secured funds and helped import machines from abroad. In 1952, MITI and the Ministry of Finance (MOF) jointly enacted and enforced the Law of Firm Rationalization and reduced corporate tax in order to promote industrial rationalization. Japan's heavy and chemical industries welcomed the rationalization measures implemented under the leadership of MITI. Moreover, the Japan Productivity Center (a foundation, now Japan Center for Socio-Economic Productivity) was established as a private organ for the purpose of the stabilization of industrial relations (see Section 7.3).

In 1952, MITI suggested a curtailment of output to each cotton-spinning company in order to escape an industry depression and as a result it experienced a conflict with the Fair Trade Commission. MITI argued that this curtailment would not violate the Antimonopoly Law because it was not a plot designed and agreed on by industrialists. Rather it was an application of the system of foreign exchange control and was needed to establish quotas for future imports of cotton for the company whose production exceeded a reasonable operating level. Thus MITI authorized its 'suggestions'. The quota system of foreign currencies was enforced until 1960, and was an extremely strong policy tool for MITI. 'The suggestion of curtailment' was part of the policy measures, which have been called administrative guidance since the 1960s. It certainly fostered cartel formation in each industry. Some types of administrative guidance are still under way causing some conflicts with the Fair Trade Commission as well as a few lawsuits.

As influential economists joined the Industrial Rationalization Council, Martin Bronfenbrenner, who had stayed in Japan first as a SCAP member and then as a member of the Shoup Taxation Mission, reported on the professional schizophrenia of Japanese economics. Bronfenbrenner (1956: 396) said: 'A man with an outside job arranging dumping or price fixing for a sewing-machine or shipbuilding cartel will preach in class the virtues of pure competition and free trade, with as many diagrams and equations as you please.' Let us quote a possible counter-argument from the statement of Ichiro Nakayama, who was one of the leading Japanese economists of the day. Nakayama said: 'I understand the problem very well. However, the world of free trade has never existed in reality before. Although it is said that free trade reached the summit when Britain gained the hegemony of the world, the reduction of tariff rates was at issue. There has never been one world of ideal free trade on earth' (Nakayama *et al.* 1950: 43). In short, Nakayama would have refuted Bronfenbrenner in the following way: 'It is true that free trade is an ideal in policy making. Yet Japan alone does not have to commit itself to free trade because other countries do not do so in reality.' In fact, Japan's trade with the pound sterling area was affected by the delay of Britain's regaining the convertibility of sterling as well as by the sterling crisis after convertibility was regained.

On the other hand, the electricity industry had been under private ownership but run by the government during the war. In 1951, its business was divided into nine electricity companies and regulated by MITI. The research organization for the study of Japan's energy and economy was promptly set up. In 1951 the Institute for Power and Technological Research was established, and in 1952 reorganized into the Central Institute for Power Research, including the establishment of the Institute for Power and Economic Research, in order to promote both technological and economic studies in the field of energy.

In April 1952, the Peace Treaty was enacted, and the Temporary Law for the Adjustment of Supply and Demand of Materials, which was the basis for economic control, became void. The Japanese economy was supposed to shift gradually from a controlled economy to a free market, and MITI was reshuffled. Later MITI gradually lost powerful policy tools such as foreign exchange control in the liberalization of trade and (direct) capital imports.

In March 1954, the Study Group of Japan's Industrial Structure was organized by those who had joined the Section of Industrial Structure within the Industrial Rationalization Council, and chaired by Ichiro Nakayama. The total number of participants was more than seventy, including economists, business leaders, researchers from private manufacturing companies, and officials from MITI, MOF, Economic Council Agency (now Economic Planning Agency), Ministry of Agriculture and Forestry, Ministry of Labor, Ministry of Health and Welfare, Defense Agency, and Bank of Japan. The Research Department of MITI and the Institute for Electric Power and Economic Research served as secretariat. Their purposes were stated as follows:

1. We must comprehend the characteristics of the structure of our national economy, select the most relevant conditions for rational economic growth with adaptation of international environments, and synthesize both. It requires not only theoretical research of interdependence of economic quantities but also policies to promote the optimal industrial structure.

2. We must swiftly strengthen the export capabilities of our industries, fully utilize our domestic resources, and minimize our imports in order to cope with the increase in competition for worldwide exports when the world economy restores its normalcy. In order to absorb increasing employment based upon limited capital and natural resources and to promote exports, we should not count on short-run conditions but rationalize our industrial structure under certain conditions from a long-term perspective, and then find out the way to maximize the efficiency in our national economy. (Author's translation, Research Institute of Electric Power 1956: xix–xx).

Nine subcommittees were formed to discuss the following matters of industrial structure:

1. Japan's industrial structure and trade partners, and its relations to the structural changes in the world economy;
2. the conditions for the optimal industrial structure for the attainment of international balance;
3. the relations of Japan's industrial structure to agriculture, forestry, and marine products industries;
4. the relations of resource allocation to the industrial structure;
5. the relations of primary and new industry to the industrial structure;
6. the relations of employment and national income to the industrial structure;
7. productivity and technological standards;
8. the relations of industrial investment to the industrial structure;
9. the rationalization of industrial structure and its relations to industrial plans.

Government economists and university economists in the field of applied research of economic policy were all lined up. The list of members included not only Hiromi Arisawa and Seiichi Tobata at the top, but also Miyohei Shinohara, who invented 'the income elasticity criterion' and 'comparative technological progress criterion' used for the promotion of the heavy and chemical industries by MITI. It also included Yonosuke Goto, the first government economist of Japan, as well as Yoshihiko Morozumi, who was the head of the Research Department of MITI and later became known as a MITI 'economist' in the mid 1960s. Their research report was published in 1955 under the title *Assignment for Japan's Industrial Structure*, in two volumes, and made the greatest contribution to the understanding of Japan's economic and industrial conditions of the day from the perspective of export promotion.

Their report discussed Japan's (growth) policies for desirable industrial structure in the following way. They did not calculate the balance of economic quantities including the (physical) quantities of materials, but rather suggested the orientation for qualitative structural policies because '[Japan] is a free society in which individual companies act on their own decision and judgement' (Institute for Power and Economic Research 1956: vol. 2, 699–700). They took for granted the further industrialization and rationalization of the Japanese economy, and placed emphasis on the promotion of heavy and chemical industries, the nurturing of newly emerging industries such as the petrochemical industry, the strengthening of export industries, and the breaking of domestic bottlenecks. They also urged the utilization of domestic resources and the enlargement of the production scale in each industry. In short, they aimed 'to solve problems through development as well as increasing trade, especially exports' (Nakayama 1956: 16). In conclusion, they warned that these policies for industrial structure should be harmonized with the improvement of international balance, the increase in employment and national income, and especially the enhancement of the demand side and living standards. The desirable industrial structure was attained by relevant investment policies which, they hoped, would attract commercial funds.

Since then MITI has been spending its efforts and time in studying the current conditions of Japan's economy and industries and those policies necessary for growth. The targets of Japan's economic policies have been diversified since the mid 1960s. In the 1990s, when deregulation was under way, MITI continued to study the present state and the future of the Japanese economy, and relevant policies.

5.2.5 *Establishment of the Economic Planning Agency*

In late March 1952, the Agency of Prices (the agency which controlled prices) was abolished and in late July 1952, the Economic Stabilization Board, which had acted as the main bureau on economic control and planning was abolished. In July the Economic Council Agency was established with the aim of making long-term economic plans, comprehensive economic policies, the adjustment of economic policies among ministries and agencies, and an analysis of the contemporary economy. The Economic Council was established at the same time as an attached organ to the agency and was composed of fewer than 15 learned and experienced people, including a few economists. Its members could give the prime minister their opinions about important economic policies and planning. Japanese economists have been formally involved in the making of long-term economic plans. In May 1955, the Hatoyama cabinet reorganized the Economic Council Agency into the stronger Economic Planning Agency (EPA) and decided the first Five-Year Plan for Economic self-support in December.

In this process, Japanese economic data have been collected and processed, and the quality of the data was improved substantially. Yuzo Yamada's *Materials for the Estimation of National Income in Japan* (1951) provided for the first time an estimation of national income consistent with other important economic data. In the 1950s, not only the Economic Council Agency, but also MITI and the Ministry of Agriculture and Forestry compiled tables of inter-industry relations. The three organs worked independently of each other and finished up with three tables of the Japanese economy of 1951 in 1955. The project by MITI was the largest and led by Shinichi Ichimura, who had studied in the United States at MIT. About 25 experts and 10 assistants worked for some 20 months to complete the table. During 1958–9, the Economic Planning Agency, Ministry of Agriculture and Forestry, Ministry of Construction, the Agency of Administrative Management, Statistics Bureau at the Agency of Management and Coordination cooperated to compile the consolidated table of inter-industry inputs. Thus, the government and economists found a new way of collaboration (Ikeo 1994: 96–202).

5.3 Problems in 'economic plans'

This section considers characteristics of Japanese 'economic plans' while taking account of development of economic thought in Europe and North America. It is noteworthy that the United Nations has been strongly interested in economic development and development planning and Jan Tinbergen, one of the first Nobel Prize winners, played an important role in spreading the ideas and procedures of central planning.

5.3.1 Economic policies and 'economic plans'

In Japan, most economic policies pass through a layered deliberation process until their implementation. Within a single year budget, the government set measures of discriminatory exchange rates (until 1949), the allocation of foreign currencies or foreign exchange controls (until 1960), regulations, favorable or discriminatory taxation, discriminatory rates of interest, government expenditures, and fiscal and loan investment.[5] Sakakibara (1991: 51) said: '[The] Japanese government is heavily involved not in the private sector, but in public works such as the construction of infrastructure in agriculture and fishery, forestry, transportation, and telecommunication'. Yet Japan was not an exception; as De Wolff (1965: 137) said, 'Governments anxious to develop the economy as a whole will naturally be interested in infra-structure investment in transport and electric power, which are the government's special concern in nearly all the countries.' Again, Sakakibara (1991: 53) describes Japanese policy making in relation to budget compilation procedure as follows:

> [Most] of the government's policy decisions are made in relation to budget compilation and are packaged into one giant appropriation bill. Here, economic policy making is almost synonymous with budget compilation. As such, policy formulation is both a decentralized and cumulative process . . . Budget appropriations from the central government are crucial. The role of the politician is to comply with the wishes of local governments and the agricultural and other cooperatives that are the major force in his constituency and to request appropriations from the central bureaucracy.

Yet it can be said that a project planned by local government tends to come to pass if the target was consistent with the central target, especially in the case of a big project.

From a perspective of the history of economic thought, whether private or public, physical investment has two economic effects. One is to increase production capacity and therefore future supply. Another is that the increase in investment will increase effective demand and therefore trigger the multiplier process. This is the effect that was to be expected as the effect of Keynesian fiscal policies. These policies came out of the experiences of the Great Depression of the 1930s, such as the Tennessee Valley Authority (TVA) program in the United States, the public investment policy by Nazi Germany, and deficit financing done by Korekiyo Takahashi in Japan (Ikeo 1997). After WWII, many market-oriented countries believed that they could enjoy stable economic prosperity by incorporating the effects of public investment as planned. The concept of 'government failure' did not appear until the 1970s.

Not only Japan but also many other countries made central economic plans and the United Nations supported central planning by publishing *Manual on Economic Development Projects* (1958) and *Planning for Economic Development* (1965). The World Bank called upon econometricians like J. Tinbergen to prepare a study on the problem of priorities of individual projects as related to economic development programs (UN 1958: xiv). Until around the mid-1960s, many Europeans and Japanese believed in their governments' ability to make relevant economic plans. Especially in Japan, the majority of economists were Marxist or Marxian economists from 1945 until the late 1960s (Ikeo 1998). They were worried about big business wielding too much power over the market and believed in the central government's superior planning ability in the allocation of scarce resources and the creation of a more equitable distribution of wealth and income compared with the market mechanism. The remaining economists of the day were not neoclassical, market-oriented economists, but development economists. They believed in the important role of the central government and local municipal governments in economic development, although they trusted entrepreneurship in the private sector.

In the United States, it was determined that another major depression like that of the 1930s must not be permitted and as a consequence the Employment Act of 1946 was enacted. The Act stated that the responsibilities of the Federal Government were:

> to coordinate and utilize all its plans, functions, and resources for the purpose of creating and maintaining, in a manner calculated to foster and promote free competitive enterprise and the general welfare, conditions under which there will be afforded useful employment opportunities, including self-employment, for those able, willing, and seeking to work, and to promote maximum employment, production, and purchasing power.

However, this does not mean that the Federal Government should interfere directly with the operation of free markets by central planning. For instance, USA (1965: 222–3) put an emphasis on a reliance on general monetary and fiscal policies for the government to reach the goals of maximum employment, production and purchasing power. It can be said that USA (1965) endorsed the policy lines of the neoclassical synthesis, which was first suggested in the third edition of Paul Samuelson's *Economics* (1955). 'Planning of economic development in the United States of America' (USA 1965: 231, 237) gave a clear view of the market and planning of economic development as follows:

> A free market system works effectively to allocate resources to meet most pressing needs and to produce efficiently only if there is a reasonable degree of competition. The United States Government – perhaps more than any other in the world – has worked to protect and extend the area of competition. (p. 231)
>
> The idea of economic planning – usually thought of as planning by the Federal Government – attracts very little support in the United States. ...

Few Americans have any wish for individual freedom to be subjugated to authoritative, rigid planning imposed from above. Yet, through a little-noticed and little-disputed process of evolution, American society has adjusted pragmatically to deal with problems as they have arisen. In many cases, solutions have been found which strengthened and perfected the environment for effective private planning. In other situations, governments have assumed responsibility where private planning was unable to cope with developing problems. (p. 237)

Looking back on the history of economic planning, the Soviet Union, the first socialist country, was naturally the first to embark on central planning, which was supposed to replace the market system based on economic decisions made by decentralized individual producers and the coordination of economic activities stimulated by the price mechanism. On the other hand, in countries with market economies, individual producers are guaranteed to make individual decisions in production and investment, and therefore central planning will not fully affect individual decisions.

A number of countries with market economies made economic plans together when they aimed at economic reconstruction after the ravages of WWII. The Netherlands was the first country to set up a Central Planning Bureau and started the reconstruction program under the leadership of Tinbergen while reflecting the fact that the Netherlands had a dense population and heavily depended on international trade (like Japan). Exports are necessary for the exchange of imports of what the country does not produce. De Wolff (1965: 133–4) said:

> Planning is ... important if foreign financial assistance is required. The existence of a sound and efficient development plan assures the donor countries that the best use will be made of the aid they have to offer. At one time, in 1948 and following years, the European countries participating in the European Recovery Programme were asked to draw coherent five-year plans showing the way in which American aid would enable them to reach 'viability'.

It is noteworthy that the United States requested the recipient countries to draw an economic plan, while it did not wish the Federal Government to interfere in decentralized decision making in the US.

In Japan, the Economic Planning Agency (EPA) attends to the compilation and promotion of long-term economic plans, the compilation of basic policy for administration of the overall economy and annual outline of economic plans, the planning and promotion of basic policy for price stability, and the coordination of basic economic policies. As mentioned, the Economic Council is attached to the EPA, and it has now less than thirty members. It also has the Subcommittee for Following-up Economic Planning, the Committee of Long- and Mid-term Economic Analysis, and the Econometric Committee. A few economists joined each committee.

Looking at Table 5.1, 'Japan's Economic Plans', there were thirteen economic plans which had been approved in the Cabinet meeting from the first Five- Year Plan for Economic Self-support (1955), to the last Economic-Social Plan for Structural Reform (1995). The purposes of each plan were very political as they represented the attitude and targets of the current Cabinet. The Income Doubling Plan (Table 5.2) (10 years, the longest term) especially reflected public opinion for the enhancement of economic life. The politicians absorbed it wisely, and managed to turn public eyes to economic growth after the renewal of the United States–Japan Security Treaty.[6] It also aimed to prepare for the international tide for the liberalization of trade and capital imports (see Chapter 7). Moreover, it is true that Japan's economic plans tended to have a please-everyone characteristic because a cabinet decision requires unanimous approval and therefore support by every minister (Minato *et al.* 1967: 45).

5.3.2 *Income doubling plan*

In November 1959 the Prime Minister, Shinsuke Kishi, submitted a question about 'the possibility of a long-term economic plan which targeted the doubling of national income' to the Economic Council, and asked the Economic Planning Agency to draw up a plan. In addition to the existing subcouncil on Comprehensive Policy (chaired by Ichiro Nakayama), the Economic Council formed three subcouncils on the Government and Public Sector (chaired by Hidezo Inaba), on the Private Sector (chaired by Kamekichi Takahashi), and on the Econometric Analysis (chaired by Yuzo Yamada) in order to examine the possibility. The Subcouncil on the Government and the Public Sector had 10 task forces and the one on the Private Sector 7, including participation by 30 permanent members, 18 *ad-hoc* members and 191 expert members. They were economists, business leaders, directors of economic organizations, journalists, and representatives of workers or consumers, as well as expert officials from the government including MITI. After a series of layered discussions, Ichiro Ishikawa, the chair of the Economic Council, gave the answer to the Prime Minister Hayato Ikeda.

In aiming to double the real national income in ten years and to attain full employment, the Income Doubling Plan listed several targets including the preparation of infrastructure and social capital, guidance for the enhancement of industrial structure, the promotion of international trade and cooperation, the enhancement of human abilities and the promotion of sciences, the easing of the dual structure problem, and social stability. The 'guidance for the enhancement of industrial structure' was taken up seriously in order to prevent an increase in the trade deficit, because it was thought that there was a tendency that the increase in demand for the secondary and tertiary products was relatively larger than the increase in demand for primary products, and that the demand for heavy and chemical products would increase relatively faster than any other secondary products (Economic Council 1960: 173). For the first time, the plan took a kind of dichotomous approach to planning by regarding the 'planned' numbers for the private sector as just a guide whereas those for the public sector were 'real' plans. The policy measures which the government used for the execution of the plan were not traditional price controls or foreign exchange controls, but council and administrative guidance in addition to regulation, taxation and public finance (and the fiscal investment and loan program) (Economic Council 1960: 187, 211, 215). On the other hand, 'excess competition should be avoided at the same time when new manufactures should be allowed to enter the industry in a rational manner' (Economic Council 1960: 216). The concept of 'excess competition' was often used for the foundation of MITI policies and certainly it protected Japan's cartel constitution.[8]

The Income Doubling Plan was discussed at the joint meeting of the Japanese Association of Theoretical Economics and the Japanese Econometric Society in October 1960. In the session on 'The Japanese Economy', Osamu Shimomura of the Japan Development Bank gave his paper entitled 'The basic problems of growth policy', Isamu Miyazaki of EPA his 'The methodology of the Income Doubling Plan', and Shin-ichi Ichimura his 'The structure and growth of the Japanese economy'. Yuichi Shionoya, Keinosuke Baba, Miyohei Shinohara, Shuntaro Shishido and others discussed these papers. Shimomura's paper and the comments appeared in *Kikan Riron Keizaigaku* (*Economic Studies Quarterly*, Volume 11, number 3/4). Yet in the first footnote on page 1 said, '[Miyazaki's paper] is not included in this issue because it was mostly published in Saburo Okita's *Introduction to the Income Doubling Plan* (in Japanese, Nihon Keizai Shimbunsha)'. Okita of EPA was one of the important officers in charge of drafting the Income Doubling Plan. The treatment of copyright of public reports written by government officials has been very ambiguous; it is hard to determine what sources these reports relied on because there used to be no list of references. It is hard for outsiders to find how much the results had come out of a layered process of deliberations through a series of meetings in councils and subcouncils, because there was no obvious evidence for the differences in opinions inside the meetings. It is hard to judge how much the Japanese economists contributed to the drawing of the Income Doubling Plan, although it can be said that Nakayama's support for wage doubling in his New Year essay had some influence on the making of the original idea (see Chapter 7).

5.3.3 *Effectiveness of economic plans*

What about the effectiveness of economic plans? It is apparent that no economic plan was completed before the following plan started, when we collate the ending point of an economic plan and the beginning point of the following plan. The reason was that the actual figures were different from the planned ones. When economic plans were revised several times before their completion, the usefulness of economic plans was doubted. As we saw, the Japanese government's economic 'plans' did not serve as real plans. Therefore from late 1968 to early 1969, the Economic Council and its General Subcouncil decided to form the Committee to Study Basic Issues in Economic Planning. The committee had Kazushi Ohkawa (1908–94) serving as the chair and six other members, namely Saburo

Table 5.1 Japan's economic plans

Year/month	Period (fiscal year)	Name	Purposes	Cabinet
1955/12	1956–60	Five-Year Plan for Economic Self-Support	Economic viability Full employment	Hatoyama
1957/12	1958–62	New Long-Term Economic Plan	Maximum growth The enhancement of economic life Full employment	Kishi
1960/12	1961–70	Income Doubling Plan	Maximum growth The enhancement of economic life Full employment	Ikeda
1965/1	1964–68	Midterm Economic Plan	The correction of distortion	Sato
1967/3	1967–71	Economic-Social Development Plan: Challenge Showa 40's	Development to balanced, enriched economic society	Sato
1970/5	1970–75	New Economic-Social Development Plan	The construction of comfortable Japan through balanced economic development	Sato
1973/2	1973–77	Basic Plan for Economic Society: For Vital Welfare	Simultaneous attainment of national welfare and international cooperation	Tanaka
1976/5	1976–80	Economic Plan for the Last Half of the 1970s: For a Stable Society	For a stable economic development and enriched national life	Miki
1979/8	1979–85	New Economic-Social Plan for 7 Years	Shifting to a stable growth path For enriched quality of national life Contribution to international economic and social development	Ohira

Date	Title	Goals	Prime Minister
1983/8	Projection and Guide for Economic Society in the 1980s	The formation of peaceful and stable international relations The formation of vital economic society The formation of safe and rich national life	Nakasone
1988/5	Japan Living with the Rest of the World: Five-Year Plan for Economic Management	Correction of international imbalance and the contribution to the world For a national life with the feeling of richness Development of balanced local economic community	Takeshita
1992/6	Five-Year Plan for the Enhancement of Living Conditions: For the Coexistence of Global Community	Enhancing living conditions The coexistence of global community The preparation of developmental basis	Miyazawa
1995/12	Economic-Social Plan for Structural Changes: For a Vital Economy with Security	The creation of free and vital economic society The creation of rich and safe economic society Participation in local communities	Murayama

Source: Based on Material 9 'Japan's Economic Plans' in Economic Planning Agency (1997: 927) with a little change.

Table 5.2 Taskforces for making the Income Doubling Plan within the Economic Council in 1960

In the Subcouncil of Public Sector	*In the Subcouncil of Private Sector*
Allocation of investment funds Industrial location and industrial basis The establishment of a rational and comprehensive transport system The installations of residential and living conditions The improvement of mountains and rivers for the preservation and efficient use of national land The establishment of a rational energy policy The education of science and technology and technological development The institution of education and vocational training Social security and the enhancement of social welfare Public and commercial finance	The role of the government in the private sector The advance in manufacturing industry The promotion of trade and international economic cooperation Modernization of agriculture, forestry and fisheries, and the promotion of workers' mobilization among industries Policies for middle- and small-sized companies The improvement of wages and employment The enhancement of living standards

Okita, Masao Sakisaka, Yasuo Takeyama, Hiroshi Tanimura, Yuzo Yamada, and Shigenobu Yamada. Their report became available in Japanese as *Japan's Economic Planning* in June 1969, but could not wipe out the doubts about central planning. Nonetheless, they argued that central planning had three important functions. Later Okita summarized them as follows:

> First is the educational and informative role centering on economic forecasting. With economic plans providing an overview of the outlook for the economy, private-sector companies are then able to formulate their own long-term plans with this in mind. Second is the statement of long-term commitments centering on practical planning. Every plan includes policy programs to be carried out by the government, including the distribution of investment in the major public sectors. As such, the plan is a statement of the administration's long-range policy directions. And third is its role in mediating among different interests. The Economic Council, which deliberates on these plans, includes industrialists, labor leaders, journalists, academic economists and other people representing a broad range of interests. As a result, the Council's deliberations serve to mold compromises among these conflicting interests and to forge popular consensus on what kind of a society and economy Japan should strive to be. (Okita 1989: 180)

Yet, labor leaders did not join the Economic Council until the late 1960s (see Section 3.4).

In retrospect, it is true that planning technology was greatly improved by the advancement of computers and the spread of low-priced machines. The plan became consistent among various economic policies by the use of both macro-econometric models and inter-industry analysis, and thus added something to our knowledge of how the economy worked. The Income Doubling Plan (1960) adopted the method of supposed growth rate, which considered the conditions necessary to attain the desired growth rate, but did not consider the relationship between the macro-numbers and the numbers for various industries. Therefore, it was soon found that the plan itself had numerical errors because there was inconsistency between the scope of heavy and chemical industrialization and the supposition of investment demand. The Midterm Economic Plan (1965), for the remaining period of the Income Doubling Plan, was created by linking the midterm macro-econometric model and the inter-industry model. For this purpose, the Econometric Subcommittee was first formed under the chairmanship of Ichiro Nakayama. Kazushi Ohkawa, Hiroya Ueno, Tadao Uchida, Kotaro Tsujimura, Masao Baba, Kennichi Miyazawa, Akira Yajima, Yasuhiko Yuize, Masahiro Tatemoto, and Tsunehiko Watanabe created the midterm macroeconomic model and the inter-industry model with the cooperation of Shuntaro Shishido, engineer of the Economic Planning Agency, by using the latest computing technology. The plan finally looked very scientific.

However, the Midterm Economic Plan was abolished in a year and had the shortest life of all the official plans. The following economic reasons were listed. First, the increase in the rate of consumer price inflation was estimated at 2.5 percent per year but it was 4.5 percent in FY1964 and 6.1 percent in FY1965. Second, the real increase in private investment was estimated at 9.9 percent but was 15.4 percent in FY 1964 and private investment fell 6.3 percent in FY1965. Third, the plan did not recommend deficit financing but national bonds were issued to finance fiscal policy.[9]

In addition to these reasons, there were political factors such as the Cabinet change, and the maneuvering or ignoring of planned numbers calculated from scientific procedures. In the last half of the 1960s, the active econometricians such as Uchida and Tatemoto vehemently criticized these politicians' manipulation of estimated numbers in economic plans. Tatemoto (1967: 155) defended the Midterm Economic Plan as follows:

> The only change in fundamental conditions was the government's deficit financing by issuing public bonds. Consumer prices rose more than the figures in the plan, because the planners have secretly switched to a less sensitive function for the changes in consumer prices than the original one which had been estimated by the Econometric Subcommittee. We would have produced numbers closer to actual ones if we had used the original function. Therefore, it was not a serious defect of the plan. [Author's translation]

However, no committee for econometric modeling was formed in drawing the next Economic-Social Development Plan (1967), which was to replace the

Midterm Economic Plan (1965). The new plan became the target of criticism by economists.[10] The prime minister Eisaku Sato consulted about the plan with the Economic Council, which was chaired by Kazutaka Kikawada of Keizai Doyukai (Japan Committee for Economic Development, now the Japan Association of Corporate Executives) and cooperated by other industrialists as members of the Subcommittee on Planning. First, these industrialists suggested that the restructuring of industries and large-scale companies was needed in the face of the liberalization of capital imports. Second, they drew attention to 'social development' by including the prefix 'social' in the name of the plan. They advocated the construction of an affluent regional society, the securing of residence with improved living conditions, the control of industrial pollution, etc. Third, they advocated 'stable prices' and conceived both economic growth and price stability at the same time. They aimed not only at keeping international trade in balance, but also at reducing the growth rate down to 8.2 percent and the increase in consumer prices down to 3 percent.

Uchida and Tatemoto examined the planned numbers designed by the Economic Council by using the econometric models created by the former Econometric Subcommittee and vehemently criticized the inconsistency among the 'planned' numbers (Uchida 1967; Tatemoto 1967). Uchida (1967: 38) said:

> Assume that the planned increases in labor and capital come off, and that the production function which the Econometric Subcommittee estimated prevails during the term, then the economic growth rate calculated from the production side should be near 10 percent. This rate is much larger than the 8 percent rate which was calculated from the so-called macro-econometric model.

In retrospect, Uchida's estimation was closer to what occurred in reality. The Japanese economy grew at more than 10 percent in real terms on average and enjoyed the so-called Izanagi boom from 1967 through 1970. Consumer prices rose more than 6 percent, the trade surplus went up sharply, and social overhead capital became conspicuously scarce. Then another economic plan was required while the Committee to Study Basic Issues in Economic Planning was established.

The third Sato Cabinet approved the New Economic-Social Development Plan (6-year term) in 1970. The subtitle was 'Creating human economic society'. It took up a stance for improving the international status of Japan, further promoting internationalization, and examining the social basis of people's lives. The numbers in the new plan were supposed to fall under some range, but the economic growth rate was targeted at 10.6 percent in the midst of the Izanagi boom. Shortly after the plan was decided, a recession followed and in retrospect marked the end of the high-growth period. A double-digit rate of growth has never again occurred since then. Thus the expectation of economic growth rate as calculated by the macroeconometric model was missed by a wide margin. In the 1970s, the expected rate of economic growth forecasted by the macroeconomic model based on the economic data of the 1960s turned out to be too optimistic. This was a bitter experience for applied econometricians. The Econometric Committee of the Economic Council (1980: preface) summarized the importance of the macroeconomic and inter-industry model as follows: 'The use of macroeconometric models has enabled us to examine the consistency among planned variables, to quantify the effectiveness of a policy, to analyze and evaluate the plans ex-post. These models have been improved significantly and played a great part in making and promoting economic plans.' In other words, economic plans were trusted except for economic forecasting. The next economic 'plan' was the Basic Plan for Economic Society with the subtitle of 'For Vital Welfare' in 1973.

Nonetheless, in Table 5.3 (shown later) the Econometric Committee has survived at least when economic plans are created since the late 1960s. Most of members of the committee are university economists but it also includes a few trained government economists and engineers. No industrialists, labor leaders, or consumers have ever joined the Econometric Committee.

In the 1960s, an econometrician's job was first to build a model which represented an economy, input data into it, and then clarify how accurate the model was. Then econometricians predicted the growth rate of national income and simulated the results of discretionary policies. Econometrics had made good progress since Ragner Frisch created the term in the late 1920s. In 1969, Sveriges Riksbank, the central bank of Sweden, established the Nobel Prize for economics. Two econometricians Frisch and Jan Tinbergen, were among the first Nobel Laureates. But before then, it was found that econometric models in each country performed rather badly. Tinbergen (1992: 42–43) said: 'I am afraid that the first subject I tackled in my work for the League of Nations, namely to explain the fluctuations in investment activity, never has become a great success. In the Netherlands Central Planning Bureau we found it safer, after some years, to ask industrialists for their investment programs rather than rely on an econometric explanation.' In Japan, industrialists drew an economic plan in 1967 but inconsistency among planned numbers was found in the plan. On the other hand, planning based on econometric modeling failed as well in the early 1970s.

In the 1970s, it was found that not only the market could fail, but that the government could fail also. Discretionary policies did not achieve the desired results because private economic agents would change their activities in responding to government policies, as Robert Lucas maintained. In Japan, economic planning became less glorious than before, while the period of rapid growth came to end.

5.4 Economists and the Economic Council

This section focuses on the functions of councils and the role of economists in the process of making economic policies. OECD's *Social Science Policy in Japan* (1977) stated in the chapter 'The use of social science study and the influence of policy making' that deliberation councils were considered to be the most important place for social scientists to participate in policy making, and reward attention to the members of the Economic Council (the Japanese version: 227). Therefore, we cannot ignore the place of economists in councils when we examine economists' roles in economic policy making.

5.4.1 Deliberation councils

On 1 July 1998, there were 212 councils for deliberation, inquiry and examination attached to ministries or government agencies in Japan. The Administration Agency began to publish *The Summary of Councils* in Japanese every four years around 1975. In 1983 the Management and Coordination Agency took over the job and the interval was shortened to two years. *The Summary of Councils* gives us information on councils such as competent ministries or agencies, legal foundation, purposes, prescribed number of regular members, their term, their names, and recent inquiries and answers. The councils relating to economic policies are scattered among many ministries and agencies such as the Management and Coordination Agency, the Ministry of Wealth and Welfare, the Ministry of Agriculture, Forestry and Fishery, the Ministry of International Trade and Industry, the Ministry of Transport, the Ministry of Posts and Telecommunication, the Ministry of Labor, the Ministry of Construction, and the Ministry of Home Affairs. The councils that, relatively, many economists join include the Economic Council and the National Lifestyle Council (both attached to the Economic Planning Agency), the Industrial Structure Council (the Ministry of International Trade and Industry). The term of regular members is two years as in many Japanese councils. Economists also join the related committees and subcommittees.

The process of policy making and the role of councils have been eagerly examined by scholars in public administration and political science. Michio Muramatsu in his *Japanese Bureaucrats after WWII* (in Japanese, 1981) used an interesting questionnaire to find the most important perceived role of councils. He asked those questioned to select one out of four choices that was considered to be of the most importance and received answers from 55 high-ranking officials, 195 mid-ranking officials, 50 LDP house members and 51 non-LDP house members. The most selected choices as a whole were to make policies and administrative decisions fair, and to coordinate social interest and conflict. Each accounts for 30 percent. In both sets of high-ranking officials and LDP members, the fairness of policy making came first, whereas in the set of middle-ranking officials the coordination of interest came first. The third choice as a whole was to acquire expertise and new ideas, and was 25 percent. The fourth as a whole was to authorize administrative decisions. In the set of only non-LDP house members the first was the acquisition of expertise, the second was authorization, the third was fairness in policy. However, each choice accounts for only 22–27 percent respectively.

The above four choices are very important although different councils are expected to function differently. Thus there have been layered processes of deliberation in councils in making economic plans and policies. Yet this kind of procedure has been taken for central planning in Europe as well. Tinbergen

(1964: 14) recommended the 'procedure', indicating the nature and time order of all contacts with the outside world, contacts with ministries, lower public authorities, regional or sectional planning agencies, business organizations, trade unions, and research institutions needed in the planning process. Tinbergen (1964: 14) continued as follows:

> [T]here are two main reasons why a considerable number of outside contacts are preferable. On one hand, detailed information on the economic process and its elements can better be obtained from a number of outside experts, including those handling these elements. Additionally, outside contacts make it possible to exchange opinions with those operating the economy at its various levels and hence may introduce some features of democracy, which are not customary within the single enterprise, but obviously are valuable. Among other things this element of democracy may help to facilitate the acceptance of a plan by parliament as well as its execution.

We will pay attention to the two councils that, relatively, many economists join and especially examine the Economic Council's members and organization.

5.4.2 Economic Council

The Economic Council was established in 1952 and attached to the Cabinet Planning Bureau at the Economic Planning Agency. It is supposed to respond to the Prime Minister's inquiries and is allowed to give opinions on long-term economic planning, important economic policies and plans. Its members should be learned and experienced persons and the currently prescribed membership is 30 or fewer. The Economic Planning Agency kindly gave us the formation and relations of committees within the Economic Council and the list of members.[11]

Table 5.3 lists the committees, the chairs and the number of members at the time when the past 13 economic plans were approved at cabinet meetings. The Economic Council always has several subcommittees and taskforces, some of which continue to the making of the next plan while others are abolished. The names of subcouncils tell us the problems to be handled at the time. In July 1996, there are the Subcouncil on the Promotion of Structural Changes, the Special Subcouncil, the Committee on Action Programs, the Committee on Transferring the Function of Capital City, the Committee on the World Economy of the 21st Century, and the Econometric Committee. In July 1994, there were the Subcouncil for the Following Up of the Economic Plan, the Committee on Mid- and Long-Term Economic Analysis, and the Econometric Committee. The only committee that has survived is the Econometric Committee. The Economic Planning Agency makes it a rule to summarize the relations of subcouncils and committees in a diagram at least when an economic plan is decided, although Table 5.3 does not necessarily tell you the complete relationship. Otherwise the number of subcouncils and committees may easily increase and the Economic Council would expand indefinitely.

Table 5.3 Subcouncils and committees in the Economic Council (when each plan was approved at a Cabinet meeting)

	Date of approval					
Name of Plans	12/1955 Five-Year Plan for Economic Self-Support	12/1957 New Long Term Economic Plan	12/1960 Income Doubling Plan	01/1965 Midterm Economic Plan	03/1967 Economic-Social Development Plan	05/1970 New Economic-Social Development Plan
Chair	I. Ishikawa	I. Ishikawa	I. Ishikawa	I. Ishikawa	K. Kikawada	K. Kikawada
Number of committees	25	30	30	30	30	30
Sub-councils / Chairs / Number of members	General / I. Ishikawa / 26	General / I. Nakayama / 30	Comprehensive Policy / I. Nakayama / 42	Planning / H. Aoyama / 21	Comprehensive Policy / J. Enjoji / 41	General / J. Enjoji / 29
	Production / Y. Watanabe / 35	Mineral and Manufacturing / S. Kurata / 37	Public sector / H. Inaba / 95	Policy / S. Okita / 18	Prices / K. Kono / 22	Planning / T. Fukura / 20
	Construction and Transportation / H. Kurushima / 22	Energy / S. Kojima / 21	Private Sector / K. Takahashi / 76	Econometric / K. Ohkawa / 10	National Life / K. Imai / 23	International Economy / T. Minakami / 32
	Life and Employment / H. Arisawa / 26	Agriculture, Forestry and Fisheries / Y. Kusumi / 24	Econometric / Y. Yamada / 19	National Life / K. Imai / 14	Industry / H. Inaba / 29	Life / K. Imai / 35
	Trade / K. Takagaki / 24	Construction and Transportation / K. Uemura / 31		Working / K. Baba / 18	Agriculture, Forestry and Fisheries / S. Tobata / 27	Industry / H. Inaba / 44
	Public and Commercial Finance / T. Kawakita / 23	Employment / H. Arisawa / 25		Mineral and Manufacturing / H. Tokunaga / 23	Middle and Small Sized Companies, and Distribution / S. Kitano / 31	Public and Commercial Finance / T. Morinaga / 30

National Life	Middle and Small Sized Companies, and Distribution	Public and Commercial Finance	Econometric
S. Tobata		T. Morinaga	M. Baba
18	17	18	6
Trade	Agriculture, Forestry and Fisheries	Social Capital	Land Policy
K. Takagaki	T. Ogura	S. Shihara	H. Takayama
30	18	20	9
Public and Commercial Finance	Social Capital	International Balance	Prices, Wages, Income and Productivity
T. Kawakita	H. Inaba	T. Minakami	K. Baba
26	15	25	4
	International Balance	Working	Industrial Location
	T. Minakami	K. Baba	K. Tsuchiya
	14	19	15
	Public and Commercial Finance		Basic Problems of Economic Planning
	K. Kawano		K. Ohkawa
	14		
156	182	255	224
232			14
242			426

Total members
Total subcommittees
Total members

Table 5.3 Continued

	Date of approval						
Name of Plans	02/1973 Basic Plan for Economic Society	05/1976 Economic Plan for the Last Half of the 1970s	08/1979 New Economic-Social Plan for 7 years	08/1983 Projecting and Guide Economic Society in the 1980s	05/1988 Japan Living with the Rest of the World	06/1992 Five-Year Plan for the Enhancement of Living Conditions	12/1995 Economic-Social Plan for Structural Changes
Chair	K. Kikawada	K. Kikawada	J. Enjoji	J. Enjoji	G. Hiraiwa	G. Hiraiwa	G. Hiraiwa
Number of committees	30	30	30	27	27	26	26
Sub-councils / Chairs / Number of members	General / J. Enjoji / 35	General / J. Enjoji / 35	General / 36	General / S. Ishihara / 36	Steering / 15	Steering / 18	Steering / 15
	Investigation / S. Okita / 8	Planning / S. Ishihara / 17	Planning / Y. Tanimura / 22	Planning / T. Yano / 20	Planning and Public / J. Yoshikuni / 35	Planning and Public / M. Nagaoka / 42	Planning / M. Nagaoka / 26
	Planning / S. Ishihara / 13	Econometric / K. Tsujimura / 14	Econometric / K. Tsujimura / 14	Econometric / K. Tsujimura / 21	National Life / K. Tsujimura / 25	Rich Life / I. Miyazaki / 30	Free and Vital Economy / S. Toyoda / 31
	Public and Commercial Finance / T. Morinaga / 21	International Economy / T. Minakami / 31	International Economy / T. Minakami / 23	International Economy / K. Saeki / 40	Regions and Industry / S. Akasawa / 25	Developmental Basis / T. Sekimoto / 41	Rich and Safe Life / Y. Shionoya / 30
	Life / H. Aoyama / 20	Industry / H. Inaba / 48	National Life / M. Yamamoto / 29	National Life / S. Tsutsumi / 30	International Economy / S. Tabuchi / 25	Global Assignments / Y. Kobayashi / 37	Global Society and the Role of Japan / K. Moroi / 30
	Environment and Regions / M. Sakisaka / 24	National Life / M. Sumiya / 22	Industry / K. Ueno / 50	Industry / H. Tokunaga / 71	Econometric / K. Tsujimura / 19	Econometric / A. Amano / 17	Next Generation / Y. Kobayashi / 16

Industry H. Inaba	Living Environment Regions M. Sakisaka	Public and Commercial Finance S. Sumita	Regions and Living Environment M. Sakisaka		High Speed Communication Information Society K. Kawakatsu
28	25	25	27		21
International Economy T. Minakami	Public and Commercial Finance Y. Tanimura	Regional Economy M. Sakisaka	Public and Commercial Finance J. Yoshikuni		Econometric A. Amano
15	23	13	28		17
Econometric M. Baba	Prices and Demand Management T. Otsuki	Projection of Supply and Demand of Energy K. Ueno	Energy Y. Morozumi		
12	7	8	18		
NNW Development M. Shinohara					
7					
National Preference M. Shishido					
7					
Total members					
Total subcommittees					
Total members					
190	187	220	291	129	167	171

The criteria for selecting and reselecting council members is a little different from one council to another. In the case of the Economic Council, there are no explicit criteria other than that 30 or fewer members should be selected from learned and experienced people. A person is selected because he/she is believed to be needed from time to time, sometimes from the point of view of affiliations, at other times from the personal judgement that he/she is hard to replace. With regard to the criterion for reselection, there is the oral agreement in a cabinet meeting of 1963 that the limit of reselection should be two terms for a council member with a four-year term in the case of deliberation councils attached to the Management and Coordination Agency. Applying this to a council member with a two-year term, 'The limit of reselection for an Economic Council member should be 4 terms for 8 years'. Yet there is an exception that a person can assume the chair or a council membership with a cabinet agreement if he/she is judged to be hard to replace by another. In fact, there were a couple of persons who have assumed the chair or council membership for longer than 8 years.[12] Table 5.3 shows that Ichiro Ishikawa served as the chair for more than 10 years. Table 5.5 shows that Ichiro Nakayama was a council member for about a quarter of a century and Seiichi Tobata for a little more than 20 years.

Table 5.4 has 24 kinds of affiliations. Most of the council members who are affiliated with universities are economists. But there are a few engineers and sociologists because economic policies and 'economic plans' cover a wide range of activities, including a large number of public works projects and target a balanced development between economic and social elements. Table 5.5 includes Masaji Suzuki, who was a port engineer and had worked for the Ministry of Internal Affairs, and Hideka Takayama, urban engineer. The origin of urban planning can be traced back to an ancient time, but no beautiful city was planned in the pre-modern period. In other words, there was time enough for carrying out a piecemeal construction in harmony with the whole into consideration and to result in a balanced look for the city. In contrast, the ideal of architects and urban planners often conflicts with economic rationality and the phenomenon of urban sprawl associated with the spread of capitalism looked especially ugly to their eyes. Takashi Mukaibo specialized in industrial chemistry and materials for atomic furnaces, and had assumed the Presidency of the University of Tokyo. Kunio Otaka specialized in industrial sociology, Sadako Ogata in international politics, and Chie Nakane in cultural anthropology.

When we look at the titles of members, there are many managers in large companies. Especially, the chair of the Economic Council is always a top manager. Ichiro Ishikawa, the first chair, was a member of the Chemical Control Society (Kagaku Toseikai) during WWII. Since 1945, he had assumed the Presidency of Keidanren and then the chair, a member of the Atomic Energy Commission, the first President of Japan Nuclear Vessel Development Undertaking Body and then the chair. The second chair of the Economic Council was Kazutaka Kikawada, who was the President of Tokyo Electric Power Company and then became the chair. Kikawada supported Yasuzaemon

Table 5.4 Affiliations of Economic Council members (when economic plans were approved)

Year	1955	1957	1960	1965	1967	1970	1973	1976	1979	1983	1988	1992	1995	1998
University	3	3	2	2	3	5	5	5	5	4	5	5	2	2
Research institute			2	2	2	1	1		1	1		1	2	3
Fisheries				1	1	1								
Mineral industry	2	2		1	1									
Manufacturing	8	9	9	7	7	6	4	2	3	3	5	4	5	5
Energy	1	2	2	2	2	2	2	2	2	1	1	2	2	2
Transportation	1	1	1	1	1	2	1							
Finance	1	2	2	7	6	4	4	4	4	5	3	4	5	6
Trading companies	2	2	2	1	1	1	1	1	1					
Distribution						1								
Real estate							1	1	1					
Construction										1				
Newspapers and broadcasting	1	1	1	1	1	1	1				1			
Keidanren	1	2	2	1	1		1	2	1	1	1	1	1	1
Chamber of Commerce						2	1	1	1	1		1		
Workers' groups							2	3	3	3	3	3	3	3
Consumers' groups								1	1	1	1	1	1	1
Other groups												1		
Public institution	4	4	4	4	4	2	4	4	6	4	6	3	3	2
Investigative institute	1	2	3			2	3	3		1	1		2	
Other councils									1					
Critics and others										1				2
No titles								1						
Total	25	30	30	30	30	30	30	30	30	27	27	26	26	27
# Women	0	0	0	0	0	0	1	1	1	1	2	2	3	3

Table 5.5 The Economic Council members who belong to universities or research institutes (when economic plans were approved)

Year/month	1955.12	1957.12	1960.12	1965.1	1967.3	1970.5	1973.2
Universities (U)	H. Arisawa (U. of Tokyo)	H. Arisawa (U. of Tokyo)	M. Suzuki (*Nihon U.)	M. Suzuki (*Nihon U.)	K. Ohkawa (Hitotsubashi U.)	H. Aoyama (Kyoto U.)	H. Aoyama (Kyoto U.)
	S. Tobata (U. of Tokyo)	S. Tobata (U. of Tokyo)	I. Nakayama (Hitotsubashi U.)	I. Nakayama (*Hitotsubashi U.)	M. Suzuki (*Nihon U.)	K. Ohkawa (Hitotsubashi U.)	K. Otaka (*U. of Tokyo)
	I. Nakayama (Hitotsubashi U.)	I. Nakayama (Hitotsubashi U.)			I. Nakayama (*Hitotsubashi U.)	M. Suzuki (*Nihon U.)	H. Takayama (*U. of Tokyo)
						S. Tobata (*U. of Tokyo)	S. Tobata (*U. of Tokyo)
						I. Nakayama (*Hitotsubashi U.)	I. Nakayama (*Hitotsubashi U.)
Research Institutes (RI)			K. Takahashi (TIER)	K. Takahashi (TIER)	K. Takahashi (TIER)	K. Takahashi (TIER)	T. Ogura (IDE)
			S. Tobata (IDE)	S. Tobata (IDE)	S. Tobata (IDE)		

	Year/month						
	1976.5	1979.8	1983.8	1988.5	1992.6	1995.12	1998.7
Universities (U)	H. Aoyama (Kwansei Gakuin U.)	S. Kawano (U. of Tokyo)	S. Kawano (U. of Tokyo)	S. Ogata (Sophia U.)	M. Kaji (U. of the Air)	M. Kaji (U. of the Air)	S. Kumon (International U.)
	H. Kumagai (Osaka U.)	H. Kumagai (Kansai U.)	H. Kumagai (Kansai U.)	M. Kaji (U. of the Air)	Y. Sazanami (Keio U.)	Y. Sazanami (Keio U.)	Y. Sazanami (Meikai U.)
	S. Tobata (*U. of Tokyo)	M. Sumiya (Shinshu U.)	M. Shinohara (Seikei U.)	K. Tsujimura (Keio U.)	K. Tsujimura (TEWU)		
	I. Nakayama (*Hitotsubashi U.)	I. Nakayama (*Hitotsubashi U.)	T. Mukaibo (U. of Tokyo)	C. Nakane (*U. of Tokyo)	C. Nakane (*U. of Tokyo)		
	T. Mukaibo (U. of Tokyo)	T. Mukaibo (U. of Tokyo)		K. Itsumi (*U. of Tokyo)	K. Itsumi (TEWU)		
Research Institutes (RI)		S. Sasaki (NIRA)	S. Sasaki (NIRA)		I. Miyazaki (Daiwa RI)	Y. Shionoya (ISS)	Y. Kosai (JERC)
						K. Mizuguchi (Nomura RI)	S. Hoshino (NIRA)
							K. Mizuguchi (Nomura RI)

Notes

* Professor emeritus

IDE - Institute for Developing Economies
JERC - Japan Economic Research Center
TEWU - Toyo Eiwa Women's University
TIER - Takahashi Institute for Economic Research
ISS - Institute for Social Security

Matsunaga, who advocated the privatization of the state-run electric business after WWII, and managed to distribute the assets among nine electric companies once the privatization project was passed in the Diet. He assumed the Presidency of Keizai Doyukai as well. Jiro Enjoji was the President of Nihon Keizai Shimbunsha. Gaishi Hiraiwa was the President of Tokyo Electric Power Company, and Shoichiro Toyota, the current chair of the Economic Council, is the chair of Toyota Automobile Company. Both businessmen assumed the Presidency of Keidanren, too.

Looking at the distribution of professions among the council members, we find that manufacturers have been always the largest group, and accounted for one-third from the 1950s until around 1960. The number of council members from the financial business was increased in the mid-1960s. In fact it can be said that there was a qualitative change in members of the Economic Council, because (two) large commercial bank(s) and a large securities company sent their heads to the Economic Council for the first time. In 1965, the council members from commercial banks included Jun Usami, the President of Mitsubishi Bank, who was the President for the Federation of Bankers Associations of Japan (Zenginkyo) at the time. One of the reasons for the change could be that large commercial banks were vehemently opposed to, and managed to scrap, the Special Measures Law for the Promotion of Designated Industries (Tokushin-hoan) which was proposed to the Diet by the Ministry of International Trade and Industry in 1963. Therefore, the government began to communicate closely with influential bankers.[13] The Economic Council began to have members represented from workers' groups in the late 1960s and from consumers' groups such as the Japanese Consumers' Co-operative Union (Nihon Seikyo Rengo) and the Japan Housewives Association (Shufuren) as late as the mid-1970s.

As we have seen already, the Econometric Committee is the only group that has survived in the Economic Council since the late 1960s. Japanese economists began to play a different role in the technical job of creating econometric models from other learned and experienced people.

5.4.3 Industrial Structure Council

The Industrial Structure Council is the largest of all deliberation councils in its number of members and subcommittees. It has been attached to the Ministry of International Trade and Industry (MITI) since its establishment in 1964. Its function is 'to examine and discuss important matters on industrial structure with respect to the queries offered by the International Trade and Industry Minister'. The number of members must be 130 or fewer and their term is two years. There are 43 members in the General Subcouncil as of July 1996. At the time there were subcouncils on industrial finance, distribution, industrial location, the information industry, the housing industry, WTO, the treatment of wastes and its re-utilization, the promotion of continuing education, global environment, economic cooperation, security and trade management, consumer economy, and textiles.

Looking at the prehistory of the Industrial Structure Council, we find the Industrial Rationalization Council established in December 1949, and the Industrial Structure Investigation Council established in 1961 for the next three years in order to examine and discuss the basic problems regarding industrial structure. The Industrial Investigation Council had 12 subcouncils on general matters, small and mid-sized companies, trade, industrial finance, industrial technology, industrial system, heavy industry, chemical industry, textile and miscellaneous goods, nonferrous metals, and energy in general. The council had 331 committee members and expert assistants (MITI 1994: 424). In November 1963 the chair, Shinichi Kojima, the President of Yawata Steel, gave the Minister the report 'The policy line and targets for the policy of industrial structure', which suggested the promotion of heavy and chemical industries. In March 1964, both councils were abolished and the Industrial Structure Council was established as a permanent organ to examine and deliberate on the basic problems in industrial structure. The number of members was prescribed 130 or fewer, and Kojima, the President of Yawata Steel, became the first chair for the new council. After 1964 industrial policies were supposed to go through the exchange of information and the coordination of interests. The Industrial Structure Council is described as 'MITI's number one official channel to the business community' (Johnson 1982: 102).

The Industrial Structure Section of the Industrial Policy Bureau in MITI could not give us the lists of members and subcommittees of the Industrial Structure Council. Therefore, unfortunately, we are unable to make a quantitative analysis. It is necessary to arrange basic materials on the council itself with response to the recent requirement for the accountability of actions by the government and administrators. Moreover, the system of organization tends to expand unless it is examined occasionally.

5.5 Period of major administrative reform

Several administrative reforms have been executed in order to rationalize the administrative organ intensively since 1955. For example, the Public Company of Telephone and Telecommunication was privatized and became Nippon Telegram and Telephone (NTT) in 1985. The Japan National Railroad was privatized and divided into regional Japan Railway (JR) companies in 1987. Moreover, it is worthwhile mentioning the proposals made from the administrative reform for 1994–97.

In November 1994, the Hashimoto Cabinet established the Committee for Administrative Reform and then the committee established the Taskforce for the Disclosure of Administrative Information, the Subcommittee for Deregulation, and the Subcommittee for Demarcation of the Public and the Private Sector Activities. Although the Committee for Administrative Reform did not have neoclassical economists, the last two committees included active ones. Some of 'The Promotion Plan for Deregulation' proposed by the Subcommittee for Deregulation has been already undertaken (Management and Coordination

Agency 1997). The Subcommittee for Demarcation of Public and Private Sector Activities was asked to define the criteria for sorting out jobs between the public and the private sector. It means that the role of the government and market were questioned and discussed seriously for the first time in the history of Japanese economic thought. 'The Standards for Appropriate Administrative Intervention' (December 1996) summarized the merits of the market mechanism and declared the principle of private activities, the rationalization of administrative activities, the assumption of responsibility of the administrative service, and accountability. It was the first government report that declared the policy of private activities first and keeps the scope of the administrative intervention to a minimum by considering government failure. This trend has been under way in the process of Japanese deregulation. We can paraphrase the committee's understanding of the current issues by adding a few words to their own 'Awareness of the Issues' as follows:

> Looking back over the past 50 years, the period from the end of WWII until the mid-1970s was a phase of catching up to the advanced nations of North America and Europe. The Japanese government coined the slogan 'catch up and pass (the West)' and caught the heart of the Japanese who desired an improvement in their daily lives. It implemented growth policies by emphasizing the enhancement of production and the supply side in order to increase GNP and then to improve people's lives. It often intervened in individual economic decision-making by giving some sort of guidance. When Japan has become a 'front-runner' among the world's top-level economic powers, it means that the Japanese economy has become part of the global economy and been tightly linked to the rest of the world. As the Japanese economy grew rapidly, people's needs and taste has become greatly diversified and 'catch up' is not a national target any more.
>
> In spite of these dramatic economic changes which have happened to the Japanese economy, the government continues to extend its role greatly. The results include the 'high-price, high-cost syndrome', causing tangible distortions everywhere in Japanese society and its economy. Moreover, as the principle of self-accountability was distorted due to excessive government interference, market discipline did not necessarily function efficiently. Therefore we dare not delay administrative reform by even a moment. (Partially translated by the author based on the Administrative Reform Committee 1997: 5, 279)

Moreover, the committee pointed out that commercial companies should also establish the principle of self-accountability and disclose their activities to the market in order for shareholders and investors to judge the real situation of the companies. It argued that the back-scratching alliance of government and big business should be rectified on the side of the private sectors as well as the public sector. It argued that individual business people would naturally circumvent the principle of self-accountability unless the government intervenes (The

Administrative Reform Committee 1997: 129). At least there is a consensus that the government and administration does not have the advantage of economic information over the private sector any more and therefore an economic policy should take the working of markets into consideration in its making and implementation.

Conclusion

Just after the end of WWII, Japanese economists collaborated with government officials and offered their expertise and current judgement, and made significant contributions to the handling of the reparation problem and the drawing of economic reconstruction plans. Japanese economists joined numerous deliberation councils such as the Economic Council and the Industrial Structure Council as learned and experienced persons after around 1955, when various institutions were mostly stabilized. We do not have much to say about their specific role in policy making because their discussion was not disclosed until recently. Moreover, Japan's official 'economic plans' were not real economic plans. Econometric modeling has become an important job done by economists although there was some trial and error in the making of 'economic plans' in the last half of the 1960s. Thanks to the innovation of information technology the linkage of a national economy to the rest of the world is greater in the second half of the 1990s, making it harder for a domestic policy maker to ignore the market mechanism. Individual economic agents now closely watch the government's actions, anticipate the outcome of its policies, and therefore sometimes will not act in the way the government expected them to act. The government should make and implement its policies by paying attention not only to the working of supply and demand but also to the incentive mechanism which rules each individual agent.

Notes

I thank Paul Pecorino for giving me his comments on an early English version.

1 See Arisawa (1989b: 93) about the influence of input-output analysis on his thought.
2 Shigeru Yoshida (1878–1967) was a liberal politician, pro-Anglo-American, and pro-business managers. He was ambassador to Britain from 1936 till 1941. He was in principle opposed to economic controls and related policies. Nonetheless he believed that economic control was needed for the reconstruction of the post-WWII Japanese economy. Although there had been no word like 'recalcitrance' (Futei no yakara) in an earlier draft for the new year's radio address prepared by Arisawa etc., the word was included in the final draft read by Prime Minister Yoshida. Yoshida welcomed the word and read it out with feeling, because workers were resorting to strikes to protect their lives from severe inflation. As a result, the people who had joined the lunch-time meetings left Yoshida. See Arisawa (1989a: 186), Arisawa and Nakamura (1990).
3 Y. Goto stayed in Washington DC from 1958. He died less than two weeks after he came back due to illness. See Sugita (1989: 224–33).

4   The promotion of heavy and chemical industries was Japan's policy for a long time. Yet American economists like M. Bronfenbrenner and C. Johnson were critical of the policy and called it a Stalinist policy. See Shinohara (1967: 81), Johnson (1995), and Ikeo (1998: 143).

5   See Kosai (1989a, b) and MITI *et al.* (1994: 273–323).

6   The Kishi cabinet was negotiating with its US counterpart the renewal of the US–Japan Security Treaty with a slight change from 1958 and completed it in January 1960. However, the contents ignited a protest movement against the treaty (called *Anpo Toso*) from April till June 1960. The LDP government pushed the treaty and related laws to a vote without prudent discussion in the House of Commons (Shugiin) on May 19, and the treaty was fully approved in a month without submitting it to the House of Councilors (*Sangiin*). Thus the new treaty was concluded. On the other hand, President Eisenhower's visit to Japan, which was scheduled for June, was canceled and the Kishi Cabinet resigned on July 15.

7   H. Ikeda was the International Trade and Industry Minister under the Kishi Cabinet.

8   There were many economists who were critical of 'excessive competition', although Tsuneo Iida (1961) agreed with it (see Chapter 7). P. Trezise described Japan's situation as follows, '[A]nother feature of Japan's industrial policy has been the MITI's chronic preoccupation with excessive competition as being a threat to economic order and well-being. . . . Antitrust has not been a part of Japan's political heritage. The MITI's skeptical philosophy toward competition had fairly consistent support in high political circles and in the business world as well. Cartels naturally have often attracted individual companies and industries that are anxious for relief from competitive difficulties.' (Patrick and Rosovsky 1976: 802, 804)

9   It was the Finance Minister Takeo Fukuda who decided to resort to deficit financing (in FY1965) for the first time since the end of WWII. Fukuda worked for the Ministry of Finance in the 1930s and saw Korekiyo Takahashi, the Finance Minister of the time, resorting to deficit financing in order to stimulate the depressed Japanese economy. Fukuda persuaded the Prime Minister Eisaku Sato to take a similar measure to pull the Japanese economy out of recession (Fukuda 1995: 166). Yet Fukuda was not a Keynesian because he had production-centered leanings and did not like Ikeda's consumption-centered ideas.

10   Weekly Toyo Keizai (Oriental Economist in explicit English) featured the controversy on the Social-Economic Development Plan by publishing special issues. Economists like Ryutaro Komiya, Masahiro Tatemoto, and Ryuichiro Tachi unanimously criticized the plan. See Chapter 8.

11   Mr Yasuhiro Wachinaga of the Planning Section of the Comprehensive Planning Bureau at the Economic Planning Agency sent me the details of subcouncils and committees within the Economic Council and their members at the time a new plan was decided. We thank Mr Wachinaga and the section that allowed him to prepare the information for this project.

12   This is based on the explanation given by Mr Wachinaga on the phone with response to my queries through facsimile (13 April 1998).

13   See Yoshida (1995: 925–6), Oyama (1996: 148, 153), and the Federation of Bankers Associations of Japan *et al.* (1997: 108).

References and further reading

Administrative Reform Committee, Secretariat (ed.) (1997) *Gyosei no Yakuwari wo Toinaosu* (Questioning the Role of Administration: Standards for Appropriate Administrative Intervention), Tokyo: Ministry of Finance, Printing Bureau.

Administrative Reform Committee, OB Group (ed.) (1998) *Sori heno Teigen* (Proposals to the Prime Minister: Deregulation, Disclosure and the Demarcation of the Public and Private Sector Activities), Tokyo: Administrative Research Center.

Arisawa, H. and T. Nakamura (eds) (1990) *Shiryo: Sengo Nihon no Keizai Seisaku Koso* (Documents: The Ideas of the post-WWII Economic Policies), 3 volumes, Tokyo: Todai Shuppankai.

Arisawa, H. (1989a) *Gakumon to Shiso to Ningen to* (Learning, Thoughts, and Men), Tokyo: Todai Shuppankai.

Arisawa, H. (1989b) *Rekishi no nakani Ikiru* (Living in a History), Tokyo: Todai Shuppankai.

Bronfenbrenner, M. (1956) 'Economic thought and its application and methodology in the East: the state of Japanese economics', *American Economic Review* 46: 389-98.

Coats, A.W. (ed.) (1996) *The Post-1945 Internationalization of Economics*, Durham, NC: Duke University Press

De Wolff, P. (1965) 'Planning for economic development in the Netherlands'. In UN (1965), Part 1, 133–142.

Economic Council (1960) 'Shotoku Baizo Keikaku' (Income Doubling Plan). In Okita (1960).

Economic Council (1967) 'Keizai Shakai Hatten Keikaku' (Economic-Social Development Plan: Challenging Showa 40s).

Economic Council, Econometric Committee (eds) (1980) *Shin Keizai Shakai 7kanen Keikaku notameno Tabumon Keiryo Moderu* (Multi-sector Econometric Model for the New Economic-Social 7 Year Plan), Tokyo: Ministry of Finance, Printing Bureau.

Economic Council, General Subcouncil and the Committee to Study Basic Issues in Economic Planning (ed.) (1969) *Nihon no Keizai Keikaku* (Japan's Economic Plans), Tokyo: Ministry of Finance, Printing Bureau.

Economic Planning Agency (ed.) (1965) *Chuki Keizai Keikaku* (Midterm Economic Plan), Tokyo: Ministry of Finance, Printing Bureau.

Economic Planning Agency, Comprehensive Planning Bureau (ed.) (1967) *Zusetsu: Keizai Shakai Hatten Keikaku* (Charts: Economic-Social Development Plan), Tokyo: Shiseido.

Economic Planning Agency (ed.) (1997) *Sengo Nihon Keizai no Kiseki* (Tracing the Post-WWII Japanese Economy: A Fifty Year History of the Economic Planning), Tokyo: Ministry of Finance, Printing Bureau.

Economic Stabilization Board [1947–50] (1987) *Keizai Hakusho* (Economic White Paper), Reprint, Tokyo: Nihon Keizai Hyoron-sha.

Federation of Bankers Associations of Japan (Zenginkyo) and Bankers Association of Tokyo (eds) (1997) *Ginko Kyokai 50nenshi* (A Fifty Year History of Bankers Association), Tokyo: Federation of Bankers Associations of Japan and Bankers Association of Tokyo.

Fujii, S. [1954] (1988) 'Keizai jiritsu to boeki kozo' (Economic viability and international trade), Japan Economic Policy Association (ed.) (1988): 202–16.

Fukuda, T. (1995) *Kaiko 90nen* (90 Years in Retrospect), Tokyo: Iwanami Shoten.

Gyoten, T. (1997) 'Japan and the World Bank'. In Kapur *et al.* (eds) (1998).

Iida, T. (1961) 'Kato kyoso to niju kozo' (Excess competition and dual structure), *Economic Studies Quarterly*, 11 (3/4): 23-31.

Ikeo, A. (1994) *20seiki no Keizaigakusha Network* (The Network of Economists in 20th

Century), Tokyo: Yuhikaku.

Ikeo, A. (1996a) 'Shiron: Nihon niokeru seifu ekonomist shudan no tanjo' (The birth of government economists in Japan, *Kokugakuin Keizaigaku* 44(2): 389–412.

Ikeo, A. (1996b) 'The internationalization of economics in Japan'. In Coats (ed.) (1996).

Ikeo, A. (1997) 'Keynes and Keynesian economics in pre-WWII Japan', *Transaction of the Institute for Japanese Culture and Classics* (Kokugakuin University) (80): 271-308.

Ikeo, A. (1998) 'Economic development and economic thought after World War II: non-Marxian economists on development, trade and industry'. In *Economic Thought and Modernization in Japan*, edited by S. Sugihara and T. Tanaka, Cheltenham: Edward Elgar.

Japan Economic Policy Association (ed.) (1988) *Keizai Seisakugaku no Tanjo* (The Birth of Economic Policy Science), Tokyo: Keiso Shobo.

Johnson, C. (1982) *MITI and the Japanese Miracle: The Growth of Industrial Policy, 1925–1975*, Stanford: Stanford University Press.

Johnson, C. (1995) *Japan: Who Governs?: The Rise of the Developmental State*, New York: Norton & Company.

Kanamori, H. (ed.) (1970) *Boeki to Kokusai Shushi* (Trade and International Balance), Tokyo: Nihon Keizai Shimbun-sha.

Kapur, D., J. P. Lewis and R. Webb (eds.) (1998) *The World Bank: Its First Half Century*, 2 volumes, Washington D. C.: Brookings Institute Press.

Kim, H.-K., M. Muramatsu, T. J. Pempel and K. Yamamura (1995) *The Japanese Civil Service and Economic Development: Catalysts of Change*, Oxford: Clarendon Press.

Kashima Peace Research Institute and T. Hagiwara (eds) (1972) *Kowago no Gaiko* (Diplomacy after 1952: Economy) (Nihon Gaikoshi 30), Kashima Kenkyuujo Shuppankai.

Kernell, S. (1991) *Parallel Politics: Economic Policy Making in Japan and the United States*, Tokyo: Japan Center for International Exchange; Washington: Brookings Institution.

Kosai, Y. (1989a) 'Kodoseicho heno Shuppatsu' (Starting rapid growth), Nakamura (ed.) (1989) chapter 6.

Kosai, Y. (1989b) 'Kodo seichoki no keizai seisku' (Economic policies during the rapid growth period), Yasuba and Inoki (eds) chapter 5.

Management and Coordination Agency (ed.) (1994, 1996, 1998) *Shingikai Soran* (Outline of Councils), Tokyo: Ministry of Finance, Printing Bureau.

Management and Coordination Agency (ed.) (1997), *Kiseikanwa Hakusho* (White Paper on Deregulation: For a Radical Change in Ideas), Tokyo: Ministry of Finance, Printing Bureau.

Minato, M., S. Okita and K. Kojima (1967) 'Keizai shakai hatten keikaku' (The Economic-social Development Plan: three questions), *Shukan Toyo Keizai* 3/11:41–48.

Ministry of Finance (MOF) (1982) *The Financial History of Japan: The Allied Occupation Period, 1945–52*, Tokyo: Toyo Keizai Shinposha.

Ministry of International Trade and Industry, editorial Committee for the History of International Trade and Industry (1994), *Tsushosangyo Seisaku-shi* (History of International Trade and Industrial Policies), volume 1, Tokyo: Tsushosangyo Chosakai.

Muramatsu, M. (1981) *Sengo Nihon no Kanryosei* (Japan's Bureaucratic System after WWII), Tokyo: Toyo Keizai Shinposha.

Nakamura, T. (ed.) (1989) *Keikakuka to Minshuka* (Planning and Democratization) (Nihon Keizaishi 7), Tokyo: Iwanami Shoten.

Nakayama, I. (1956) 'Nihon sangyo kozo no kenkyu ni josu' (Introduction to the study of Japan's industrial structure), Institute of Electric Power and Economic Research ed.

(1956) volume 1, 4–17.

Nakayama, I. and Economic Planning Agency, Editorial Room for the Post-WWII Economic History (eds) [1964] (1993) *Keizai Antei Honbushi* (The History of the Economic Stabilization Board) (Sengo Keizaishi7), Reprint, Tokyo: Hara Shobo.

Nakayama, I., H. Arisawa, S. Tobata, Y. Morita, and S. Tsuru (1950), 'Zadankai: Nihon Shihonshugi no Unmei' (The destiny of Japanese capitalism), *Keizai Hyoron*, May, 2–108.

OECD (Organization for Economic Cooperation and Development) (1972) *The Industrial Policy of Japan*, Paris: OECD.

OECD (1977) *Social Sciences Policies in Japan*, Paris: OECD.

Okita, S. (1960) *Shotoku Baizo Keikaku no Kaisetsu* (Outline of the Income Doubling Plan), Tokyo: Nihon Keizai Shimbun-sha.

Okita, S. (1981) *Tohon Seiso* (Constantly On the Move: My Personal History), Tokyo: Nihon Keizai Shimbun-sha.

Okita, S. (1989) 'Japan'. In J. A. Pechman (ed.) *The Role of the Economist in Government: An International Perspective*, NY: New York University Press.

Oyama, K. (1996) *Gyosei Shido no Seijikeizaigaku* (Political Economy of Administrative Guidance), Tokyo: Yuhikaku.

Patrick, H. and H. Rosovsky (1976) (eds) *Asia's New Giant*, Washington D.C.: The Brookings Institution.

Research Institute of Electric Power and the Study Group of Japan's Industrial Structure (eds) [1955] (1956) *Nihon Sangyo Kozo no Kadai* (The Issues in Japan's Industrial Structure) 2 volumes, Tokyo: Chuo Koronsha. Tokyo: Institute of Electric Power Economic Research, 1955.

Sakakibara, E. (1991) 'The Japanese politico-economic system and the public sector'. In Kernell (1991).

Samuelson, P. (1955) *Economics, an introductory analysis*. Third edition. McGraw-Hill.

Shimomura, O. (1961) 'Seicho seisaku no kihon mondai', *Kikan Riron Keizaigaku* 11 (3/4): 1–15. 'Basic problems in economic growth policy', *Translation Series*, no. 37, Calcutta: Indian Statistical Institute, 1963.

Shinohara, M. (1967) *Keizaigakusha no Hatsugen* (The Statements made by an Economist), Tokyo: Nihon Keizai Shimbun-sha.

Shinohara, M. (1982) *Industrial Growth, Trade, and Dynamic Patterns in the Japanese Economy.* Tokyo: University of Tokyo Press.

Society for Industrial Studies (ed.) (1995) *Sengo Nihon Sangyoshi* (The Post-WWII History of Japanese Industries), Tokyo: Toyo Keizai Shinpo-sha.

Sugita, H. (1889) *Showa no Ekonomisuto* (Economists in Showa Era), Tokyo: Chuo Keizai-sha.

Tatemoto, M. (1967), 'Keizai ni yowai naikaku no keizai keikaku' (The economic plan made by the cabinet which is weak at economic thinking), *Chuo Koron* 82 (6): 152–63.

Tinbergen, J. (1964) *Central Planning.* CN: Yale University Press.

Tinbergen, J. (1969) 'The use of models: experience and prospects'. In Lindbeck, A. (ed.) (1992) *Nobel Lectures: Economic Science, 1969–1980*, Singapore: World Scientific.

Uchida, T. (1967) 'Keizai shakai hatten keikaku' (The Economic-Social Development Plan: Three questions), *Shukan Toyo Keizai* 3/11: 34–40.

United Nations (UN) (1958) *Manual on Economic Development Projects.* NY: United Nations.

United Nations (1965) *Planning for Economic Development.* 2 volumes. NY: UN Publications.

United States of America (USA) (1965) 'Planning for economic development in the United States of America'. In UN (1965) Part 1.

Wilts, A. (1998) 'Changes in Dutch economics in the 1930s'. In P. Fontaine and A. Jolink (eds) *Historical Perspectives on Macroeconomics: Sixty Years after the General Theory*, London: Routledge.

Yamada, Y. (1951) *Nihon Kokumin Shotoku Tokei Suikei Shiryo* (Materials for the Estimation of National Income Statistics in Japan), Tokyo: Toyo Keizai Shinposha.

Yasuba, Y. and Inoki, T. (eds) (1989) *Kodo Seicho* (Rapid Growth) (Nihon Keizaishi 8), Tokyo: Iwanami Shoten.

Yoshida, A. (1995) 'Ginkogyo' (Banking), Society for Industrial Studies (ed) (1995), 916–41.

6   Bureaucrats and economics

Kiichiro Yagi

6.1 Jurisprudence and economics in Japanese administrative bureaucracy

In Japanese central government after 1945, such ministries as the Ministry of Finance (MOF) and the Ministry of International Trade and Industry (MITI), which are related to economic policies, have increased their power and prestige. However, it is not the graduates in economics but graduates in law, particularly those of the Law Faculty of the University of Tokyo (*Todai*), that occupy the main stream of government officials even in those ministries. A small group of bureaucrats are called sometimes 'bureaucrat economists'. Their analysis based on econometrics is respected in and out of the administrative bureaucracy. But they are in essence experts that have no access to influential positions in real policy making.[1] Indeed post-1945 Japanese bureaucrats talk much on economic matters, in clear contrast to the pre-war bureaucrats, but most of them are lawyers in their educational background. Even 'bureaucrat economists' are in many cases lawyers that studied economics after entering administration.

Lawyers' dominance in the Japanese civil service has historical roots. Some researchers doubt the relevancy of the detailed judicial knowledge demanded by the appointment examination of higher officials to their general administrative task. However, since the Meiji period the Japanese public law system has left administrative bureaucracy a relatively wide area of discretion to complement the written law. In such areas of quasi-legislative functions, judicial training has been directly useful in the daily service of administrative officials. The training of interpreting articles and writing answers in legal language has been easily transferred to the work of drafting and reporting policy under the order of the superior. Some researchers add further that even when the real task is totally divorced from the specialized knowledge acquired in student years, the record of success in the most difficult examination is respected immensely by specialist officials in the lower ranks (Muramatsu 1981: 65–6).

The lawyers' dominance in the administrative bureaucracy of Japan has been criticized since the 1940s. This criticism influenced the post-1945 reform of the civil service. But the Commission on Social Sciences Policy sent to Japan by OECD in 1976 repeated the warning against the lawyers' dominance and specialists' lack of independence in the administrative system of Japan.[2] Considering the academic situation that in Japan politics is usually taught as a minor course or as a minor department within law faculties, it is economics that is suited to compete with jurisprudence as an alternative background for government officials.

By the appointment examination of government officials of the 'Class I' that was performed in June and July 1996, planned recruitment from the division 'Economy' was announced to be ca. 100, while 'Administration' was ca. 45 and 'Law' ca. 180. Those who are appointed from the successful applicants in these three exam divisions are called 'career bureaucrats', namely bureaucrats on the elite course.[3] Those who passed the exam were: 142 in 'Economy', 65 in 'Administration', and 247 in 'Law'. Real appointment is decided by each ministry and agency on the list of successful applicants who express their choice of ministries and agencies and are enlisted in the order of their exam scores. In the beginning of the new fiscal year (1997), 95 from the applicants in 'Economy' were appointed, with 33 from those in 'Administration', and 157 from those in 'Law'.[4]

Table 6.1 shows the distribution of these new people among ministries and agencies. Some ministries such as the MITI and the Ministry of Post and Telecommunication appointed 'Economy' applicants that rivaled 'Law' applicants in number. Needless to say, the difference between successful applicants in examinations and real appointees comes from the mismatch of the applicants' wishes and the ministries/agencies' decision. It is also possible for successful applicants to postpone enlisting for various reasons (mismatch, illness, or entering graduate courses). In the exam that was performed in 1997, following the downsizing policy of the administration reform, the planned recruitment from 'Economy', 'Administration' and 'Law' were reduced to ca. 70, ca. 30, and ca. 140, respectively. The number of successful applicants and appointees of these three divisions were also reduced to, respectively, 110, 58, and 206 in the former, and 78, 23, and 158 in the latter.

According to the questionnaire of higher-position officials that was performed in 1976–7, economics-related knowledge was judged as 'the necessary knowledge for administrative officials' at nearly the same rate with law (politics included) related knowledge (Muramatsu 1981: 67). It is natural that appointees from 'Economy' preferred economics-related knowledge, but 38 percent of the appointees from 'Law' also judged economics-related knowledge as the most necessary. This preference for economics is intensified as the positions become higher (see Tables 6.2, 6.3).

Economics is thus considerably appreciated within the administration and recruitment is institutionalized. Nevertheless, it does not seem to have successfully undermined the traditional dominance of the generalist with a judicial background. In the Ministry of Finance, elite bureaucrats from the 'Economy' have a tendency to gather in the section of finance. But they cannot encroach on the overwhelming power of lawyers who are centered in the section of state finance and occupy the personnel chamber. It is said that economists cannot be

Table 6.1 Composition of the appointees from the successful applicants of FY1996

Divisions of Class I	Admin.	Law	Econ.	Other Divs	Total
Board of Audit	1	1	3	0	5
National Personnel Authority	2	1	0	1	4
Prime Minister's Office	1	2	1	0	4
Fair Trade Commission	0	2	2	0	4
National Police Agency	1	15	2	12	30
Imperial Household Agency	0	1	0	1	2
Management and Coordination Agency	3	4	2	2	11
Hokkaido Development Agency	0	1	2	12	15
Economic Planning Agency	0	0	9	0	9
Science and Technology Agency	0	3	0	15	18
Environmental Agency	0	4	1	10	15
National Land Agency	0	0	2	1	3
Ministry of Justice	4	8	2	16	30
Public Security Investigation Agency	1	2	1	0	4
Ministry of Foreign Affairs	0	0	0	1	1
Ministry of Finance	0	17	5	0	22
Local Finance Bureaus	0	3	5	0	8
Custom House	2	2	2	0	6
Mint Bureau	0	0	0	1	1
Printing Bureau	0	1	0	1	2
National Tax Administration	1	2	5	5	13
Ministry of Education	9	8	2	15	34
Ministry of Health and Welfare	1	9	5	19	34
Ministry of Agriculture, Forestry, and Fisheries	0	10	4	20	34
Ministry of International Trade and Industry	2	9	11	18	40
Agency of Industrial Science and Technology	0	0	0	10	10
Patent Office	0	0	0	53	53
Ministry of Transport	0	12	7	30	49
Maritime Safety Agency	0	0	0	4	4
Meteorological Agency	0	0	0	8	8
Ministry of Post and Tele-communications	1	9	9	20	39
Ministry of Labor	2	9	5	14	30
Ministry of Construction	2	10	2	68	82
Ministry of Home Affairs	0	12	6	0	18
Fire Defense Agency	0	0	0	3	3
Total	33	157	95	495	780

Source: Annual Reports of the National Personnel Authority, 1997.

Table 6.2 Exam divisions and judgment of essential knowledge for administrators

Exam division	Essential knowledge					
	Humanities (history, sociology, philosophy, etc.)	Law (law, politics, etc.)	Economy (economics, management, etc.)	Natural sciences, others	Sum (%)	Number of answers
Law	9	45	38	8	100	160
Econ. and admin.	21	19	44	16	100	43
Natural sci.	21	24	29	26	100	38

appointed to administrative vice-minister, though they can attain the rank of councilor. Further, also among officials from the 'Economy', a cleavage exists between senior bureaucrats who are accustomed to the patronizing administration and stick to regulations and the young or middle-aged that know neo-classical economics and favor deregulation policy.

6.2 Postwar reform of the administrative personnel system

Similarly with postwar reforms in other areas, the postwar reform of the Japanese civil service was a mixture of intentions and efforts by both the Japanese and Americans. On the Japanese side, the concept of reform can be traced back to the proposal of the Imperial Rule Assistance Association (1941) that demanded the constitution of a central personnel agency, introduction of systematic training, and the abolition of the dominance of lawyers. From the viewpoint of this chapter, it is also noteworthy that the significance of the sensitive administration in the industry and economy was stressed in particular by the Chamber of Commerce and Industry. The need of the administrator with expertise in economic matters was felt severely during wartime. This technocratic tenet colored the efforts of the

Table 6.3 Positions and judgment of essential knowledge

Position	Humanities	Law	Economy	Natural sciences, others	Sum (%)	Number of answers
Vice-Minister, Director	7	29	55	9	100	55
Councilor	9	32	41	18	100	22
Senior Chief	15	38	38	9	100	47
Chief	15	42	28	15	100	127

reform in Japan up to the visit of the Hoover Commission (United States Personnel Advisory Mission to Japan) in November 1946.[5]

In clear contrast to the Japanese government that merely sought modification of the system, Americans considered from the beginning 'the fundamental reform of the bureaucratic administration' as 'one of the first-ranked objectives' of the occupation. In their view, creation of a new civil service system that united 'efficiency' and 'democratic elements' was 'one of the preconditions for the future welfare of the Japanese nation'. The pre-1945 Japanese bureaucrats were *Kanri* (state officials) whose loyalty was to the emperor. The introduction of the American idea of the 'public servant' shocked the Japanese who were accustomed to the pre-1945 authoritarian administration.[6] After six months of intensive work, Blaine Hoover submitted his Mission's final report (June 1947) that contained the draft of a new law (of Japan's civil service) to Gen. MacArthur. Apart from the conceptual switch from the 'official of the Emperor' to the 'servant of the people', the main pillars of Hoover's draft were the constitution of the 'National Personnel Authority (NPA)', democratic reform of the appointment examination, and introduction of the open position-classification system.

Besides the NPA's united personnel administration, the antipathy to the classification of positions that accompanied an open appointment examination was strong among bureaucrats. They were afraid of the dissipation of ministerial bureaucracy that was based on the career promotion system of the closed elite bureaucrats. Further, a progressive group within the SCAP (office of the Supreme Commander of Allied Powers) was opposed to Hoover's treatment of workers in the government sector under severe disciplinary restraint of public officials. As a result, the first National Civil Service Law of 1947 that was legislated during Hoover's temporary absence was not in accord with Hoover's original concept. After returning to Japan, Hoover pushed Gen. MacArthur to write an official letter to the Japanese Prime Minister that ordered the revision of the new law.

American ideals of an open and democratic civil service met resistance and sabotage from all bureaucrats. Though the appointment examination for the higher positions was once carried out in 1948, the second was postponed by the resistance and it was finally abandoned when Japan recovered independence. Denying the elitism of the pre-1945 Upper-Level Civil Service Examination', all divisions of examination were equal in principle under the new Civil Service Law. However, by the second year (1949), the recruitment examination to the vacancy of the sixth grade positions was considered as the substitute of appointment examination of elite bureaucrats. In 1957 this acquired the name of the 'Higher Examination'. In the age of rapid economic growth this was also divided into the 'Higher A' and the 'Higher B' (1960). This division was introduced in order to fill the gap in the freshman's salary of the 'very excellent university graduates' ('Higher A') compared with the standard of big business. In 1967 the double application to the 'Higher A' and 'Higher B' was prohibited. At last the 'Higher A' was renamed the 'Class I'. The so-called 'career bureaucrats' are those who entered public service from three administrative divisions (Administration, Law, and Economy) of the 'Higher A' and 'Class I' later.

We will borrow an overview description of the rehabilitation process of the elite examination from the NPA's retrospect of its first two decades.

> In the fiscal year 1954, the administration system became gradually stabilized. Massive recruitment to fill the urgent need for staff was over. The necessity of planned recruitment for the future cadres was recognized. Each ministry had made its annual recruitment from three administrative divisions, Administration, Law, and Economy flat. As a result, annual total appointees from the three administrative divisions have numbered ca. 250 constantly. . . . Looking into the schools of the successful applicants and appointees, graduates of the University of Tokyo increased year by year and occupied the majority in particular in the appointees from three administrative divisions. They maintained a strong tradition and chain of seniors in the world of government officials, though not so strong in the period of the old Upper-Level Civil Service Examination. Graduates of other ex-Imperial Universities, Kyoto, Tohoku, Kyushu and so on showed moderate increases. Appointees from the graduates of private universities and new national universities were apparently rare (Jinjiin 1968: 122).

6.3 Economics in appointment examinations

6.3.1 *The old Superior Examination of Administrators*

Economics courses were not excluded in the pre-war appointment examination of higher officials. The Upper-Level Civil Service Examination that was first introduced in 1888 contained 'Public Finance' and 'Economics' in its seven prescribed examination areas. Others were 'Constitution', 'Civil Law', 'Commercial Law', 'Administration', and 'International Law'. Since candidates had to take three areas from these, the Meiji state could admit a two-thirds economist as its bureaucrat. In 1894, 'Economics' was included in the six obligatory areas while 'Public Finance' became one of the four optional areas. The highest share of economy-related courses in a candidate's choice was thus reduced to two-sevenths. This was not changed in the revision of the Upper-Level Civil Service Examination in 1918.

Due to the criticism of the 'lawyer's domination', the share was recovered up to four-sevenths in 1929. 'Economics' was ranked within the four obligatory areas together with 'Constitution', 'Administrative Law', and 'Civil Law'. The 20 optional areas – candidates had to take three – included not only 'Public Finance' as well as 'Economic History', 'Agricultural Policy', 'Commerce Policy', 'Industrial Policy', and 'Social Policy'. But in the revision of 1941, only 'Public Finance' remained. When the last Upper-Level Examination was performed in 1947, 'Economics' was one of the three obligatory areas beside 'Constitution' and 'Administrative Law'. The optional 12 areas (four to be chosen) included 'Public Finance', 'Economic Policy' and 'Social Policy'. The highest possible share was thus the same (four-sevenths) with that of 1929–40.

Table 6.4 Composition of successful applicants in the Upper-Level Civil Service Examination in 1934

School	Todai (law)	Other imp. univ. (law)	Priv. univ. (law)	Law grad. in total	Todai (econ.)	Other imp. univ. (econ.)	Tokyo Univ. of Com.	Priv. Univ. (econ.)	Econ grad. in total	Total number
Successful applicants	156	52	22	248	12	8	3	1	27	302
Appointees*	86	39	15	160	8	5	1	1	17	198

Source: Senzenki Kanryosei Kenkyukai (1981)

Note
* Those who entered the Ministry of Justice, Imperial Household Ministry, Military, Local Governments, semi-public companies, Manchuria are excluded.

On the side of universities, it was in 1919 that economics was separated from the Law Faculty in the imperial universities in Tokyo (*Todai*) and Kyoto (*Kyodai*). After a while, in the late 1920s, the inflow of economics graduates to the administration had formed a stream, however small. Table 6.4 presents the composition of the successful candidates and appointees of the Superior Examination that was performed in 1934. Economics graduates' share in both cases was 8.9 and 8.6 percent respectively. The graduates' number in the two imperial universities in the corresponding year is shown in Table 6.5. In this year two imperial universities sent 11 economics graduates (106 law graduates) to the government, while they had supplied in the accumulated figure 306 economics graduates (law graduates 2,998) until that year.

A half of the economics graduates in the pre-1945 state administration were those of the *Todai*. The remaining positions were occupied by the graduates of other imperial universities (Kyoto, Kyushu, Tohoku) and Tokyo University of Commerce. Graduates of private universities were very rare.

Out of this year's 17 appointees of economics graduates, 7 entered the Ministry of Railways, 4 the Ministry of Finance, 2 the Ministry of Commerce and Industry, 2 Taiwan Administration, 1 the Ministry of Agriculture and Forestry, and 1 Korea Administration. This year, in addition, the Ministry of Justice, Guandong Territory, Manchuria, and Aichi Prefecture each recruited one economics graduate though they were not counted as the appointees of the central government. The private institutions that recruited successful candidates were: Mitsui Trust Fund, the *Asahi Shimbunsha* (newspaper), Yokohama Class Bank, Tokyo Horse Race, Federation of Export Associations, and Kyosai Life Insurance (one each).

Three economics graduates in the Ministry of Finance were promoted finally to the Chief of Printing Office, Member of Policy Board of the Bank of Japan, and Board Member of the Public Corporation of Tobacco and Salt, respectively. The one that entered the Ministry of Commerce and Industry became Chief of the Tokyo Regional Bureau. The best of the seven economics graduates in the Ministry of Railways became Chief of the Niigata Regional Bureau. All of these successful economist bureaucrats were graduates of the Economics Faculty of *Todai*. But the law graduates of *Todai* that entered the MOF in the same year included Shinichi Ishino who became the Administrative Vice-Minister of the MOF and Yasumi Kurogane who became the Chief Cabinet Secretary. Ei Isozaki, who became the President of the Japanese National Railways, and Haruo Maekawa, who presided over the Bank of Japan, were also law graduates of *Todai* who entered the administration in the same year (1935). Even within the ranks of the *Todai* graduates, economics graduates were still marginal in the promotion race.

Particular economics graduates near this entry year were Osamu Shimomura (graduated *Todai* and entered the Monopoly Sales/Ministry of Finance in 1934) and Masayoshi Ohira (graduated the Tokyo University of Commerce to enter the Deposit Department/Ministry of Finance in 1936). The former is a famous bureaucrat economist who was the brains behind Hayato Ikeda (politician from the MOF bureaucracy: prime minister 1960–64). The latter was the bureaucrat politician who succeeded Ikeda's clique and became prime minister in 1978–80.

Table 6.5 Law and economics graduates of the *Todai* and *Kyodai* in the pre-war bureaucracy

	Todai (law)		Todai (econ.)		Kyodai (law)		Kyodai (econ.)	
	New graduates	Accum.	New graduates	Accum.	New graduates	Accum.	New graduates	Accum.
Total	622	16,309	356	3,880	429	6,127	217	2,827
Administrators	93	2,660	8	177	13	338	3	129
Judicial officials	39	1,036	0	2	5	449	0	7
Imp. House officials	1	61	0	2	0	7	0	0
Public servants*					16	199	4	102
Lawyer and patent lawyer	5	1,408	0	12	1	408	0	7
Invited by foreign government or companies	4	39	0	0	3	55	0	24

Source: The 63rd Report of the Ministry of Education of the Great Empire of Japan (Apr. 1935–March 1936)

Note
* This item appears only in the table of *Kyodai*.

Shimomura's career anticipated that of post-war bureaucrat economists in respect of experiencing a stay in the United States (1937) and working for research sections in the Price Agency and the Economic Stabilization Board (predecessor of the Economic Planning Agency) after the war. Ohira spent some time in Mongolia (1939) and worked for the Economic Stabilization Board as the chief of the public enterprise section. Though it resembles Shimomura's career in appearance, Ohira's career was related to the most important concerns of MOF's interest. While Shimomura entered the Policy Board of the Bank of Japan in 1953 and acquired a Doctorate in economics, Ohira ran for election in 1952 after being the chief of the accounting section of MOF and the secretary of the minister. Ohira's career was very similar to another bureaucrat politician, Takeo Fukuda (law graduate of *Todai*) who entered the MOF eight years earlier and became prime minister directly before him (1976–8).

6.3.2 *Changes after 1945*

Due to the war the Upper-Level Civil Service Examination was dropped in the financial years 1944 and 1945. The first examination after Japan's surrender was that of FY1946 and was carried out in April 1947. It supplied 173 successful candidates. As they were not enough for the demand, the examination was repeated in December of the same year and produced 189 successful candidates. Further, a special examination for administrators that had entered ministries in the later phase of the war (1944–5) was carried out twice in April 1947 (with 120 successes and in February 1948 with 109). Though these examinations were officially still the old Upper-Level Examination, alterations were made in examination areas. In obligatory areas, 'Civil Law' was transferred to the optional group, and 'Japanese History', that had been added to the obligatory group during war, was abolished. In optional areas, 'Political History', 'Sociology', 'Economic Policy', 'Social Policy', and 'Foreign Language' were added and 'Philosophy' dropped. 'Economics' joined also in areas of the oral examination beside 'Constitution' and 'Administrative Law (or International Civil Law)'. Previously, oral examination had dealt with 'Administrative Law and two areas taken from examination areas'.

Probably reflecting the alterations in the examination areas, successful economics graduates increased to 24 in the total of 173 in the first appointment examination (April 1947). But in the second, they were marginalized by the resurgence of law graduates from *Todai*. Economics graduates numbered only 12 in the total of 189 successful candidates. Since law students also could take economic courses in the curriculum of ex-imperial universities, six months' preparation seems to have been enough for the examination-suited talent of law students of *Todai*.

The first appointment examination under the new National Civil Service Law was carried out in January 1949. The examination for general administrators ('Class A: Administration Job') was separated from that for professionals ('Class B: Professional Job') that consisted of 17 divisions. The 'Law' as well as the

'Economy' were among them. The double application to Class A and B was permitted, but taking plural divisions in the Class B was impossible. Originally, two species were introduced to separate courses of generalists and specialists. Ironically, however, the Class A could not succeed the glorious tradition of Upper-Level Examination for Japanese administrators. The separation of two Classes was abolished in 1951. 'Administration' became of the same rank with 'Law' and 'Economy'.

The ratio of applicants to planned recruitment has been remarkably high in the division of 'Administration' in every year. Since the questions in 'Administration' are not so specialized as in 'Law' or 'Economy', many candidates apply for this division while aiming also at the appointment examination of local government services. Ministries and agencies did not intend to increase the appointments from this division. As a result, in recent years, successful candidates and appointees from this division amount to only a half of those from 'Economy' and a quarter of those from 'Law'.

Appointees from 'Economy' exceeded one hundred constantly since 1985. In the 1990s it amounts to over 50 percent of those from the 'Law'. However, the applicants for the 'Economy' show a declining tendency. Most economics students are not so much surrounded by the civil service oriented atmosphere as law students. But it is also true that current organization and style of administration has not improved much in its appeal to economics students.

Table 6.6 Application, success and appointment of the higher examination, 1948–63

Fiscal year	Application	Success	Appointees
1948	12,305	3,684	1,032
1949	7,961	1,952	833
1950	10,599	1,416	713
1951	14,250	2,148	523
1952	29,976	2,142	961
1953	29,301	1,980	665
1954	32,256	1,488	569
1955	25,754	1,314	635
1956	25,862	1,504	591
1956sp*	672	92	58
1957	25,289	1,801	621
1958	23,770	1,751	761
1959	20,892	1,596	716
1960	16,364	1,370	664
1961	12,637	1,530	827
1962	15,465	1,533	823
1963	17,757	1,835	1,004

Source: Jinjiin (1968)

Note
* Specially carried out for the appointment of the Patent Office and the Agency of Industrial Science and Technology

Table 6.7 Applications and success of the appointment exam for higher government officials*

Year	All-divisions		Administration		Law		Economy		Economy/Law	
	Application	Success	Application	Success	Application	Success	Application	Success	Application	Success
1964	15,904	1,434	1,943	64	3,807	298	1,750	99	46%	33%
1965	21,125	1,624	2,076	43	4,411	299	2,572	99	58%	33%
1966	24,759	1,507	1,989	38	4,843	290	2,958	98	61%	34%
1967	21,567	1,364	1,070	28	4,293	269	2,402	109	56%	41%
1968	20,483	1,313	1,088	29	3,496	266	1,772	95	51%	36%
1969	17,973	1,306	988	30	4,032	251	1,838	98	46%	39%
1970	17,637	1,353	1,025	30	3,998	252	1,894	96	47%	38%
1971	23,532	1,401	1,428	30	5,093	261	3,021	100	59%	38%
1972	27,429	1,349	1,425	29	5,238	242	3,150	99	60%	41%
1973	30,129	1,410	1,658	30	6,227	249	3,222	100	52%	40%
1974	30,688	1,375	1,773	30	6,227	249	3,222	100	52%	40%
1975	37,825	1,206	2,895	25	7,556	237	4,134	83	55%	35%
1976	44,518	1,136	2,803	25	8,238	235	4,741	79	58%	34%
1977	48,314	1,206	3,224	30	8,729	240	5,060	89	58%	37%
1978	55,972	1,311	3,924	35	10,630	245	5,826	89	55%	36%
1979	51,896	1,265	4,136	30	10,034	229	5,363	90	53%	39%
1980	45,131	1,254	3,625	30	9,694	229	4,549	91	47%	40%
1981	40,770	1,361	3,462	42	9,644	226	3,955	101	41%	45%

1982	36,856	1,383	3,401	35	8,837	237	3,751	90	42%	38%
1983	34,854	1,478	3,547	40	8,421	221	2,974	95	35%	43%
1984	34,089	1,562	3,288	40	8,321	220	3,203	94	38%	43%
1985	36,072	1,655	3,975	50	8,915	242	3,332	110	37%	45%
1986	32,675	1,718	3,828	55	8,043	251	2,901	119	36%	47%
1987	32,308	1,696	3,856	50	7,666	250	2,912	121	38%	48%
1988	28,833	1,814	3,340	52	6,728	266	2,511	134	37%	50%
1989	27,243	1,983	3,050	52	6,443	270	2,354	146	37%	54%
1990	31,422	2,047	4,925	68	7,341	271	2,739	133	37%	49%
1991	30,102	2,200	5,491	66	6,955	287	2,390	155	34%	54%
1992	30,789	2,075	5,487	74	7,008	286	2,372	167	34%	58%
1993	35,887	1,893	6,783	74	7,822	272	2,728	162	35%	60%
1994	41,433	1,725	7,890	72	8,990	261	3,119	147	35%	56%
1995	43,431	1,636	8,961	68	9,138	258	2,938	148	32%	57%
1996	45,254	1,583	9,958	65	9,461	247	2,789	142	29%	57%
1997	39,863	1,297	9,609	58	8,356	206	2,404	110	29%	53%
Sum	1,136,963	51,920	127,921	1,517	244,635	8,612	106,846	3,788	44%	44%

Note
* 'Higher A' in 1964–1984, 'Class I' since 1985.

Regrettably, we could not acquire the classified data of the appointment examination from FY1948 to FY1963. Table 6.6 shows only the total numbers of the applicants, successful candidates, and appointees of the higher class examination in this period. Table 6.7 represents classified figures in three administrative divisions after FY1964.

Table 6.8 shows the distribution of questions in the 'Specialized Examination' of divisions of 'Administration', 'Law', and 'Economy' in FY1997. Changes in the distribution of 'Specialized Examination' of the division 'Economy' are shown in Table 6.9.

In the FY1996, questions of the first-stage examination (multiple-choice questions) for the candidates 'Class I, Economy' were made by two professors of national universities (economics graduates of the Hitotsubashi University and the *Todai*) and three bureaucrat economists (all economics graduates of the *Todai*). As for the free-style specialized examination in the second stage, eight academic economists served as examiners for 'Economic Theory' and 'Labor Economics' in the division 'Administration' and for 'Economic Theory', 'Public Finance', and 'Economic Policy' in the division 'Economy'. Three of them were graduates of the Hitotsubashi, two of the Osaka University, one of *Todai*, one of the Tohoku University, one of the Keio University. Their current positions were professors of Hitotsubashi (3), Osaka University (2), Keio University (2), and St Sophia University (1). The longest tenure was 8 years.

As seen from this result of our hearing at the National Personnel Authority, professors of *Todai* did not occupy influential positions in the appointment examination. Still, *Todai* graduates provided nearly a half of the successful candidates. It was a coincidence that all three bureaucrat economists were *Todai* graduates, but it was also evidence of the large share of *Todai* graduates in government bureaucracy.

Table 6.10 compares the distribution of the appointees from three administrative divisions among ministries and agencies. Despite the continuing dominance of lawyers, appointments from 'Economy' showed an increase in some of them. The Economic Planning Agency intensified its specialization in 'Economy'. The Ministry of Post and Telecommunications increased appointees from 'Economy' so that they rivaled those from 'Law'. The former reflects the consolidation of EPA as the center of bureaucrat economists, while the latter represents MPT's growing self-confidence about the economic ministry in respect to information and finance.

6.4 Economics in training after entry

6.4.1 Training of the NPA

All the appointees from the successful Class I candidates take freshman's training and after six months' probation take basic level administrative training. Training in the first year was carried out by the NPA to nourish the confidence and general knowledge that is needed for a responsible administrator. NPA practices also

Table 6.8 Areas and numbers of questions in the specialized exam for the administrative divisions of Class I

Exam division	Specialized exam (multiple choice)	Specialized exam (descriptive method)
Administration	Choose 7 Areas (49 questions) out of 10 Areas (7 questions each: in total 70 questions)* below: Politics (Theory/Ideas), Politics (History/Institution/Reality), Administration, Constitution, Administrative Law, Civil Law, Economics, Public Finance, Labor Economics, Social Security, International Relations, Sociology	Choose 3 Areas (1 question each) out of the 7 Areas: Politics, Administration, Constitution, Economic Theory, Labor Economics, International Relations, Sociology
Law	In addition to Constitution (6), Administrative Law (12), and Civil Law (12), choose 15 out of 20 questions in the areas of Commercial Law (5), Criminal Law (5), Labor Law (5) and International Law (5). Further, choose 5 out of 10 questions in the area of Economics and Public Finance. In total answer 50 questions.*	One question each from Constitution, Administrative Law, and Civil Law.
Economy	In addition to Economic Theory (17), Public Finance and Economic Policy (7), Economic History and Economic Conditions (9), choose 12 out of 17 questions in the areas of International Economics (5), Statistics and Econometrics (7), and Management (5). Further, choose 5 out of 10 questions in Constitution (5) and Civil Law (5). In total answer 50 questions.**	One question each from Economic Theory, Public Finance, and Economic Policy

Notes
* Until 1996, choice of 50 out of 65 questions.
** The choice of questions is introduced in this year.

Table 6.9 Areas of questions in the division of the 'Economy'

	Name	Questions	Time (min.)	Areas	Descriptive exam
1948	Exam of Public Servants	80	210	Obligatory: Economics, History of Economic Thought, Public Finance, Economic History, Statistics, Accounting, Economic Policy, Economic Situation, Management, Constitution, Civil Law, Commercial Law*	—
1949	Position of Grade 6	80	?	Obligatory: Economics, History of Economic Thought, Public Finance, Economic History, Statistics, Accounting, Economic Policy, Economic Situation, Management, Commercial Law*	—
1950	Position of Grade 6	80	210	Obligatory: Economics, History of Economic Thought, Public Finance, Economic History, Statistics, Accounting, Economic Policy, Economic Situation, Social Policy, Management, Constitution, Commercial Law*	—
1951	Position of Grade 6	80	180	Obligatory: Principles of Economics, History of Economic Thought, Public Finance, Statistics, Economic Policy, Economic Situation, Financial Economics, Management, Commercial Law	—
1952	Position of Grade 6	100	240	Obligatory: Principles of Economics, History of Economic Thought, Public Finance, Economic History, Economic Policy and Economic Situation, Constitution, Commercial Law, Civil Law	—
1954	Position of Grade 6	100	240	ibid.	Descriptive: Principles of Economics, Public Finance, Economic Policy

Year	Exam			Areas	
1957	Higher Exam	100	240	Obligatory: Principles of Economics, History of Economic Thought, Public Finance, Economic History, Statistics, Economic Policy, Economic Situation, Constitution, Civil Law, Commercial Law	ibid.
1960	Higher A	100	240	ibid.	ibid.
1962	Higher A	80	210	ibid.	ibid.
1967	Higher A	70	210	ibid.	ibid.
1971	Higher A	60	210	ibid.	ibid.
1985	Class I	60	210	ibid.	ibid.
1991–	Class I	60	210	Obligatory: Economic Theory, Public Finance and Economic Policy, International Economics, Econometrics, Economic History and Economic Situation, Constitution and Civil Law	Descriptive: Economic Theory, Public Finance, Economic Policy
1996**					

Source: Materials provided by the NPA

Notes

* No announcement of the areas was made in the exams of 1948–50.

** See Table 6.8 for the change in FY1997.

Table 6.10 Appointments of the successful applicants in administrative divisions

Fiscal years	1971–73			1981–83			1991–93			1995–1997		
Divisions	Admin.	Law	Econ.	Admin.	Law	Econ.	Admin.	Law.	Econ.	Admin.	Law	Econ.
Board of Audit	0	11	6	0	7	6	0	5	3	3	4	5
National Personnel Authority	2	11	0	4	7	2	3	9	1	3	6	2
Prime Minister's Office	3	3	3	5	4	1	3	7	3	5	5	1
Fair Trade Commision	0	4	2	0	5	3	2	7	7	0	7	6
National Police Agency	0	41	0	4	50	5	4	52	7	3	43	5
Imperial Household Agency	…	…	…	…	…	…	…	…	…	0	1	0
Public Security Investigation Agency	0	1	0	…	…	…	5	6	0	1	8	3
Management and Coordination Agency	0	12	2	5	3	5	5	14	10	8	14	2
Hokkaido Development Agency	1	6	3	0	2	0	2	5	3	1	3	5
Economic Planning Agency	1	6	16	0	1	18	0	1	25	1	1	23
Science and Technology Agency	0	2	1	1	5	0	2	4	1	2	5	0
Environmental Agency	0	7	3	3	5	2	4	5	4	1	9	5
Ministry of Justice	5	22	0	2	9	0	10	30	3	7	33	3
Ministry of Finance	3	37	27	3	50	24	2	41	24	1	40	20
Local finance bureaus	5	4	2	3	6	3	2	11	14	2	6	13
Custom House	0	4	1	3	2	1	4	3	3	3	3	4
Mint Bureau	…	…	…	…	…	…	2	1	1	1	1	0
Printing Bureau	…	…	…	…	…	…	1	2	1	0	2	1
National Tax Administration	0	15	13	3	10	10	2	10	16	2	10	10

Ministry of Education	7	28	0	8	26	6	16	31	6	18	35	7
Ministry of Health and Welfare	5	24	8	8	21	6	1	28	9	1	31	11
Ministry of Agriculture, Forestry, and Fisheries	0	32	18	0	33	10	2	30	16	0	28	13
Ministry of International Trade and Industry	0	38	24	2	43	37	2	51	21	4	32	30
National Land Agency	...	...	...	...	...	...	1	1	2	0	0	5
Ministry of Transport	0	39	17	2	39	7	2	43	15	1	35	17
Ministry of Post and Telecommunications	1	30	4	1	27	12	5	34	32	4	27	30
Ministry of Labor	3	17	7	4	21	9	6	20	13	5	28	15
Ministry of Construction	3	29	12	0	34	10	2	30	14	3	25	11
Ministry of Home Affairs	3	38	4	0	38	6	6	53	4	3	37	12
Recommended organizations	8	18	8	...	...	...	...	...	...	...	...	...
Total	51	472	179	60	448	185	96	535	253	84	479	259

Source: Annual Reports of the National Personnel Authority

administrative training that is oriented to policy making at the levels of supervisor, section vice-chief, and section chief of ministry. This administrative training is a combination of collective research on the policy agenda that is based on the lectures of experts and individual policy researchers. In both cases, team discussion was emphasized in this MPA training. Policy agendas in economic problems are adopted very often.

6.4.2 Training within ministries and agencies[7]

MPA's training aims at the development of a broad perspective in administrators on the basis of communications beyond ministries and agencies or beyond the borders of government and private sectors. The continuous training that deepens specialized knowledge and skill is not guaranteed by NPA's training. Most ministries organize special courses by employing insider experts and academic staff in metropolitan areas as lecturers. One of the reasons for constituting research institutes within ministries (Institute of Fiscal and Monetary Policy (1985), Research Institute of International Trade and Industry (1987), and Research Institute of Post and Telecommunications (1989)) lies in the theoretical training of young and middle-ranking officials. Further, numerous unofficial study groups are organized among administrators. They often cause the formation of cliques within the ministerial bureaucracy.

As an example of a well-developed training system, we have a glance at that of the National Tax Administration (National Tax Administration c. 1992). First, immediately after entering the Administration, the 'Class I' appointees take a week's 'basic training for the Class I' and 'learn jobs and tasks of the departments of the Administration and acquire basic knowledge for a tax(wo)man'. Then in the second year they are sent to the Tax College to take a month's 'higher tax training'. In this training they 'acquire essential knowledge for the Class I appointees such as that of corporate tax law, bookkeeping, financial statements'. Further, after two years' service as officials of departments, they are supposed to take six months' 'theoretical training in taxation'. This course covers 'not only the theory and knowledge of taxation in general but also high-level understanding of the administrative law, public finance, and economics, improvement of communication in English, and writing a treatise'. This course 'intends to acquire the capability of coping with problems of tax administration on the basis of theoretical background'. The six months' 'theoretical training' completes the first stage of training for Class I appointees.

The training of the next stage is performed individually by recalling appointees to the President Chamber's Office and sending them to overseas universities or to one-year domestic training. In addition to the Law School of Harvard University (Section of the International Taxation) with which Tax Administration keeps a close relation, the Tax Administration has sent its officials to various American graduate schools (Yale University, Syracuse University, South California University and so on). In the case of domestic training, a graduate-school-level training is given at the Training Center of

International Trade together with trainees from other ministries, private firms, and foreign governments. Seminars and discussions in the field of international economics, international jurisprudence, and practical problems in international trade are held in English. Further, the Tax Administration ensures its officials enrich their international experience by sending them to the 'International Seminar for Tax Administration', the forum of young tax-men of the world, or to the Institute of Tax Administration in Los Angeles and the overseas branches of the Japan External Trade Organization (JETRO). Thus, in this system all the Class I appointees of the Tax Administration are supposed to acquire a theoretical background at a graduate-school level as well as sufficient international experience to compete with their foreign colleagues.

6.4.3 Overseas training programs

As already seen in the case of Tax Administration, a high-class level of training over a year is usually given by granting opportunities for study abroad. Recently, enrollment to graduate schools of domestic universities has emerged as an alternative.

The NPA has two programs for the study abroad of government officials. 'The Long-Term Researcher Abroad Program for Administrators' was introduced in 1966 to provide officials with less than six years' service with the chance to study for two years at graduate schools of overseas universities. The researchers are selected by the NPA out of applicants that are recommended by ministries and agencies. Up to FY1997 a total 1,152 officials were given the chance to study abroad on this program. The numbers who went to various countries were: 794 officials to the United States, 171 to the United Kingdom, 108 to France, 43 to Germany, 26 to Canada, 10 to Australia. Out of the 73 researchers that were selected in FY1988, the MITI accounts for 12, the MOF 11, the Ministry of Agriculture, Forestry and Fisheries 7, National Police Agency 5, the Ministry of Transportation 5, and so on. The United States is an overwhelmingly popular destination.

Before the introduction of this program most ministries and agencies sent promising young officials to study abroad independently. Even now ministries keep the option of overseas training open as well as using the NPA's program. The MOF has a policy of offering all the appointees to the third service year the chance to study abroad. For this policy MOF uses the training program of the JETRO as well as that of the World Bank etc. Overseas posts of JETRO are used also by the MITI. In MITI's case about two thirds of the Class I administrative appointees are sent to study abroad.

Study abroad is a good opportunity for economics graduates to advance the study that they had to interrupt to enter public service. It is also a chance for law graduates in the economy-related ministries to learn economics systematically. However, it must be added that study abroad results in a considerable number of young officials leaving public service for the sake of entering academic careers as well as getting positions in private firms.

Another NPA program is the 'Short-Term Researcher Abroad Program for Administrators' that was introduced in 1974. This program provides for six months' or one year's overseas training for officials with over six years' service. Selection is made by the NPA from the applicants recommended by ministries. From 1974 to 1977 this program sent 801 officials to government organizations of foreign countries or to international organizations. A breakdown of 801 officials shows: 399 to the United States, 155 to the United Kingdom, 49 to Australia, 43 to France, 42 to Germany, 41 to Canada, and 72 to other countries. The share of the United States is smaller than in the case of the 'Long-Term Program'.

6.4.4 Domestic Researcher Program

Recently, the course at graduate schools of Japanese universities, the 'Domestic Researcher Program for Administrators', has been institutionalized with the involvement of the NPA. Administrators with from two years' to less than 16 years' service are sent to the master course of graduate schools in Japan for two years. To realize this program the severe restrictions for the enrollment to the graduate course and the psychological resistance of academicians to the administrators had to be eliminated. In the 1970s when these barriers were removed, many universities moved to establish special graduate courses for the re-education of occupational students. Some universities have endeavored to establish relations with ministries and agencies in this respect. The Graduate School of Management and Policy Science of the Tsukuba University began accepting administrators in FY1976, and the Graduate School of Policy Science of the Saitama University followed the next year. After an interval, traditional universities such as *Todai* (1992) and *Kyodai* (1994) changed their policies and welcomed researchers sent by ministries and agencies.

The researchers sent 247 in total. The numbers sent to each destination are as follows: Graduate School of the Tsukuba University 94, Saitama University 91, Yokohama National University (since 1990) 24, the University of Tokyo 31, Kyoto University 7. However, the main field of Tsukuba and Saitama is policy science, in the case of the Yokohama National University international economic law, and in *Todai* and *Kyodai*'s case law and politics. The domestic training program in economics proper has not yet started. As for training in economics, the graduate schools of American universities are still predominant.

6.4.5 Promotion

By our hearing at the NPA, its official admitted that an appointee from the 'Economy' seldom reaches the top of the ministerial bureaucracy (vice administrative minister). According to Muramatsu *et al.*'s research, while 37 out of 153 appointees from the 'Law' reached the position of vice minister and directors of sections, only four out of 41 appointees from the 'Economy' and 'Administration' in the same year reached that level (Muramatsu 1981: 61).

Is there a career promotion route for specialist ('bureaucrat economists') administrators from 'Economy'? As mentioned already, the Economic Planning

Agency, whose appointees are now monopolized by successful candidates in 'Economy', has the nature of a training center for bureaucrat economists. In other ministries also there is a possibility to develop the skill of economic analyst by continuously working at research sections. Another is the promotion route via such sections as the financial sections of the MOF where officials from 'Economy' have dominance both in administrative positions as well as experience as economists. In MOF's case economists usually occupy the position of financial director that is ranked highest next to the vice administrative minister.

Recently in-office economists have begun to publish their views on journalism. However, officially, no specialist careers exists in the public service. They are all under the control of their superiors. The critical comments of the OECD Mission on the lack of respect for the expertise of specialists and their independence seems to be still valid in the case of economists in government.

> The place of specialists' section (research sections etc.) is not fixed within the organization of the public service. In addition to their own activities, research and planning sections collect data and prepare materials for decision makers at a superior level and for the deliberation of the Diet. However, in the final decision on policies, the opinion of the general administrative sections tends to have more influence than the analytical results of these specialists' sections. (OECD 1972: 248)

In contrast to the American system that encourages the entry of academics into public service, Japanese bureaucracy has supplied many economists to Japanese universities. Most cases involve experienced senior bureaucrat economists. There are, however, cases where talented middle-aged bureaucrats acquire academic jobs temporarily or permanently. Sometimes they keep in touch with their home ministries by serving as expert economists. This mixture of academic independence and ministerial loyalty might be an individualistic solution to the problem that was criticized by the OECD mission.

6.5 Present administrative reform

It is true that the significance of economics is recognized among government officials especially in economy-related ministries and agencies. This is confirmed by the numbers of appointees from the examination division 'Economy' as well as the content of various courses after the appointment. However, under the voluntaristic administrative style based on discretionary power, and under the exclusive elite career system, administrators with knowledge in economics stand apart from the main stream. The relative unpopularity of the civil service among economic students might be a reflection of this situation. Bureaucrat economists' independence is also not sufficiently consolidated. Probably the closed career system of elite administrators in Japanese public service itself is inconsistent with the independence that is needed for the task of the economist.

By the reduction of government personnel under the policy of the Administrative Reform, it is hopeless to expect the extension of specialist careers within ministerial bureaucracy. On the contrary, backed by growing criticism of bureaucracy, personnel exchanges with the academic world and private sectors are demanded from several sides.[8] One of the main aims of the proposal is the utilization of economics as a policy science. Without a general rehabilitation of the democratic ideals of the postwar civil service reform, this will end only as a temporary mobilization of economics/economists for crisis control from above.

Notes

1. Under the so-called 'joint colonial control' of MOF and MITI that had continued till 1969, the citadel of 'bureaucrat economists', Economic Planning Agency (EPA), could not have an administrative vice minister who had progressed from within. After the retreat of MITI, personnel policy of EPA was all the more dominated by lawyers of MOF (Kawakita 1991:112–14).

2. 'The proportion of lawyers is still large. Particularly the number of officials with the educational background of law is conspicuous in ministries in charge of economic policies, such as the Ministry of Finance and the Ministry of International Trade and Industry. . . . One reason is that administrators spend a considerable part of their office hours in the drafting and implementation of legislative rules. . . . Another reason lies in the peculiar historical development of the social sciences in Japan. The center of human and social sciences has been traditionally occupied by law faculties, especially by that of the University of Tokyo. . . . Accordingly, the dominance in the recruitment of higher officials is a reflection of the personnel policy of the government that prefers generalists to experts in each area' (OECD 1978: 237).

3. In addition, the recruitment of 15 officials from the exam division 'Agricultural Economy' was announced this year. However, most of them were destined to work as specialists in the Ministry of Agriculture, Forestry, and Fisheries.

4. The fiscal year of Japanese government begins in April and ends in March. The appointment examination for 'Class I' is usually carried out in June and July in two stages and the final result is made public in the middle of August. After the decision of ministries and agencies the appointees enter public service on 1 April of the next year.

5. As for the historical roots and the process of post-war civil service reforms, see Ide (1974), Okada (1997) and Kim *et al.* (1995).

6. In Hoover's view even the Emperor (Tenno) was a 'public servant' so long as he survived in the new Japanese constitution. Almost all Japanese were shocked when they saw the emperor in the list of public servants in Hoover's final report.

7. In (2), (3), (4), data are mainly taken from the annual reports of the NPA.

8. In its report of 22 August 1998 the NPA demanded the institutionalization of the temporary appointment of civilians with conditions appropriate to their expertise. One month before (17 July) the Meeting on the Administration of the Ministry of Finance (headed by Ryuzo Sejima) also submitted its report to the Finance Minister, in which the midway appointment, personnel exchange with universities and private firms, and improvement of the research institute by distinguished economists are proposed.

References and further reading

Ide, Y. (1974) 'Sengo kaikaku to Nihon kanryo-sei' (Postwar reforms and Japanese bureaucracy). In Tokyo Daigaku Shakaikagaku Kenkyujo (ed.) *Sengo Kaikaku* (Postwar Reforms) vol. 3, *Seiji Katei* (Political Process), Tokyo: Tokyo Daigaku Shuppankai.

Jinjiin (National Personnel Authority) (1968) *Jinji Gyosei 20-nen no Ayumi* (20 years of the Personnel Administration), private.

Jinjiin (1998) Komuin Hakusho Heisei 10-nen ban (White Paper on Civil Service for 1998), Tokyo: Ministry of Finance, Printing Bureau.

Kawakita, T. (1991) *Tsusan-sho* (The Ministry of Trade and Industry), Tokyo: Kodan-sha.

Kawakita, T. (1999) *Kanryo-tachi no Nawabari* (Territories of Bureaucrats), Tokyo: Shincho-sha.

Kim, Hyung-ki, M. Muramatsu, T. J. Pempel and K. Yamamura (1995) *The Japanese Civil Service and Economic Development*, Oxford: Clarendon Press.

Kokuzeicho (National Tax Administration) (c. 1992) *Kokuzeicho: Kokka-Komuin-Saiyo-Ishu-Shiken wo jyukensareru Minasanhe* (National Tax Administration introduces the applicants for Class I to the appointment examination for government service), Tokyo: Kokuzeicho.

Komiya, R. and K. Yamamoto (1981) 'Japan: the officer in charge of economic affairs' in A. W. Coats eds., *Economists in Government*, Durham, NC: Duke University Press.

Muramatsu, M. (1981) *Sengo Nihon no Kanryo-sei* (Japanese Bureaucracy after WWII), Tokyo: Toyo Keizai Shinpo-sha.

OECD (Organization for Economic Cooperation and Development) (1978) *The Industrial Policy of Japan*, Paris: OECD.

Okada, A. (1997) *Sengo Nihon Kanryo-sei no Seiritsu*, Tokyo: Hosei University Press

Senzenki Kanryosei Kenkyukai/Hata Ikuhiko (1981) *Senzenki Nihon Kanryo-Kiko no Seido, Soshiki, Jinji*, Tokyo University Press.

7   From reconstruction to rapid growth

Takeo Minoguchi (Sections 7.1 and 7.4), Tamotsu Nishizawa (Section 7.3), and Aiko Ikeo (Section 7.2)

Introduction

Japan declared war against China in the summer of 1937, and then the United States and the United Kingdom in December 1941. As seen in Chapter 5, when the Pacific Campaign was over in August 1945, some Japanese had already started preparing for the reparation problem and the reconstruction of the Japanese economy. This chapter focuses on the two important economists, Ichiro Nakayama and Seiichi Tobata, who participated in the Special Investigation Committee set up in the Ministry of Foreign Affairs in November 1945, and the Economic Council, which was established in 1952, for the longest period.

7.1 Ichiro Nakayama and the Japanese economy

When Ichiro Nakayama died on 9 April 1980 at the age of 81, the then Prime Minister Masayoshi Ohira described his contributions to Japan's economic development as follows:

> One cannot speak of the recovery and development of our country's postwar economic society without mentioning the Sensei (Professor Nakayama). Most importantly, during the period when postwar labor-management relations were severely shaken, he expended every effort as chief of the Central Labor Relations Commission. Through the fair and balanced judgements of Sensei, many major disputes were skillfully brought under control and guided to resolutions, and even now the memories remain as new. In recent times our country's labor-management relations have proceeded in a manner more sound than can be seen in any foreign country. I believe that this is nothing other than the fruition and the realization of the Sensei's long years of guidance in bringing the trust between labor and management together as one.
>
> Further, the Sensei participated in the policy formulations of successive governments, and here left major marks as well. He was engaged in numerous public positions, notably as chair of the Price Stabilization Policy Council, and also chair of the Tax System Investigative Council, and chair, and then

later president, of the Transportation Policy Council. His attitude of always taking his responsibilities very seriously earned him high praise and deep respect from all sides. (Nakayama 1981: 10–11)

As stated in the funeral oration, Nakayama's economic contributions can be categorized in two broad ways. One was his role in promoting peace and stability in industrial relations, and the second was his role in participating in and leading economic policy making in successive governments. In this chapter, we will focus on introducing the second role.

7.1.1 Nakayama's relationship with the government

Nakayama wrote of his ties to the government, 'I have become a member of the newly formed Labor Committee. This is the first time that I have become a member of a government-connected committee or come to be connected to a policy deliberation council' (Nakayama 1981: 11).

However, Nakayama had already been involved with the government to some extent in the prewar era. Prior to the war, he had established himself as one of Japan's preeminent economists through such works as *Pure Economics* (1933a), *Equilibrium Theory and Capital Theory* (1938), and *An Equilibirum Analysis of Developing Process* (1939) (all in Japanese). His first ties to the government were formed through the Economic Research Institute (generally known as the Akimaru Institute), established within the Ministry of the Army in 1940. Nakayama took charge of the Domestic Section, and during this time stated in a report that 'Our studies have demonstrated through labor power, productive power, and other aspects that Japan's economic capacity will be hard pressed to endure a war of any greater scale' (Nakayama 1983: 391). At the same time, the Britain–America Section was headed by Hiromi Arisawa, who was one of the so-called 'trio of economists'. Nakayama's opinion was heard but ultimately not heeded. Accordingly, Japan suddenly entered the Second World War. Nakayama later wrote in his recollections that 'I had a great sense of fear that this declaration of war had at last brought Japan into a war beyond its means' (Nakayama 1981: 391).

Nakayama's ties to the Central Labor Commission also date from the wartime era, resulting from his participation in a research group on postwar management organized one or two years before the war ended. Nakayama stated, 'There was a research group in which Shinchichi Miura, an advisor to the Bank of Japan, was one of the active leaders, and I took charge of the issue of Germany's demobilization of its soldiers after World War I. That was because that was the first problem Japan had to confront after losing the war. That research created the reason for having me named as a member of the Commission' (Nakayama 1981: 10).

The importance of Nakayama's research activities from the prewar era was acknowledged, and at the end of the war he promptly became a participant in policy making for economic reconstruction. To begin with, he became a member of the Postwar Currency Policy Committee at the request of Finance Minister

Keizo Shibusawa. The Committee decided that the old yen should be frozen and replaced by a new yen. Nakayama also participated in the Postwar Japan Economic Reconstruction Research Group, which operated within the Economic Bureau of the Foreign Ministry under the then Foreign Minister Shigeru Yoshida. Yoshida believed that 'Economic management under the occupation needed, as in Britain and the US, to secure the cooperation of first-rate economists' (Wakimura 1981: 238). In addition to Nakayama, other prominent members of the Committee included Hyohe Ouchi, Hiromi Arisawa, Seiichi Tobata, Kiyoshi Tsuchiya, and Hidezo Inaba. Another participant, who served as the committee secretary, was a future foreign affairs minister named Saburo Okita. The Committee issued its report, 'Japan's Economic Reconstruction,' in 1946.

In addition, Nakayama was a participant in the informal lunchtime meetings held by Yoshida upon becoming Prime Minister in 1947. Other members included, in addition to Nakayama, Hiromi Arisawa, Seiichi Tobata, Shunichi Uchida, Yoshiaki Hori, Jiro Shirasu, and Hiroo Wada. The idea for the Production Priority System, a pillar of Japanese economic policy during the early postwar era, emerged from these meetings.

Nakayama accordingly observed, 'The war was the occasion for me to become directly involved in Japan's economic issues, and if the war had not occurred during this generation, my career as an economist might have taken a different course' (Nakayama 1973: II).

Nakayama described his relations with the government in the following statement:

> In the postwar period alone I was involved with many deliberation councils and committees. I have memories of the Postwar Currency Policy Committee of the immediate postwar era in 1945. I was involved in the Statistics Committee, which was founded the following year, 1946, for over 17 years, even after it was renamed the Statistics Council. I was a member of the Central Labor Commission, also established in 1946, for exactly 15 years until resigning in 1960 when I was the chair. In 1959 I became chair of the Tax System Investigative Committee, where I participated until resigning in 1965. I have participated continuously in the Economic Council from its establishment in 1953 to the present, and am presently chair of the Price Stabilization Policy Council, which was founded as the Price Issues Discussion Group in 1963. I have important memories of the Ministry of Education's University Establishment Council, MITI's Industrial Rationalization Council, and the Ministry of Labor's Central Minimum Wage Council. (1973: iii–iv)

Thus Nakayama served as chair, president, and committee member in a great variety of policy deliberation councils, discussion groups, investigation groups, councils, and committees, but it is difficult to judge the usefulness of his work to Japan's economy. As Nakayama states:

What purpose was served by becoming a member of those deliberation councils and committees? Leave aside for the moment the issue of what I myself contributed, that is, objectively speaking, what kinds of contributions did I make to deliberation councils and committees, as this is generally difficult to answer. The committees, like in the Statistics Committee or the Central Labor Committee in the beginning, for example, had the characteristics of administrative agencies; further, even when they were termed councils, like the University Establishment Council or the Central Minimum Wage Council for example, their policy decisions were called advice, but in reality some of the committees held strong administrative powers. (1973: iv)

Nakayama participated in two government-related areas in which he obviously made important contributions to the Japanese economy. One was the Central Labor Commission which he chaired from 1950 to 1960 and the other was the formation of policy towards rapid economic growth, in which he was active in the ten years from 1960. The following section describes these roles.

7.1.2 *Nakayama and postwar rapid economic growth*

It was in 1955 when production recovered to its prewar level and the so-called rapid growth era began. From 1960, when the Ikeda cabinet announced the National Income Doubling Plan, economic growth accelerated further, with GDP growth averaging 10 percent from 1960 to 1965 and 11.3 percent from 1965 to 1970. From 1955 until 1970, production levels reached 3.5 times those of the prewar era.

The basis for the Ikeda cabinet's Income Doubling Plan was Nakayama's 'wage doubling thesis' which appeared in the Yomiuri Newspaper on 1 January 1959. There is a wealth of material which attests to this point. To begin with, there is the following statement by Tetsuzo Nakajima in the Collected Memorial Writings on Professor Nakayama entitled *A Straight Path for Eighty Years.* 'The Sensei added the phrase "wage doubling thesis" to a certain paper . . . The "wage doubling thesis" soon bloomed as the Ikeda cabinet's income doubling policy' (Nakayama 1981: 95–6). Another case is the postscript to the 16th volume of *The Complete Works of Nakayama Ichiro* by Miyohei Shinohara.

On the 1 January 1959 Yomiuri Newspaper the phrase 'propose wage doubling' was written. The prime minister inquired to the Economic Council about the income doubling plan in November 1959, and the report was completed in November 1960, so it can be seen that the income doubling hint really originated in Nakayama's ideas. I think that there are also a surprisingly large number of people who remember discussions with Professor Nakayama on television or then Prime Minister Ikeda talking about 'what Nakayama-san calls the monthly wage doubling thesis'. (Shinohara 1973: 557)

Nakayama's wage doubling thesis needs to be described. Nakayama, at the beginning of 'The Wage Doubling Proposal', explained it as follows:

> When we think about future images of the Japanese economy, the most comprehensive expression, in abstract form, is welfare state. . . . When we are in this state of impoverishment, how can we approach our ideal of the welfare state? When we confront this issue it is all the more imperative to give concrete form to our future images. For that concrete form, I daringly propose the wage doubling economy. However, the prerequisite for doubling wages is that productive capacity must be doubled. For the reinforcement of productive capacity an accumulation of capital is necessary. Trade relations are necessary, and finding markets is a general precondition.

He concluded, 'The objective of doubling wages, first, as a mutual objective of labor and management, and, by and by, as an objective of national policy, could serve as an effective first step towards a concrete future of the Japanese economy' (Nakayama 1973: 32, 42).

However, Nakayama's income doubling thesis offered no prediction as to what year doubling could be achieved. He said only, 'As long as the growth rate continues at the current rate, the wage level could increase several times. Not just two but even three or four times. Whatever stage is reached, first making it an objective and then moving toward it should make a superb strategy' (Nakayama 1973: 33). The Ikeda Cabinet's vision of the 'plan for doubling incomes', which it proposed to accomplish 'within ten years', was fundamentally different from the income doubling thesis.

Nevertheless, Nakayama committed himself to the Income Doubling Plan, as noted by Saburo Okita (1981: 107). 'Professor Nakayama really took care of matters in his capacities as general section chair of the Economic Council and as the real leader in planning the Income Doubling Plan'. According to the plan proposed by the Economic Planning Agency, under Nakayama's guidance, wages would double in ten years if they grew at a 7.2 percent rate. The Ikeda cabinet, on the other hand, called for the higher rate of 9 percent. The main reason that the Economic Planning Agency adopted the 7.2 percent figure was simply that a high growth rate, such as that of the Jinmu boom of 1956, 'would generate contradictions in the structure between the economic base and the superstructure' (Nakayama 1981: 37). At that time, three factors – transport, steel, and electric power – created limiting factors for growth. The thinking was that strengthening these core industries would bolster growth and make the 7.2 percent target attainable. A second reason was the belief that excessive growth would lead to a shortage of foreign exchange because of Japan's high reliance on imports. A third reason was concern that excessive growth would create income differentials between industries whose productivity could be quickly raised and whose productivity was difficult to improve. That would likely lead in turn to productivity-gap inflation as incomes were standardized. The proposal of the Economic Planning Agency aimed not merely at growth, but at stable growth. Therefore, 7.2 percent rather than 9 percent was chosen as the targeted rate.

Whatever plan was adopted, it cannot be denied that making a public promise to double incomes in ten years or less eliminated future uncertainty and stimulated investment and consumption. In 1960, the first year of the plan, GNP grew at a real rate of 13.1 percent, and it grew at 11.6 percent in 1961, both figures well above the 9 percent specified in government plans. As predicted, this brought deterioration in the balance of payments, leading to a tightening of fiscal policy in 1962 and the appearance of a Japanese-style recession.

However, rapid economic growth created favorable conditions for realizing the income-doubling thesis and its successor the Income Doubling Plan. To begin with, the cheap yen created an advantage for a trading nation like Japan.

> The foremost of the fortuitous factors promoting growth was the decision to fix the exchange rate at 360 yen to the dollar. The rate was fixed in 1949, when Japan's productive capacity was at its lowest level. From that time until the present the productivity of manufacturing industries has increased three times. During the course of this three-fold expansion, quality improved and new products appeared continuously while prices fell as fast as products grew. Moreover, the rate was fixed at 360 yen, which was advantageous to exports. What is advantageous to exports should be disadvantageous to imports, but here also we were able to make great use of another fortuitous factor. That is the fact that the price of imports stagnated or else fell. For this reason, Japan's ability to import increased much more than the norm. Over these ten years, exports grew, the balance of payments strengthened, which is how we can explain the conditions which became pillars of high growth. (Nakayama 1973: 37)

A second factor underlying high growth was investment in modern equipment which made possible productivity improvements.

> Equipment was destroyed in the war, and we emerged destitute, but we then built all the first-rate, large-scale equipment we desired. The Western countries were hindered by a sense of conservatism, and the replacement and modernization of equipment failed to progress. (Nakayama 1973: 64)

A third factor was an expanding market that could serve as an outlet for productive capabilities. Nakayama points out that:

> Until very recently, America possessed exceedingly great and expanding economic power, and it was for this reason that Japan was able to maintain its very strong export performance. This was a major factor in keeping Japan's economy afloat. In short, the global economy freed the market so that Japan's economy could bloom, and this was the reason that Japan's economy could grow steadily on its own. (Nakayama 1973: 134)

These factors, the introduction of equipment incorporating the newest technology and the advantage of the fixed exchange rate of 360 yen to the dollar, made it possible for Japan to master the skills of international competitiveness, to export its steel, ships, and automobiles first to the US, and then to the rest of the global market, and to experience rapid growth. In other words, Japan's rapid growth was investment- and export-led. However, this pattern of rapid growth based on rapid productivity gains in core industries created the distortion of rising consumer prices. Solving the inflation problem became Nakayama's next task, and the fight against inflation became the central issue of the second half of the high growth era.

7.1.3 Nakayama's fight against inflation

Nakayama became chair of the Price Problem Discussion Group, which served as a personal advisory body to the head of the Economic Planning Agency, in September 1963. He was then successively appointed to head the Price Stability Promotion Council in March 1967 and the Price Stabilization Policy Council in July 1969.

We must specify the period for which we discuss Nakayama's fight against inflation. He was head of the Price Stabilization Policy Council in 1974 when Japan suffered the OPEC oil embargo-induced 'crazy inflation'. at which time Nakayama told the Budget Committee of the Diet's House of Councilors that the country needed to adopt a tight fiscal policy and postpone tax cuts. However, in the sixteen-volume collected works of Nakayama, the oldest essays on inflation date from 1963 and the newest go up only through 1972. Thus the materials on Nakayama's role in fighting inflation cover only the high-growth era.

An important characteristic of inflation during the high-growth era was that it applied only to consumer prices while wholesale prices, which affected exports, remained stable. Thus consumer prices rose 34 percent in the five-year period from 1960–65 (6 percent annually) while wholesale prices rose only 2.1 percent (0.4 percent annually). The figures for 1965–70 were 30.3 percent (5.4 percent annually) and 11.3 percent (2.2 percent annually), respectively. The highest consumer price increases were recorded by agricultural products, at 50.4 percent and 42.5 percent, in the 1960–65 and 1965–70 periods respectively, and by the service sector, at 44.5 percent and 33.8 percent, respectively. In contrast, the wholesale prices of manufactured goods fell one percent and then rose 9.7 percent during the two five-year periods.

We can explain rising consumer prices and stable wholesale prices by the following factors. The first is differences in weighting in the way that price indexes were then compiled. The wholesale price index covers transactions between companies, so manufactured goods, almost all of them produced by large firms, account for 83.6 percent of the index, while services are totally excluded. In contrast the consumer price index covers products and services purchased for consumption. Thus industrial products account for no more than

45 percent of index compilation, and products from small- and mid-size firms account for a large share. Agricultural products account for 14 percent and services 34 percent.

Consequently, the costs of foodstuffs and small- and mid-size firm products, which did the most to force up prices during the high-growth era, were not included in the wholesale price index. But why did these prices rise so much faster than large firm products? The reason involves two characteristics of the high-growth era economy. The first was a tight labor market, which meant that wages rose regardless of firm size and moved toward standardization. This factor forced up wage costs in the service sector and in small- and mid-size firms. The second factor was that large firms greatly improved their productivity through high investment, which smaller firms and the agricultural and service sectors failed to do. The high rise in consumer prices and the stability of wholesale prices can be explained by these two factors.

Agricultural and small- and mid-size-firm products and services are important components of consumer prices. But even as these sectors' wages rose their productivity did not increase, making price rises inevitable. On the other hand, the weight of industrial products, particularly those produced by large firms, is quite important. Further, while wages in large firms increased, productivity improved prodigiously, so that wage increases were absorbed by productivity increases and not carried over as price increases. Therefore, since inflation during the high growth era was caused primarily by the productivity differential between agriculture, smaller firms, and services on the one hand and large industrial firms on the other, it was termed productivity growth rate differential inflation by Yoshihiro Takasuka.

What kind of policy measures can be used to suppress inflation generated by such differentials in rates of productivity increase? In general, increases in productivity are absorbed by three factors: rising wages, increasing profits, and falls in prices. From this observation we can make the following inference. First, assuming differentials in rates of productivity increase as a precondition, we may suppose that if prices fall in industries with high rates of productivity increase, then overall prices may remain stable. As Nakayama stated:

> In brief, in industries where productivity is low, or where significant productivity rises cannot be expected, and which exhibit mechanisms for high wage standardization because there is high productivity elsewhere, then the prices of the products of those industries must somehow rise; in order to cover those price rises with price stability, that is to maintain stability of the currency, then the prices of the high productivity industries must somehow fall. (Nakayama 1973: 293)

But how should the prices of high productivity industries be lowered? Nakayama believed that in such cases the intervention of the Fair Trade Commission was necessary to ensure that competition reverted to its proper form.

> Even profits made from vigorous productivity are eaten up by unfair competition cartels and never ultimately come back as benefits for consumers. The Fair Trade Commission is above all an institution for restoring such distorted competition to fair competition. I would like the government to extend the internal and external support necessary for this committee to be able to perform its full activities. (Nakayama 1973: 340)

This is a criticism of the point that productivity increases are not reflected in price decreases but absorbed by wages and profits.

However, Nakayama did not believe that differences in rates of productivity increases were always a precondition. When productivity increases were low, it was because of those industries' lack of effort to raise productivity, he thought, and any productivity increases they made should not be converted into higher prices. As Nakayama saw it, the worst problem was the rice price. The means of deciding the producer price for rice assumed the necessity of 100 percent self-sufficiency in rice, and used a formula for guaranteeing production costs and income guarantees. Nakayama believe that this formula prevented improvements in productivity.

> Looked at in this regard, does the present means of deciding the producer rice price and production cost and income guarantee formulae as well as such things as index formulae ultimately actually perform the task of encouraging productivity to rise? What matters is that the present rice price setting formula is based on the producer rice price, but, in a word, it rests on self-sufficiency. . . . Judging from conditions at present, I do not think that 100 percent self-sufficiency is possible. Instead self-supply could be held to 90 percent or 85 percent, and an approach of using imports to cover the rest should be adopted. (Nakayama 1973: 314–15)

In other words, the partial liberalization of rice imports could generate competition in rice production and bring about stronger efforts to increase productivity. He believed that this would contribute to price stability.

Further, Nakayama advanced comprehensive proposals for promoting price stability. These included introducing an incomes policy which would provide guidelines indicating how high wages could rise; in this way rises in high productivity sectors would not bring out rapid rises in low productivity sectors. He also suggested holding down growth funds which promoted growth but also tended to bring about labor shortages, and policies for suppressing demand. Despite his efforts, prices did not stabilize, leading Nakayama to lament 'This was regrettable' in his personal record (Nakayama 1981: 40).

7.1.4 Theoretical background to Nakayama's economic thought

As a youth, Nakayama studied general equilibrium theory at the University of Bonn under Joseph A. Schumpeter. Later in his student days he conducted research on the mathematical economics of A. Cournot, H. H. Gossen, and L. Walras under the guidance of Tokuzo Fukuda. The result of this work was *Pure Economics* (in Japanese), which appeared in 1933. The early Nakayama was, simply stated, a Schumpeterian. However, Nakayama's economic thought underwent a major change when John Maynard Keynes' *General Theory* appeared in 1936. According to Nakayama's seminar students, Nakayama selected *General Theory* as his seminar text practically the moment it was published (Nakayama 1983: 347). That was in 1936. In 1939, Nakayama published *Commentary on Keynes' General Theory* (in Japanese) through the publisher Nihon Hyoron-sha. During this period, the main theme in Nakayama's economics came to be 'stability and progress'. He explains the process of choosing this watchword as follows:

> I remember that it was around 1938–39 when I made stability and progress the catchwords for my future, and the motivation was Keynes. Keynes' General Theory was published in 1936, and it was in that form that Keynes' revolution influenced the world. One way that it did so was in being a major revision of the classical school, and yet a second was that it posed economic meaning for policy. . . . Immediately following its publication, *General Theory* was reviewed in nearly every economics journal in the world, which is to say that they heightened the wave of the Keynesian revolution. Among these was the review of Dennis Robertson. The words stability and progress appeared at the end of his review. These words struck me like a veritable bolt of lighting. For I, who had been searching for a foothold toward changing pure economics theory into real policy, these words at once enabled me to readily surmount the fence between theory and policy. . . . Further, for me who had been lost, this phrase was the mentor. (Nakayama 1983: 7–8)

Thus Keynes' economics made possible the application of economic theory to the real economy. By examining the numbers of citations of economists and references made to them by Nakayama in 'Observations on the Japanese Economy' in his *Complete Works* (*Zenshu*), vol. 16, we can see the important influence of Keynes on Nakayama's economics. There were 26 citations and references for Keynes, 16 for Schumpeter, 11 for Marshall, 8 for Galbraith, 6 for Smith, and 6 for Triffin. Around ten of Keynes' numerous citations and references concern currency systems, along with the relationship between currency systems with economic growth and with inflation.

As is well known, Keynes believed that capitalist economies should be freed from the restraints of the gold standard, and that flexible provision of currency under a managed currency system should be instituted in order to realize full employment. His calls for a managed currency system began with *Tract on Monetary Reform* (1923) and continued in *A Treatise on Money* (1930) and in *General Theory*. Keynes argued that monetary reforms would enhance the effectiveness of central banks' use of monetary policy to realize full employment. Nakayama believed that this was the greatest contribution of Keynes' economics.

The person who argued for changing the monetary system from the gold standard to a managed currency system and who posited the utility of fiscal deficits for achieving full employment, the basis of economic policy, was Keynes. Through his series of publications, *Tract on Monetary Reform* (1923), *A Treatise on Money* (1930), and *General Theory* (1936), he emphasized freeing currency from gold and for the necessity of a monetary system which could freely provide the amounts of money necessary to realize and maintain full employment. This was the outcome which Keynes ingeniously extracted from his experiences starting with the First World War, while the world, at least from the 1931 Great Depression and after, actually obeyed Keynes' appeals to adopt these policies. (Nakayama 1973: 461)

Moreover, a comparison of the gold standard era with the managed currency era shows that during the latter economic growth was two times faster at 5 to 6 percent annually. This was because previously the 3 percent annual growth of the gold supply had limited economic growth (Blaug 1995: 23). Still, the managed currency system was a double-edged sword, for while it proved a superb means of achieving high growth and full employment, there was the fear that a small error would trigger inflation. This led to the aggravating problem of trying simultaneously to stabilize prices, maintain full employment, and pursue economic growth. Under the managed currency system, full employment was achieved but price stability was sacrificed.

The meaning of Nakayama's catchphrase 'stability and progress' under the managed currency system came to mean 'price stability and full employment' or 'price stability and economic growth'. During the early postwar era, full employment and growth were comparatively easily achieved because of favorable economic conditions in Japan. This applied above all to the strategic variable of investment, which is decisive for national income. In Japan's case, fortunately, investment for modernization was necessary and therefore abundant. Otherwise, the only problem was to provide the money necessary for investment. In the first half of the high-growth era, therefore, Nakayama's economics functioned smoothly. As prices began to rise in the second half of the high-growth era, however, there was increasing ambiguity in the policy course.

Nakayama failed to develop a consistent policy line. With regard to price stability, he sometimes argued, based on quantitative monetarism, for controlling currency supply; sometimes he argued, based on wage push theory, for instituting wage policies. Shinohara explains this inconsistency as follows:

For example, today the trend among monetarists is not to believe in wage push inflation, so few people believe in the need for incomes policies. On the other hand, however, the stance that 'quantitative monetarism will not die' existed even during the heyday of Keynesian economics and is firmly embedded in Nakayama economics. Nonetheless, Professor Nakayama argued that, depending on circumstances, some type of income policy might be necessary. So in the Nakayama structure, the two were not contradictory.

> . . . While Professor Nakayama was advocating the position that Keynes' theories be accepted from beginning to end, he was also a person who emphasized the value of quite old quantitative monetary theories. . . . Thus the professor himself made free use of the theoretical weapons of the most brilliant first-rate scholars. (Nakayama 1983: 301)

Shinohara terms this contradiction in policy lines 'general equilibrium theoretical harmony'. Below is his explanation of this term.

> Rather, thinking in terms of the general equilibrium of the entire economy where price levels are determined by both supply and demand, emphasizing only the demand-pull inflation of the total currency approach means looking at only one dimension; while being concerned only about cost-push inflation means overlooking the demand side so that also is too limited. Therefore, for a policy to resolve the contemporary inflation of the postwar, a comprehensive demand policy is important, and when inflation becomes a problem incomes policies are also important. (Shinohara 1973: 559)

Thus Nakayama's economics was a magnificent structure based primarily on Keynesian economic thought but it also included opposing economic thoughts within a 'general equilibrium'.

7.2 Ichiro Nakayama on international trade

This section discusses the controversy between pro-trade and pro-domestic development advocated by Ichiro Nakayama, Hiromi Arisawa and others from the viewpoint of Nakayama. Nakayama rightly argued that Japan had to promote international trade in order to enhance the living standard, because he understood the reconstruction of the Japanese economy from the international perspective. The discussion and debate among Japanese economists of the day depended heavily on the international environment brought about by the Cold War from 1947. The fact was that Japan's international trade was unable to increase, or more precisely, Japan could not import more due to its continual trade deficit because it could not export more. This was the reason why Japan's government implemented exchange control. Therefore, we have to look carefully at the situation evolving over time and to clarify the real differences in opinions.

From 1945 until the late 1960s the majority of economists in Japan were Marxist or Marxian economists. The remaining economists of the day were called modern economists (*kindai keizaigakusha*). Yet they were not neoclassical, market-oriented economists, but rather development economists, who paid careful attention to the 'real world' in recommending economic policies. They believed in an important role of the central government and local municipal governments in economic development. Nakayama was the target of criticism by the majority, Marxian economists. He wrote many articles and essays on the current conditions of the Japanese economy for various journals and magazines, and later had them published in book form. It is noteworthy that he was always calm and his writings were objective and encouraging.

It is well known that there was a big controversy between pro-trade and pro-development around 1950 (Table 7.1). Hisao Kanamori included part of the papers written by Nakayama and Arisawa in *Boeki to Kokusai Shushi* (Trade and International Balance) (Kanamori ed. 1970), and Kimihiro Masamura summarized the controversy in *Sengoshi* (A Post-War History) (Masamura 1985: 363–6). However, it seems that few have discussed the whole process of the controversy except for Ikeo (1998), which unfortunately had a mistitle of an important article. There seem to be three reasons. First, the monthly magazine *Hyoron* (review in English), which carried Nakayama's 'Nihonkeizai no kao' (The face of the Japanese economy) and H. Arisawa's 'Nihon shihonshugi no unmei' (The destiny of Japanese capitalism), was issued only from February 1946 till April 1950. It was abolished a couple of months after it carried their articles and only a few complete copies remain now. Second, it is hard to trace the controversy because it took place in scattered magazines. Third, Nakayama himself made a mistake and put the wrong year, 1949, for the publication of his 'Sekai shijo to nihon keizai' (The world market and the Japanese economy), which was first published in *Keizai Hyoron* (Economic Review in English) in 1950, when he included the article under the different title 'Boeki-shugi to kokunai-kaihatsu-shugi' (Pro-trade and pro-development) in Nakayama's *Nihon Keizai no Kao* (The Face of the Japanese Economy) (1953). The mistake was left as it was when volume 12 of *Complete Works of Ichiro Nakayama*, including his *The Face of the Japanese Economy*, was published in 1972. It seems that no one realized the mistake.[1]

When we focus on the economic debates around 1950, we have to look carefully at the background, international environment, and the situation evolving over time. Japan was occupied by the Allies led by the United States, while the US was retreating in East Asia after the Cold War centered around the antagonism between the US and the Soviet Union started in 1947. When the People's Republic of China was established under the leadership of the Chinese Communist Party, Japanese economists were shocked because China was one of the two major trade partners before China and Japan began to fight in 1937. Twenty percent of Japan's international trade prior to 1937 was with China, with another important trade partner being the US. Naturally the US became Japan's far largest trading partner from the occupation period. It was expected that Japan's trade with China would not regain as much as the period prior to 1937. In fact, the issue in the controversy of pro-trade versus pro-domestic development was the difference in expectation of the future course of Japan's international trade. Nakayama argued that Japan had to expand international trade in order to maintain the current living standard, while he agreed with the economists of pro-domestic development like Arisawa that Japan needed to develop its own resources and industries. Therefore, there was no discrepancy about the importance of domestic development for both sides.

The controversy began with Nakayama's 'Nihon keizai no kao' (The face of the Japanese economy), which was published in a monthly magazine *Hyoron* in December 1949. What Nakayama had in mind was Schumpeter's memorial

Table 7.1 The controversy between pro-trade and pro-development

December 1949	I. Nakayama 'Nihon keizai no kao' (The face of the Japanese economy), *Hyoron* (Review, Kawade Shobo) (38), 1–9.
January 1950	T. Suzuki, K. Kimura and S. Tsuru 'Zadankai: Nihon keizai no kao' (Round table: The face of the Japanese economy), *Hyoron* (Kawade Shobo) (39), 33–44.
February 1950	Arisawa 'Nihon shihon-shugi no unmei' (The destiny of Japanese capitalism), *Hyoron* (Kawade Shobo), (40), 5–14.
March 1950	S. Tsuru ' "Keizaigaku" no hitori-aruki ha abunai – "Nihon-keizai no kao niyosete" ' (It is dangerous for economics to walk alone), *Hyoron* (Kawade Shobo), (41), 13–23.
	I. Nakayama 'Sekai shijo to nihon keizai' (The world market and the Japanese economy), *Keizai Hyoron* (Economic Review) March, 1–9. [This article was included in the section entitled 'Boeki-shugi to kokunai-kaihatsu-shugi' (Pro-trade and pro-development) of Nakayama's *The Face of the Japanese Economy* (in Japanese, 1953) and volume 12 of *Nakayama's Zenshu*. The year of publication 'Showa 24' (1949) on page 128 and 94 respectively was wrong. Ikeo (1998: 139, 150) mistakenly wrote the later title of a section in the book 'Boeki-shugi to kokunai-kaihatsu-shugi' for the title of the original article.]
April 1950	I. Nakayama 'Keizai hatten to chingin no mondai' (Economic development and the problem of wages), *Kaizo* (Transformation) 31 (4), 49–53.
May 1950	I. Nakayama, H. Arisawa, S. Tobata, Y. Morita, and S. Tsuru 'Toronkai: Nihon Shihon-shugi no unmei' (Round table: Japanese capitalism and its destiny), *Keizai Hyoron* May, 2–108.
June 1950	K. Matsui, 'Sengo no boeki seisaku' (Post-war trade policy), *Chuo Koron* (Public Opinion) (736), 4–18.
	S. Tsuru *Keizaigaku heno Hansei* (Reflection to Economics), Jiji-tsushin-sha.
April 1951	S. Tsuru '8000man nin to kokunai shigen' (80 million population and domestic resources), *Chuo Koron* (746), 19–30.
	K. Matsui 'Boeki shugi no unmei' (The destiny of pro-trade), *Chuo Koron* (746), 19–30.
	H. Inaba 'Keizai jiritsu keikaku no mukeikakusei' (A wrong planning of economic viability), *Chuo Koron* (746), 31–40.
October 1951	K. Akamatsu, Y. Nakano, T. Nawa, and S. Yabe 'Zadankai: Zenmen kowa to tandoku kowa no taiketsu' (Round table: the peace treaty with all the nations or only with the western bloc) *Chuo Koron* Special Issue (753), 114–28.
June 1952	M. Toyosaki, K. Kojima *et al.* 'Kokumin keizai kaigi: dai-4 bukai: tai-chuso boeki ha nantokadekinaika' (National Economic Conference: The Fourth Group: The problem of trade with China and the Soviet Union) *Chuo Koron* Special Issue (763), 62–71.
April 1953	I. Nakayama 'Boeki-shugi to kokunai-kaihatsu-shugi sairon' (Pro-trade and pro-development, reconsidered) *Tsusho Sangyo Kenkyu* (Study of International Trade and Industry) (1), 2–7.
July 1953	S. Tsuru 'Nihon boeki-seisaku no shuyo mondaiten' (Major problems of Japan's trade policy), *Keizai Kenkyu* (Economic Review) 4 (3), 195–202.
December 1953	H. Arisawa *Saigunbi no Keizaigaku* (Economics of Rearmament), Tokyo Daigaku Shuppankai.
	I. Nakayama *Nihon Keizai no Kao* (The Face of the Japanese Economy), Nihon Hyoronsha.

lecture 'The face of the German economy' (c. 1930) for the anniversary of the establishment of the University of Bonn. Nakayama argued that the Japanese economy must frown, beset with deflation under the so-called Dodge Line or the Nine-Part Directive on Stabilization. The Dodge line was implemented by the Allied Occupation Force in order to achieve fiscal, monetary, price and wage stability and to maximize production for exports. After implementation of the plan, commodity prices began to decline in the black markets and finally the price level was stabilized, but accompanying formidable social instability, including massive unemployment.

In his 1949 paper, Nakayama utilized the three statistical data describing the face of the Japanese economy understandable to non-Japanese economists: population, international trade, and national income. First, Nakayama called attention to the fact that Japan had 80 million people and its population was increasing at 2 percent per year. This fact was important and surprised the world. Italy had 48 million people and its population was increasing at 1 percent per year, which was the fastest pace among European countries. Criticizing Malthus's pessimistic, biological viewpoint on population, Nakayama argued that an occupational, industrial viewpoint was more relevant and that the increase in population was a positive result of social and economic phenomena such as the increases in productivity. Nakayama (1972: 9) said: 'Thanks to the increase in productivity, which has been enabled by the industrialization since the Meiji era [1868–1912], Japan's population has increased from 30-odd million in 1868 up to 80 million.'

Second, calling attention to Adam Smith's absolute advantage theory of trade and idea of international division of labor, Nakayama confirmed that the benefit of international trade was common sense. Japan lacked iron ore, cotton, and crude oil, which were to be brought to Japan by international trade. He argued that the imports and the exports, which were needed to secure the imports, were the basis for Japan's industrialization and the increase in its population. Third, Nakayama regarded the level of national income as the best measure to describe the face of a national economy. He examined the historical changes in Japan's real income per hour and compared it to other countries. Japan's real income per hour had more than sextupled from 0.03 in 1900 to 0.19 in 1937. In 1944, Japan's figure was 0.18, USA 0.96, UK 0.61, and France 0.21. He said that National Income was already found in textbooks such as Hicks's *The Social Framework of the American Economy* (Hicks and Hart 1945) and Samuelson's *Economics* (1948).

In the issue of January 1950, the magazine *Hyoron* featured the round-table discussion of Takeo Suzuki, Kihachiro Kimura and Shigeto Tsuru. In 'Zadankai: Nihon keizai no kao' (Round-table: The face of the Japanese economy), they put forward a critical argument and questioned why Nakayama had chosen these three data. Yet the focal point of their discussion was gradually moved toward international trade. Arisawa's 'Nihon shihonshugi no unmei' (The destiny of Japanese capitalism, February 1950) and Tsuru's 'Keizaigaku no hitori aruki ha abunai' (It is dangerous for economics to walk alone, March 1950) appeared in the same magazine *Hyoron*.

Nakayama defended his points in his 'Sekai shijo to nihon keizai' (The world market and the Japanese economy, March 1950), which appeared in *Keizai Hyoron* (Economic Review). He misnamed his position as pro-trade (boeki-shugi) and the critics as pro-domestic-development (kokunai-kaihatsu-shugi), because he knew that both sides agreed that it was necessary to develop the domestic economy even though there was disagreement on the future prospect and importance of international trade. Nakayama (1972: 83) defined pro-trade as solving economic problems in a country from a perspective of the world economy, or from a global perspective in a recent terminology, and targeting to build a country based on international trade. On the other hand, Nakayama (1972: 84) defined pro-domestic development as putting energy and resources on the domestic development given the limitation of international trade. Nonetheless it seems that Nakayama called his position pro-trade because he thought it necessary to emphasize the importance of international trade.

Nakayama repeatedly emphasized the importance of international trade. He admitted that both the conditions of the world market and Japan's trade items were changed over the period experiencing two world wars. Nakayama (1972: 83) also admitted that it was hard for Japan to promote international trade because of a mountain of problems surrounding Japan. Nevertheless, he argued as follows. It was easy to understand that Japan needed to engage in international trade, when one looked at the long sheet of international balance in *Industrialization in Japan and Manchuria* (1940) edited by E. B. Schumpeter and the Nine-Part Directive's policy of promoting exports first for the purpose of securing imports.[2] This reflected Japan's economic conditions. Japan had a large population compared with its territory and so could not supply enough food for its people to live in isolation. It had few natural resources. Its living standards were still low. The world economic conditions should determine whether one country would import food or produce more food on its own.

Nakayama continued. There were two groups. One considered the future of the Japanese economy to stand on international trade, while the other put more weight on domestic economic development with supposition of a limit on international trade. Nakayama argued that Japan did not have capital accumulations large enough to promote either trade or domestic development yet. He rebutted the critics point by point. First, exportable goods had changed compared with the pre-WWII period because of technological development. Silk was replaced by nylon, rubber goods by artificial materials. Second, GATT was signed by a number of countries because the expansion of multilateral trade was expected to maintain high employment and enhance national income, and to contribute to the development of productive resources in each country. Nakayama understood the critics' points. Japan was not allowed to join the GATT group because of the British government's strong opposition and its exports to the sterling bloc were strictly limited.[3] Its exports to China and the Soviet Union would not expand substantially because Japan joined the Western bloc led by the USA and the Cold War would continue. He agreed that Japan could learn a way of economic planning for domestic development from the experiment of the TVA in the USA of the 1930s.

Nonetheless, he concluded that the future course of the Japanese economy must be founded in the expansion of international trade. He pointed out that the prosperity of the British economy, whose mainland was smaller than Japan's, depended on international trade and the import of food, and that no country had prospered in isolation. Referring to the 1949 annual report of the World Bank, he suggested that Japan needed capital imports as well, although everyone knew that no one was willing to lend money to Japan at the time.

The entire May 1950 issue of *Keizai Hyoron* featured a round-table discussion on the destiny of the Japanese economy with participation by Nakayama, Arisawa, Tobata, Yuzo Morita and Tsuru. Referring to Morita's latest economic data, they discussed the current economic conditions in both the world and the Japanese economy. Nakayama repeated his arguments that there were not big differences among the participants, although Arisawa and Tsuru were pessimistic about the future of a capitalist country. Their round table spawned a series of reviews and discussions among other economists and businessmen.

The question of trade was shifted to the political arena, and the issue became whether Japan should sign the San Francisco Peace Treaty with Western liberal or capitalist countries, including the United States and Western Europe, or should it wait for an overall treaty including China and the Soviet Union. Non-Marxians, including Kaname Akamatsu and Nakayama, supported Japan's prompt return to international society by the treaty in order for Japan to secure the natural resources which Japan lacked, because they did not attach so much economic importance to China (and Korea), which did not have many kinds of resources which Japan lacked (Akamatsu *et al.* 1951: 123). The Japanese government signed the treaty in September 1951.

In April 1952, the occupation was over and Japan was back into international society. However, in 1952 Japan's export was 1,273 million dollars, import was 2,027 million dollars, and its trade deficit amounted to 754 million dollars. The deficit did not show any change. In April 1953, the Ministry of International Trade and Industry began to issue the monthly magazine *Tsusho Sangyo Kenkyu* (Study of International Trade and Industry). Sankuro Ogasawara, the International Trade and Industry Minister of the day, called for the cooperation of the business world based on Nakayama's position of trade support. Ogasawara (1953: 1) said:

> We need a further increase of export, the reduction of import, the promotion of domestic industries, and the curtailment of national consumption in order to attain economic viability as soon as possible. Especially we need to strengthen the international competitiveness of our industries by constructing infrastructure, and to promote and expand international trade in order to attain international balance. ... We have decided to issue *Tsusho Sangyo Kenkyu*, which aims to contribute to the study of important problems in international trade and industry and to the prompt propagation of government policies while reflecting the opinion of business people. We really hope that our magazine will play a sound role and become the guideline for the policies of international trade and industries. [Author's translation]

Nakayama contributed his 'Boeki-shugi to kokunai-kaihatsu-shugi sairon' (Pro-trade and pro-development, reconsidered) to the first issue of *Tsusho Sangyo Kenkyu*. He criticized the economists of pro-domestic development and picked up three causes for Japan's inactive exports. First, the world economy was in depression, which was not a reason to oppose pro-trade. International cooperation was needed instead. Second, import restrictions in the Sterling area; Japan's export was about 40 percent of what it had been prior to 1937. Yet there was hope in the principle of mutual benefit in trade. Third, Japan's spinning industry, which used to be the top exporter, had to curtail its operation sharply due to the decrease in export and production. Nakayama (1972: 96) believed that it was important to make a relevant prospect of future trade. In this respect, Nakayama agreed with the economists of pro-domestic development. Nakayama (1972: 100) explained as follows:

> First, when domestic resources are developed as expected, then the result of the development has to be exported. Second, even if all the textiles are to be created from minerals, the products will have to be traded. Thus pro-domestic development should be complemented by pro-trade. There is no contradiction at all. [Author's translation]

Nakayama, Arisawa, Tsuru and the other economists of their generation agreed that Japan should develop domestic resources in order to enhance the international competitiveness of its industries. However, this kind of developmentalism was criticized by the economists of the next generation (see Chapter 8). In the 1950s, Japanese society saw political conflicts and class struggles rather than economic development. In this severe environment, workers and employers reached a consensus for the introduction of labor-saving technology in production lines, because both sides looked for the salary raise with the increase in productivity. This consensus and cooperation became the basis for economic growth in the 1960s.

7.3 Ichiro Nakayama and stabilization of labor-management relations

7.3.1 Nakayama and the Central Labor Commission

Ichiro Nakayama, who had become prominent for his works *Pure Economics* (1933a) and *Equilibrium Analysis of the Developing Process* (1939), started his postwar activity with involvement in Japan's postwar industrial relations through the Central Labor Commission. Under Japan's Labor Union Law, established after the war, the Central Labor Commission was created in March 1946 to serve as a body which would include labor, management, and an impartial third party. Nakayama was named a member of the impartial party (or public representative), along with Shotaro Miyake, Izutaro Suehiro, Iwao Ayusawa, and Susumu Katsura. Since labor issues, from wages to employment, were economic issues, it was natural for one of the impartial party members to be an economist. Nakayama's ties to the government through the wartime era are recounted in Section 1, but an immediate cause of his appointment to the Central Labor Commission has been said to be partly due to persuasion by his former pupil, Soichi Togashi, an official at what was then the Labor Administration Bureau of the Ministry of Welfare (later the Ministry of Labor; Togashi became its vice-minister). Further, from 1939 through 1949, a period of ten years spanning the prewar, wartime, and postwar eras, Nakayama, along with Seiichi Tobata, assumed the duties of teaching economic policy at the Faculty of Law of the University of Tokyo. This course combined theory with practical policy, and Nakayama used it to expound upon what he regarded as the conditions necessary for 'stability and progress'.[4]

Nakayama's deep involvement with labor-management relations really began in 1946, an intense year which witnessed the Toshiba Dispute, and it lasted until his resignation from the Labor Commission in 1961. During this fifteen-year period, he served as president of the Commission for ten years from 1950, when he succeeded Suehiro. Nakayama helped to resolve some 90 labor disputes, including Oumi Kenshi Company, and many other major clashes involving militant unions such as Kokuro (National Railway Workers Union), Zentei (Postal Workers Union), Densan (Electric Power Related Industry Workers Union), and Tanro (Coal Miners Union). For this work, he was called 'a god of the moment' by Minoru Takita, a leader of Zensen Domei (Federation of Textile, Garment, Chemical Mercantile and Allied Industry Workers Union) and later Sodomei, the moderate labor federation. Nakayama was praised by Hajime Maeda of the Japanese Federation of Employers (Nikkeiren) for his tenacious negotiating style, which he termed 'Kameude-style'. Maeda also stated that 'his knowledge, his sincerity, his ability to bring people together were decisive, and his superb timing was a gift from heaven'. Nakayama was closely involved in industrial relations and industrial disputes from the stormy wartime years through the age of stability, making contributions to stabilizing labor-management relations, and in so doing promoting industrial development in general. A book edited by the Central Labor Commission states, 'President Nakayama, over a period of fifteen years following the war, provided a leadership unsurpassed in the area of labor-management relations for our country, and was the man who brought together an era in the history of Japan's industrial relations'.[5]

The Central Labor Commission was at the center of a most painful era during which the old practices had collapsed and no new ones were created yet. Nakayama even compared it to the Paris Commune.[6] In looking back over those fifteen years, he stated the following:

> It would be hard to forget my work as a member of the Central Labor Commission for some fifteen years, including the ten as commission chair. I knew militants from the Communist Party, and I also experienced the 2-1 [February 1st] General Strike. As a democracy, in the abstract the outlines were easy to understand, but being able to follow them in concrete form was

an experience difficult to gain for a person through study...What was hard was being caught between unions, with their many powers and managers with the power of capital behind them, while having not a bit of power myself and so being charged with resolving problems with knowledge alone ... stated in an exaggerated way it was the sense of powerlessness of scholarly learning. However, there was nothing better than learning for springing back from this sense of powerlessness and opening new paths of resolution. (Nakayama 1979: 22–3)

Nakayama and Suehiro were emblematic of the Central Labor Commission's role in the transition from stormy era to an era of order. Labor law scholar Suehiro played a major role in systematizing the Central Labor Commission in its early years in the midst of numerous industrial disputes, laying the foundations for labor and management to resolve problems by using the commission's rules, and establishing a system to which both sides would willingly submit. Nakayama, the economist, first appeared in the spotlight on that foundation during the Densan (Electric Power Related Industry Workers Union) dispute. When the Commission became involved in wage disputes, which were essentially economic issues, it was Nakayama rather than Suehiro who played the leading role. He pioneered, and insisted on using, the CPS (consumer price surveys) and CPI (consumer price index) in Commission dealings. At the start of arbitration, Nakayama's attitude was pro-labor, and leaned toward getting a favorable resolution for the workers. At that time, the Densan workers' wages were double the usual wage level and the wage determination standards were clear (being based on the cost of living as a minimum wage standard). The so-called Densan-type wage system emerged from Nakayama's mediation. It was the Central Labor Commission which had come to determine Japan's wage system, and it was Nakayama who led the commission. The nine-month long Densan strike and the 63-day Coal Miners Union strike were major conflicts which impacted on Japan's energy supply, so the determining of the workers' wages and stabilizing labor-management relations in those industries amounted to 'major labor policies regarding Japanese capitalism'.[7]

In the preface to Volume 13 of his *Complete Works* (*Zenshu*) entitled 'A New Era for Managers and Workers', Nakayama noted that J. M. Keynes himself evinced no direct concern for labor problems, but observed, 'The policy-related nature of that sort of economics, through the issues of employment and wages, naturally comes close to the heart of the labor question'. He stated that the transition from economics to sociology which would include labor issues left few individual scholars quite surprised, and that as a result of research on the labor movement in particular, one would graduate from pure economics to the realm of social dynamics studies, to borrow Kenneth Boulding's term. At the same time that he served on the Central Labor Commission, Nakayama served also as chairman of the Central Advisory Council on Wages, preparing a proposal that became the basis for establishing the minimum wages law. In addition, he served as vice-president of the Japan Productivity Center, chairman of the Standing Committee for the Labor-Management

Consultation System, and as a representative for Japan at the International Labor Organization. After resigning from the Central Labor Commission he was named president of the Japan Labor Association (Nihon Rodo Kyokai). Finally, he wrote numerous works on industrial relations theory and human relations theory such as *Atarashii Keieisha, Atarashii Rodosha* (New Managers, New Workers, 1958), *Roshi-kyogisei* (The Labor-Management Consultation System, 1958), *Nihon no Kogyoka to Roshi-kankei* (Japan's Industrialization and Industrial Relations, 1959), and *Roshi-kankei no Keizai-shakaigaku* (The Economic Sociology of Industrial Relations, 1974). Nakayama wrote: 'Speaking of public activities in the way of activities, I was rather inclined to be engaged in scholarship,' and during the course his pure economics evolved to become 'a social and human science in the broad sense'.[8]

7.3.2 Nakayama and labor issues

'My economics started with teacher Tokuzo Fukuda. . . . If I had not listened to the lectures of teacher Fukuda, I would never have become an economist'. Thus Nakayama's involvement with labor problems probably began with Tokuzo Fukuda. He warmly praised the pioneering achievement of *Rodo Keizai Ron* (Labor Economics) (1899), co-authored by Fukuda and Lujo Brentano, in the memorial lecture entitled 'Kosei keizaigaku to Fukuda Tokuzo' (Welfare economics and Tokuzo Fukuda) which was delivered on the 100th anniversary of Fukuda's birth. Brentano had researched British labor problems and compared it to the German case. He argued that in order to achieve Britain's level of prosperity, and also pursue the optimal course of economic development, Germany needed to raise wages, shorten working hours, and raise labor productivity. Upon reading this, Nakayama stated that Japan still faced the problems of one hundred years before, namely whether Japan was able to provide high wages and shorten working hours. (Nakayama 1979: 12; 1978: 63–6).

Fukuda made concrete labor issues the background for his welfare economics from the beginning, and in his 'Kakaku toso kara kosei toso he' (From price struggles to welfare struggles: labor struggles as welfare struggles, 1921), he criticized A. Marshall and A. C. Pigou. 'We conduct research on prices not for its own sake, but in order to know their relationship to economic welfare, so by studying this field we hope to advance research on welfare'. According to Fukuda, Pigou neglected the issue of whether income distribution, and particularly labor's share, was equitable. It was in order to supplement this share that labor struggles as welfare struggles occurred. Fukuda believed that labor movements existed and labor disputes took place because they played the vital role of enabling labor to receive a legitimate share of original income and ensure proper working hours. This argument appeared in *Rodo Keizai Ron* (Labor Economics), the work which launched Fukuda's welfare economics research and social policymaking, and Nakayama believed that it distinguished Fukuda's welfare economics from those of Pigou, which 'in the first place, have very little sense of the workers' (Fukuda 1922: 189; Nakayama 1974a: 69–72).

Nakayama was born in 1898 in Mie Prefecture. After attending Kobe Higher School of Commerce, he entered the newly opened Tokyo University of Commerce in 1920, 'Hitotsubashi in its Golden Age', where he studied under Fukuda. He then went to study at Bonn University in Germany under Joseph A. Schumpeter. Schumpeter had already finished his early trilogy work, and was lecturing on economic sociology, which was to serve as the draft for *Capitalism, Socialism, and Democracy* (1949). Nakayama found the basis for his life's work both in Schumpeter, who made the general equilibrium theory of Walras into 'German without the mathematics' and parted ways with 'Papa Marx', and in Fukuda who insisted on the importance of welfare economics.

At the strong recommendation of Fukuda, Nakayama was posted to Home Office's Social Bureau in 1930, immediately upon his return from Germany. There he developed and conducted surveys on unemployment. Fukuda, Izutaro Suehiro, and Ginjiro Fujiwara at that time made up the Consultative Council of the Social Bureau and they used it to assist survey research on wages, employment, labor unions, and the highly conspicuous unemployment problem. Fukuda had become a councilor to the Home Office in 1923. He, Hiroshi Ikeda, Toru Nagai, and Toyohiko Kagawa, had exerted themselves to produce a proposal for establishing facilities for labor exchange (the Nationalized Labor Exchange). Fukuda discerned the underlying basis of the unemployment problem and used the Consultative Council to emphasize the need for survey research. Nakayama undertook the work based on this proposal, from first draft to final collection of data, at Fukuda's behest. Nakayama believed that the experience he gained in conducting the survey was 'extremely valuable', after until then having 'only meditated at my desk'; it was 'absolutely because of it that I later came to have a multifaceted understanding of surveys and empirical evidence'.[9]

After Fukuda's death, Nakayama undertook lectures on economic theory in tandem with Kinnosuke Otsuka's Marxian economics. Nakayama published *Junsui Keizaigaku* (Pure Economics) in 1933. At the same time he wrote many pieces on unemployment and unemployment statistics, and put forth a conception of economic sociology. It was 'Keizai riron to keizai shakaigaku' (Economic theory and economic sociology) which Nakayama wrote in the collected eulogies to Fukuda. In 'Keiki kenkyu niokeru keizaigaku to tokeigaku tono kosho' (connection between economics and statistics in the business studies cycle, (1932)) he stated that it was 'all of an economic sociology of immense meaning in which economic theory was also included, and here was nothing other than a demand for an economics for the present age, which is an age of change [reform]' and proposed the conception for 'an empirical proof-based economics program' (Nakayama 1933b; 1932: 353–5).

7.3.3 Labor management consultation system and the productivity movement

Nakayama eschewed the use of the management-centered terms 'labor management' and 'labor policy' in favor of labor-management relations, and during his tenure on the Central Labor Commission promoted as key words 'labor movement as a modern system' and the formation of 'new managers and new workers' as 'democratic partners'. If both managers and workers became strong, 'then shunto (spring offensive) would become a festival'.[10]

Nakayama believed that the preconditions for labor-management consultation were the formation of 'new managers and new workers' and of 'new workers and new labor unions', 'especially human relations' (Nakayama 1958a: Chapter 2). In the postscript to the new edition of *Atarashii Keieisha, Atarashii Rodosha* (New Managers, New Workers, 1963), he stated the following about the changed social status of labor unions:

> To say in a word how unions have become big and become strong, or how they advanced from that point, it is that unions grew to where they had to take responsibility for their own actions. As core actors in modern industrial relations, unions at the beginning had an absolutely non-Japanese existence. Having emerged in modern society as non-Japanese, unions soon concentrated their full powers on trying to confirm that status. A history of struggle succeeded by struggle and opposition succeeded by opposition started here. Labor-management relations as a history of disputes first originated in the unions' nature of being non-Japanese. Striving in struggles brought soon forth results in various forms. The establishment of the Factory Law and the Labor Standards Law, and the affirmation of the rights of collective action, collective bargaining, and striking through the Labor Union Law were the major successes, and along with those successes the unions also achieved full recognition of their social status. The status of a labor union in a modern industrial state was to be able to move beyond the creation of social reformers of 100 years ago. The affirmation and expansion of this status bestowed a major change in the character of unions. That was that unions were no longer the non-Japanese of society, but important and also Japanese. Being also Japanese, they grew to the point where they had to become conscious of their responsibility. (Nakayama 1958a [1963]: 182-3)

Labor-management relations moved from the chaos of the early postwar era to a stable and calm era on account of economic reconstruction and recovery. The major trends of global industrial relations indicated a progression 'from the struggle-centered relationship up to now to a mutual sharing of responsibility, and the cooperation based thereon'. The US carried out technical assistance plans while Britain and the rest of Europe promoted productivity movements, and Japan established its own Productivity Center in February 1955. A direct cause of its establishment was partly because W. C. Haroldson, from the US Embassy, had offered to support the founding of a productivity center, and had first spoken with Nakayama. In the same year, Nakayama had attended the annual congress of the ILO as the government's representative, where he had proposed establishing an international labor-management issues research association. He emphasized that the productivity movement should both include and 'unify managers and workers as well as persons of academic experience'. Nakayama and Shigeo Nagano were named vice-presidents of the new organization (the president was Taizo Ishizaka and the general secretary was Kohei Goshi). Nakayama headed a management inspection mission that visited the US from September 1955. In 1957, he was appointed chairman of the Productivity Center's Standing Committee on Labor-Management Consultation, a position in which he served until his death.[11]

Beginning in the fall of 1957 Nakayama wrote a series of articles 'Korekara no roshi-kankei' (Industrial relations from today) for *Asahi Newspaper*, and in 1958 from those he developed *Atarashii Keieisha, Atarashii Rodosha* (New Managers, New Workers) and further published *Roshi Kyogisei* (The Labor-Management Consultation System), as one of the Productivity Library. In the 1 January 1959 edition of the *Yomiuri Newspaper*, he published his well-known article 'Chingin nibai wo teisho' (A proposal to double wages: It's not a dream if production increases).

> When thinking about the future of Japan's economy, in abstract form the most comprehensive phrase is welfare state. . . . But how can we move toward the ideal of the welfare state just when we are poor, when facing this problem ... in concrete form, I want to boldly advocate doubling wages.
>
> It is natural that a management that has grown used to production and exports under a low standard of living, that is low wages, will raise voices of protest against suddenly making income doubling a goal. Stated the other way around, however, it is a problem of productive efficiency. If one valued the increase in capability of productive efficiency at twice that of wages, the result is that there would be no reason to deny a doubling of wages. . . . If lousy labor relations are a major cause of production impediments, then I believe that calling for the workers' cooperation under this slogan would be a wise way of doing things. Doubling incomes, first as a mutual goal of labor and management, and at last as a purpose of national policy, could be an effective first step toward a concrete future vision of Japan's economy. (*Zenshu*, vol. 16, pp. 32–4)

The cooperation and harmony of labor was necessary for the development of the productivity movement. However, the national labor federation, Sohyo, had criticized the Productivity Center even before its start, accusing it of being 'a link in the MSA remilitarization economic policy, a mechanism within which managers using the beautiful names of labor-management cooperation and raising productivity will study ways to intensify labor and hold down wages'. Kohei Goshi argued against this view in an *Asahi Newspaper* article entitled 'Seisansei no kojo to rodo-kumiai' (Productivity raising and labor unions: after fattening the chicken, the egg). Unlike the rationalization and efficiency raising practiced until then, in the case of productivity raising: 'the benefits will be bestowed equally upon consumers, workers, and managers'. Raising productivity would 'enrich the wellsprings of livelihoods and wages', that is, 'fatten the goose'. Sohyo's objective in its struggles were always wage increases, but, asked Nakayama rhetorically, 'without raising productivity, how could wage increases be possible?'[12]

234 Takeo Minoguchi, Tamotsu Nishizawa and Aiko Ikeo

The First Productivity Contact Council meeting, held in May 1955, decided on three principles that the members believed were necessary for the productivity movement to develop as a national movement. The three principles also derived from Nakayama's conceptions, and expressed his basic doctrines on labor-management relations. They were:

1. Productivity improvement would ultimately expand employment, but redundant workers would be transferred in the most efficient manner possible from a national economic perspective, while unemployment would be prevented by private- and public-sector cooperation and adoption of appropriate measures.
2. According to the concrete proposals drafted for the purpose of raising productivity, consultations would be held to make adjustments to the conditions of all enterprises and to further cooperative labor-management research into these matters.
3. The fruits of productivity raising would, according to the conditions of the national economy, be fairly distributed among managers and workers as well as consumers.[13]

The Productivity Center publicized its activities by publishing *Seisansei Kojo Nyusu* (Productivity Raising News) twice a month from April 1955, and in May it began to put out *Seisansei Kojo Shiriizu* (Productivity Raising Series) every ten days in order to 'generally disseminate correct productivity consciousness'. In no. 7 of the latter, Nakayama's article 'Seisansei no riron to jissai' (The theory and reality of raising productivity) appeared. In the second half of the article, Nakayama discussed the three principles, focusing on the need to emphasize human relations in enterprises. In economic practice up to that time:

> All effort was concentrated on production costs or cost relations, and in comparison no effort was made toward the conditions of labor. On the labor side, enough consideration was given toward wage costs, but apart from that, with regard to human conditions, only extremely inadequate attention was given. Speaking of rationalization, the natural outcome of this situation was that one could think readily of dismissals. However, this cannot be done in today's economy. In the contemporary economy with its calls for human relations and industry relations, even in computing enterprise costs it is clearly seen that neglecting the human relations of labor is something that cannot be done. (Nakayama 1956, pp. 97–8)

The productivity movement could not develop without its two pillars, labor and management, fully comprehending its spirit and execution, hence cooperative labor-management consultation became indispensable. The thinking led to the establishment in November 1956 of a Special Committee, connected to the Productivity Center and headed by Nakayama. In June 1956, the Special Committee announced its 'Way for a Labor-Management Consultation System

Related to Productivity' idea, and later added basic directions for the labor-management consultation system. In November, the Standing Committee on the Labor-Management Consultation System was established, with Nakayama as chairman, to serve as an executive committee to set up guidelines for the consultation system and guide its dissemination. In October 1959, the Standing Committee published *Nihon no Roshi Kyogisei* (Japan's Labor-Management Consultation System) and announced that it would bring an end to 'old-style industrial relations issues' where collective bargaining meant dividing the pie, and bring forth 'absolutely new and different issues' so that raising productivity would mean increasing the size of the pie. Further, it would call for 'self-conscious and cooperative measures by labor and management', necessitating 'rational consultation on an equal basis by labor and management'. From that time on, the Standing Committee has made major contributions to realizing the diffusion and institutionalization of the consultation system in enterprises nationwide (Nihon Seisansei Honbu 1985: 304, 307–8, 313–16; 1959: 1–2).

As emphasized in the manual 'Way to a Productivity-Oriented Labor-Management Consultation System', there was a distinction made between collective bargaining and a mutual labor-management understanding based on a self-conscious realization of 'the social responsibility of enterprises'. It was also emphasized that the foundation for labor-management cooperation did not rest on using productivity to increase corporate profits, but in enhancing the welfare of the nation as a whole. Making up the foundation of cooperation were three conditions:

1. mutual recognition between labor and management,
2. a fair distribution of benefits, and
3. employment security.

With regard to condition 1, managers needed to realize the 'social-ness (*shakaisei*) of the enterprise' as well as to be properly cognizant of 'the social function of labor unions'. Similarly, workers needed to recognize 'the social responsibility they exercised toward the national economy' while not ignoring the economic bases of their enterprises. Condition 2 called for a 'labor-management concord' resting not on a power relationship focused on 'collective bargaining for the sake of raising wages', but rather on an objective 'recognition of rewards' along with 'rational wage systems' and 'particular profit-distributing methods' reflecting productivity increases (Nihon Seisansei Honbu 1985: 304–7). The 'social mission of the enterprise' and the 'social responsibility of the enterprise' evident in these ideas accorded with the 'new management ideal' espoused by Keizai Doyukai in its book *Keieisha no Shakaiteki-sekinin no Jikaku to Jissen* (The Recognition and Practice of Social Responsibility by Managers, 1956).

In 1955, the same year that the Productivity Center was founded, two new political parties were also established. The Japan Socialist Party (now the Japan Social Democratic Party) brought together the progressive parties while the conservative parties banded together to form the Liberal Democratic Party, resulting in the creation of the new political order that supported high economic growth. In the following year, the successful economic recovery prompted the government-produced *Keizai Hakusho* (Economic White Paper) to make the memorable observation that 'this is no longer the postwar era'. At its national convention in November 1955, held just as the two major party system was getting under way, Keizai Doyukai adopted a 'Resolution in Defense of Parliamentary Democracy'. Along with lauding the importance of a two-party system for promoting sound parliamentary politics (parliamentary democracy), the resolution stressed the following points for economic actors. 'Enterprises exist for the sake of the development of the national economy, and the fundamental idea of management must be that managers hold a responsibility to respond to the needs of the nation'. Further, defense of parliamentary politics required the fulfillment of certain economic conditions, and the resolution stated, 'We plan for the establishment of industrial peace, and will strive to improve productivity' (Keizai Doyukai 1976: 70–74).

It was at this national conference that Keizai Doyukai asserted that 'social responsibility' was a management concept and that enterprises were a 'public organ'. The declaration of Sohei Nakayama created an important legacy for the development of a new era of ideals for Keizai Doyukai by stressing the traditions of enterprise democratization and the Economic Reconstruction Council. The declaration went as follows:

> The present era calls for a new management concept. . . . What is the new management concept? I believe that it is social responsibility. The thinking of managers until now was that their task was to increase the profits of individual enterprises for the sake of individual enterprises, so they focused on the pursuit of enterprise profit as their goal. In contrast, the new management concept demands responsibility towards shareholders, responsibility towards employees, and responsibility towards the public.

Therefore, it was natural that there be a new perception on the part of workers also.

> Not only must enterprises bear a social responsibility, but it is natural for the labor movement as well to make the prosperity of enterprises a precondition. . . . Labor and management together, by mutually sharing the gains made through raising productivity, shall develop the economy.

Takeshi Sakurada stated, 'At present . . . it is persons who make abundant use of intelligence and technology who contribute to the welfare of the public, it is the managers who take charge of business as a true public institution. This is what we call the management era'. He declared, 'The basis of the manager's spirit is total application of the belief that we managers truly treat that enterprise as a public institution'. Two elements were involved in treating firms as public institutions. First, owners had to suppress their self-interested motivations and stabilize ownership for the long term. Second, since firms had to be managed for the benefit of the public welfare, 'to give in to the arbitrariness of a group of workers is contrary to the desire of managers to treat (enterprises) as public institutions'. According to Sakurada, 'Management and labor under democratic rules must contend properly and first respect the rules of check and balance; since company-controlled unions are not possible, for the same reason management interference into unions is not possible, it is important that labor and management be aware and be persuaded that they, from an equal position, must attend to various responsibilities and respond to the needs of the people' (Keizai Doyukai 1976: 416–18; Sakurada 1982: I, 13–18).

These statements of Sohei Nakayama and Takeshi Sakurada were to develop into the arguments about 'the social responsibilities of unions' by Kazutaka Kikawada. *Nihon Rodo Kyokai Zasshi* (The Journal of Japan Labor Association) published three special issues in April, May, and June, 1962, dealing with the topic of 'The Social Responsibility of Labor and Management'. In the April issues Kaoru Ota and Minoru Takita, leaders of the left-wing Sohyo and right-wing Zenro labor federations, respectively, debated 'The Social Responsibility of Managers,' while Masaru Hayakawa of the hard-line employers association, Nikkeiren, debated with K. Kikawada of the moderate employers association, Keizai Doyukai, on the topic 'The Social Responsibility of Labor Unions'. In the May issue, the pairs reversed topics, with Hayakawa and Kikawada debating management responsibilities, while Ota and Takita engaged on unions. In the June issue, prominent labor relations specialist Kazuo Okochi summarized the debates under the rubric 'The Social Responsibility of Labor and Management', and Ichiro Nakayama presided over a round-table discussion between the four labor and management representatives.[14]

Stability grew as a new balance between labor and management developed. In terms of world history, Japan's labor-management relations are still relatively new. However, Nakayama stated that, 'Japanese labor-management relations are not necessarily backward in terms of form . . . from the end of the war rapid modernization proceeded, and the cutting-edge trend of world industrial relations in that way became an issue of Japan'. In *Nihon no Roshi-kyogisei* (Japan's Labor-Management Consultation System, 1963), Nakayama argued in its first section entitled 'Labor-Management Consultation System as an Expression of Human Relations,' that the consulting system was 'an expression of human relations between workers and managers' and 'the realization of democracy at the site of production'. He added:

> This can be a system that is the core of collective bargaining, and can further therefore be its extension in resolving labor-management problems, especially conflictual relations, and deal head on with industrial relations as human relations. . . . It is in trying to consider Japan's industrial relations from the aspect of the labor-management consultation system, precisely in this sphere of issues, that the distinctive qualities of Japanese labor relations appear.[15]

At the same time, Nakayama described collective bargaining and consultation in the following manner. The two main pillars supporting labor-management relations were collective bargaining and consultation. The principal task of collective bargaining was to serve as the forum for resolving disputes over distribution issues, while consultation mainly undertook problems related to production and served as the mechanism for resolving them at the enterprise level. The two pillars had been regarded as independent until that time, he stated, but it had become impossible for them to be separate. What had brought their unification were changes in the capitalist economy and the growth of unions. In Japan's case, however:

> The sudden progression of immature collective bargaining and the immature consultation system from their actualization toward unification could not have been hoped for, but even if, say, one had desired it, an enormous danger awaited. In order to conduct collective bargaining effectively and entrust it to settle distribution, it has been necessary to make a much harder effort at nurturing proper adversarial bargaining. Trying to blur this point and conduct the consultation system alone would simply have the result of weakening the productive output of the laboriously built consultation system. Given the enterprise-based nature of Japan's labor unions, the development of the consultation system is highly desirable. However, in order that it truly contributes to production, and further therefore that it brings improvement in labor-management relations, it is necessary to confirm very clear distinctions between rights and responsibilities. If not, it will not be possible to defend the consultation system from counter-movements, much less hope to expand the system and unify it with collective bargaining. (Nakayama 1958 [1963]: 188–9)

7.4 Seiichi Tobata and Japanese agriculture

7.4.1 Tobata's early career

Like Ichiro Nakayama, Tobata was born in Mie Prefecture. He was born in 1899, just one year later than Nakayama. He graduated from the Number Eight Higher School in Nagoya, and entered a newly opening institute, Agricultural Science Section Two of Tokyo University's Department of Agriculture. Tobata chose Section Two over Section One because it had added economics and other social science content. Tobata specialized in agricultural economics but one of his reasons for choosing this major was the rice riots of the previous year. During this time he reflected:

> Apart from research, I, a mere student, received a bad shock. The 'masses' I had until now hardly thought about, but now I knew of their real existence. Further, I knew that they bore a vast energy. Social science was for the research of this existence I thought. (Tobata 1979a: 33)

Tobata graduated in 1922, submitting a graduation thesis entitled 'The Ricardians' Land Socialism,' and subsequently entered graduate school. He was promoted to researcher in a year and a half and then to assistant professor in another year. During this time, the strongest influence on Tobata was *Era and Agricultural Administration* (in Japanese) by the renowned anthropologist Kunio Yanagita. This was the first book on Japanese agriculture to conduct economic analysis. In a section of the book on 'The Custom of Paying Farm Rents with Rice,' Yanagita argued that the system of paying farm rents in kind hampered independent activity by the farmers (Tobata 1979b).

In 1926, Tobata received a one-year fellowship from the International Education Foundation (later the Rockefeller Foundation) and ventured forth to the University of Wisconsin. There he entered the Department of Agriculture and studied under famed institutional economist John Commons. Then, from 1928 through 1930, he studied at the University of Bonn where he met Nakayama, who had arrived there one and a half years earlier. Like Nakayama, Tobata studied under Schumpeter, and from Nakayama he received his initiation into neo-classical economics. However, what Tobata learned from Schumpeter and his *Theory of Economic Development* (1912) was not so much equilibrium theory as economic dynamics. In looking back at this time Tobata reflected:

> Under Professor S[chumpeter] I learned just a little equilibrium theory, but this was not all. There is the great work *Theory of Economic Development*. This purported that dynamic theory is the theory of destruction of the above-mentioned equilibrium. Moreover, so far the destruction of economic systems has been outside the sphere of an economy, so that if we start, for example, from natural disasters, wars, populations increase, and technological advance, then the applicability of dynamic economic theory to these sorts of external drives has come to be argued. Here Professor S's case differs from theories up to now. Collapse starts from inside an economy. This means an important issue for economics. This is the realization of a new production function, and for its structure, the central pieces of the enterprise members, the measure of creating trusting trust, and further the genuine profits and interest of capitalism are born. Finally in this sort of destruction can be seen the replacement of the old by the new. This means that economic change always means on the one hand that the creation of new things accompanies the destruction of old things – first there is this type of dynamic theory. After one year in Bonn, I have at last been able to master Schumpeter's theories. (Tobata 1979a: 63)

As will be explained later, the distinction between 'entrepreneurs' (kigyosha) and 'mere businessmen,' which became a central conception in Tobata's agricultural economics, was taken from Schumpeter's *Theory of Economic Development*.

Promoted to full professor in 1933, Tobata took charge of lecturing on both agricultural administration and the second course in economics. The main focus of Tobata's research at this time was:

in connection with national economics, analyzing agricultural issues using pure economic means, especially price mechanisms of course, . . . as can be seen in many works, I research across many areas, including the problems of independent farmers, the problems of industrial unions, agricultural village life, farmers leaving their villages, the problems of wives in agricultural villages and so on. (Tsuchiya 1978: 27)

From 1939 until the end of the war, he assumed a concurrent post as professor in the Department of Economics and lectured on colonial policy. During this period the Department of Agriculture made great strides in modern economic research on agriculture.

To Kamiya's efforts around 1941 to use Douglas-type production functions to measure the productivity of agricultural workers, to Kazushi Ohkawa's foodstuff demand functions and research into agricultural production functions and so on, and not only to the global agricultural economic academic community but also to the econometric community he [contributed] achievements of which he could be proud as both a direct and as an indirect participant. (Tsuchiya 1978: 27)

From 1942, Tobata participated in the Philippine Island Survey Committee, which was headed by Shozo Murata, the leading advisor on the affairs of the occupied territory. Also taking part were Masamichi Royama, Hiroshi Suekawa, and Kozo Sugimura. In 1944, they produced *Report on the Philippine Survey*. At that time Tobata and Sugimura were both members for economic relations. As a result of performing that task, Tobata also served in 1953 as sole member of a fully empowered committee on reparations to the Philippines.

After the Second World War, it is not so much Tobata's research activities which were remarkable as his participation as an authority on agricultural administration in a large number of government and private research institutes, investigation groups, and committees. Next, let us turn our attention to Tobata's contributions to Japan's economy.

7.4.2 *Tobata and the Japanese economy*

Immediately upon the end of the war, Tobata was asked to become minister of agriculture and forestry in the first Shigeru Yoshida government, but declined because of his unease with politics. However, this initial contact became the opportunity through which Tobata later served as head of all types of committees, investigation groups, and policy deliberation councils for the government, in which capacity he played an important role in shaping economic and agricultural policies. In addition, he contributed to the training of a number of excellent younger scholars as the head of various research institutes.

First, let us examine his roles as the director of two government-run research institutes, the General Institute for Agriculture, founded in 1946, and the Institute for Developing Economies, founded in 1959; the latter he headed after reaching the mandatory age for retirement at the University of Tokyo.

Director of the General Institute for Agriculture

This institute was a social science research institute developed from numerous proposals formulated by Hiroo Wada, a prominent official at the Ministry of Agriculture and Forestry (Wada also served as Yoshida's first agriculture and forestry minister). A large number of research institutes were already tied to the various government ministries, but this was the first such institute to conduct social science research. Tobata took charge of its establishment.

The purpose of the institute was to conduct research on reviving agriculture following the postwar land reform. Therefore, it was necessary to select as staff persons able to conduct the relevant research. For this reason, Tobata stressed the following three points:

1. Until [the founding of the institute], Japanese agriculture had agricultural operations but there was very little importance placed on making agricultural management central to agriculture. There is no use in saying 'This is life so obey' to agricultural workers in the postwar era. Farmers able to exercise their own talents and capacities for choice are needed. This means research emphasizing the study of management and book-keeping. Masao Otsuki and Nobufumi Kayo are those kinds of people. They assisted the operation of the General Institute for Agriculture.

2. There was almost no economics at the Ministry of Agriculture and Forestry. From prewar through wartime, the supreme order was to increase the supply of food, and for that reason the emphasis was placed on spiritual rather than economic approaches, so that it became an 'economic' kamikaze and Imperial agricultural village movement. Postwar conditions have completely changed, so that Korea and Taiwan, which contributed greatly to the Japanese food supply, have become foreign countries. The adoption of parity formulae because of rice controls, preparations for rice production statistics, and, further, the decision making on exchange rates, which has a strong impact on raw silk thread exports – all of these types of useful economic tools were rare at the Ministry of Agriculture and Forestry. The General Institute for Agriculture must compensate for this. Keinosuke Baba has become a researcher, and has made major contributions to agricultural and forestry administration, which comprises the core of research into these areas. In addition, Yasuo Kondo is from the university and will serve concurrently as the newly appointed director of the statistics bureau; we must not forget that his major revolutions in agricultural and forestry have promoted economic research.

3. People with command of technology have moved into economic fields and have opened new perspectives. In Japan in the past the two fields

were too separate. Shigeo Hosono, who is an expert in agricultural technology, and Hisao Shishido, an engineering expert, have joined the institute. (Tobata 1979a: 92–3)

In the fifty years which have passed since the end of the war, there have been major changes in the conditions of Japanese agriculture. The period when the General Institute for Agriculture was founded was one of food shortages but today there is an abundant supply. Moreover, the greater part of our country's food supply is imported, and the self-supply ratio has fallen below 40 percent. Given these conditions, Tobata stated with regard to the future of the General Institute for Agriculture, 'It is imperative to think intently about the position of Japanese agriculture in the world' (Tobata 1979a: 95).

Asia Research Institute

The Asia Research Institute (later renamed the Institute of Developing Economies in English) was originally conceived to train experts on developing nations, in accordance with proposals by the Ministry of International Trade and Industry. However, numerous jurisdictional disputes ensued between it and the Ministry of Foreign Affairs, which had numerous contacts with such nations, so the institute was launched as a special corporation (tokushu hojin). As at the General Institute for Agriculture, the first task Tobata faced was deciding on what research areas to establish. Moreover, there were no positions on developing countries in Japanese universities at that time, so the Asia Research Institute was initially forced to create its own experts from scratch.

For that reason, beginning in 1959 we employed some ten-plus fledgling researchers every year. Then a few years later we would send these fledglings to different locations where they would enter universities or research institutes and start their research careers, master the local language, and establish ties with the local society. They all discovered problems and found ways to resolve them. (Tobata 1979a: 106)

Tobata explained the reason for adopting this personnel training method as follows:

In general, there are two attitudes to research on developing countries. The first is to regard them as backward and to conduct meditative research at one's desk. The other is to adapt oneself to the location in some way, and to start conducting investigation and research. Then afterwards begin trying to transform the developing countries. Which is better is rather hard to decide, but from my own experience the foundations of the first approach are shallow, and its intensity weak. With the latter, the researchers who master one country and later arrive at a general theory are the most secure, and therefore I think that they can cultivate the seeds of future developmentalism. (Tobata 1979a: 107)

The institute's name has been changed to the Institute of Developing Economies in English. It includes a staff of over 280 persons, making it one of the largest research institutes on developing economies in the world.

Tobata also served as director of the Policy Science Research Institute and of the Finance Research Institute. Tobata's second most important contribution to the Japanese economy was serving as head of governmental meetings, investigative groups, deliberation groups and so on, thereby helping to shape economic and agricultural policy making. These activities all took place during Japan's high-growth era, and the most pressing problem was trying to find ways to eliminate the income gap between manufacturing industry and agriculture. The major forums for debating this problem were the Agriculture, Forestry, and Fisheries Technology Group and the Agricultural Basic Issues Research Group, leading to the enactment of the Basic Agricultural Law in 1961.

First, the Agriculture, Forestry, and Fisheries Technology Group (the Technology Group) was established in the Ministry of Agriculture and Forestry in 1956, and Tobata served as its president until his retirement in 1963. At its inception, the conception of the Technology Group's task was that it reconsider the agricultural sector in the perspective of rapid economic growth, and find out if high growth was possible in the primary industries as well. For that, the most important need was technological development. This perception then led agriculture and forestry minister, Ichiro Kono, to conduct an inspection tour in Britain, leading to significantly accelerated development of agricultural technology.

Seeking to respond to the demands of the Technology Group, Tobata worked to engage leading persons from the natural sciences community as group members. Thus the development of agricultural technology has not developed from agricultural sciences in the narrow sense, but rather finds its sources in the development of many fields, such as physics and chemistry. Among the main contributors were Seiji Kaya, former head of Tokyo University's Department of Science, Kinichiro Sakaguchi of a famed sake-making enterprise, and Yoshiji Tokari, a Tokyo University biological sciences professor.

Enhancing research at agricultural testing centers and linking such research to agricultural and forestry administration were made prime functions of the Technology Group. In order to enhance research, Tobata augmented and improved equipment and facilities at testing centers rather than increase personnel. At that time, there were around 5000 persons employed in testing centers, but the total funds allotted to each researcher for both assistants and equipment was some 500,000 yen per year. Also important was the relevance of the research projects, leading Tobata to make the following pronouncement:

> Speaking of crops and livestock, a differentiation must be made between large American-type farms and Japan's small establishments. There are crops and livestock on small establishments. In the case of agricultural machinery, in contrast to large farms, the strong pattern of small establishments is toward hand-held tools. From this point, we must shift our attitude to one of changing

> our perspective away from plants, and then away from crops, and towards the crops of small establishments and towards tackling [small establishments'] problems. (Tobata 1979a: 117)

With regards to research testing on small establishments and its connection to agricultural and forestry administration, Tobata stated:

> In order to maintain very close relations with every testing center, here and there individual researchers were appointed as adjustment officers to the Technology Group for the purpose of fostering communication on research among the testing centers and coordination between test research and the agriculture and forestry administration. (Tobata 1979a: 114)

Tobata also believed that it was necessary to elevate the status of engineers within the agriculture and forestry administration. In short, it was necessary to comprehend the importance of agricultural technology. Among the government ministries and agencies of that period:

> There were few cases where [there was so strong a sense that] the administrative section opposed the technical section, and that the status of the administrative section was low relative to that of the administration, as in the Ministry of Agriculture and Forestry. It was necessary not to think that low [status] was inevitable. When we can imagine that a great agriculture rests on strong technology, then that inevitability will destroy itself. (Tobata 1979a: 118)

When Tobata retired as head of the Technology Group, he called for the founding of a research institute to work on plant viruses, and prevailed on the Ministry of Finance to provide the funds.

Second, the Basic Agriculture Problems Investigative Committee was established in 1959. Its purpose was stated as follows:

> Nearly ten years after the completion of the land reform, the high-growth era began. The purpose for which this investigative committee was created was to conduct what can be termed a follow-up to the land reform in order to learn what agriculture needed to do during the high-growth stage. (Tobata 1979a: 119)

This committee became quite large, with 50 members, and an administrative bureau was established inside the Ministry of Agriculture and Forestry under the direction of Buichi Ogura. Two main points outline the issues undertaken by the investigative committee.

> The first was the domestic issue, aiming at a so-called balance (of income) between the agriculture and non-agriculture sectors. Others were cultivating

the competitive capability of domestic agriculture against foreign agriculture during a period of intensifying trade liberalization. (Tobata 1979a: 120)

For that reason it was necessary to make agriculture a member of the core economic community, or, stated differently, to make it into a sound industry.

> In that respect, emphasis was placed on the restructuring of agriculture and on selectively expanding livestock production according to the demands of high economic growth. The most important structural reform was to internalize agricultural productivity, and to introduce an 'economy of expanded managerial scope' in agricultural execution. Even if large-scale management cannot soon be achieved, the merits of scale can be achieved through the expansion of business cooperation. By chance, along with high growth it became common for farmers to leave their villages, and so they have abandoned the agricultural land for cultivation, and I thought that this was useful for those who remained to be able to expand management scale. (Tobata 1979a: 120)

The investigative committee sent the government a report about one year after its founding, and received a response within a year. As a result, the Basic Agricultural Law of 1961 was enacted, and the Basic Agricultural Problems Investigative Committee was reborn as the Agricultural Administrative Issues Investigative Committee. Naturally, Tobata continued to be committee director. However, the concept of the 'economy of expanded managerial scope' conceived by the Basic Problems Investigative Committee failed to develop at all, and the fundamental concept of the Basic Law fell apart. Tobata explained why he believed it failed.

> There were many circumstances but the most important points are the following. Farmers leave agriculture to work away from their homes, and the pay is much greater than in farming. By working one day, they could earn the value of 60 kilos of grain [wheat], which was then an astonishing amount. To produce 60 kilos of grain required a total of some three days of labor. While it did not easily mesh with farming, work away from home made possible an improved lifestyle. Even if one dared to leave farming, there was no need to leave the village. By working in both industry and farming, families were able to remain in the countryside. The most important factor encouraging this trend was the nationwide surge in land prices caused by excess liquidity. As a result, farmers did not cut loose from their farm land but held on to it as their most valuable asset. As a result of these circumstances, both agricultural improvement and expanded management utterly fell to pieces. (Tobata 1979a: 121)

The combination of excess liquidity and the Kakuei Tanaka Cabinet's plan for remodeling the Japanese archipelago fanned speculation in land across the nation and caused property prices to soar. As a result, people did not dispose of their land and the plan to increase the size of farm operations failed to develop, but that fault lay in politics rather than with the investigative committee. Nonetheless, Tobata felt responsible for never having discussed the 'land problem' in the committee, and he resigned his post as committee chair.

Tobata also headed the Rice Price Council, the Economic Council, the National Lifestyle Council, and the Tax System Investigative Committee, but these groups played only a limited role in the modernization of the agricultural sector.

7.4.3 Tobata's agricultural economic theory

In the final section we will examine Tobata's economic doctrine, which formed the basis of his economic policies. For this purpose, we may consult three of his works, *The Evolutionary Process of Japanese Agriculture* (1936), *The Shape of Japanese Agriculture* (1953), and *The Shapers of Japanese Capitalism* (1964) (all three in Japanese).

The evolutionary process of Japanese agriculture

The Evolutionary Process of Japanese Agriculture was published by Iwanami Shoten in 1936. A reprint edition entitled *Collected Famous Works on Early Showa Agricultural Administration and Economics*, edited by Yasuo Kondo and published by Noson Gyoson Bunka Kyokai, appeared in 1978. According to the 'Bibliographical Introduction' by Keizo Tsuchiya:

> This book covers principally the Taisho period around 1936, and represents an attempt to understand the essence of agricultural village problems by investigating how Japanese farming developed, and what the nature of that development was. ... The question of who exactly bore the burden of Japanese agriculture is one that Tobata seeks to clarify in this work. (Tsuchiya 1978)

The main burden bearers of Japanese agriculture were the cultivators and farmers; while some might mention the agrarian landlords, Tobata claimed that they were no more than 'mere businessmen' and not 'entrepreneurs' who could reshape economies. The phrase 'mere businessmen' was borrowed from Schumpeter, indicating that Tobata learned the basis of his agricultural economic theory as a student at the University of Bonn. According to Ichiro Nakayama in a monthly report of the reprint edition, this point was proven by the following:

> Tobata placed great importance on [Schumpeter's] development theory, and focused on dealing with it. *The Evolutionary Process of Japanese Agriculture*, published in 1936, was the result. There he makes a clear distinction between mere industrialists and entrepreneurs, and conducts an analysis with the development of Japanese agriculture as his subject. This was clearly a Schumpeterian point of view, and it opened a new perspective in agricultural

economics. I want to say that he had already learned this foundation during his period at the University of Bonn. (Nakayama 1978)

According to Schumpeter, the entrepreneur is the main force in economic development. The entrepreneur stimulates economic change by (a) creating products of a new kind and quality, (b) introducing new production methods and new commercial practices, (c) developing new markets, (d) obtaining new resources and new sources of raw materials, and (e) creating new forms of enterprise organization. However, by simply mechanically cultivating their land in the same manner year after year, farmers effect no progress. Further, landowners do not attempt to gain efficiency profits by improving efficiency, but rather pursue a conservative economic pattern of seeking to gain scarcity profits by limiting the amount of production. This type of economic actor is not an entrepreneur but a 'mere businessman'.

If those engaged in agricultural production are not really entrepreneurs, then who in fact are the entrepreneurs? According to Tobata, they are the food-processing industrialists and the government. Why can processors be entrepreneurs?

> In order to obtain the most appropriate assorted raw materials for their own manufacturing processes, they take the initiative in providing seeds, nurseries, and resources to farmers; they often provide guidance in the use of production technologies or else order that they be used, and afterwards they monopolize those procurements. (Tobata 1936 [1978]: 80–1)

> Further, the reason why government can be an entrepreneur is because it operates the agricultural testing centers through which newly developed agricultural technologies and new products are applied to production. Further, the government is able to provide subsidies and low interest loans to farmers. However, the government is not like a private industry able to stimulate the farmers, but is rather a 'non-risk-bearing entrepreneur'. (Tobata 1936 [1978]: 117)

Tobata added, 'There is a strong tendency to do desk work and paperwork which cannot soon revitalize agriculture and forestry administration, which cannot deal forcefully with vital issues, and does not reflect real issues' (Tobata 1936 [1978]: 117).

However, *The Evolutionary Process of Japanese Agriculture* was written during the prewar era, while the 1945 land reform turned the 'mere businessmen' rent-paying farmers into farmers able to [with the potential to] combine the roles of land owner, worker, capitalist, and entrepreneur in single individuals. For that reason, states Tsuchiya, the writer of the reprint edition's 'Bibliographical Introduction,' to Tobata's theory utilizes a contemporary evaluation.

There were three reasons why Tobata believed that prewar Japanese farmers were 'mere businessmen'. To begin with, 'Japanese farmers had few opportunities for training in commercial economy or monetary economy' (Tobata 1936 [1978]: 75). In the postwar era, however:

> With the increase in concurrent jobs, the advance of investment in mechanization, farmers could not avoid becoming part of the monetary economy. Farmers could not avoid making economic calculations for the procurement of purchasing capital and methods of repayment, and became incorporated into the monetary economy. (Tsuchiya 1978: 19)

The second reason was that it was not possible for millions of farmers to engage in full competition and to become price shapers, so with regard to changes in price they were 'fatalistic and passive, and could not perceive that they could be, or be inspired to become, movers' (Tsuchiya 1978: 76). But in the postwar era:

> Most agricultural products such as rice, grains, and livestock are covered by price supports, underpayment systems, and price stabilization zone systems, and at present it is estimated that price systems in which the government participates cover 80 percent of all agricultural output. Price collapses like those of the prewar era cannot occur, and further, as can be seen in the rice price and milk price competition, farmer power helps to shape prices. (Tobata 1936 [1978]: 20)

Finally, the third reason given by Tobata was:

> Additional provisions of capital are necessary in the process of economic development and creation. . . . Unfortunately, the vast majority of our farmers have little accumulated capital, and what is more they lack the opportunities and the ability to obtain it through forms of personal trust relations. (Tobata 1936 [1978]: 76–7)

After the war, however:

> Farm village finance was transformed in 1953 with the establishment of the Public Financial Fund for Agriculture and Forestry. Today, institutional funding for capital for general equipment and so on are plentiful, and the lending capabilities of systems such as Agricultural Modernization Capital and the Agricultural Cooperative Union have greatly expanded. Capital accumulation by farmers has increased, and trusts relations have developed greatly, so that major change has been achieved compared to the prewar era. (Tsuchiya 1978: 20–1)

As the above passages indicate, Tobata's use of the three reasons why farmers were 'mere businessmen' to illuminate postwar conditions shows how greatly the environment has changed, and how new conditions have enabled the 'mere businessmen' to shed their previous roles. Tsuchiya concluded:

> However, independently operating farms (those providing an income equivalent to those earned by persons in other industries) amounted to no

more than ten percent of the total number of farms in Japan in 1977, so it must be admitted that the nurturing of entrepreneurial farms still has far to go. ... If one focuses only on the agricultural side, farms which engage in side businesses are followers of the government and the few farms dedicated only to farming, so we might say that their character of being mere businessman is reinforced. ... The major factor preventing farmers from shedding their previous roles has been the sharp rise in the price of farm land which has reinforced the desire of farmers to keep their land as assets, making it difficult to increase farm size. (Tsuchiya 1978: 20–1)

Britain in 1846 took the step of abolishing the Corn Laws which restricted wheat imports, leading to an expansion in the size of farm fields which in turn brought an increase in productivity and a structural shift in production from wheat to livestock as well as a shift to horticultural production. These changes represented various entrepreneurial efforts which responded to the liberalization of agriculture. When I read this book, I feel that our country should also be exposed to the full brunt of foreign competition, and that Japanese agriculture should be forced to stand alone so that it can become truly independent because it is necessary that farmers shed their roles as mere businessmen and become entrepreneurs.

The Shape of Japanese Agriculture

The Shape of Japanese Agriculture (in Japanese) was published by Nihon Hyoron-sha in 1953. The content is a collection of articles from various journals and speeches, and is not well organized. Let us turn our attention to a section entitled 'Research institutes and agricultural and forestry administration' which deals with the change in policy of around 1897 which sought to enhance agricultural self-sufficiency and increase output by excluding foreign competition.

The 1890s were a period when national policy revolved around the objective of 'Rich nation, strong army,' when a large war indemnity gained from China enabled Japan to participate in the gold standard and stabilize its currency, and when exports of light manufactured products increased steadily. During this period, policy making emphasized increasing national self-sufficiency and domestic output in order to satisfy the growing domestic demand. However, Japan had to rely on imports because of poor rice harvests. Therefore, boosting farm production became a major policy goal, and a number of agricultural testing centers were established.

However, there came to be a change in the circumstances of the testing centers. At first, thinking centered on whether self-sufficiency should be achieved in order to increase output or whether output should be increased in order to achieve self-sufficiency. Then conditions changed. There was a change in policy toward self-sufficiency in order to hold down output capacity somewhat so that development that needed to be achieved was not accomplished. (Tobata 1953: 277)

Tobata explains why emphasis came to be placed on self-sufficiency policies.

> The circumstances were as follows. When food from foreign countries first entered Japan, it became clear that it was very cheap. Consequently, this created very difficult pressure on domestic rice production. In order to put an end to that pressure, absolutely don't bring [it] in from abroad. In cases where it had to be brought in, neutralize it with customs duties so that it would pose no threat to the interior. (Tobata 1953: 277)

By shifting toward this sort of self-sufficiency policy and establishing a domestic farming monopoly, Japan suppressed rather than raised productivity capacity, and kept agricultural prices high while creating so-called scarcity profits. The 1918 rice riots were a long-term result of 'over-protectionist policy' for agriculture.

In the contemporary era, however, the environment for Japanese farming has continued to change. Tobata believed that this created the possibility that entrepreneurs would emerge.

> Today, as is well known, self-sufficiency in the domestic foodstuff supply cannot be achieved. Also competition from overseas must be accepted. This would be one motivation to make it essential for Japanese farming to conduct technological development. (Tobata 1953: 283)

Further, with regard to agrarian reform,

> Unlike the conditions of the previous farmers, relations have become simple and they are able to be direct actors in shaping production capacity. We must have an agricultural administration which can adjust conditions to awaken the desire to increase production capacity. (Tobata 1953: 283)

The Shapers of Japanese Capitalism: various economic actors

The Shapers of Japanese Capitalism was published by Iwanami Shoten in 1964. To the earlier distinction between mere businessmen and entrepreneurs it added Diligentia and Industria. Diligentia means 'effort at pure production,' and as a result of this effort: 'Even though there is accumulation of old and traditional things, it is not creation of things through leaps of new development'. Thus: 'There was nothing which was such a source of stagnation in the Japanese economy and especially in Japanese agriculture, and further, which suppressed the will to escape this stagnation, as the philosophy of diligentia diligence' (Tobata 1964: 92–4).

Industria was derived from the economic philosophy of Schola, and it means creative diligence. Thus Tobata wrote, 'This is a necessary, and the most tightly appropriate, economic element to support the existence of capitalism' (Tobata 1964: 93). But what would be required to instill the philosophy of industria in place of diligentia? Tobata believed that it was education. 'It is through education that our eyes are opened to our desire for progress. We know that this is a prerequisite for an orderly society. Without it, there is no development of industria' (Tobata 1964: 102). The 'education' mentioned here is surely not the education taught through words. One of the beliefs about Japanese agriculture which runs through all of Tobata's written works is that there is an element of stagnation in Japanese farming, and that its conceptual [ideological] origins are in 'mere businessmen' and 'diligentia diligence'. The origin of this ideology was the government's policy of overprotection of agriculture. This suggests that a practical education demonstrate the need to subject farming to foreign competition.

Notes

1. I thank Shiro Sugihara and Takenori Inoki for their suggestions, which encouraged me to a thorough investigation of the related literature. I was lost when I could not find the relevant articles in *Hyoron* issued throughout 1949.
2. Other contributors were G. C. Allen (1900–82), M. S. Gordon and E. F. Penrose. Allen taught at Nagoya for three years in the 1920s. See Ikeo (1996).
3. Japan became a member of GATT in September 1955 and of the United Nations in December 1956.
4. Katsumi Yakabe, 'The Nakayama Era in the Central Labor Commission', in Chuo Rodo Iinkai (1981: 3).
5. Minoru Takita, 'Sekiryotaru Omoi: Nakayama Sensei wo Ushinatte' (Lonely thoughts: losing Prof. Nakayama), Chuo Rodo Iinkai (1981: 51). 'Zadankai Nakayama Ichiro shi wo kataru' (Round-table discussion: Speaking of Ichiro Nakayama), Chuo Rodo Iinkai (1981: 84). See also page 5 of the same publication. 'Geppo Zadankai III. Sengo Nihon no Roshi Kankei' (Monthly Round table III, Postwar Japan's Labor-Management Relations), *Nakayama Zenshu*, Supplement, pp. 82–3.
6. Nakayama, 'Churoi Kaikan no Tatemono to Rekishi to Kioku' (Building, History, and Memories of the Central Labor Commission Hall) (1965), in Chuo Rodo Iinkai (1981: 226-7).
7. 'Zadankai – Nakayama Ichiro shi wo kataru', pp. 84–96. 'Geppo Zadankai III. Sengo Nihon no Roshi Kankei', *Nakayama Zenshu*, supplement, pp. 82–7.
8. Nakayama's preface to vol. 13 of his *Zenshu*, pp. iv-v. Nakayama (1979: 23–4).
9. Fukuda (1924), preface 2. Nakayama's preface to vol. 13 of his *Zenshu*, pp.ii–iii. On Fukuda's involvement with the Social Bureau of the Home Office, see Chiho Zaimu Kyokai (1971: 396).
10. 'Zadankai – Nakayama Ichiro shi wo kataru', *Nakayama Zenshu*, supplement, pp. 102–5.
11. On the process of establishing the Productivity Center, see Okazaki *et al.* (1996: 100–3). 'Geppo Zadankai III. Sengo Nihon no Roshi Kankei', *Nakayama Zenshu*, supplement, pp. 94–7.
12. Nihon Seisansei Honbu (1985: 108–10). *Asahi Shimbun*, 21 February 1955. Nakayama (1963: 123).
13. Noda (1975: 577). Tetsuzo Nakajima, 'Omoidasu mama wo' (Way as I am remembering), in Nakayama (1981: 97).

14. See *Nihon Rodo Kyokai Zasshi* (April 1962), p. 27.
15. Nakayama's preface to vol. 13 of his *Zenshu*, p. vii. See also *Zenshu*, vol. 13, pp. 509–11. Nakayama (1975: 203–6).

References and further reading

Akamatsu, K., Y. Nakano, T. Nawa, and S. Yabe (1951) 'Zadankai: Zenmen kowa to tandoku kowa no taiketsu' (Round table: the peace treaty with all the nations or only with the western bloc), *Chuo Koron* Special Issue (753), 114–28.

Blaug, M., ed. (1995) *The Quantity Theory of Money*, Cheltenham: Edward Elgar.

Chiho Zaimu Kyokai (1971) *Naimusho shi* (History of the Home Office), vol. 3, Chiho Zaimu Kyokai.

Chuo Rodo Iinkai (1981) *Nakayama Ichiro Sensei to Rodo Iinkai* (Professor Ichiro Nakayama and the Labor Commission).

Fukuda, T. (1922) 'Kakaku toso yori kosei toso he' (From price struggles to welfare struggles: especially labor struggles as welfare struggles), in *Shakai seisaku to kaikyu toso* (Social policy and class struggles), Tokyo: Okura Shoten.

Fukuda, T. (1924) *Fukko keizai no genri oyobi jakkan mondai* (Principles and recovering economies and some problems), Tokyo: Dobunkan.

Hicks, J. R. and A. G. Hart (1945) *The Social Framework of the American Economy: An Introduction to Economics*, New York: Oxford University Press.

Ikeo, A. (1996) 'The advent of marginalism in Japan', *Research in the History of Economic Thought and Methodology.* 14: 217–45.

Ikeo, A. (1998) 'Economic development and economic thought after World War II: non-Marxian economists on development, trade and industry'. In S. Sugihara and T. Tanaka (eds) *Economic Thought and Modernization in Japan*, Cheltenham: Edward Elgar.

Kanamori, H. (ed.) (1970) *Boeki to Kokusai Shushi* (Trade and International Balance), Tokyo: Nihon Keizai Shimubun-sha.

Keizai Doyukai (1956) *Keizai Doyukai Ju-nen shi* (Ten-year history of the Keizai Doyukai), Tokyo: Keizai Doyukai.

Keizai Doyukai (1976) *Keizai Doyukai Sanju-nen shi* (Thirty-year history of the Keizai Doyukai), Tokyo: Keizai Doyukai.

Keynes, J. M. (1923) *Tract on Monetary Reform*, London: Macmillan.

Keynes, J. M. (1930) *A Treatise on Money*, London: Macmillan.

Keynes, J. M. (1936) *The General Theory of Employment, Interest and Money*, London: Macmillan.

Kondo, Y. (ed.) (1978) *Showa-zenki Nosei Meisakushu* (Collection of Major Works on Early Showa Agricultural Administration), 3 volumes, Tokyo: Noson Gyoson Bunka Kyokai.

Masamura, K. (1985) *Sengoshi* (A Post-War History) vol. 1, Tokyo: Chikuma Shobo.

Nakayama, I. (1932) 'Keiki kenkyu niokeru keizaigaku to tokeigaku tono kosho' (Connection between economics and statistics for business cycle studies), *Zenshu*, vol. 5.

Nakayama, I. (1933a) *Junsui Keizaigaku* (Pure Economics), Tokyo: Iwanami Shoten.

Nakayama, I. (1933b) 'Keizai riron to keizai shakaigaku' (Economic theory and economic sociology). In *Fukuda Tokuzo Hakase Tsuito Ronbunshu: Keizaigaku Kenkyu* (Collected Essays in Memory of Professor Tokuzo Fukuda, Economic Studies), Tokyo: Moriyama Shoten.

Nakayama, I. (1938) *Kinko Riron to Shihon Riron* (Equilibrium Theory and Capital Theory), Tokyo: Iwanami Shoten.

Nakayama, I. (1939) *Hatten-katei no Kinko-bunseki* (An Equilibrium Analysis of Developing Process), Tokyo: Iwanami Shoten.

Nakayama, I. (1953) *Nihon Keizai no Kao* (The Face of Japanese Economy), Tokyo: Nihon Hyoronsha (also in Nakayama (1972), vol. 12).

Nakayama, I. (1956) 'Seisansei no riron to jissai' (The theory and reality of productivity). In *Seisansei no riron to jissai* (The theory and reality of productivity) I. Tokyo: Nihon Seisansei Honbu.

Nakayama, I. (1958a) [1963] *Atarashii Keieisha, Atarashii Rodosha* (New Managers, New Workers), 2nd edition, Tokyo: Nihon Rodo Kyokai.

Nakayama, I. (1958b) *Roshi Kyogisei* (The labor-management consultation system). Tokyo: Nihon Seisansei Honbu.

Nakayama, I. (1959) 'Chingin nibai wo teisho: Seisan nobaseba yume de nai' (A Proposal to double wages: it's not a dream if production increases), vol. 16 of *Zenshu*.

Nakayama, I. (1972–3) *Nakayama Ichiro Zenshu* (Complete Works of Ichiro Nakayama), 18 volumes, one supplementary volume, Tokyo: Kodansha.

Nakayama, I. (1973) 'Introduction to the 16-volume Complete Works,' in *Speaking on the Japanese Economy*, vol. 16 of *Zenshu*, Tokyo: Kodansha (in Japanese).

Nakayama, I. (1974a) [1978], 'Kosei keizaigaku to Fukuda Tokuzo' (Welfare economics and Tokuzo Fukuda), in Takeo Minoguchi and Tadashi Hayasaka eds. *Kindai-keizaigaku to Nihon* (Modern Economics and Japan), Tokyo: Nihon Keizai Shimbun-sha.

Nakayama, I. (1974b) *Roshi kankei no Keizai-shakaigaku* (The economic sociology of industrial relations), Tokyo: Nihon Rodo Kyokai.

Nakayama, I. (1975) 'Roshi kankei no sanjunen' (Thirty years of industrial relations), in Zenkoku Rodo Iinkai Renraku Kyogikai, *Rodo Iinkai no Sanjunen* (The Labor Committee's Thirty Years), 1976.

Nakayama, I. (1978) 'Geppo' (Monthly Reports), appended to Tobata (1978).

Nakayama, I. (1979) *Waga-michi Keizaigaku* (My Economic Path), Tokyo: Kodansha.

Nakayama, I. (1981) *Ichiro Hachijunen: Nakayama Ichiro Sensei Tsuiso Kinen Bunshu* (Ichiro's Straight Path for Eighty Years: Collected Essays in the Memory of Professor Ichiro Nakayama), privately published.

Nihon Seisansei Honbu, Roshi Kyogisei Jonin Iinkai (1959) *Nihon no Roshi Kyogisei – sono Rekishi, Genjo oyobi Mondaiten* (Japan's Labor-Management Consultation System: Its History, Present Situation and Problems), Tokyo: Nihon Seisansei Honbu.

Nihon Seisansei Honbu (1985) *Seisansei Undo 30-nen shi* (30-year History of the Productivity Movement), Tokyo: Nihon Seisansei Honbu.

Noda, N., chief editor (1975) *Seisansei Jiten* (Productivity Dictionary), Tokyo: Nihon Seisansei Honbu.

Ogasawara, S. (1953) 'Sokan ni atatte' (Introduction to the Study of International Trade and Industry) *Tsusho Sangyo Kenkyu* (1), 1.

Okazaki T., S. Sugayama, T. Nishizawa, and S. Yonekura (1996) *Sengo Nihon Keizai to Keizai Doyukai* (The Postwar Japanese economy and the Keizai Doyukai), Tokyo: Iwanami Shoten.

Okita, S. (1981) 'Kyosei ochite sabishita hitoshio' (It is terrible to lose the giant star) in Nakayama (1981).

Sakurada, T. (1982) *Sakurada Takeshi Ronshu* (Collected essays of Sakurada Takeshi), 2 volumes, Sakurada Takeshi Ronshu Kankokai.

Samuelson, P. (1948) *Economics: An Introductory Analysis*, New York: McGraw-Hill.

Schumpeter, E. B. (ed.) (1940) *The Industrialization of Japan and Machukuo, 1930–1940: Population, Raw Material and Industry*, New York: Macmillan.

Schumpeter, J. A. (1912) *Theorie der wirtschaftlichen Entwicklung,* Leipzig: Dunker & Humblot. Second edition, 1926. *Theory of Economic Development,* MA: Harvard University Press, 1934.

Shakai Keizai Seisansei Honbu (1996) *Roshi Kankei Hakusho 30-nen shi – hakusho ni miru waga kuni roshi kankei no kiseki –* (Thirty-year White Paper History of Industrial Relations: the locus of industrial relations seen through White Papers), Tokyo: Shakai Keizai Seisansei Honbu (Socio-Economic Productivity Center).

Shinohara, M. (1973) 'Koki' (Postscript) in Nakayama (1972), vol. 16, pp. 551–64.

Tobata, S. (1936) [1978] *Nihon Nogyo no Tenkai Katei* (The Evolutionary Process of Japanese Agriculture), Tokyo: Iwanami Shoten.

Tobata, S. (1953) *Nihon Nogyuo no Sugata* (The Shape of Japanese Agriculture), Tokyo: Nihon Hyoronsha.

Tobata, S. (1964) *Nihon Shihonshugi no Keiseisha* (The Shapers of Japanese Capitalism: Several Economic Actors), Tokyo: Iwanami Shoten.

Tobata, S. (1979a) Watashi no Rirekisho (My Life History), Tokyo: Nihon Keizai Shimbun-sha.

Tobata, S. (1979b) 'Noseigakusha toshiteno Yanagita Kunio' (Agricultural administrator Kunio Yanagita: memories of my teacher), in Tobata (1979a).

Tsuchiya, K. (1978) 'Kaidai' (Bibliographical introduction), in Tobata (1978).

Wakimura, Y. (1981) 'Kokoronokori no koto futatsu' (Two things to regret), in Nakayama (1981).

8 External liberalization and 'industrial structure policy'

Asahi Noguchi

8.1 Policies for external liberalization and the 'two generations' among economists

Japan's economy enjoyed a period of spectacular development in the 1960s which has been called the 'High-Growth Era.' It was also a time during which economists in Japan played important roles in developing economic policies within and outside the government. Policy subjects at the time can be largely divided into two classes: those connected with the growth of the Japanese economy (and 'planning' toward it) and those connected with external trade and capital liberalization. This chapter exclusively deals with the latter subject. The purpose of this chapter is to examine the ways in which Japanese economists related to and argued about a series of economic policies which the government and the administration formulated to cope with ongoing external liberalization in the 1960s.

In 1960, the Ikeda Cabinet announced the 'Income Doubling Plan.' The extent to which this introduced Japan's period of 'High Economic Growth' in the 1960s remains a subject of debate. Estimating the growth potential of the Japanese economy was, to be sure, one of the focal subjects at that time, and a great number of prominent economists inside and outside the government were willing to join in the debate. Naturally, the Income Doubling Plan, formulated in such an atmosphere, was intended to be a kind of 'national project.'[1] As Komiya (1975: Ch. 10) insists, however, 'National Economic Plans' in postwar Japan, including the Income Doubling Plan, were substantially little more than 'official forecasting.' If we interpret the word 'plan' to mean a set of constraints on economic activity in the private and public sectors, these were not 'plans' at all. Therefore, it is doubtful that Japan's 'High Growth' was promoted by ingenious economic planning. However, it remains possible that the slogan 'Income Doubling' had some economically important impact on people's minds.

By contrast, the significance of trade and capital liberalization for the Japanese economy was far more substantial. In the first place, Japan's rapid economic development after the Meiji Restoration had been achieved under the 'forced free trade regime' that the unequal treaties signed with Western countries in the closing days of the Tokugawa shogunate had initiated. The Meiji government had made great efforts to revise these treaties, and finally obtained tariff autonomy in 1899, four years after the conclusion of the Sino-Japanese War. In spite of this, the government remained strongly committed to free trade, so that Japan continued to charge low tariffs (Harada and Kosai 1987: 59). After the 1930s the situation changed drastically. As the world economy moved toward a 'bloc' or wartime economy following the start of the Great Depression in 1929, the Japanese economy also evolved into self-sufficiency. In spite of various economic reforms following Japan's defeat in WWII, the Japanese economy remained essentially autarkic in nature. As Tsuruta (1982: 86) points out, therefore, Japan's external liberalization in the 1960s was really an 'epoch-making event' through which the open economy regime replaced the existing closed-economy regime. This process took in total about thirty years, including the wartime and the postwar period of reconstruction, and the beginning of the high economic growth period.

If external liberalization can be defined as the removal of barriers preventing various goods and factors of production from moving across borders, its effect for a national economy is almost self-evident. As in international trade textbooks, if the relative prices of goods differ across countries, every country can maximize its income under the constraints of given factor endowments by promoting production specialization according to its comparative advantage. And if remuneration rates of the production factors (e.g. labor, capital, and various managerial resources) differ across countries, each can utilize its production factors most efficiently by promoting international factor movements.[2] Therefore, most academic economists tend to think that international movements of goods and factors of production should be promoted in principle (e.g. Tatemoto 1969a: 131–2). Furthermore, they should not be restricted by policies except in a transitional adjustment process or 'market failure' situation. Analogous to Japan's external economic liberalization in the 1960s, the NIEs and the ASEAN countries took steps to abolish their previous protectionist policies and adopted external liberalization policies during and after the 1970s. The miraculous economic growth which took place in these countries suggests that the above economic reasoning represents some aspects of the real world. In this sense, we may safely say that Japan's external liberalization in the 1960s was one of the most significant factors influencing high economic growth throughout this decade.

In reality, however, the measures taken by Japan's policy authorities were not necessarily based on this type of economic reasoning. An inner motivation to make the Japanese economy more competitive and efficient was not at the root of the external economic liberalization at the time. Instead, it was primarily a compromise to 'gaiatsu', pressure directed toward Japan from other countries. This pressure came from such arenas of international economic negotiation as GATT (General Agreement on Tariffs and Trade), the IMF (International Monetary Fund), and the OECD (Organization for Economic Cooperation and Development). In fact, government officials and policymakers at the time thought that external liberalization was a cost which Japan could not avoid paying in order to occupy a position in the international economic society to which Japan had just returned. Therefore, they thought that economic liberalization should be introduced as slowly as possible unless such reluctance aroused criticism from foreign countries. This is exactly the way the authorities actually acted.

This negative motivation for external liberalization was not so much a perception peculiar to policy officials as a reflection of the general consciousness in business circles and the Japanese public as a whole. As the then-popular metaphor that 'the second black ship is coming' shows, most Japanese thought that their economy was far more backward than the economies of the Western countries. They feared that Japanese enterprises would be driven away if the domestic market were opened up to foreign enterprises. It is precisely such fears that motivated most of the policies pioneered primarily by MITI (the Ministry of International Trade and Industry) in this decade. Among these policies were attempts to construct a 'New Industrial System' based on the Special Measures Law for the Promotion of Designated Industries, the institutionalization of the 'Industrial Policy' through administrative guidance, and the inducement of the 'reorganization of industries' by promoting industrial mergers. These policies were all formulated or implemented with the notion that domestic industries (or companies) could not survive without strengthening their 'international competitiveness.'

In short, we may say that the actual purpose of Japan's external liberalization policies in the 1960s was not to liberalize the domestic economy, but to reduce the influence of liberalization as much as possible. In this sense, they were not so much liberalization policies as policies 'against' liberalization. During the introduction of capital liberalization, for example, policy authorities made it a rigid rule to apply it only to some 'secure' industries where liberalization would not have any effect. Authorities made tremendous efforts to retard liberalization in other industries, arguing that 'competitiveness is not enough.' In the event that an industry was to be liberalized against its will, on the other hand, authorities enforced industrial reorganization policies in the name of 'strengthening the international competitiveness' of the industry.

In the following sections of this chapter, we will examine how Japanese economists at that time thought about and behaved toward these policies. To make clear the precise meaning of their behavior, we must first investigate the background of this era. The period during which external liberalization took place was also an epoch-making period involving the great change described as the 'alternation of generations' among policy oriented economists. The 'older generation' played a leading role in policy making during the postwar economic rehabilitation, whereas the 'newer generation' had been brought up with neoclassical economics (or the 'neoclassical synthesis'), as systematized and institutionalized in postwar America. In this chapter, we will call the older generation the 'first generation' and the newer generation the 'second generation,' following the terminology used in Komiya (1986).[3]

In the first half of the 1960s, when trade liberalization was a primal policy subject, the first generation still preserved a dominant influence on the making of policy. As Komiya (1986: 22) describes, 'Up until about 1965 Japan's industrial policy, implemented primarily by MITI, was based on the ideological groundwork laid by this generation.' These economists thought that Japan could not go on resisting external economic liberalization indefinitely. At the same time they believed that some 'key industries,' such as heavy industries (or heavy and chemical industries), must be under direct governmental protection and promotion to encourage development of the Japanese economy. They made policy suggestions from this viewpoint within the Industrial Structure Investigation Council (and the Industrial Structure Council) in MITI.

With the focus shifting from trade to capital liberalization in the second half of the 1960s, however, the second-generation economists gradually became conspicuous. Contrary to the notion peculiar to the first generation and the policymakers under their influence, the second generation thought that the external liberalization of the Japanese economy should not be treated as a mere compromise to 'gaiatsu,' but as a task that Japan must undertake voluntarily. They also pointed out the lack of basis of many fears about economic liberalization. One of their principal targets was a then widely circulated caution that 'with the liberalization going on Japan's industries would be dominated by foreign capital and the national interests would be injured.' They also insisted that the 'industrial reorganization' initiated by MITI could have the negative effect of impeding competition in markets since its policy intention was the creation of monopolies. For the second generation, therefore, it was not the liberalization but the policies against liberalization promoted by the policy authorities that should be restricted.

To summarize, there were two factions among economists at that time: those who had actively participated in formulating the 'industrial structure policy' initiated by MITI, and those who had strongly opposed them. Thus there sometimes occurred severe conflicts between the former group, the first generation, and the latter, the second generation. At the peak of these conflicts was a campaign provoked by many of the second-generation economists against the merger, between the two biggest steel companies at that time, Yawata Steel and Fuji Steel. As Komiya (1986: 23) describes, this confrontation over the 'Giant Merger' problem was really a 'clash that stands out even today in the history of Japanese economic thought.' At the same time, this opposition by the second-generation economists 'provoked the interest toward the anti-trust policy nationally, and made an incentive to put it forward beyond the intentions of those who were concerned with the merger' (Ando *et al.* 1994: 381). From this time on, the stance of policy authorities also gradually approached the notion commonly held by the second-generation economists, namely that the government should rely on the function of the market mechanism as much as possible, and confine its role to the correction of certain defects.

8.2 Trade liberalization and 'new industrial system'[4]

8.2.1 External circumstances and internal responses concerning trade liberalization

On 24 June 1960, the cabinet adopted the 'Outline of the Plan for the Liberalization of Trade and Foreign Currency Exchange' (Keizai Kikakucho

1960). This marked the first time the Japanese government prescribed a specific scheme for trade liberalization. At that time, Japan's liberalized trade share was only 40 percent when estimated as the proportion of the customs value of liberalized items to the total customs value of imports (excluding those imported by the government). The aim of this plan was to raise this share to 90 percent within three years, which was not at all an easy goal to achieve considering the many obstacles to liberalization. The external circumstances at the time moved Japan toward a bold change.

As argued before, pressure from foreign countries was a driving force influencing Japan's trade liberalization reforms. Japan was admitted to the IMF and GATT in 1952 and 1955 respectively. A major objective of these two organizations was to extend indiscriminate transactions of trade and foreign exchange around the world, thus preventing a recurrence of bloc economies such as proliferated before WWII. Contrary to this general principle, many countries, including Japan, that were suffering from a dollar shortage had to resort to foreign exchange controls and import restrictions. These exceptional measures were based on the 'transitional' clause (Article XIV) of the IMF Agreement, or on Article XII of GATT, allowing a country in external financial difficulty to restrict imports.

At the end of the 1950s, when the problem of the dollar shortage had been relieved worldwide, the US government began persistently to ask the recovering countries to proceed with liberalization. In response, most leading European countries restored currency convertibility in 1958, and took a step toward substantial trade liberalization in 1959. As a result, Japan became the only major country continuing foreign exchange and trade restrictions. This situation inevitably made Japan the target of criticism from other countries, who demanded liberalization on such occasions as the general meeting of the IMF held from September to October 1959, and that of GATT, held from October to November in the same year. It is at this stage that the Japanese government started to outline various arrangements for trade liberalization. These finally emerged as the 'Outline of the Plan for the Liberalization of Trade and Foreign Currency Exchange' adopted in June 1960.

Although this 'Outline' was ambitious for Japan at the time, other countries thought that the pace of '90 percent liberalization within three years' mentioned in it was too slow. As a result, Japan was continually asked to enforce liberalization more rapidly at subsequent IMF and GATT meetings. On 5 August 1961, the US government also insisted that Japan should liberalize 16 items dealing with exports to the US. Under these circumstances, the Japanese government adopted the 'Plan for Promoting the Liberalization of Trade and Foreign Currency Exchange' which was enacted to advance the liberalization measures prescribed in the former 'Outline.' The subsequent trade liberalization was generally executed according to this 'Plan.'

Although this worldwide force pushing Japan toward trade liberalization was irresistible by the end of the 1950s, domestic responses to it were initially unusual. The tone of the press was dominated by sensational expressions such as *gaiatsu* pressing Japan' or 'black ship coming.' Although stubborn objections to trade liberalization stemming from such sentiments had never vanished, the consensus of opinion gradually changed afterwards. Two views roughly summarize opinions at the time. One held that 'now that liberalization has become a general tendency of the world, Japan has no option but to proceed with liberalization in order not to be regarded as a nuisance.' Most of the 'liberalization proposals' formulated and announced around that time by business and academic leaders were mainly based on this kind of thinking.[5] The other was that 'since the Japanese economy is still too weak to accept substantial liberalization, it must be accompanied by definite countermeasures by the government.' The previous 'Outline' had already mentioned such policy direction. It stated that the government should 'help companies to cooperate with each other in order to overcome transitional difficulties accompanying liberalization, and take measures to facilitate the enlargement of firm size, the establishment of specialized production, the coordination of capital investments, and the rationalization of material procurement.' This line of thinking was later denoted 'consolidation of the industrial order,' and became the most focal subject of policy controversies relating to the 'New Industrial System' and the Special Measures Law for the Promotion of Designated Industries.

8.2.2 *Special Measures Law for the Promotion of Designated Industries and the Industrial Structure Investigation Council*

On 22 March 1963, the cabinet decided to bring the 'Special Measures Law for the Promotion of Designated Industries' (below abbreviated as the Special Measures Law) before the Diet. Its principal purpose was to designate the industries that required certain measures to strengthen their international competitiveness in the coming age of trade liberalization. Its additional purpose was to promote mergers and rationalizations within these industries, involving cooperative efforts between the government and private companies. The original title of the bill was the 'Special Measures Bill for Strengthening the International Competitiveness of Designated Industries,' which describes its precise intention better. These legislative attempts were largely motivated by a characteristic notion, commonly held among the policy officials at that time that the backwardness of Japan's economy expressed itself most conspicuously in such phenomena as 'smallness of firm size' and the resulting 'excess competition.' Terms such as 'new industrial system' or 'new industrial order' were frequently used at the time to represent the desirable industrial system that would overcome these defects and realize 'effective competition' through 'enlargement of firm size.'[6]

The Special Measures Law was peculiar in that it was primarily initiated by MITI bureaucrats. This explains why it caused various criticisms in the Diet, and was shelved and finally discarded as a 'bill without a sponsor.' This unusual story was later made popular by a famous novel. A motive for MITI itself to adhere strongly to the Special Measures Law was very apparent. In the former period of strict trade regulations, MITI monopolized the authority to allocate limited amounts of foreign currency to each industry. This authority operated as the source of power with which MITI could effectively dominate and manipulate private industries.[7] Since trade liberalization had inevitably deprived MITI of its most vital power source, MITI had been in great need of another role that would provide it with well-grounded authority.

Though MITI was a primary force in putting forward the Special Measures Law, an additional force came from the public. As mentioned above, most people at that time, including business and academic leaders, were extremely anxious about the outcome of liberalization. Naturally they became sympathetic to the notion behind the Special Measures Law, and to its slogans such as 'upgrading the industrial structure' or 'consolidating the industrial order.' This explains the reason why a framework of policy thinking laid out by the 'Industrial Structure Investigation Council' continued to remain influential even after the discarding of the Special Measures Law, and was frequently referred to as a primary source of guidance for 'industrial structure policy.' This council, members of which were mostly prominent business and academic leaders, took an active part in the process of preparing the Special Measures Law.

The Industrial Structure Investigation Council was established as an auxiliary institution of MITI on 1 April 1961. Its principal purpose was to 'prepare a system for investigating various problems associated with trade liberalization.' During its existence, the council organized 12 committees (and 32 subcommittees) including the 'General Committee' whose chairman was Ichiro Nakayama. Of all the committees, the most important in the formulation of the Special Measures Law was the 'Industrial Order Committee' whose chairman was Hiromi Arisawa.

In a recent study Kosuke Oyama (1996: Ch. 5) sheds some light on the process of discussion within the Industrial Order Committee. He examined documents stored in MITI, which had long been kept closed to the public. His study shows that debate in the committee was not superficial and uncritical as has usually been thought, but in fact the discussion that occurred there actually affected the drafting of the Special Measures Law (Oyama 1996: 123). The direction of policy changed significantly as a result of severe criticism by committee members, including the chairman, Hiromi Arisawa. Reflecting the intentions of the Enterprises Bureau of MITI that formulated it, the initial draft of the Special Measures Law was strongly oriented toward 'bureaucratic control.' Members of the committee questioned this, and forced MITI to depart from its original intention and move toward 'private-public cooperation' (Oyama 1996: 127–9).

Although the Enterprises Bureau of MITI and committee members disagreed as to how the policy should be enforced, both groups shared the same general understanding about the existing conditions of and the required measures for Japan's economy. Most committee members, like the bureaucrats, thought that the greatest problem for Japan's economy facing liberalization was the 'smallness of firm size' and its accompanying 'excess competition.' They felt that 'appropriate firm size' and 'effective competition' must be realized to overcome these defects. They also believed that MITI should promote mergers and concentrations within industries to achieve this goal. As well, in order that MITI might activate these policy measures, the Antimonopoly Law should be relaxed or an exemption from the Antimonopoly Law should be allowed.[8]

The Industrial Structure Investigation Council finished its main tasks by submitting the Report (Sangyo Kozo Chosakai 1963) on 29 November 1963. The major motif of this Report was the familiar one that it was necessary to 'upgrade the industrial structure' and 'consolidate the industrial order' to strengthen international competitiveness. Nevertheless it contained one novel idea which was to lay the foundation for MITI's 'Industrial Structure Policy' afterwards. It defined the meaning of 'upgrading the industrial structure' precisely as promoting heavy and chemical industry. Furthermore two 'criteria for constructing optimal industrial structure' were provided to justify this definition, one of which was the 'income elasticity criterion' while the other was the 'productivity growth criterion.'

According to the Report, 'The doctrine of comparative advantage and international division of labor has various limitations as a guiding principle.' As such, intentional industrial structure policies with a long-term perspective might be required in case 'the outcome fulfilled solely through the working of price mechanism in the present stage does not coincide with the demands of the national economy.' Moreover, the Report argues, 'In order to upgrade the industrial structure, it is desirable from a demand side to develop an industry whose product has a high income elasticity of demand, and from a supply side an industry which has high productivity growth or higher potential for technological developments'. The Report thus concludes that heavy and chemical industries might fully satisfy these two criteria.[9]

The Special Measures Law was scrapped after all, since MITI could not clear away a deep-rooted suspicion among business leaders that the law might actually aim at 'bureaucratic control,' rather than 'private-public cooperation' as it claimed. Yet business leaders were not necessarily opposed to the notion which motivated the Special Measures Law. Like the MITI bureaucrats, business leaders maintained that legislative restrictions on corporate mergers and cartels should be relaxed because competition with foreign enterprises was becoming more and more intense. In fact, they aspired to weaken the Antimonopoly Law more so than MITI. Their real intention was to initiate corporate mergers and cartelizations not by 'bureaucratic initiative,' but by 'self-coordination' within private industry.

Such strong resistance to the Special Measures Law and its eventual abandonment obliged MITI to compromise with private industry. This marked a turning point, after which MITI gradually altered its policy orientation to one that involved less compulsion and more inducement. Later, this kind of administrative style was systematized as 'industrial policy through administrative guidance' with which MITI became prominent.

In relation to the Special Measures Law it should be pointed out that there were few, if any, criticisms aimed directly at the ideas behind the law. Whether through bureaucratic initiative or self-coordination, what MITI meant by 'realization of effective competition through enlargement of firm size' was actually policy-induced monopolization of the economy. Such a policy direction apparently contradicted the idea behind the Antimonopoly Law. Nevertheless, those who questioned monopolization numbered very few in those days.

This is demonstrated by the fact that the Fair Trade Commission, the authority operating the Antimonopoly Law, made no serious objections to MITI over the Special Measures Law. The Fair Trade Commission could only announce that it would admit cartels for rationalization, showing that there was no need for further legislation to circumvent the Antimonopoly Law (see Ando *et al.* 1994: 299–300).

This prevailing apathy toward antimonopoly policy at the time helped to keep alive a notion of a 'New Industrial System' that had been proposed in the Special Measures Law and the Report of the Industrial Structure Investigation Council. In fact the notion 'had revived completely in connection with the capital liberalization commencing around 1966 or 1967' (Konishi 1973: 136). One difference between that time and the previous trade liberalization was that a group of second-generation economists emerged as a decisive opponent.

8.3 Confrontation between the 'two generations' over capital liberalization and the giant merger

8.3.1 Controversy over capital liberalization

In Japan, the term 'capital liberalization' denotes a relaxation of regulations on 'direct inward investment.' This is a stock acquisition by a foreigner with participation in management or establishment of a subsidiary company, which began at the end of the 1960s. Japan responded to this problem by reluctantly bowing to foreign pressure, as during the time of trade liberalization. Capital liberalization began in July 1967 and was completed in December 1975, taking almost ten years to complete the process. Japan's timidity in proceeding with capital liberalization often made other countries indignant. Domestic sentiment toward capital liberalization also showed the familiar pattern of evolution from the 'unjust *gaiatsu*' and 'awful black ship' arguments to sayings such as 'We have no option because it's the general tendency of the world.' However, a domestic fear that foreign capital would dominate Japan was so fundamental that the pace of liberalization was even slower than before.

It was not until Japan was admitted to the OECD (Organization for Economic Cooperation and Development) in April 1964 that capital liberalization became a serious issue for Japan. The OECD had established an agreement on liberalization of invisible current transactions and international capital flows for the purpose of realizing its initial aims. These included worldwide economic growth, support for developing countries, and the expansion of free trade. When Japan joined the OECD, however, it declined to accept eighteen items prescribed in this agreement, one of which was related to liberalizing direct inward investment. In subsequent OECD meetings, this became a target of criticism among other countries, who insisted that Japan present a detailed schedule for liberalization. The US government also made similar requests repeatedly in the Japan–US Joint

Committee on Trade and the Economy. The fifth meeting of this committee, held in July 1966, gave a decisive impetus for the Japanese government to begin capital liberalization in earnest.

Following the requests made by the US government during these negotiations, MITI asked the Foreign Capital Council how capital liberalization should be undertaken. MITI also set up a 'Capital Transactions Liberalization Counter-Measures Special Committee,' chaired by Hiromi Arisawa, within the General Committee of Industrial Structure Council. In June 1967, the Foreign Capital Council submitted a report indicating the direction toward capital liberalization, which began the following month.

About the time when these first measures of capital liberalization were brought into practice, various arguments and controversies were underway domestically. In contrast to those over trade liberalization, these arguments took place between two groups of different economic thinking. MITI's bureaucrats and the economists emphasized the threat of foreign capital for Japan's economy and advocated the necessity of industrial reorganization and the relaxation of the Antimonopoly Law. The other group comprised the economists who pointed out the advantages of capital liberalization and the possible harmful effects of the policies that MITI proposed.

This marked the beginning of successive controversies between the first-generation and the second-generation economists. The climax took place the following year over the 'Giant Merger' between Yawata Steel and Fuji Steel. These two camps of economists and bureaucrats had debated intensely over capital liberalization in such economic journals as *Shukan Toyo Keizai* (Weekly Oriental Economist) and *Economisuto* (Economist). Miyohei Shinohara and Ryutaro Komiya stood out for the first and the second generations respectively. The two most representative bureaucrats who had been preaching the policy directions of MITI at the forefront of the debate were Shintaro Hayashi and Yugoro Komatsu.

The fundamental thinking of MITI was actually a revision of the 'New Industrial System,' which flourished during the period of trade liberalization. The idea was that strengthening international competitiveness through corporate mergers and enlargement of firm size was needed in order to repel foreign capital. MITI, and particularly its spokesman Shintaro Hayashi, frequently announced that capital liberalization would necessitate more effective counter-measures than trade liberalization because foreign enterprises had more 'capital power' than domestic ones (see Mitsuharu Ito's interview with Hayashi in Ito 1977: 113–19).

Among the economists active at the time, the most representative proponent of MITI's position was Miyohei Shinohara. Shinohara argued that ongoing capital liberalization would bring about a situation where 'foreign capital itself will flow into the country and participate in management, and superior technologies will disturb domestic enterprises' (Shinohara 1967a: 27). He also maintained that the meaning of capital liberalization was totally different from that of trade liberalization since 'absolute differentials of capital power and technology power would play the most decisive role' in the former. According to his view, enlargement of firm size would therefore be a reasonable counter-measure to capital liberalization, though it seemed contradictory to the principle of comparative costs (Shinohara 1967a: 26). From these standpoints, Shinohara warned that neglecting appropriate measures in capital liberalization would necessarily lead to a circumstance where 'each industry would be dominated by a world enterprise, and the independent development of national industries and national technologies would be hindered by so-called "technological imperialism"' (Shinohara 1967a: 28).[10]

The second-generation economists immediately voiced their opposition to this kind of argument by MITI. *Shukan Toyo Keizai*, an economic journal, described this situation as follows: 'the greater part of the arguments stems mostly from political and business circles who sense that foreign capital would dominate Japan's industries. But modern economists, who appreciate the effect of capital liberalization on the growth of Japan's economy and the improvement of national welfare, are showing strong hostility' (*Shukan Toyo Keizai*, Rinjizokan, 28 September 1967: 2).

The most influential criticism was the argument made by Ryutaro Komiya in his *Economics of Capital Liberalization* (1967). According to Komiya, the essence of foreign direct investment is the international movement of managerial resources: the technology, know-how, patents, and brands, that a firm cannot do without. Like other factor movements, these resources necessarily move from countries where their marginal productivity is lower to those where they are higher. Therefore, it is apparent that both a host and a home country will gain from foreign direct investment. Komiya maintains that capital liberalization is desirable in principle, and downplays the fear that national interests will be injured by the domination of foreign capital over domestic industries.

He also points out the fact that most of the arguments presented by those stressing the danger of foreign capital domination are constructed on such economically dubious concepts as 'capital power (*shihonryoku*)' and 'technology power (*gijyutsuryoku*).' As a result, Komiya argues, inappropriate 'counter-measures' are commonly taken. Representative of these is industrial reorganization and the relaxation of the Antimonopoly Law put forward by MITI, business leaders and their associated economists. These measures are in fact harmful because they are based on the unsound notion that 'It is necessary to establish monopoly in order to compete with monopoly.' If the possibility of monopoly domination by worldwide enterprises really exists, then according to Komiya the most important counter-measure is the strict application of the Antimonopoly Law to any enterprise regardless of its home base.

Komiya also illustrates the lack of foundation of familiar arguments such as the following: 'Capital liberalization is not beneficial because foreign enterprises will not obey administrative guidance. So self-coordination within industries and private-public cooperation will be more difficult.' Komiya writes, 'if this effect is strongly marked, it will not be a disadvantage but will rather be one of the greatest advantages of capital liberalization' (Komiya 1967: 28).

Although Komiya's main intention was to deliver his viewpoints on capital liberalization as a pressing issue, his analysis served as a frame of reference afterwards. He had constructed a rigorous theory of the mechanism of foreign direct investment, which had not been sufficiently developed at the time, and previously had been regarded as 'a blind spot of the economic theories' (Komiya 1967: 15). The following comment illustrates the impact of this article: 'It reached the highest level in its academic content and surpassed the previously published literature on capital liberalization in its originality' (Iida 1967: 50). In fact, Komiya's idea that foreign direct investment should be primarily treated as an economic phenomenon associated with the movement of managerial resources later became one of the sources for theories of multinational corporations.

8.3.2 Economists' criticism of the giant merger

Although an attempt to construct the 'New Industrial System' through the Special Measures Law had collapsed, MITI did not abandon its goal, and made a consistent effort both to direct the economy by means of administrative guidance, and to relax the Antimonopoly Law. The first-generation economists, perennial supporters of MITI, were closely involved in formulating this 'industrial structure policy' through such channels as the Industrial Structure Council. In contrast, the second-generation economists voiced strong opposition to MITI's plans on capital liberalization. This confrontation reached its peak in the subsequent controversy over the 'giant merger' between Yawata Steel and Fuji Steel.

On 17 April 1968, the newspaper *Mainichi Shimbun* released the story that the presidents of both Yawata Steel and Fuji Steel had agreed to merge their companies. Immediately after this, the giant merger problem between these two steel companies became a focal issue of policy debate. It also caused an unprecedented upheaval in which business, academic, and political circles as well as MITI and the Fair Trade Commission were involved.

Until this time, these two companies had been ranked first and second respectively within Japan's steel industry. Moreover, a merger between them might have resulted in the creation of the biggest steel company in the world. Taking all these circumstances into consideration, it was apparent that the legitimacy of this merger was questionable viewed from the antimonopoly policy. In fact, the Fair Trade Commission was quite against this merger plan from its outset. As a result of the burdensome legal procedures which had been imposed by the Fair Trade Commission, it took about a year and a half for the merger to be finally admitted (Tsuruta 1982: 147–9).

One reason why the merger between these two private steel companies caused such a furore was that the political pressure to put forward the merger was extraordinarily strong. Many political figures, particularly those in the ruling Liberal Democratic Party, as well as the business elite, actively attempted to hasten this merger. These political manipulations seemed especially malignant in the eyes of the second-generation economists who were of the view that the merger should be judged from the viewpoint of policies for promoting competition based on the Antimonopoly Law.

When this merger plan was revealed, MITI issued an immediate favorable comment. To MITI, this merger looked like an ideal case of 'industrial reorganization' which had come forward by itself. Thus there was no reason for MITI to hesitate to support it. Many cabinet ministers at the time, for example Prime Minister Eisaku Sato, minister of the Economic Planning Agency Kiichi Miyazawa and MITI minister Etsusaburo Shiina, also made favorable comments in the Diet. Among business leaders, the most overt supporter of this merger was Sohei Nakayama, then the president of Japan Industrial Bank, the largest shareholder and main bank to both steel companies.[11] In August 1968, the Special Committee on the Fundamental Problem, previously established in MITI's Industrial Structure Council, published a 'Note' (Sangyo Kozo Shingikai Kihon Mondai Tokubetsu Iinkai 1968) attempting to demonstrate the necessity of giant mergers.[12]

Amid this steady progression toward the merger, protest against it was made on 15 June 1968. The 'Note on the Giant Merger' was issued by the Gathering for Discussion on Antimonopoly Policy.[13] Ryuichiro Tachi and Masahiro Tatemoto were among the organizers of this group. This gathering consisted of economists, mostly of the second generation, who were opposed to MITI's policies and sympathetic to the Fair Trade Commission. Almost every newspaper printed a front-page report on this 'declaration against the giant merger by a group of academic economists' the next day. The contents of their 'Note on the Giant Merger' can be summarized as follows:

1. There is a strong suspicion that the 'Giant Merger' is against Article XV of the Antimonopoly Law, in the sense that it will lead to a substantial restriction of competition.

2. The proponents of this merger insist that it will generate economies of scale through the enlargement of firm size. The possibility of realizing this advantage is, however, very small.

3. Some cabinet members and policy officials in MITI are frequently and actively expressing their approval of the 'Giant Merger'. These actions interfere with the Fair Trade Commission, who should judge this case fairly. Therefore they must be regarded as actions exceeding the boundary of administrative authority.

4. A movement supporting the 'Giant Merger' is also active in such policy councils as the Economic Council and the Industrial Structure Council. However, the arguments made there are largely made by the interested parties, and can scarcely reflect the opinions of scholars who have expertise on this problem and can view it objectively. Therefore, the views issued by these councils are not acceptable as authorized ones.

5. If the various measures to restrict competition and to facilitate private monopoly were allowed by modifying the current antimonopoly law, it would necessarily lead to the decline of competition among enterprises. Since competition has been an engine for growth in Japan's economy, the future development of Japan would be greatly hindered by suppressing it.

The second-generation economists evidently stressed the significance of antimonopoly policy for maintaining a competitive economic system. They also severely denounced the government, MITI, and the policy councils that disregarded it. Masahiro Tatemoto, a leading figure in the movement against the merger, wrote: 'We acted in order to demonstrate theoretically how important the "principle of competition" is for the growth and development of Japan's economy. ... It is not the "trifling target" of Yawata and Fuji, those inefficient monsters, that modern economists are really opposed to, but the great evil called "industrial reorganization" or "industrial control"' (Tatemoto 1969b: 25).

The second-generation economists stressed the importance of competition in the market mechanism. They attacked the policy authorities and the economists of the former generation, who failed to understand the significance of competition and tried to violate it by promoting monopolistic policies in the name of 'strengthening competitiveness'.[14] These actions by the second-generation economists were meaningful since 'they initiated the removal of industrial policy, publicized widely the significance of antimonopoly policy, and contributed greatly to formulating competition rules for Japan's economy' (Tsuruta 1982: 154).

8.4 Economic evaluation of the 'industrial structure policy'

With external economic liberalization in the 1960s, Japan's economy gradually changed from its former autarkic and closed nature, and became a part of the international economy. For the policy officials and economists who had actually been concerned with policy-making, however, it was not easy completely to abandon the policy thinking that had been fostered during the closed-economy regime, which spanned thirty years before and after the war. It was not until the younger generation, armed with completely different economic training, won a battle with the older generation that this inward-oriented policy thinking declined considerably. A focal point of this confrontation between the two generations was, needless to say, MITI's 'industrial structure policy' which characterized the 1960s, the era of external liberalization for Japan. This section examines how we should evaluate the industrial structure policy from an economic standpoint.

As has been mentioned, much of the policy thinking behind MITI's industrial structure policy had been derived from the first-generation economists who had played a decisive role in policy-making in the postwar economic rehabilitation. Therefore, it is a matter of course that later generations of economists who have a different policy orientation tend to deprecate the notions of the first generation, as shown in Tatemoto (1966; 1969a; 1969b), Komiya (1966; 1986; 1988), Konishi (1966; 1973), Kaizuka (1968), and Tsuruta (1982).

The reason why the later generations of economists were critical of the policy stance of the first generation is very simple. The policy arguments made by the first generation and the policymakers seem incomprehensible on the one hand,

and awkward or harmful on the other, when viewed with the economics which the later generations accepted as a standard framework.[15]

Perhaps the most aggressive criticism of this sort can be seen in the writings of Ryutaro Komiya. He ironically calls the three prominent economists of the Industrial Structure Council, Hiromi Arisawa, Ichiro Nakayama and Miyohei Shinohara, the 'three giants of the prehistoric period.' He designates the essays of Yoshihiko Morozumi (1966) and Nobuyoshi Namiki (1973), both of whom were outstanding MITI bureaucrats in charge of industrial policy, as policy arguments belonging to the 'prehistoric' era (Komiya 1988: 21). According to Komiya, for example, notions like 'criteria for constructing optimal industrial structure,' which were the main thrusts of the 1963 Report by the Industrial Structure Investigation Council, are nothing but 'prehistoric,' falling short of standard economic knowledge. He writes, 'If goods are produced by an industry in which rapid productivity increase is occurring and for which the income elasticity of demand is high, then the industry will grow on its own. Hence there is no reason why, due to these two criteria, such an industry should be made a particular object for promotion' (Komiya 1988: 7).[16]

As is pointed out in Komiya (1988: 5), although the officials responsible for industrial policy in postwar Japan frequently argued that Japan required an industrial policy to improve the 'international competitiveness of domestic industry,' they never explained the economic grounds for this idea. Therefore, Komiya writes, 'Until about the mid-1970s, it was hard to have a dialogue among scholars and policymakers about industrial policy.'[17] Among the economists, 'There was little in common between the arguments of those who worked from the standpoint of economic theory and those of the older generation who operated in the "prehistoric" period' (Komiya 1988: 5).

As can be seen in Hayashi (1967b) and Shinohara (1967b), those who cautioned that a rapid progress of capital liberalization would damage national interests tended to emphasize the existence of 'differential technology power' between domestic and foreign enterprises. They also pointed out the danger of 'technological domination' by foreign enterprises.[18] From a purely economic standpoint, however, this 'national loss' argument is dubious. If there is a differential of factor rewards, say wage rates, between the home country and a foreign country due to differential technologies, both countries can increase their incomes either by a technology transfer or by a factor movement, in this case an emigration of labor. Therefore, differential technologies are not a factor indicating the perils of technology transfer, but rather they indicate its desirability through such measures as foreign direct investment.

In this regard, it is most striking that no policy officials seemed to have an accurate grasp of the way wage rates and other factor rewards were determined. Apparently they did not understand that wage rates were determined by the marginal productivity of labor, and that a low wage rate was usually a result of low productivity owing to poor technology. Policy officials such as Shintaro Hayashi and Yugoro Komatsu typically argued that the export competitiveness of, say, the steel industry, was due only to Japan's low wage rate compared to those of the other developed countries. Further, capital liberalization would provide foreign enterprises possessing advanced technologies with a chance to exploit Japan's cheap labor freely (Ito 1977: 118–22 and Nagano *et al.* 1968: 29). They were convinced that such 'technology invasion' must be prevented since it would conflict with Japan's national interests. Their stubborn assertions on the danger of capital liberalization and on the necessity of giant mergers were all based on this kind of inward-looking economic thinking. From an economic standpoint, however, this assertion is the same as saying that it is desirable that Japanese workers should be equipped with poorer technologies, so that their marginal productivity, and thus wage rates, should be lower. There is no doubt that they never dreamed of making such an assertion themselves.

Those belonging to what Komiya called the 'prehistoric' era conflicted sharply with later generations over 'excess competition' as well. Policy officials at the time argued that the weakest point of Japan's industries was their 'smallness of firm size,' and that competition among these small firms was excessive (see, for example, Morozumi 1963: 'Current State of Japan's Industrial Order'). The 'New Industrial System' described earlier in this chapter was formulated on this line of thinking. Because of this, its principal goal was the construction of a 'desirable industrial system' by promoting the enlargement of firm size through private-public cooperation. A slogan favored by MITI's policy officials in those days was 'From Excess Competition to Effective Competition.'

In contrast, the second-generation economists were dubious about the validity of the 'excess competition' hypothesis, as expressed in Tatemoto (1966; 1969b: 36–42) and Konishi (1966). They regarded 'effective competition' as a 'genuine upside-down fake' that had been used to pervert the original industrial organization theories (Tatemoto 1966: 31). According to Tatemoto, these theories were not a 'justification for structuring a system of oligopoly through mergers, rationalization, and grand combinations as in the industrial system arguments,' but rather the positive notion that competition is effective in a real economy. Tatemoto argues that the 'Policy intentions of MITI and the Economic Council are as follows: stirring up an excessive crisis atmosphere toward capital liberalization, insisting that heavy and chemical industry, which has been already fully oligopolized, is an "excess competition" industry, and pushing forcefully policies for restricting competition by monopolization and rationalization on this premise' (Tatemoto 1969a: 39). Tatemoto goes so far as to say that the "Japanese type of excess competition argument is nothing more than a "fake money" created to justify these policies for restricting competition.'

The thought of the second-generation economists such as Tatemoto and Komiya was quite the opposite of their opponents. If 'excess competition' really exists, they argue, it is due not so much to too much competition as to some kind of rationing by policy authorities.[19] For example, 'If plant and equipment investments were rationed with administrative guidance or self-coordination within the private industries, every company would necessarily rush to make an ambitious investment plan with an intention to get more' (Tatemoto 1969a: 43). Thus, Tatemoto concludes, 'Competition sometimes described as excessive is actually the outcome of such rationing.' Komiya also argues that 'A real cause of excess competition in investment lies in the fact that existing size of production equipment has been used as a kind of criterion in the past when executing direct control, administrative guidance, and cartelization' (Komiya 1975: 315).[20]

From this perspective, therefore, what was most required to overcome excess competition was to reduce administrative guidance and administrative intervention, and to establish a principle of self-responsibility for economic decision-making among private companies (Konishi 1968: 120). However, MITI's policy officials at the time resisted the reduction of administrative authority by touting the usefulness of 'private-public cooperation,' and insisting on the necessity of relaxing the antimonopoly law to ease 'excess competition' (see, for example, Hayashi 1967a: 52–60). The policy measures taken from such a standpoint were naturally both bizarre and potentially harmful in the eyes of second-generation economists.

8.5 What was this thing called 'industrial policy'?

Policy officials in the 1960s and the economists close to them had a tendency to downplay the virtues of external liberalization and market competition. Instead, they tended to regard these as dangerous. Simply speaking, MITI's 'Industrial Structure Policy' in the 1960s, or 'Industrial Policy' as it is generally called, was formulated based on this 'crisis sentiment' combined with the economic pessimism peculiar to first-generation economists.

It is difficult to understand why first-generation economists came to have such a pessimistic view unless we take into consideration the historical background which forged their economic outlook. Among the common properties that stand out in the economic thinking of the first generation we can discern a distrust of the market economy, an inclination to guiding economic development through government policy, and pessimism toward the future of the international economy. These characteristics are closely related to the history they had experienced. This history included a time of unprecedented economic difficulty lasting from the Great Depression to the regulated economy of wartime and the postwar period. Hiromi Arisawa and Ichiro Nakayama, the two giants of the first generation, had both struggled under these historical circumstances. It is understandable, therefore, that they found it difficult to abandon the way of thinking these experiences engendered.

In the previous chapter, we discussed the debate between the pro-trade stance and the pro-domestic-development stance, in which Ichiro Nakayama was a representative proponent of the former view. Examining this debate, it appears that at least Ichiro Nakayama, among the other first-generation economists, succeeded in freeing himself from their common economic pessimism. As argued in the previous chapter, however, the pro-trade stance of Nakayama was actually a trade-oriented developmentalism, which had little in common with the free-trade doctrine of the classical and neoclassical economists. Admitting on the one hand the existence of such divergent views within the first generation, Komiya thus concludes as follows: 'As a whole this generation was unaffected by the micro- and macroeconomic theories that are internationally dominant today. This is not to say that they had never come in contact with these theories, but their arguments on industrial policy show hardly a trace of such influence' (Komiya 1986: 23).[21] We can regard this as a typical assessment by a second-generation economist, who constructed policy arguments within the framework of neoclassical synthesis.

The first-generation economists also differed greatly from the second generation in that 'Most of them had little regard for and less understanding of antimonopoly policies aimed at promoting competition' (Komiya 1986: 23). They often regarded the enlargement of firm size and the monopolization of industries as irresistible events with favorable consequences for an economy. This apparently reflects a trace of the Marxian view that 'concentration and centralization of capital is an inevitable historical tendency.'[22]

Statements by Ichiro Nakayama to Ryutaro Komiya regarding the 'giant merger' problem illustrate this (Nakayama and Komiya 1968). Nakayama argued as follows: 'The world is more monopolized, and enterprises become larger and more consolidated. A big enterprise with a nationalistic background tends to increase monopolization. Therefore, we may say that now is the era of monopoly capitalism, as left-wing intellectuals used to say.' To justify the giant merger Nakayama grounded his assertion on this 'development of global nationalism' (Nakayama and Komiya 1968: 123–6). Behind the positive attitude of the first generation toward the merger between Yawata Steel and Fuji Steel lay this dogma of the 'inevitability of monopoly capitalism,' one of the characteristic economic views of this generation.

Since the book written by Chalmers Johnson (1982), a popular view is that Japan's 'economic miracle' was due to MITI's industrial policy. Economists influenced by this idea argue that development policy guided by bureaucrats, which is most conspicuous in Japan but is also seen in other East Asian countries, is a general model of a growth strategy called 'state-initiated development strategy' or 'developmentalism.'[23] In this chapter we have seen that Japan's 'industrial structure policy' gradually disappeared due to the severe criticism made by the second-generation economists. However, there is no support for this kind of 'efficiency of bureaucratism' hypothesis. Japan's industrial policy was more likely the last bloom of the obsolete economic idea that placed more trust in government than in the market. The internationalization of Japan's economy ended the influence of these ideas.

Notes

1.   In the 'New Long-Range Economic Plan' preceding the Income Doubling Plan, the Japanese economy's 'planned annual growth rate' over the said period was estimated at 6.5 percent. The so-called 'Growth Controversy' over the appropriateness of this figure took place between Osamu Shimomura and Saburo Okita. Thereafter, Miyohei Shinohara, Shigeto Tsuru, Toshihiko Yoshino, Yoshizo Yoshida, Tadao Uchida, and Tsunehiko Watanabe joined in the debate. Major

articles associated with this controversy are contained in the anthology edited by Kinyu Zaisei Jijyo Kenkyu-kai (1959). It is said that there were two sources behind the Ikeda Cabinet's idea of 'income doubling.' One was the 'doubling monthly salary' proposition which Ichiro Nakayama had announced in the Yomiuri Shimbun (see Chapter 7), and the other was the '10 percent growth estimation' which Osamu Shimomura advocated in the controversy.

2. However, as the 'factor-price-equalization theorem' tells us, if the production functions of the countries are identical, there is no inducement for international factor movements within an incomplete specialization international equilibrium after free trade, since each factor reward of the countries will equal each other in this case. If the possibility remains that the income of each country can be increased by international factor movements even after trade, it is mainly the case that there are technological differentials among the countries so that factor rewards among them are not completely equalized after trade. Moreover, if the technology itself is internationally transferable, as are many managerial resources accumulated in a firm, the same benefits can be obtained from international transfer of technology as international factor movement. It is apparent that foreign direct investment by multinational corporations is the most typical way of transferring technology across national borders.

3. According to the characterization by Komiya (1986: 22–3), the 'first generation' comprises the 'economists educated before or during the war, represented by such figures as Hiromi Arisawa and the late Ichiro Nakayama,' and the 'second generation' includes 'people who had studied in the West, where they had been exposed to economic theories that were fresh and novel to Japan at the time.'

4. For the historical materials contained in the following sections of this chapter, we owe much to Tsusansho (1990; 1991), and Ando *et al.* (1994).

5. An example of this can be seen in the 'Joint Proposal for Liberalization' announced on 7 August 1959, written by eight renowned figures including Hiromi Arisawa, Ichiro Nakayama, and Yoshizane Iwasa. It said that 'If Japan has no option at all but to remain as a member of the Free World, we must follow the trend of liberalization in the world.' Further, 'It will be to our own advantage to take part in this trend' (*Nihon Keizai Shimbun,* 7 August 1959).

6. A representative demonstration of this line of thought, peculiar to MITI, is an article written by Yoshihiko Morozumi (Morozumi 1963), then director of the First Enterprise Division at the Enterprise Bureau of MITI. He also played a principal role in formulating the Special Measures Law.

7. In the 1950s, Japan's imports were under strict administrative regulations. Every importer had to apply to MITI for each item imported to obtain a ration of foreign currency (except for some nationally indispensable imports such as food and raw materials for which foreign currency rationing was immediately available). MITI often refused to ration foreign currency to imports competing with home products, so that this exclusive authority actually operated as a potent policy measure to protect domestic industries. Every company thus had to anticipate the intention of MITI as long as it wanted to import raw materials or other goods.

8. One exception was Tadao Uchida, then associate professor of Tokyo University, who presented a remark in opposition to the relaxation of the Antimonopoly Law (see Oyama 1996: 132).

9. Shinohara (1957) first argued that Japan's policy for protecting and promoting

heavy and chemical industry should be founded on such 'criteria for constructing industrial structure.' Shinohara states that a 'criterion of comparative costs' is essentially a 'static' one, and that from a long-term perspective it is desirable for Japan to specialize in a heavy and chemical industry which is then in a state of comparative disadvantage but whose product has high income elasticity of demand. It is apparent that the 'criteria for constructing optimal industrial structure' appearing in the Report were derived from Shinohara's 'criteria for constructing industrial structure,' although the term 'productivity growth criterion' did not appear in Shinohara's presentation. Later, Shinohara himself endorsed the 'productivity growth criterion' used in the Report (see Shinohara 1967b: 81–4).

10. The same line of argument can be seen in a report made by the 'General Policy Researching Group' (Arisawa and Tsuchiya 1967). This report argues that 'We should not fail to see a positive phase in which trade liberalization will fundamentally coincide with the interest of Japan's economy rather than seeing it as a *gaiatsu*' (Arisawa and Tsuchiya 1967: 35). In policy arguments, however, its stress was directed as follows: 'Foreign capital, specifically US capital, which is supposed to enter into Japan with the progress of capital liberalization is far superior to a company of this country in its general competitiveness. The differentials of technology-development power and capital power between them and us are especially obvious' (Arisawa and Tsuchiya 1967: 161). As a consequence, the report concludes that it is necessary for Japan to reorganize, that is to merge and consolidate enterprises, so as to protect Japan's economy from the 'technological colonialism of the United States.' It is remarkable that the very names of Yawata Steel and Fuji Steel are mentioned as an example of a combination in the section where the necessity of rationalizing the steel industry was asserted (Arisawa and Tsuchiya 1967: 112–15).

11. Around that time, many attempts for supporting the 'industrial reorganization' were made simultaneously within business circles. Examples include the 'Japan Economic Research Institute' whose representative committee members were Kogoro Uemura, Ichiro Nakayama, and Shigeo Nagano, and the 'Society for the Study of Industrial Problems' whose 'research subject' was 'excess competition in the steel industry.' Sohei Nakayama took an active part in most of these connections. Nakayama revealed his role in the attempt to merge the steel companies in an interview with Mitsuharu Ito (Ito 1977). The policy direction initiated by the business circle was already apparent in the circumstances surrounding the 'Economic and Social Development Plan' announced in February 1967, which replaced the preceding 'Medium-Term Economic Plan.' A notable difference between both plans is that the Medium-Term Economic Plan was formulated with the assistance of econometricians belonging to the second generation (see Ch. 5), whereas the Economic and Social Development Plan was initiated mainly by business practitioners acting without economists' cooperation. In the latter plan, one objective was attaining 'economic efficiency' by reorganizing industries and restricting competition within them. Naturally, this plan became a target of severe criticism from Tadao Uchida and Masahiro Tatemoto who developed the macro-econometric model on which the former Medium-Term Economic Plan was based (see Uchida 1967 and Tatemoto 1967). This confrontation between the second-generation economists and the business circle on the 'Economic and Social Development Plan' was a prelude to the

subsequent controversies over capital liberalization and the giant merger. Minato, Okita and Kojima (1967) discuss related circumstances from the view of the business practitioners.

12. See Sangyo Kozo Shingikai Kihon Mondai Tokubetsu Iinkai (1968). However, the policy direction of this Note is very ambiguous. Although it emphasized 'positive effects of corporate mergers' through enlargement of plant and equipment investment, strengthening of technology-development ability, and so on, the 'possibility of restricting competition' was also pointed out as a problem with the giant merger. The Note was actually a compromise between both groups, as described in Komiya's comment (Komiya 1968). After the Special Committee on the Fundamental Problem was established, a 'declaration against the giant merger by a group of academic economists' appeared as shown below. Until that time, 'there was no committee member who held a somewhat different notion about the previous policy ideology of MITI,' so that 'the committee personnel were supposed to be a gang plotting together for a merger' (Komiya 1968: 15). The sudden appearance of the 'declaration against the giant merger' shocked MITI and the Industrial Structure Council, moving them to conciliate the 'group of academic economists.' They hastily included in the Special Committee on the Fundamental Problem two economists, Hisao Kumagai (then a professor at Osaka University) and Kotaro Tsujimura (then at Keio University), both of whom worked on this declaration. As a consequence, 'the "Note" came to bring about some messages added as a compromise with the academic economists' (Komiya 1968: 15).

13. The writers of 'Note on the Giant Merger' were Hideo Aoyama, Kenjiro Ara, Kenichi Imai, Hiroya Ueno, Hirofumi Uzawa, Tadao Uchida, Hisao Kumagai, Ryutaro Komiya, Ryuichiro Tachi, Masahiro Tatemoto, Kotaro Tsujimura, Shigeto Tsuru, Chiaki Nishiyama, Kazuo Noda, Masao Fukuoka, Shozaburo Fujino, Yasusuke Murakami, and Tsunehiko Watanabe.

14. In a commentary on the debate (Nagano *et al.* 1968) over the 'Giant Merger' by representative economists, business leaders, and policy officials, *Shukan Toyo Keizai* described the situation as follows: 'This special issue is sure to create a broad sensation. On the one side are the business leaders and MITI officials who are supporting the giant merger, and on the other side are the modern economists who are opposing it. Both parties show a strong hostility to each other. A perception gap between the older and the newer generation on the logic of economic policy and a distrust toward the administration of MITI seems evident' (*Shukan Toyo Keizai*, Rinjizokan, 3 July 1968: 2).

15. In the mid-1960s, Tachi and Komiya (1964) represented the policy reasoning based on the 'neoclassical synthesis,' a standard framework of economic thinking for the second generation. Later, Kaizuka (1968) argued that there could be no ground for 'industrial policy' within the policy arguments of the neoclassical synthesis, and gave the famous definition that 'Industrial policy is the policy done by MITI' (Kaizuka 1968: 48). In a symposium on the Yawata-Fuji merger problem (Komiya *et al.* 1968), Yasusuke Murakami stated: 'Now we are forced to choose one of the two optional policy stances. The one is a stance based on the "neoclassical synthesis", or "new economics" in other words, whose principle is to use the competitive mechanism of the market as far as possible, and to supplement it with a Keynesian counter-cyclical policy if need be. The other is a regulatory stance where a centrally planned policy authority makes a guideline for every industry,

and coordinates it. Generally speaking, the stance we are taking is the former, whereas most of the people who are promoting the merger seem to be heading for the latter' (Komiya *et al.* 1968: 122). This shows that most of the second-generation economists grounded their policy arguments in the 'neoclassical synthesis' at the time.

16. As a famous criticism made by Murray Kemp (1960) to the 'Mill-Bastable Infant-Industry Dogma' indicates, if an industry which is unprofitable thus far is sure to make profit in the future, it does not necessarily need government protection since a firm in this industry can compensate for the current loss with future profit. Therefore, those who thought that the government should designate such an industry with the 'criteria for constructing industrial structure,' and protect and promote it nationally, would believe in what Komiya and Amano (1972: 198) disdainfully called the 'intelligence of bureaucrats hypothesis.' This hypothesis assumes that the government, not private entrepreneurs, can foresee correctly which industries will prosper in the future. In other words, the 'criteria for constructing industrial structure' is justifiable only if one can provide plausible grounds to guarantee that the policy authority is always superior to most of the private entrepreneurs in judging a possible future increase of demand or technological progress.

17. The debate on the giant merger mentioned in note 14 shows 'how hard it was for the scholars to have a dialogue with the policymakers and the business practitioners.' A typical example depicting a perception gap between the camps is the confrontation between MITI official Yugoro Komatsu and scholars Komiya, Watanabe, and Uchida. Komatsu asserted that international competitiveness of the steel industry depended solely on Japan's cheap labor, while the scholars pointed out the vagueness of the 'international competitiveness' concept in view of comparative advantage (Nagano *et al.* 1968: 29–31).

18. For example, Shinohara maintains that capital liberalization should operate under some restraints because 'it would interrupt the smooth execution of the national economic plan if it led to excessive domination of foreign capital over our industries,' and because 'it would have the additional undesirable effect of making Japan technologically colonized' (Shinohara 1967b: 154–5).

19. Komiya (1966) seems to be the first to point out this causation in the Japanese literature.

20. Echigo (1967) clarifies a similar argument about excess competition. According to him, there is evidence that 'a problem of excessive equipment can be observed only in such process industries as steel or petroleum refinery in which the unit of equipment capacity is definite, but it is scarcely observed in industries such as automobile or heavy electric machinery for which rationing is not applicable.' Therefore, Echigo concludes that 'the harm of capital investment competition is not so much excessive competition as reduced competition' (Echigo 1967: 68).

21. This judgment by Komiya on the first generation is completely parallel to the observation made long ago by Martin Bronfenbrenner (1956), in which Bronfenbrenner noted the ailment of 'professional schizophrenia' in Japanese economics professors. By the term 'schizophrenia,' Bronfenbrenner intended to denote the situation in which a professor teaching pure economics in class seemed to have no sense of insincerity when doing his ordinary out-of-class job of forming policy advice in favor of artificial price fixing or industrial cartelization.

22. The majority of Japanese Marxian economists at that time continued to neglect,

or sometimes to ridicule, the criticism which the second-generation non-Marxian economists directed toward the giant merger. Hayasaka and Masamura (1974) explained: 'Behind the silence to which the majority of Marxian economists confined themselves were both the traditional perception of capitalism and the traditional perception of socialism. The former holds that the concentration of economic power is inevitable in capitalism. The latter is that the socialist economy which is to emerge in the future should be constructed by shifting this concentrated economic power into the hands of an economically centralized state' (Hayasaka and Masamura 1974: 125). However, there were a few Marxian economists who opposed the giant merger at the time. They include Kazuo Takenaka, Sekio Sugioka, and Kimihiro Masamura. It is apparent from their writings, e.g., Takenaka (1968) and Sugioka and Masamura (1968), that their arguments had much in common with those of the second-generation non-Marxian economists rather than those of the other Marxian economists.

23. This 'revisionist' view on economic development was a focus of research attention in the 'East Asian Miracle' project sponsored by the World Bank (World Bank 1993: Ch. 2). Gao's work (1997) is the most recent attempt to interpret the policy-making process in Japan, specifically that of the 1930s to the mid-1960s, from this 'developmentalism' perspective.

References and further reading

Ando, Y., Y. Imuta, H. Kanamori, M. Sakisaka, M. Shinohara, K. Takenaka, T. Nakamura, and A. Hara (eds) (1994) *Showa Keizaishi* (Economic History of Showa), Tokyo: Nihon Keizai Shimbun-sha.

Arisawa, H. and K. Tsuchiya (eds) (1967) *Shihon Jiyuka: Sono Honshitsu to Taisaku* (The Liberalization of Capital: Its Essence and Counter-measures), Tokyo: Shakaishiso-sha.

Bronfenbrenner, M. (1956) 'Economic thought and its application and methodology in the East: the state of Japanese economics', *American Economic Review*, 46, 2: 389–98.

Echigo, K. (1967) 'Sangyo saihensei ron wo hihan suru: dokkin seisaku yogo no tachiba kara' (Criticizing the industrial reorganization discourse: from a standpoint of defending the antimonopoly policy), *Economisuto*, 20 April: 66–73.

Gao, B. (1997) *Economic Ideology and Japanese Industrial Policy: Developmentalism from 1931 to 1965*, Cambridge: Cambridge University Press.

Harada, Y. and Y. Kosai (1987) *Nihon Keizai Hatten no Big Game: Rent-Seeking Katsudo wo Koete* (Big Game of Japanese Economic Development: Beyond Rent-Seeking Activities), Tokyo: Toyo Keizai Shinpo-sha.

Hayasaka, T. and K. Masamura (1974) *Sengo Nihon no Keizaigaku: Hito to Gakusetsu ni Miru Ayumi* (Economics in Postwar Japan: The Course in View of Biographies and Theories), Tokyo: Nihon Keizai Shimbun-sha.

Hayashi, S. (1967a) 'Sengo no Nihon keizai to dokusen kinshi seisaku' (The postwar Japanese economy and the antimonopoly policy) in H. Inaba and T. Sakane (eds) *Shihon Jiyuka to Dokusen Kinshiho* (Capital Liberalization and Antimonopoly Law), Tokyo: Shiseido.

Hayashi, S. (1967b) 'Shihon jiyuka no riron to genjitsu: keizai ronso no zenshin no tameni' (Theory and reality of capital liberalization: for the purpose of advancing the economic controversy'), *Economisuto*, 19 September: 14–24.

Iida, T. (1967) 'Yaburetari meikokueki ron' ('False national interest advocacy is defeated), *Shukan Toyo Keizai*, Rinjizokan, 28 September: 50–7.

Ito, M. (ed.) (1977) *Sengo Sangyoshi heno Shogen (1): Sangyo Seisaku* (Testimony on the Postwar Industrial History (1): Industrial Policy), Tokyo: Mainichi Shimbun-sha.

Johnson, C. (1982) *MITI and the Japanese Miracle: The Growth of Industrial Policy 1925-75*, Stanford: Stanford University Press.

Kaizuka, K. (1968) 'Shinkotenhasogo no taichiba kara mita seisaku taikei' (Policy structure in view of the neoclassical synthesis), *Shukan Toyo Keizai*, Rinjizokan, 11 December: 42–9.

Keizai Kikakucho (1960) 'Boeki Kawase Jiyuka Keikaku Taiko' (Outline of the Plan for the Liberalization of Trade and Foreign Currency Exchange) in H. Kanamori (ed.) *Boeki to Kokusai-shushi* (Trade and Balance of Payments), 1970, Tokyo: Nihon Keizai Shimbun-sha.

Kemp, M. C. (1960) 'The Mill-Bastable Infant-Industry Dogma', *Journal of Political Economy*, 68, 1: 65–7.

Kinyu Zaisei Jijyo Kenkyu-kai (ed.) (1959) *Nihon Keizai no Seichoryoku: 'Shimomura Riron' to sono Hihan* (Growth Potential of the Japanese Economy: 'Shimomura Theory' and its Criticism), Tokyo: Kinyu Zaisei Jijyo Kenkyu-kai.

Komiya, R. (1966) 'Mushiro hikoritsuka no osore' (Danger to be more inefficient), *Shukan Toyo Keizai*, Rinjizokan, 6 December: 35–7.

Komiya, R. (1967) 'Shihon jiyuka no keizaigaku' (Economics of capital liberalization), *Economisuto*, 25 July: 14–29.

Komiya, R. (1968) 'Chusho ron yori jissho kenkyu wo' (Do more empirical studies than abstract arguments), *Economisuto*, 3 September: 14–20.

Komiya, R. (1975) *Gendai Nihon Keizai Kenkyu* (A Study of the Contemporary Japanese Economy), Tokyo: Tokyo Daigaku Shuppankai.

Komiya, R. (1986) 'Industrial policy's generation gap', *Economic Eye* (Keizai Koho Center, Japan), 7, 1: 22–4.

Komiya, R. (1988) 'Introduction'. In R. Komiya, M. Okuno and K. Suzumura (eds) *Industrial Policy of Japan*, New York: Academic Press.

Komiya, R. and A. Amano (1972) *Kokusai Keizaigaku* (International Economics), Tokyo: Iwanami Shoten.

Komiya, R., T. Uchida, K. Takenaka, Y. Murakami, K. Imai, and T. Konishi (1968) 'Futatabi Yawata-Fuji gappei ni hantai suru: symposium' (Opposing again the merger between Yawata and Fuji: a symposium), *Shukan Toyo Keizai*, Rinjizokan, 11 December: 74-122.

Konishi, T. (1966) 'Nihon-teki "yuko kyoso" no genri' (Principle of Japanese style of 'cooperative competition'), *Shukan Toyo Keizai*, Rinjizokan, 6 December: 33–4.

Konishi, T. (1968) 'Ogata gappei Shijisetsu ni miru botsuronrisei' (The illogicality of discourse supporting the giant merger), *Shukan Toyo Keizai*, Rinjizokan, 3 July: 116–25.

Konishi, T. (1973) 'Nihon no kyosoizi seisaku' (Competition-sustaining policy in Japan) in M. Shinohara and M. Baba (eds) *Gendai Sangyo Ron (3): Sangyo Seisaku* (Modern Industry (3): Industrial Policy), Tokyo: Nihon Keizai Shimbun-sha.

Minato, M., S. Okita, and K. Kojima (1967) 'Sangyo taisei no koritsuka wo megutte: zadankai' (The way to make the industrial system more efficient: a conversation), *Shukan Toyo Keizai*, 11 March: 41–8.

Morozumi, Y. (1963) 'Sangyo taisei ron sono 1: Tsusansho gawa no ichi teian' (Industrial system discourse, no.1: a proposal from MITI) in Y. Chigusa (ed.) *Nihon Keizai no Genjyo to Kadai, Vol. 4: Sangyo Taisei no Saihensei* (The Current State and the Problems of the Japanese Economy, Vol. 4: Reorganization of the Industrial System), Tokyo: Shunjyusha.

Morozumi, Y. (1966) *Sangyo Seisaku no Riron* (Theory of Industrial Policy), Tokyo: Nihon Keizai Shimbun-sha.

Nagano, S., T. Doko, S. Nakayama, M. Minato, Y. Komatsu, M. Shinohara, T. Uchida, T. Watanabe, R. Komiya, and S. Okita (1968) 'Ogata gappei to kokumin keizai' (The giant merger and the national economy), *Shukan Toyo Keizai*, Rinjizokan, 3 July: 4–39.

Nakayama, I. and R. Komiya (1968) 'Kyoso genri to kigyo gappei: taidan' (Competition principle and corporate merger: a conversation), *Chuo Koron*, June: 116–26.

Namiki, N. (1973) 'Kigyokan kyoso to seisaku kainyu' (Interfirm competition and policy intervention) in M. Shinohara and M. Baba (eds) *Gendai Sangyo Ron (3): Sangyo Seisaku* (Modern Industry (3): Industrial Policy), Tokyo: Nihon Keizai Shimbun-sha.

Oyama, K. (1996) *Gyoseishido no Seiji-keizaigaku: Sangyo Seisaku no Keisei to Jisshi* (The Political Economy of Administrative Guidance: Formulation and Implementation of Industrial Policy), Tokyo: Yuhikaku.

Sangyo Kozo Chosakai (1963) 'Toshin' (Report) in H. Arisawa and H. Inaba (eds) *Shiryo Sengo 20-nenshi (2)* (Literature on Twenty Years' Postwar History (2)), 1966, Tokyo: Nihon Hyoronsha.

Sangyo Kozo Shingikai Kihon Mondai Tokubetsu Iinkai (1968) 'Sangyo no kozo kaikaku to kiggyo gappei ni tsuiteno iken' (Note on structural reform of industry and corporate merger), *Economisuto*, 3 September: 29–35.

Shinohara, M. (1957) 'Sangyo kozo to toshi haibun' (Industrial structure and investment allocation), *Keizai Kenkyu*, 8, 4: 314–21.

Shinohara, M. (1967a) 'Sangyo seisaku to dokkin seisaku no shomondai: shihon jiyuka ni taisho suru michi' (Problems on industrial policy and antimonopoly policy: a way to cope with capital liberalization), *Economisuto*, 20 April: 26–34.

Shinohara, M. (1967b) *Keizai Gakusha no Hatsugen* (Opinion of an Economist), Tokyo: Nihon Keizai Shimbun-sha.

Sugioka, S. and K. Masamura (1968) *Ogata Gappei wo Kokuhatsu Suru* (Prosecuting the Giant Merger), Tokyo: Tokuma Shoten.

Tachi, R. and R. Komiya (1964) *Keizai Seisaku no Riron* (Theory of Economic Policy), Tokyo: Keiso Shobo.

Takenaka, K. (1968) 'Yonin dekinu shijyo shihaigata gappei' (Market-dominating merger is unacceptable), *Shukan Toyo Keizai*, 4 May: 57–60.

Tatemoto, M. (1966) 'Sakadachi shita yukokyoso ron' (Upside-down effective competition discourse), *Shukan Toyo Keizai*, Rinjizokan, 6 December: 30–2.

Tatemoto, M. (1967) ' "Keizai ni yowai" naikaku no keizai keikaku' (An economic plan of the 'weak in economy' Cabinet), *Chuo Koron*, May: 152–63.

Tatemoto, M. (1969a) *Nihon Keizai wo Ikasu Mono: Kigyo to Seifu no Arikata* (The Way to Give Life to the Japanese Economy: The Role of an Enterprise and Government), Tokyo: Nihon Keizai Shimbun-sha.

Tatemoto, M. (1969b) 'Kindai keizai gakusha teiko no tsumeato: kasen taisei wo ureete' (A trace of resistance by modern economists: deploring the oligopolistic structure), *Asahi Journal*, 16 November: 21–5.

Tsuruta, T. (1982) *Sengo Nihon no Sangyo Seisaku* (Postwar Industrial Policy of Japan), Tokyo: Nihon Keizai Shimbun-sha.

Tsusansho (MITI) (1990) *Tsusho Sangyo Seisakushi, Vol.10: Daisanki, Kodo Seichoki (3)* (The History of the Policies of Trade and Industry, Vol. 10: The Third Period of High Growth (3)), Tokyo: Tsusho Sangyo Chosakai.

Tsusansho (1991) *Tsusho Sangyo Seisakushi, Vol.8: Daisanki, Kodo Seichoki (3)* (The History of the Policies of Trade and Industry, vol. 8: The Third Period of High Growth (1)), Tokyo: Tsusho Sangyo Chosakai.

Uchida, T. (1967) 'Shinkeikaku heno mitsu no gimon' (Three doubts on the new plan), *Shukan Toyo Keizai*, 11 March: 34–40.

World Bank (1993) *The East Asian Miracle: Economic Growth and Public Policy*, Oxford: Oxford University Press.

Name index

Institution index

Subject index